The Politics of Religious Tourism

CABI Religious Tourism and Pilgrimage Series

General Editors:
Dr Razaq Raj, Leeds Business School, Leeds Beckett University, UK
Dr Kevin Griffin, School of Hospitality Management and Tourism, Dublin Institute of Technology, Ireland

This series examines the practical applications, models and illustrations of religious tourism and pilgrimage management from a variety of international perspectives. Pilgrimage is not only a widespread and important practice in Islam, Judaism and Christianity, but also in other major religious traditions such as Buddhism, Hinduism and Sikhism.

The series explores the emergence and trajectories of religious tourism and pilgrimage. Inclusive of all denominations, religions, faiths and spiritual practices, it covers evaluations of religious tourism and pilgrimage, management guides, economic reports and sets of represented actions and behaviours within various cultural, management and marketing contexts. A key strength of the series is the presentation of current and diverse empirical research insights on aspects of religious tourism and pilgrimage, juxtaposing this with state-of-the-art reflections on the emerging theoretical foundations of the subject matter.

The series illustrates the principles related to religion, pilgrimage and the management of tourist sites. It aims to provide a useful resource for researchers and students of the subject, and increase understanding of this vital aspect of tourism studies.

Titles Available

Pilgrimage and Tourism to Holy Cities: Ideological and Management Perspectives
Edited by Maria Leppäkari and Kevin Griffin

Conflicts, Religion and Culture in Tourism
Edited by Razaq Raj and Kevin Griffin

The Many Voices of Pilgrimage and Reconciliation
Edited by Ian S. McIntosh and Lesley D. Harman

Local Identities and Transnational Cults within Europe
Edited by Fiorella Giacalone and Kevin Griffin

Religious Pilgrimage Routes and Trails: Sustainable Development and Management
Edited by Anna Trono and Daniel Olsen

Risk and Safety Challenges for Religious Tourism and Events
Edited by Maximiliano Korstanje, Kevin Griffin and Razaq Raj

Pilgrimage in Practice: Narration, Reclamation and Healing
Edited by Ian S. McIntosh, E. Moore Quinn and Vivienne Keely

Religious Tourism in Asia
Edited by Shin Yasuda, Razaq Raj and Kevin Griffin

Islamic Tourism: Management of Travel Destinations
Edited by Ahmad Jamal, Kevin Griffin and Razaq Raj

Managing Religious Tourism
Edited by Maureen Griffiths and Peter Wiltshier

Tourism, Pilgrimage and Intercultural Dialogue
Edited by Dolors Vidal-Casellas, Silvia Aulet and Neus Crous-Costa

Spiritual and Religious Tourism: Motivations and Management
Edited by Ruth Dowson, Jabar Yaqub and Razaq Raj

Dark Tourism and Pilgrimage
Edited by Daniel Olsen and Maximiliano Korstanje

Religious Tourism and the Environment
Edited by Kiran Shinde and Daniel Olsen

Pilgrims: Values and Identities
Edited by Darius Liutikas

Front cover image: shows the Hagia Sophia, Istanbul, Turkey. The Hagia Sophia has stood as one of the greatest religious buildings in the world for nearly 1,500 years. She was originally built as a church and after the Ottoman conquest of Constantinople was converted to a mosque, before finally becoming a museum in 1934. In July 2020, Turkish courts approved President Erdoðan's petition to convert Hagia Sophia back into a mosque.

The Politics of Religious Tourism

Edited by

Dino Bozonelos

California State University, San Marcos, USA

Polyxeni Moira

University of West Attica, Greece

CABI is a trading name of CAB International

CABI
Nosworthy Way
Wallingford
Oxfordshire OX10 8DE
UK

CABI
200 Portland Street
Boston
MA 02114
USA

Tel: +44 (0)1491 832111
E-mail: info@cabi.org
Website: www.cabi.org

T: +1 (617)682-9015
E-mail: cabi-nao@cabi.org

The views expressed in this publication are those of the author(s) and do not necessarily represent those of, and should not be attributed to, CAB International (CABI). Any images, figures and tables not otherwise attributed are the author(s)' own. References to internet websites (URLs) were accurate at the time of writing.
CAB International and, where different, the copyright owner shall not be liable for technical or other errors or omissions contained herein. The information is supplied without obligation and on the understanding that any person who acts upon it, or otherwise changes their position in reliance thereon, does so entirely at their own risk. Information supplied is neither intended nor implied to be a substitute for professional advice. The reader/user accepts all risks and responsibility for losses, damages, costs and other consequences resulting directly or indirectly from using this information.

CABI's Terms and Conditions, including its full disclaimer, may be found at https://www.cabi.org/terms-and-conditions/.

A catalogue record for this book is available from the British Library, London, UK.

ISBN-13: 9781800621718 (hardback)
        9781800621725 (ePDF)
        9781800621732 (ePub)

DOI: 10.1079/9781800621732.0000

Commissioning Editor: Claire Parfitt
Editorial Assistant: Lauren Davies
Production Editor: Marta Patiño and Shankari Wilford

Typeset by Exeter Premedia Services Pvt Ltd, Chennai, India
Printed and bound in the UK by Severn, Gloucester

Contents

Contributors

Silvia Aulet Serrallonga, PhD, is a professor in the Faculty of Tourism at the University of Girona. Her research line is cultural tourism and heritage management, focusing, in particular, on religious and sacred sites, but she has also worked in other related areas such as peacebuilding, intercultural dialogue and cultural accessibility. Apart from different publications on these topics, she is variously a member of the Editorial Board of the *International Journal on Religious Tourism and Pilgrimage*, the association Future for Religious Heritage, the Unitwin UNESCO Chair in Culture Tourism and Development and the Chair in Gastronomy, Culture and Tourism Calonge-Sant Antoni at the University of Girona. She is Director of the UNESCO Chair on Cultural Policies and Cooperation at the University of Girona. She has participated in several research studies both as an academic researcher and as a consultant. She has participated in different European projects like SPIRIT-Youth, INCOME Tourism, Cultsense and CAMPMASTER. Currently, she cooperates with different institutions related to religious tourism, such as Montserrat Monastery, mainly organizing training courses and seminars and developing research programmes. Email: silvia.aulet@udg.edu

Dino Bozonelos, PhD, is a lecturer in the Departments of Political Science and Global Studies at California State University, San Marcos, and in the Department of International Business at Kedge Business School. His research interests revolve around global issues, including geopolitics, religious tourism, and pilgrimage, religion and politics, and comparative political economy. He has published in several journals, including the *Academy of International Business Insights*, *Politics & Religion* and the *International Journal of Religious Tourism and Pilgrimage*, and in several edited volumes. Email: dbozonelos@csusm.edu

Valentina Castronuovo is a Postdoctoral Researcher at CNR – IRISS in the field of cultural heritage innovation. With a PhD in Tourism Geography, her research topics are oriented towards the development and promotion of religious and cultural itineraries, the design of sustainable tourism routes, the systemic enhancement of diffuse cultural heritage and, more generally, cultural and tourist development of territories. Since 2014 she has been collaborating with the Chair of Geography of Tourism at the Department of Cultural Heritage of the University of Salento. She has worked as a cultural planner for both private and public bodies and she is the author of contributions and articles in journals, books, projects and research reports, published both internationally and nationally. Email: valentina.castronuovo@gmail.com

Stefania Cerutti, is Associate Professor of Economic and Political Geography at the Department of Sustainable Development and Ecological Transition of the University of Eastern Piedmont. Her research focuses on cultural and religious heritage, local and territorial development, project management, sustainable tourism and planning. Her research and teaching activities are complemented by significant participation as a speaker and chairperson at conferences and seminars, as well as a good scientific production at national and international level. She is director of the Interdepartmental Study Centre Upontourism. Vision, strategy and research on innovative and sustainable tourism are other areas of interest. Email: stefania.cerutti@uniupo.it

Charlotte Lee, PhD, teaches topics in comparative politics, international relations and global studies at Berkeley City College. She has published broadly on topics in political science, including institutional change in China, transition in Eastern Europe and democratic peace. Her publications include *Training the Party: Adaptation and Elite Training in Reform-era China* (Cambridge University Press, 2015) and *Cadre Training in a New Socialist Countryside* (in Steven Goldstein and Jean Oi, eds., The Changing Face of Local Governance: Reform China through the Lens of Zouping. Stanford: Stanford University Press, 2018). She has been a contributing author for Open Educational Resources (OER) textbooks in comparative politics and political science research methods. She received her PhD in Political Science from Stanford University and was a postdoctoral Minerva Chair at the US Air Force Academy. Prior to that, she was a US Peace Corps Volunteer (assigned to Romania). Email: clee@peralta.edu

Panagiota Manoli is Associate Professor in Political Economy of International Relations at the Department of Political Science and International Relations, University of the Peloponnese. She graduated from the Department of Political Science and Public Administration at the University of Athens and holds a PhD in International Relations from the University of Warwick (UK) where she studied as an A. Onassis Scholar. She has been Visiting Research Fellow at the Hellenic Observatory (LSE, 2018), Visiting Professor at the European Studies Center, University of Pittsburgh (2016), and Policy Scholar at the Woodrow Wilson International Center for Scholars, Washington DC (2010). She has taught at the University of the Aegean (Rhodes, 2007–2019) and she has worked as the Director of Studies and Research at the International Center for Black Sea Studies – ICBSS (Athens, 2005–2009) and in the Economic Affairs Committee of the Parliamentary Assembly of Black Sea Economic Cooperation (Istanbul, 2000–2004). Her research interests focus on global governance, comparative regionalism, security and development, European Neighborhood and Black Sea politics. Email: manoli@uop.gr

Polyxeni Moira is Professor in Sociology of Tourism at the Department of Tourism Management, University of West Attica in Greece. She was also a Visiting Professor at the University of Ioannina, Harokopeion University, University of Aegean, National and Kapodistrian University of Athens and the Hellenic Open University. She holds a PhD in Sociology from Panteion University of Political and Social Sciences, Greece. She has BA degrees in Public Administration, International and European Studies, and Communication and Mass Media. She also holds MScs in Rural and Regional Development, Pedagogy and Administrative Law. She has been teaching in higher education over the last 30 years. She has published 20 scientific books (in the fields of Religious Tourism and Pilgrimage, Marine Tourism, Cruise Tourism, Industrial Heritage Tourism, and articles in more than 50 international and Greek journals. Her research interests include sociology of tourism, consumer behaviour in tourism and alternative forms of tourism (especially religious tourism, marine tourism, industrial heritage tourism, slow tourism, etc.). Email: polmoira@uniwa.gr

Dane Munro is a Resident Academic at the Institute for Tourism, Travel and Culture (ITTC) at the University of Malta, where he has his regular teaching load and is a supervisor of both undergraduate and postgraduate dissertations. His academic educational trajectory is marked by an MA in the Classics and a PhD in the Cultural Anthropology of Pilgrimage and Faith-based Tourism at the University of Malta. He also obtained a PhD in History at the University of Groningen, the Netherlands, regarding the culture of *memoria* and the identity of the knights of the Order of St John throughout the ages. His research in the Classics and historical research has resulted in a standard publication on St John's Co-Cathedral, *Memento Mori, a Companion to the Most Beautiful Floor in the World*. Dane is a member of the academic boards and is editor of the *International Journal of Religious Tourism and Pilgrimage* (IJRJP) and the publications of *Sacred Journeys*. He is also a Visiting Professor and pilgrimage consultant at *Turistica*, the Faculty of Tourism at the University of Primorska, Slovenia, regarding religious events and pilgrimage tourism. Munro is an active pilgrim and researcher in the field of faith-based tourism and has published many peer-reviewed articles. Email: dane.munro@um.edu.mt

Dimitrios Mylonopoulos is Professor of Tourism Law, at the Department of Tourism Management, University of West Attica (Greece). He is also a Visiting Professor at the University of Patras, at Hellenic Open University, at National and Kapodistrian University of Athens, at Piraeus University, at Hellenic Army Academy, at Hellenic Naval Academy and at Hellenic Open University. He holds a PhD in Public Law from Panteion University of Political and Social Sciences, Greece. He has studied at Democriteion University of Thrace, Panteion University, Harokopieio University, Economic University of Athens, National and Kapodistrian University of Athens and Hellenic Navy Academy. He holds BA degrees in Law, Public Administration, International and European Studies, and Communication and Mass Media. He also holds an MSc in Applied Geography and Area Management, Pedagogy, European Studies, Maritime Studies and promotion of mental health and prevention of mental disorders. He has been teaching in higher education for the last 30 years. He is also a retired senior officer in the Hellenic coast guard. He has published more than 30 scientific books in the field of law (tourism law, marine tourism and maritime issues) and articles in international and Greek journals. Email: dimilon@uniwa.gr

Daniel H. Olsen is a Professor in the Department of Geography at Brigham Young University. His research interests revolve around religious and spiritual tourism, heritage tourism, and the management of sacred sites, with secondary research interests in tourism in peripheral areas and tourism and disabilities. He is co-editor of the publications *Religion, Tourism and Spiritual Journeys, Religious Pilgrimage Routes and Trails, Dark Tourism and Pilgrimage, Religious Tourism and the Environment, The Routledge Handbook of Religious and Spiritual Tourism* and the forthcoming *New Pilgrimage Routes and Trails: Society, Peace, and Development*. Email: dholsen@byu.edu

Masahiro Omae is a Dean at the School of Behavioral and Social Sciences and Consumer and Family Studies at San Diego City College. He holds a PhD in Political Science from the University of California, Riverside. Additionally, Dr Omae served as a staff researcher for the Children's Service Division at Riverside County Department of Public Social Services where he designed and evaluated various services and programmes to improve child welfare. Email: momae@sdccd.edu

María Angélica Alvarez Orozco holds a Masters Degree in Cultural Tourism from University of Girona, Spain. She is currently a student of the PhD programme in Tourism from the same university and has a BA in Business Management from the University of Cartagena, Colombia. Her research is focused on pilgrimage, religious, spiritual and transformational tourism. Her Masters thesis was awarded in 2020 as one of the best theses with influence in tourism in Spain. She has experience in international projects, internationalization of education, tourism management and coordination of international programmes at higher education institutions. Email: maalvarez889@gmail.com

Jorge Olleros-Rodríguez is a PhD candidate in Tourism at the University of Santiago de Compostela (Spain). He has a degree in Law from the University of Navarra and solid training and experience in the world of tourism. He has a Masters in Tourism from the University of Santiago de Compostela, and is Hotel Director, former president of the Association of Hoteliers of O Grove, member of tourism in the Chamber of Commerce and councillor of tourism in the municipality of O Grove. He has published articles related to gastronomy and the de-seasonalization of the holiday season in areas of northern Spain and especially the region of Galicia. Email: jorge.olleros@hotmail.com

Spyridon Parthenis is a PhD candidate in Tourism, Politics and Public Policy (University of West Attica, Greece). He is an alumnus of the Greek National School of Public Administration, specializing in Tourism. He holds a Masters degree in Public Administration (MPA) (Neapolis University Pafos, Cyprus), a Masters Degree in Applied Geography and Spatial Planning (Harokopio University of Athens, Greece) and a Master of Science in Operations Management, with specialization in Agrotourism, Wine Tourism and Regional Development (University of West Attica, Greece). He has been a public administration practitioner in tourism for over fifteen years. His research interests are tourism public policy, policy analysis, politics of tourism, international relations and tourism, policy process theories, policy narratives, tourism and air transport, tourism mobilities and lifestyle migration. He has presented papers at academic international conferences and has published several articles and edited chapters on special interest tourism, with an emphasis on cultural and industrial heritage tourism, religious tourism, and pilgrimage as well as tourism education and training. Email: spyrosparth@gmail.com

Elisa Piva is a researcher of economic and political geography at the Department of Economics and Business Studies, University of Piemonte Orientale, Italy. She holds an international PhD in Tourism from the University of Girona, Spain. Her research activity focuses mainly on the following topics: geography of tourism, territorial development, management of tourist destinations, destination branding, territorial governance, religious tourism and pilgrimage. Since April 2015, she has been a member of the Editorial Board and Scientific Committee of the *International Journal of Religious Tourism and Pilgrimage*. She has participated in several national and international conferences as a speaker. She has been a scientific and organising committee member for many of those conferences. She has participated in various research projects and groups, enhancing collaboration with foreign universities and institutions. She is the author of different papers published in prestigious national and international journals. Email: elisa.piva@uniupo.it

Xosé M. Santos is a full professor in Geography at the University of Santiago de Compostela, in the Department of Geography. He specialized in tourist studies. He has carried out work on the recent changes in rural and urban areas and other human geographic aspects. He also dedicates his research time to developing tourist analysis referring to historic cities, cultural itineraries and pilgrimage routes. He was the Director of the Centre for Tourism Studies and Research (CETUR), at the University of Santiago de Compostela (2005–2014). He has participated in several international projects analysing the role of tourism in development. Email: xosemanuel.santos@usc.es

Francisco Singul, PhD, is chief of Jacobean Culture at Xacobeo-Tourism of Galicia, Regional Government of Galicia (Spain), and lecturer in the Heritage Masters in the Department of Art History at the University of Santiago de Compostela. His research interests are centred on the pilgrimage to Santiago: tradition, culture, history, art history and actual situation of the road to St James experience. He has published in several research journals, including *Coronica*, *Compostellanum*, *Cuadernos de Estudios Gallegos* and *Ad Limina*, and in several edited volumes and Conference Acts in Spain, Italy, Poland, France, Portugal and the USA. He is also the author of several books on the pilgrimage to Compostela edited in Spain, Brazil, Italy and Japan. Email: francisco.singul.lorenzo@xunta.gal

Anna Trono is associate professor of Political and Economic Geography at the Department of Cultural Heritage, University of Salento (Italy), and is an experienced researcher in tourism, environmental problems and urban planning in EU countries. In the last 20 years she has focused her research on environmental heritage, cultural routes and cultural/religious tourism. She has published numerous books and papers in several journals on these themes, many in connection with large-scale projects involving international universities and under the aegis of European Union research programmes. She is steering committee member of the International Geographical Union–Commission Geography of Governance and represents the Department of Cultural Heritage in the network UNITWIN/UNESCO Culture Tourism Development led by IREST. She is scientific member of the following European Routes Associations: Charles V Emperor, Via Francigena and Via Romea Germanica. Email: anna.trono@unisalento.it

Introduction

This edited volume originates out of a class that was taught at the University of Girona in 2019. I was invited by my colleague Silvia Aulet to lecture on the politics of tourism and religious tourism. While I found plenty of material on the discussion of politics and tourism, there was surprisingly little in the way of politics and religious tourism. At first, I was a bit perplexed. As a political scientist still relatively new to the study of religious tourism, I thought there would be quite a bit of literature. Sacred sites and sacred travel are 'dripping with politics' and the term politics, or political, are often written into research on religious tourism and pilgrimage, but with little formal analysis. Indeed, 'politics/political' is usually included as a catch-all phrase. It is not often that politics is comprehensively addressed in religious tourism and pilgrimage.

Why should we try to analyse and study the politics of religious tourism? At its core, politics is the study of power. It involves the struggle in any group that will give one or more persons the ability to make decisions for the larger group. Power is defined as the ability to influence others or impose one's will on a population. Where power comes from, how power is expressed and managed, the ethics of power – these are all major questions that the discipline of political science is often tasked with analysing. This broad perspective is what allows the study of politics to be applied to any subject, discipline or field of research, including that of religious tourism.

The study of politics is about who gets what, when and how. When it comes to religious tourism and pilgrimage, we ask the important questions: How is this power exercised at a religious destination? Who determines and then arranges the power relationships within sacred sites? Is it the state or is it a religious authority? Is it the market? What aspects of religious tourism are governable by institutions, such as government ministries, or religious authorities? What aspects are left to the tourist or pilgrim to govern? When is power exercised? Is it before the visitor arrives, during the experience itself, or throughout the whole visit? These questions are not just academic. They are practical as well. Policy makers, professionals and practitioners will benefit from a robust and in-depth discussion of the topic.

In addition, the salience of religious tourism will grow over time. First, the religious tourism and pilgrimage market is projected to increase to an estimated valuation of $37 billion by 2032 (see Chapter 10 this volume). Thus, as the economic importance of this phenomenon grows, so will its politics. Issues, such as overtourism and the effect of touristic policies on religious destinations, are generally better solved by elected politicians and policy makers, rather than profit-driven market actors. In addition, the rise in geopolitics and nationalism will inevitably include religion and religious sites. The recent invasion of Ukraine by Russian forces is partly driven by a religious–nationalist narrative that Kiev (Kyiv) is the birthplace of the Russian state, and that Ukraine should not exist as a separate country. Finally, religion itself is balkanizing, which leads to the breakup of a religious faith into smaller groups and denominations that are sometimes hostile to each other. We definitely see this in Western Christianity, particularly among Protestants, but this is also visible within Islam, where divisions that were once not as prevalent, have become prominent. In summary, there is not only a lot to discuss now regarding politics and religious tourism and pilgrimage, but also plenty moving forward.

The principle aim of this edited volume then is to engage in a broad study of the *politics of religious tourism*, a surprisingly neglected yet consistently present dimension of publications on religious tourism. Many management professors and practitioners who write on the topic are aware that politics is present in their writings. However, their approach has been one of benign neglect, and/or a priori assumptions about the role of politics in the management of sacred sites. Indeed, current scholarship is better understood as religious tourism *and* politics, as the literature is fragmented into various perspectives and approaches that best serve each author's disciplinary interests. This edited volume then seeks to enrich the literature on politics of religious tourism through the use of different perspectives and approaches. Some are incorporated from the discipline of political science, whereas others are from law, geography, history, management, public administration and tourism studies.

The book is divided into three parts. Part One is titled *The Politics of Religious Tourism*, and directly applies the discourses within political science to religious tourism and pilgrimage. In Chapter 1 (*Introduction to the Politics of Religious Tourism*), Dino Bozonelos and Polyxeni Moira review the existing literature on the politics of religious tourism. They provide a working definition of politics of religious tourism to better conceptualize the field. They also note that most scholarly work has focused on politics *within* religious tourism, where the words 'politics' or 'political' are used to touch upon the political context of a sacred site, with a smaller number of articles written on political science and religious tourism. This latter category is more on the application of concepts, frameworks and theories developed in political science to the phenomena of religious tourism and pilgrimage.

In Chapter 2 (*Religious and Faith Tourism and the Politicization of Sacred Sites*), Daniel Olsen explores the politicization of sacred sites and its relationship to religious and faith tourism. As centres of 'emotionally charged visions of life', in which visions of life mark places where the sacred has manifested itself within mundane space, these places are often contested by religious and secular groups in terms of control, maintenance and interpretation. First, the characteristics of sacred spaces and places that lead them to be politicized are noted. Then, three types of politicization of sacred sites are examined, followed by a discussion of how this politicization affects religious and faith tourism.

In Chapter 3 (*Human Rights: The Right to Tourism and Access to Religious Tourism and Pilgrimage Sites*), Dimitrios Mylonopoulos, Polyxeni Moira and Spyridon Parthenis firmly establish a human right to tourism as it relates to religious sites. They examine the concepts of culture and heritage and unravel the ambiguous nature of cultural heritage and its place within the human rights discourse. Tracing through the origin of modern human rights, the authors explore the equivocal character of the right of participation in cultural life as it is enshrined in international law, as well as the role of international organizations as major actors in safeguarding and promoting cultural–religious heritage and cultural diversity. The chapter incorporates a case study of Greece's Mount Athos, a UNESCO World Heritage Site, where a centuries-old ban on all women exists. The authors explore if the special status granted to Mount Athos, acknowledged by both the Greek Constitution and European Union (EU) law, violates the universally recognized principle of gender equality. Or, if it is fully justifiable on the grounds of its unique spiritual and religious nature.

In Chapter 4 (*Soft Power and Sacred Sites: The Geopolitics of Prayer*), Dino Bozonelos explores the concept of religious soft disempowerment, where the religious actions, the incorporation of religious principles or a sacred site into cultural diplomatic efforts could offend or alienates others, leading to a loss of credibility and attractiveness. This comes out of the soft power discourse within international relations, which tends to imply that cultural attraction, values or ideology function as key elements within a country's efforts to exert power. The author highlights, through a case study of the 2020 conversion of Hagia Sophia into a mosque, how a strategy of religious soft power through sacred sites can generate negative geopolitical implications that could potentially offset any positive benefits that are often associated with soft power.

In Chapter 5 (*Bringing the State Back into Religious Tourism: Institutional Logics and Religious Tourism Governance*), Dino Bozonelos analyses religious tourism governance, where various institutions at different levels, both inside and outside the government, come together to produce positive outcomes, usually in the form of public policy. This necessitates a discussion on the role of the state in religious tourism, an ignored concept within the dominant discourse of neoliberalism, which assigns a supportive role to market pre-eminence. The author discusses the impact of formal religious tourism governance and distinguishes between governance and management. The chapter wraps up with a discussion of institutional logics and how they can help guide future research on religious tourism and pilgrimage.

Part Two of this edited volume is titled *Governance of Religious Tourism* and concerns the governance and governance structures of religious tourism sites. In Chapter 6 (*Global Governance and Religious Tourism: The Role of International Organizations*), Panagiota Manoli attempts to fill in a gap in the literature by placing the study of religious tourism within the context of global governance. The author nuances the role of international organizations in shaping the development of religious tourism globally. In doing so, the chapter investigates the performance of the UNWTO, UNESCO, ICOMOS and the Council of Europe as the primary shapers of a global framework for the development of religious tourism. This includes work on framing and norm setting, stakeholder pooling and networking, capacity building, information sharing and in monitoring and assessment measures.

In Chapter 7 (*Blurring the Lines: Governance and Management in the Promotion of Religious and Spiritual Sites*), Spyridon Parthenis, Polyxeni Moira and Dimitrios Mylonopoulos highlight the relevance of national tourism administrations (NTAs) and national tourism organizations (NTOs) and explain their place within the governance of religious and spiritual sites. The authors both ask and answer a number of crucial questions: What is the contemporary role of NTAs/NTOs as public institutions and what is their mission? Where does governance stop and when does management start? Are the boundaries between governance and management blurred? What does the marketing and promotion of religious and spiritual sites and places as part of the national cultural heritage of a country consist of? The authors also seek to outline the public sector and civil society actors as well as the private travel and tourism industry stakeholders involved in the management, conservation and promotion of religious and sacred sites.

In Chapter 8 (*'Ministries of Religion' in Western Democracies: Model of Fragmented Religious Tourism Governance*), Dino Bozonelos, Stefania Cerutti and Elisa Piva explore religious tourism governance in Europe, where governmental authority for EU countries is fragmented for religious activities and largely separated for religious tourism. Even though religious activities are still an important aspect of Western societies, the surprising fact remains that for most of these countries, 'affairs of the church' are largely diffused under the regulatory authority of multiple ministries. In Europe, the needs of religious communities are tied to the ministries of interior, justice or culture. Regarding religious tourism governance, it is tied to the ministries of economics or tourism authorities. This contrasts with other countries, particularly less secular Muslim-majority countries, where specific ministries of religion exist for explicit government action and intervention. Finally, the authors include a case study of Italy to contextualize how secularism has affected this trend towards 'ministries of religion'.

In Chapter 9 (*The Multiple Scales in the Governance of the Way of Saint James*), Xosé M. Santos and Jorge Olleros-Rodriguez explore the institutional governance structures of the Way of Saint James. As a cultural itinerary, the Way of Saint James is formed by a wide network of pilgrimage routes that originate in different places in Europe that eventually end in the city of Compostela. A number of actors at various levels are involved. This includes organizations at the international level, such as UNESCO or the Council of Europe, at the national level, such as the Friends of the Way of Saint James and the Catholic Church, and local actors such as municipalities and associations of Friends of the Camino.

In Chapter 10 (*Religious Tourism in Malta between Politics, Policies and Private Enterprise*), Dane Munro applies evidence-based policy making (EBPM) and policy analytics to explore and discuss the trajectory of the phenomenon of faith-based tourism in Malta. There have been various attempts over the years to create a niche market by policy makers and stakeholders in Malta. An ongoing struggle exists on whether to force faith-based tourism into the summer mass tourism segment or to decide on a quality-based shoulder and low season special interest market. The author details how the politics, policies and the private enterprise structure of the islands can identify several areas where improvements are probable, if not possible. These policy prescriptions, based on evidence, are of pratical use to tourism policy makers in Malta.

The third and final part of this edited volume is on *Crisis, Politics and Sacred Sites*, with an emphasis on how the recent COVID-19 pandemic has affected the governance of sacred sites. In Chapter 11 (*International Efforts to Secure Sacred Sites: Capacity and Autonomy Across Countries*), Charlotte Lee, Masahiro Omae and Dino Bozonelos analyse the ambitious 2019 United Nations Plan of Action to Safeguard Religious Sites. There has been a growing call for the securitization of religious sites around the world, spurred by hundreds of high-profile terrorist acts committed at places of worship around the world. In this chapter, the authors use comparative case studies of Sri Lanka, Germany and Iraq to reveal how state capacity and autonomy determine the degree and type of protections implemented by various governments. The authors conclude that the UN Plan of Action is a necessary, but insufficient, condition for the protection of religious sites from religious terrorism. If the goals of the UN Plan are to be achieved, states must increase their capacity and, in cases of weak states such as Iraq, also increase their autonomy.

In Chapter 12 (*Closure of Sacred Sites and Autonomous Organization of Religious Ritual: Re-Thinking the Geography of Sacred Space. Policies and Restrictions in Europe in The Age of COVID-19*), Valentina Castronuovo discusses how government policies and strategies to manage the COVID pandemic have led to changes in the management of public places, most notably amongst sacred sites. As one of the main places subject to closures and restricted use, tension rose between public health norms and the freedom to enjoy essential services. After an overview of the restrictive policies affecting sacred sites by European Union Member States, the author asks if a rethink on the exercise of religious freedom in Europe is needed. The author also presents an initial characterization, from a geographical point of view, of the neo-spaces generated by alternative religious practices which, in the present as well as in the past, have reflected the resilience of the identity of religious communities.

In Chapter 13 (*Is Pilgrimage an Essential Service? The Conflict over Congregational Worship and Health Governance*), Maria Angélica Alvarez-Orozco and Silvia Aulet Serrallonga examine whether pilgrimage can be considered as an essential activity as understood through the World Health Organization's (WHO) ten Essential Public Heath Operations (EPHO). The EPHOs incorporate different dimensions of health, such as physical, mental, social well-being and spiritual. The authors point out that spirituality is closely related to well-being, which can include self-improvement by overcoming challenges, something that is often accomplished through pilgrimage walks. Through a series of in-depth interviews with representatives of pilgrimage sites, the authors suggest that pilgrimages, and their associated trails, be understood as essential services and that their governance should reflect this importance.

In Chapter 14 (*Religious Tourism as an Economic Development Policy: The Politics of Tourism Development*), Anna Trono analyses the value of religious and spiritual travel, which is increasingly recognized today as a remedy to health crises, social and environmental malaise, and the uncertainty produced by the COVID-19 pandemic. After an overview of the ancient and current meaning of religious tourism and faith itineraries, the chapter considers some tourism strategies designed to promote sustainable tourism. The author presents four case studies on how tourism and the desire for culture and religious sentiment can be reconciled not only with the search for spirituality, but also with a focus on sustainable tourism in the places visited. It will consider the need for religious tourism polices to create new market niches, new types of supply and demand, new tourist circuits and new entrepreneurial figures, acting as a dynamo of regional economic development.

Finally, in Chapter 15 (*Governing the Camino: Protecting Pilgrims during the COVID-19 Pandemic*), Francisco Singul discusses how the COVID-19 pandemic directly affected the Camino de Santiago. The author catalogues the efforts put in place by government agencies to protect pilgrims during the pandemic. These measures include transitioning to a digital pilgrimage credential and the option of insurance. The author posits that for best safety practices it is essential that governing agencies cooperate with each other at all levels, including at the regional (Galician), national (Spanish), and international as well. This cooperation must also include the Xacobeo, a public limited company that helps govern the Camino, the Catholic Church and related associations, such as the Friends of the Camino de Santiago. The author concludes that the idea of cooperation in governance is a must for management and is essential in preserving the health of both pilgrims and the local population.

This edited volume concludes with Chapter 16 (*What's Next? Politics and Religious Tourism: Emerging and Future Directions*). In this chapter Dino Bozonelos and Polyxeni Moira examine three potential growth areas. The first is the application of 'core' concepts and theories developed in political science to religious tourism. This can be subdivided through the subfields found within the discipline itself, from international relations to comparative politics to political methodology. The second is the continued research into areas that involve politics and political actors but are also tangential to the discipline of political science. This could be referred to as 'peripheral' political science. These tend to focus on sacred sites and include their role in contentious politics, the use of conflict resolution techniques regarding contested religious destination sites, and the effect of political violence, such as terrorism or wartime conditions, on religious places. Finally, it involves the implementation of such concepts and theories, or what is commonly referred to as public policy. Tourism public policy has been studied at length, yet this literature has yet to be fully extended to religious tourism and pilgrimage. Given the inherent unique qualities that exist within religious travel, religious tourism public policy needs further examination.

Dino Bozonelos
Departments of Political Science and Global Studies, California State University, USA

Polyxeni Moira
Department of Tourism Management, University of West Attica, Greece

1 Introduction to the Politics of Religious Tourism

Dino Bozonelos[1]* and Polyxeni Moira[2]
[1]Departments of Political Science and Global Studies, California State University, San Marcos, USA; [2]Department of Tourism Management, University of West Attica, Greece

Abstract
This introductory chapter reviews the existing literature on the politics of religious tourism. Building on this scholarship, a working definition of politics of religious tourism is introduced, with the intent to better conceptualize the topic. In addition, most scholarly work focuses on politics within religious tourism, where the words 'politics' or 'political' are used to touch upon the political context of a sacred site. In contrast, a smaller number of articles have been written on political science and religious tourism. This latter category is more on the application of concepts, frameworks and theories developed in political science regarding the phenomena of religious tourism and pilgrimage. Finally, concepts such as governance, institutions and policy are re-examined within the discourse of religious tourism and pilgrimage.

1.1 Introduction

In 1975, HG Matthews wrote that tourism is 'grossly lacking of political research' (Matthews, 1975). Almost thirty years later, when Hall (1994) wrote his seminal work, *Tourism and Politics: Policy, Place and Power*, he repeated the same claim. Almost another thirty years have passed, and despite the exponential increase in research, a similar argument can be made regarding religious tourism. Despite the acknowledgement that religious tourism is a product of complex religious, political and economic relationships, these processes are either mostly overlooked, or at least assumed away. As a subfield, religious tourism is overwhelmingly located in traditional tourism research clusters – schools of business management,

schools of theology or in the departments of cultural geography, with the former taking the lead in publications. Given the contemporary emphasis on the phenomenological, religious tourism is often analysed reductively, usually in understanding the motivations and experiences of travellers (Durán-Sánchez et al., 2018). The experience of the 'consumer' be it a pilgrim, religious tourist or a secular tourist just visiting a sacred site is maximized. Whereas the role of politics, including governance and governing institutions is often minimalized, deferring to neoliberal thinking on the importance of consumer behaviour.

The principle aim of this edited volume is to provide a comprehensive overview and framework of the study of the *politics of religious tourism*, a surprisingly neglected yet consistently present dimension of publications regarding

*Corresponding author: dbozonelos@csusm.edu

DOI: 10.1079/9781800621732.0001

religious tourism. Many management professors and practitioners who write on the topic are aware that politics is present in their writings. However, their approach has been one of simple contextual use, with a priori assumptions about the role of politics in the management of sacred sites. Indeed, current scholarship is better understood as religious tourism *and* politics, as the literature is fragmented into various perspectives and approaches that best serve each author's disciplinary interests. Some element of politics is brought in to understand a specific context, but the application of political science theories and understandings to religious tourism are generally missing.

Surprisingly, few political scientists research religious tourism. Governance, management and access to sacred sites for pilgrims and religious tourists is nothing but political, often the result of centuries of negotiations or compromise, among many different stakeholders. Some of this may reflect the shift in focus in political science itself from institutions to behaviour. The behavioural revolution in the 1950s almost ended discourse on institutionalism entirely. Since then, political scientists have generally focused on the individual level of analysis, using econometric approaches and utilitarian assumptions to study political behaviour, such as voter preferences or interest formation (Franco and Bozonelos, 2020). The neoinstitutionalist revival in the late 1980s and 1990s helped reorient political science back to its roots. Neoinstitutionalism is best explained by North (1991), who reintroduced the importance of institutions. All behaviour, including the market itself, is guided by norms and expectations that are strongly embedded within institutions.

Still, we do not argue that we should only view religious tourism through a political science disciplinary perspective. That would be improper. Scholarship on religious tourism and pilgrimages has increased exponentially in conjunction with increasing numbers of people who travel for religious reasons (Durán-Sánchez *et al.*, 2018; Rashid, 2018). And while political science has much to offer, religious tourism is inherently multidisciplinary and interdisciplinary. No single discipline can claim sole authority to the study of religious tourism. Just like its secular form, tourism can be studied from a variety of social science and humanities disciplines. Still, outside of economics, the application of the social sciences to the study of tourism is 'relatively weak' (Holden, 2005, p. 1). Even Holden's book, *Tourism Studies and the Social Sciences* ignored political science in favour of political economy, which has become a reoccurring theme in the research of tourism and will be discussed more at length below.

This is why Hall (1994) referred to the politics of tourism as the 'poor cousin of both tourism research and political science and policy studies' (p. 1). Through this metaphor, Hall describes this field of research as mostly ignored on purpose. He cites several reasons, including the unwillingness of decision makers to recognize the politics inherent within tourism; a lack of official interest by researchers, which stems from not taking tourism studies seriously; and the lack of comprehensive methods used to understand trends and analyses, outside of the methods used by scholars in tourism management. Holden (2005) echoed the sentiments of Hall, where he commented that social scientists often view tourism and the study of tourism as an 'area of study that is frivolous and not appropriate for mature scholars' (p. 1). And if tourism, which is arguably the largest global industry, is largely ignored by political scientists, then what are we to say about religious tourism, considered a niche market within tourism itself?

If the politics of tourism is the poor cousin of both tourism research and political science and policy studies, then the politics of religious tourism is the poor second cousin, twice removed on the stepfather's side. Given the lack of attention, the question to logically ask, is why should we even try to analyse and study the politics of *religious* tourism? As Hall (2017) notes, 'tourism is deeply embedded in politics and indeed, politics in tourism' (p. 3). Sacred sites are inherently political in nature and have been for centuries (Timothy and Olsen, 2006). Religious and political divisions directly impact religious tourism destination sites. In addition, religious traditions and political ideologies often combine to shape important characteristics and attributes, from how the space is physically arranged itself, to site management, to visitor access, and also to safety and security. Olsen (in this edited volume) explains that as sacred sites are inherently contested, they become politicized. The author refers to the 'textured or layered politics' that exist within these landscapes. Tensions can bubble up quickly and even the most minute of issues can become politicized. This is especially true when such sites are contested by different stakeholders, religious groups and/or governing authorities, and in the case of the Old City of Jerusalem, all at once (Isaac *et al.*, 2016).

Often, the question that arises is who 'owns' the site? In other words, who is the ultimate decision maker when it comes to the governance and management of the destination? Timothy and Olsen (2006) refer to this as the 'politics of place' (p. 28) and Shackley (2001) writes that sociopolitical control is one of the most significant factors governing access to sacred sites. In today's global tourism, the default answer is the private corporations and entities that are directly involved and, for many sites, that may be the case. However, governance and management are much more convoluted when the site is contested. Jobani and Perez (2020) identify several contested sites in their book: the Devil's Tower National Monument, the Babri Masjid/Ram Janmabhoomi in India, and the Western Wall, the Church of the Holy Sepulchre (Tomb), and the Temple Mount/Haram al-Sharif in Jerusalem. Other contested sites include Hagia Sofia in modern day Istanbul as well as the Temple Lot in Independence, Missouri. The politics of ownership, access and interpretation are of not just local and national political importance, but often global as well.

Tourism can be used both as a source of political power and for political capital (Hall, 1994; Shackley, 2001; Charles and Chambers, 2015). Tourism issues, such as overtourism, have emerged as salient political concerns and sources of contention. Local resentment at how tourists behave and also how tourism impacts daily regime can at times impact elections (Shackley, 2001; Novy and Colomb, 2019). As an industry, tourism is a powerful economic engine, at times accounting for 10.3% of global GDP (WTTC, 2022) and up to 10% of the world's total employment. The policy impacts of tourism are evident, particularly through tourism development, which has become a vital ingredient for economic progress (Bähre, 2007). For some countries, tourism might be the raison d'être for development, where a country might initiate a tourism site where one did not exist before. This is even more evident when it comes

to poorer countries where tourism often constitutes a larger sector of their economy (Bianchi, 2002; Stabler *et al.*, 2010; Edgell and Swanson, 2019). Finally, tourism as a practice and as an act, are tied to the cultural milieu of that state, which in turn, can be inherently political. Which historical and cultural sites a country promotes, and which sites a country demotes, are part of the cultural politics. This has become more relevant with the growth in dark tourism, a more modern development where thanatopsis can become easily controversial (Korstanje and Olsen, 2020).

Religious tourism however, can have an ever greater societal impact. The World Tourism Organization (UNTWO) has placed an emphasis on the growth of religious tourism. Secretary-General Taleb Rifai has identified three benefits of religious tourism: awareness of common heritage, local economic development and cultural understanding. Yet, politics is intimately intertwined with sacred sites. Even though the UNWTO does not specifically point to politics as a challenge, it is implied throughout (Griffin and Raj, 2017). The physical spaces are considered centres of 'emotionally charged visions of life' (Friedlander, 2010, p. 125). They have meaning beyond what would be associated with a profane tourist site, such as a beach resort, or even with a cultural tourist site, such as a monument to those who have fallen in war.

At its core, politics is the study of power. As Elliott (1997) writes, 'politics is about the striving for power, and power is about who gets what, when, and how in the political and administrative system and in the tourism sector' (p. 10). It involves the struggle in any group for power that will give one or more persons the ability to make decisions for the larger group. Power is defined as the ability to influence others or impose one's will on a population. Where power comes from, how power is expressed and managed, the ethics of power – these are all major questions that the discipline of political science is often tasked with addressing. This broad perspective is what allows the study of politics to be applied to any subject, discipline or field of research, including that of religious tourism.

This edited volume on the politics of religious tourism focuses on how power is exercised in religious tourism. If power is defined as the ability to influence or impose will, then power is often expressed through governance, institutions and policy. Governance is not an easily defined concept. As Hall (2012) writes, governance is an emerging frame in tourism public policy and planning literature. Governance can be defined by Fukuyama (2013) as 'a government's ability to make and enforce rules, and to deliver services, regardless of whether that government is democratic or not.' For religious tourism, governance has become an increasingly recognized component.

Closely correlated to governance is the concept of institutions. Institutions are defined as organizations or activities that are self-perpetuating and valued for their own sake (O'Neil, 2021). They consist of the organizations, norms and rules that structure government and public actions. Institutions are an important feature in religious tourism, where religious arrangements are baked into stone (Bozonelos, 2022). Religious leadership, religious customs and rituals and the compromises reached between increasingly secular societies and both indigenous and immigrant religions cannot be assumed away. They represent the struggles for power that are inherent in modern politics, and the institutionalization of these dimensions are featured strongly in both the governance and management of sacred sites. Scholarship on institutionalism and tourism in general has been rising (Falaster et al., 2017). Yet the lack of application of institutionalism, and more specifically neoinstitutionalism, is surprising. Institutions are 'carriers of history' and understanding the path development of current arrangements is important (David, 1994). Indeed, this may explain why case studies appear to be the most dominant method used in religious tourism research. Context is needed as each sacred destination site has unique aspects that are often not generalizable to other locations.

Out of governance and institutions comes policy and policymaking. Edgell and Swanson (2019) define policy using the Merriam-Webster dictionary: 'a definite course or method of action selected from among alternatives and in light of given conditions to guide and determine present and future decisions'. Policy is the final outcome of governance, and the execution of policy is how institutions self-perpetuate. There is no debate over how important governments are for contemporary religious tourism and pilgrimage.

This niche industry could not survive without some measure of government involvement. Governments provide political stability, security, legal frameworks, essential services and basic infrastructure that are fundamental to the perseverance of a sacred site. In addition, national governments retain sovereignty over country access. This includes immigration procedures, border controls, and flying over and into national territory.

Tourism policy can be defined when definite courses or methods of action are taken together to provide a framework from which decisions can be made that affect, develop or promote tourism (Goeldner and Brent Ritchie, 2012; Edgell and Swanson, 2019). Still, government is not the only voice. In democratic governance, multiple actors are involved. Referred to as pluralism in political science, this is an open participatory style of government in which many different interests are represented. In democracies, government policies should roughly correspond to public desires. Including interest groups such as industry associations, religious orders all come together to form the 'heavenly choir' of democracy. Of course, the comment is made that this choir sings with a distinct 'upper-middle class accent', which reflects the stronger influence that wealthier groups and individuals have in modern democracies.

The same critique could be applied to the governance of sacred sites as well, and particularly with sites that are contested. Stronger, more powerful religious groups, or groups that align with the dominant religious tradition in that democracy, will often yield more influence when it comes to religious tourism and pilgrimage policy. This is certainly the case in multireligious democracies such as India, with Prime Minister Modi's alliance with the Hindutva movement leading to government support for Hindu temples and sanctuaries, sometimes at the expense of minority religions (Iqbal, 2019). This even more true in faltering or fragile democracies such as Sri Lanka, where the government has historically relied on Buddhist monk support for oppression of Tamil Hindu guerrilla groups. Such monks would often bless the Sri Lankan soldiers and others who would prioritize and promote Sinhalese heritage and the protection of the Buddhist character of the nation (Lam, 2020).

Yet, this also tends to be true when it comes to authoritarian countries. These governments find themselves closely aligned with the more conservative elements in their societies, which, more often than not, includes religion and religious figures. We see these close connections in countries such as Russia, where President Putin has forged a close relationship with the Russian Orthodox church. We also see it in Saudi Arabia, where the al-Saud family has maintained a mutually beneficial alliance with the Salafists, a movement begun by Mohammad al-Wahab in the 1700s. This is also evident in countries where the authoritarian regime is not aligned with the dominant religion. A good example is Myanmar, where the military regime has an off-again on-again relationship with the Sangha, or Buddhist clerics. The Sangha often rally against the military regime, often followed by a reprisal. However, they cannot completely isolate the clerics as they are revered by the Buddhist majority.

1.2 What Is Religious Tourism and Pilgrimage?

The definitions of what is a religious tourist and what is a pilgrim, and the distinctions between the two, are important for the politics of religious tourism. The motivations of a religious tourist vis-à-vis a pilgrim matter. However, the institutions that envelop the sacred site are just as important. Certain religious destinations are not set up for religious tourists and are designed with the pilgrim in mind. A good example includes Mount Athos in Greece where a permit, or *diamonitirion*, is required for entry (Mylonopoulos *et al.*, 2009). Other sites are only for members of the religious community in good standing. Only Muslims can enter Mecca and only Orthodox Jews are expected to attend Lag b'Omer, a festival that celebrates Rabbi Shimon Bar Yochai, a second century Jewish mystic on Mount Meron. Still other sites are more accessible or available to non-followers or non-believers. Generally, this is the case with Buddhist religious tourism sites where efforts have been made to accommodate and market to non-Buddhists.

The distinction between the pilgrim and the religious tourist has been an issue under study for many years by the scientific community (Jackowski and Smith, 1992; Rinschede, 1992; Vukonić, 1996; Robichaud, 1999; Collins-Kreiner and Gatrell, 2006; Digance, 2006; Timothy and Olsen, 2006; Stausberg, 2011; Eade and Dionigi, 2015). According to Olsen and Timothy (2006), '... gaps exist in the perceptions of the differences between pilgrimage and tourism from the perspectives of religion, the pilgrims themselves, the tourism industry, and researchers.'

Jackowski and Smith (1992) believe that true pilgrimage takes two forms, depending on the goals and the mode of travel alike. In the first form, the driving force is the religious feeling (pilgrim) while in the second the driving force is the quest for knowledge (religious tourist). Pilgrims dedicate their time to meditating and praying, performing religious rituals, and while they travel they visit specific sancta. Most of these pilgrims are not informed about the historical or cultural (i.e. the non-religious) significance of the cities, the towns and the villages they pass through. Their initial goal is the 'special pilgrimage' to a worship centre, in which curing a sick person or saving one's soul and acceptance to heaven can occur. On the contrary, religious tourists are the individuals whose major motive to travel is to a large degree the quest for knowledge. They seek information and experiences through the journey and the communication with people, the areas and the towns they pass through. Religious tourists usually visit the area-centre and participate at least in one part of the rituals. Rinschede (1992) considers that religious tourism is a form of tourism where the participants travel either partially or exclusively for religious reasons. In fact, it is his belief that religious tourism is a subcategory of cultural tourism, highlighting the fact that those who participate in organized pilgrimages usually spend an extra day to visit selected cultural religious tourist sites (Moira *et al.*, 2009). Robichaud (1999) believes that religious tourists are a cross between tourists and pilgrims. They travel, having religious motivation but they are not aware of how to approach their spiritual goal as they are surrounded by professional travel advisors, follow predefined travel packages, participate in organized group meals, and follow standard routes, missing their real religio-spiritual goal. Their journey may be called pilgrimage but in reality, these travellers are alienated and shift from pilgrims to tourists. The wellness, the comforts, the cosmopolitan surroundings of travels and luxury hotels, the digital cameras and the video cameras which accompany many travellers, the commodification of the sacred objects, the need for lodgings, meals, organized events, etc. remove the spiritual element from the pilgrimage and restrict it to the touristic element. Smith (1992) makes a similar distinction with regard to the motives of religious tourists. She created a position framework whose two polarities are the *sacred* and the *secular*. Between the two endpoints there are unlimited possible combinations of sacred and secular. In the middle, there is what is called 'religious tourism'. In fact, this figure confirms the view expressed by Pearce (1991) that the travellers' motives are various and changing and their interests and, by extension, their activities may easily shift from pilgrims to tourists and vice versa. Vukonić (1996) claims that religious tourists, after having met their religious needs, subsequently behave as tourists, meaning that they need accommodation, food, to buy souvenirs, etc. Turner and Turner (1978, p. 20) believe that the religious tourist is half pilgrim and half tourist.

Of course, we should bear in mind that a pilgrimage is also shaped, apart from religious beliefs, by the influence of other factors prevailing each time, such as political (e.g. in Poland the church is a symbol of the national identity and unity of the Poles), economic, social, etc. (Jackowski and Smith, 1992, p. 105). Furthermore, historical factors can have a considerable impact on pilgrims (e.g. in the Holy Monastery of Agia Lavra built in 961 CE in Greece, the religious and the historical element coexist as it is the site where the Greek Revolution against the Ottomans was launched in 1821 and where the bullet-ridden Banner of the Revolution is kept today).

According to Μοίρα (2009, 2019) pilgrimage and religious tourism are two different social phenomena in which 'religiosity' is their common element, regardless of whether it is active or inactive. Thus culture, religion and tourism create a 'symbiotic' or 'complementary' relationship. These social phenomena are (a) the *pilgrimage*, where the spiritual element of faith dominates and which is manifested in the appropriate conditions distinguished by spirituality, rigour, temperance, observance of the standard, mental preparation, etc. The pilgrim is a traveller, a 'seeker' for the ultimate coveted goal, the pilgrimage. This effort is reinforced by the 'spiritual reward' he expects from the realization of the pilgrimage and the expected satisfaction from the achievement of his goal. Therefore, a pilgrimage is characterized by all the activities of individuals or groups in areas, places and monuments of religious importance with the predominant motive being the spiritual ascent from earth to heaven, i.e. pray/communicate with the deity, the fulfilment of a vow, or the substantial participation in religious ceremonies and events, as part of the individual's religion, (b) *religious tourism*, as a subcategory of cultural tourism, where the religious element of the place or event is utilized with tourist criteria as cultural heritage. The cultural aspect becomes a common component of tourism and religion. Thus, religious tourism is characterized by all the activities related to the travel of individuals or groups to areas, places and monuments of religious–cultural importance with a dominant motive of contact with the religious element of the host place as part of culture. Therefore, a religious tourist is not always a believer.

The typology and the ranking of the visitor/religious tourist or pilgrim is not only of academic interest, but also practical, as it influences his choices in all phases of the journey. Initially, the destination choice depends on whether it appears more or less attractive in relation to their desires, motivations, and needs. Then, the organization of the trip, the options during the trip, for accommodation, food, visits, souvenir purchase, etc. differ. For example, the pilgrim who wishes to fast during the pilgrimage has different needs from the needs of the religious tourist. Also, the behaviour of the pilgrim in the sanctuary is different from that of the religious tourist. Understanding the above is necessary both to meet the needs of visitors and to manage them (Moira *et al.*, 2009; Μοίρα, 2009; Μοίρα, 2019).

The distinction between a religious tourist and a pilgrim has a different meaning depending on the management body (public or private) the definition depends on each researcher's discipline (economy, sociology, politics, law etc.) and their expectation. For example, from the view of religious organizations, pilgrims generally are not considered to be tourists, because they travel for spiritual reasons. On the contrary travel agents, hotel managers, etc. consider all travellers as tourists because their presence generates economic benefits and is relevant to economic growth (Moira *et al.*, 2009; Μοίρα, 2009; 2019).

For governments, the inclusion of the pilgrim in the general category of 'tourist' emphasizes purely economic criteria, ignoring travellers' motivations. In reality, this generalization and the 'artificial increase' in tourist numbers responds to a purely 'economist' perception and the need for a constant increase in numbers. In fact, this generalization, which is truly a political action (Μοίρα, 2022) artificially reinforces the importance of the tourism sector (Bodson and Stafford, 1988).

1.3   What Is the Politics of Religious Tourism?

To properly answer this question, we must ask a preliminary question, what is the politics of tourism? The politics of tourism is understood by Hall (1994) to be the study of power arrangements, which are 'inextricably linked to a given set of value assumptions which predetermine the range of its empirical application' (p. 13). Simply stated, politics matter and policy has impact. Following Hall, we define the politics of religious tourism as '...the exercise of political power in religious tourism and pilgrimage and the study of power arrangements.'

Hall's book, *Tourism and Politics*, mostly focuses on policy development at several levels of analysis, with discussions of what the political context generally looks like at each level. One of the more relevant conceptualizations is his bifurcation of policy analysis into 'internal process orientated criteria of adequacy' and 'outcome-orientated criteria of effectiveness on impact'. The former is where academics often bring in theories to explain how such processes have developed, whereas the latter is often written by anyone who can assess the impact of governance and policy. In this latter category is where the field opens up and why we see so much interdisciplinarity when it comes to the politics of tourism.

In a later book, *Tourism and Public Policy*, Hall (1995) brings together both parts to develop the field of *tourism public policy*. This involves policy analysis where both the causes and the consequences are studied in an attempt to provide a unified approach to the subfield. Hall makes sure to note that institutional arrangements are significant in tourism. Institutions place restraints on policy makers. This is antithetical to the neoliberal notion that market forces should guide tourism and/or tourism development policy. Telfer (2015) notes that an expectation has developed that tourists and tour companies should be free to operate as they see fit across international borders. Any state intervention is seen as onerous and should be either minimized or eliminated altogether. Likewise, Sharpley (2015) notes that development is often the raison d'être for tourism. As it is such an effective source of employment and income, countries consider it a growth industry. In addition, tourism can serve as a vehicle for wealth redistribution where investment and the transfer of wealth to an underdeveloped area can have significant economic benefits. Given this view, it is logical to see why many tourism scholars are quick to dismiss or overlook institutional arrangements. It simply does not fit into their paradigmatic approaches to tourism.

These understandings are also apparent in the study of religious tourism. For example, Hall's earlier bifurcation of politics of tourism into 'internal process orientated criteria of adequacy' and 'outcome-orientated criteria of effectiveness on impact', or as I refer to them, 'looking within to explain' and 'looking outside for impact', are quite relevant for the study of the politics of religious tourism as well. Bozonelos (2022) refers to the 'looking outside for impact' approach as *religious tourism policy studies*, where outside variables are considered, such as the behaviour of the tourist and/or pilgrim, such as motivations and experiences, or the importance of the sacred site for the regional economy. This is evident in both editions of Raj and Griffin's (2015) book, *Religious Tourism and Pilgrimage Management: An International Perspective*. In both volumes, the chapters are mostly focused on consumption of the religious tourism site and how the site is managed to meet those consumer expectations. Less discussed are the institutional arrangements that may or may not bound the decisions of the consumer. Clarke and Raffay (2015), and Trono (2015) come closest to addressing the role of institutions in the second edition, with the former addressing stakeholder theory in religious tourism and the latter about how various entities work together to develop a religious site.

This discourse then leads us to bifurcate current scholarship into two areas of research when it comes to the politics of religious tourism.

Politics within religious tourism: this area focuses on the political dimensions associated with religious tourism. Politics within religious tourism is where the bulk of the scholarship is located. In this area of research, often the words 'politics' or 'political' are used to touch upon the political context of the sacred site. A good example is the seminal volume by Timothy and Olsen (2006) on religious tourism. A search for politic* in their book yielded 47 results, excluding references and author bios. In each of these instances, some form of the word politics was either used as part of the phrase, 'social, cultural, *political*, economic' and 'socio-*political*', or as a catchall phrase, such as, '...they are affected by the *politics* and social trends...' (p. 114). This trend is repeated in a myriad of other articles and books on religious tourism and pilgrimage (see Katic's book *Pilgrimage and Sacred Places in South-east Europe*, where politic* is mentioned 79 times).

Other more recent works have focused on the political contestation of sacred sites. Eade and Katic (2014) note that anthropologists have been much more willing to focus on power dynamics and resistance to those dynamics in sacred sites. Yet they notice that little attempt is made to analyse the institutions that are the repositories for that power. Their book, *Pilgrimage, Politics and Place-Making in Eastern Europe: Crossing Borders* provides much needed context to the political challenges in the region. Jobani and Perez (2020) identify several contested sites in North America, including the Devil's Tower National Monument, where Native American tribes contest how their sacred sites are imagined in modern discourse. They explore church–state governance models as context for how contested religious places are managed. Barkan and Barkey (2015) investigate state policies and how the behaviour of political authorities affect shared religious destination

sites within the former Ottoman Empire. Finally, Raj and Griffin (2017) provide a broad view of conflict and religious tourism. Their edited volume not only encompasses political contestation, but also how religious tourism development can lead to conflicts within a society.

Another research area has centred on the impact of political violence, such as terrorism, on religious tourism sites. Chowdhury *et al.* (2017) specifically discuss religiously motivated terrorism and how holy places have become uniquely targeted. Chowdhury *et al.* (2021) further discuss the impact of terrorism and link the motivations of terrorists with their targeting of specific shrines and sacred sites. Isakhan (2020) uses social movement theory to discuss how the targeting of Shi'a sacred sites in Iraq by the Islamic State led to a successful mobilization effort to protect them. This 'shrine protection narrative' has been instrumental in uniting the often fractious Shi'a militias into a potent political coalition. Finally, Korstanje and George (2021) develop the notion of religious tourism security, where the tourist and pilgrim's perception of risk is central in understanding if the site is secure. In addition, they highlight that while a pilgrim might be willing to tolerate a less secure environment, a religious tourist may not.

Political science and religious tourism: this area involves the application of theories in political science to religious tourism. Most of what has been written falls within *religious tourism policy and development*, where local, national or supranational agencies partner with religious officials and private market economic actors to use sacred sites as part of their economic growth plans. This overlaps with the religious tourism policy studies category described above, with the difference being that much of theory in these writings come in the form of political economy, where scholars study the 'ever-evolving nexus of relationships between state governance and economic transactions' (Coleman and Eade, 2018).

Reader (2014) discusses how academics often want to separate the sacred from the mundane, particularly when it comes to economic actions and decisions. However, economic forces, such as commercialization and personal consumption have always been present at pilgrimage sites. Market dynamics are crucial for the success of any religious destination site.

Pilgrimage can be built *through* the marketplace as well. Coleman and Eade (2018) add to Reader's analysis and posit that there might be multiple agencies involved in the construction of pilgrimages. Economic and political relations are used to steer pilgrims in a particular way. Proper governance is then an important feature for success. Finally, Bozonelos (2022) breaks down the recent discussions on the political economy of religious tourism. In each of these works, institutions have a central role.

1.4 Conclusion

The politics of religious tourism is fraught with complications. Understanding 'who gets what, when and how', how scarce resources are distributed, including to whom, in what amounts, and under what rules, are questions that are not always easily answered. Politics is how a society makes collective decisions. Yet when it comes to the governance of religious tourism sites, policy decisions often focus on the economic benefits, a trend that is reinforced through neoliberal discourse. However, sacred sites are not just important economically. They can have cultural importance and even national and global implications. Focusing on just the economic

benefits ignores the roles that stakeholders have in the management and promotion of sacred sites. Often expressed through institutions, these stakeholders, be it religious organizations, cultural associations, or other entities, are intimately involved in the governance of religious tourism and of destination sites.

However, this complexity should not be the major obstacle to researching the politics of religious tourism. Instead, complexity should be viewed as an opportunity to delve further into the issues. As mentioned before, there are quite a few different approaches that exist from *politics within religious tourism* to *political science and religious tourism*. In addition, there is *religious tourism policy studies* and *religious tourism governance*. Each one of these research areas can benefit from the application of theories, frameworks and concepts from political science, policy analysis, public opinion and from the respective subfields within each area. The subfields of international relations (IR) and comparative politics (CP) within political science have much to offer religious tourism. IR theories of soft power and constructivism are applicable and have already been applied in tourism. The same can be said for neoinstitutionalist writings. In sum, there is a plethora of opportunities for future research.

References

Bähre, H. (2007) Privatization during market economy transformation as a motor development. In: Burns, P.M. and Novelli, M. (eds) *Tourism and Politics: Global Frameworks and Local Realities*. Butterworth-Heinemann, Oxford, UK, pp. 33–58.

Barkan, E. and Barkey, K. (2015) . : *Choreographies of Shared Sacred Sites: Religion, Politics, and Conflict Resolution*. Series: Religion, Culture, and Public Life, Columbia University Press, New York, pp. 1–32. DOI: 10.7312/bark16994.

Bianchi, R. (2002) Towards a new political economy of global tourism. In: Sharpley, R. and Tefler, D. (eds) *Tourism and Development: Concepts and Issues*. Channel View Publications, Bristol, UK, pp. 265–299.

Bodson, P. and Stafford, J. (1988) The economic paradigm in tourism. *Téoros, Revue Québécoise de Recherche Appliqué en Tourism* 7(3), 3–5.

Bozonelos, D. (2022) The political economy of religious and spiritual tourism. In: Olsen, D. and Timothy, D. (eds) *The Routledge Handbook of Religious and Spiritual Tourism*. Routledge, New York, pp. 36–52. DOI: 10.4324/9780429201011.

Charles, E.T.A. and Chambers, D. (2015) The salience of tourism in politics. In: Chambers, D. and Rakic, T. (eds) *Tourism Research Frontiers: Beyond the Boundaries of Knowledge*. Emerald, Bingley, UK.

Chowdhury, A., Razaq, R. and Clarke, A. (2021) Impact of terrorism and political violence on sacred sites. *Journal of Islamic Tourism* 1(1), 34–46.

Chowdhury, A., Razaq, R., Griffin, K.A. and Clarke, A. (2017) Terrorism, tourism and religious travellers. *International Journal of Religious Tourism and Pilgrimage* 5(1), 1–19.

Clarke, A. and Raffay, A. (2015) Stakeholders and co-creation in religious tourism and pilgrimage. In: Raj, R. and Griffin, K. (eds) *Religious Tourism and Pilgrimage Management: An International Perspective*, 2nd edn. CAB International, Wallingford, UK. DOI: 10.1079/9781780645230.0000.

Coleman, S. and Eade, J. (eds) (2018) *Pilgrimage and the Political Economy: Translation of the Sacred*. Berghahn Books, New York.

Collins-Kreiner, N. and Gatrell, J.D. (2006) Tourism, heritage and pilgrimage: the case of Haifa's Bahá'í gardens. *Journal of Heritage Tourism* 1(1), 32–50. DOI: 10.1080/17438730608668464.

David, P.A. (1994) Why are institutions the 'carriers of history'? Path dependence and the evolution of conventions, organizations and institutions'. *Structural Change and Economic Dynamics* 5(2), 205–220. DOI: 10.1016/0954-349X(94)90002-7.

Digance, J. (2006) Religious and secular pilgrimage. In: Timothy, D.J. and Olsen, D.H. (eds) *Tourism, Religion and Spiritual Journeys*. Routledge, London, pp. 36–48.

Durán-Sánchez, A., Álvarez-García, J., del la Cruz del Río-Rama, M. and Oliveira, C. (2018) Religious tourism and pilgrimage: bibliometric overview. *Religions* 9(9), 249. DOI: 10.3390/rel9090249.

Eade, J. and Dionigi, A. (eds) (2015) *International Perspectives on Pilgrimage Studies: Itineraries, Gaps and Obstacles*. Routledge, New York.

Eade, J. and Katic, M. (2014) *Pilgrimage, Politics and Place-Making in Eastern Europe*. Ashgate Studies in Pilgrimage, Routledge, New York.

Edgell, D.L. and Swanson, J.R. (2019) *Tourism Policy and Planning: Yesterday, Today, and Tomorrow*, 3rd edn. Routledge, New York.

Elliott, J. (1997) *Tourism: Politics and Public Sector Management*. Routledge, New York.

Falaster, C., Zanin, L.M. and Guerrazzi, L.A. (2017) Institutional theory in tourism research: new opportunities from an evolving theory. *Brazilian Journal of Tourism Research* 11(2), 270–293. DOI: 10.7784/rbtur.v11i2.1310.

Franco, J. and Bozonelos, D, *et al.* (2020) History and development of the empirical study of politics. In: Franco, J., Lee, C., Vue, K., Bozonelos, D., Omae, M. et al. (eds) *Introduction to Political Science Research Methods*, 1st edn. Academic Senate for California Community College. Available at: https://socialsci.libretexts.org/Bookshelves/Political_Science_and_Civics/Introduction_to_Political_Science_Research_Methods_(Franco_et_al.) (accessed 3 May 2023)

Friedlander, L. (2010) Sacred geographies: myth and ritual in serious games. In: van Eck, R. (ed.) *Interdisciplinary Models and Tools for Serious Games: Emerging Concepts and Future Directions*. IGI Global, Hershey, PA, pp. 125–145.

Fukuyama, F. (2013) What is governance? *Governance: An International Journal of Policy, Administration, and Institutions* 26(3), 347–368. DOI: 10.1111/gove.12035.

Goeldner, C.R. and Brent Ritchie, J.R.B. (2012) *Tourism, Principles, Practices, Philosophies*. Wiley, Maitland, FL.

Griffin, K. and Raj, R. (2017) The importance of religious tourism and pilgrimage: reflecting on definitions, motives and data. *International Journal of Religious Tourism and Pilgrimage* 5(3), pp. ii–ix.

Hall, C.M. (1994) *Tourism and Politics: Policy, Place and Power*. Wiley, Maitland, FL.

Hall, C.M. (1995) *Tourism and Public Policy*. Routledge, New York.

Hall, C.M. (2012) A typology of governance and its implications for tourism policy analysis. In: Bramwell, B. and Lane, B. (eds) *Tourism Governance: Critical Perspectives on Governance and Sustainability*. Routledge, New York.

Hall, C.M. (2017) Tourism and geopolitics: the political imaginary of territory, tourism, and space. In: Hall, D. (ed.) *Tourism and Geopolitics: Issues and Concepts from Central and Eastern Europe*. CAB International, Wallingford, UK.

Holden, A. (2005) *Tourism Studies and the Social Sciences*. Routledge, London. DOI: 10.4324/9780203502396.

Iqbal, K. (2019) The rise of Hindutva, saffron terrorism and south Asian regional security. *Journal of Security and Strategic Analyses* 5(1), 43–63.

Isaac, R.K., Hall, C.M. and Higgins-Desbiolles, F. (2016) Introduction. In: Isaac, R.K., Hall, C.M. and Higgins-Desbiolles, F. (eds) *The Politics and Power of Tourism in Palestine*. Routledge, New York. DOI: 10.4324/9781315740508.

Isakhan, B. (2020) The Islamic state attacks on Shia Holy sites and the "Shrine Protection Narrative": threats to sacred space as a mobilization frame. *Terrorism and Political Violence* 32(4), 724–748. DOI: 10.1080/09546553.2017.1398741.

Jackowski, A. and Smith, V.L. (1992) Polish pilgrim-tourists. *Annals of Tourism Research* 19(1), 92–106. DOI: 10.1016/0160-7383(92)90109-3.

Jobani, Y. and Perez, N. (2020) Governing the Sacred. In: *Governing the Sacred: Political Toleration in Five Contested Sacred Sites*. Oxford University Press, Oxford, UK. DOI: 10.1093/oso/9780190932381.001.0001.

Korstanje, M.E. and George, B. (2021) Safety, fear, risk, and terrorism in the context of religious tourism. In: Olsen, D.H. and Timothy, D.J. (eds) *The Routledge Handbook of Religious and Spiritual Tourism*. Routledge, New York.

Korstanje, M.E. and Olsen, D.H. (2020) Negotiating the intersections between dark tourism and pilgrimage. In: Olsen, D.H. and Korstanje, M.E. (eds) *Dark Tourism and Pilgrimage*. CAB International, Wallingford, UK.

Lam, R. (2020) Sri Lankan government ties religious freedom to protection of Buddhism. *Buddhistdoor Global*. Available at: https://www.buddhistdoor.net/news/sri-lankan-government-ties-religious-freedom-to-protection-of-buddhism/ (accessed 26 August 2022).

Matthews, H.G. (1975) International tourism and political science research. *Annals of Tourism Research* 2(4), 195–203.

Moira, P., Parthenis, S., Kontoudaki, A. and Katsoula, O. (2009) Religious tourism in Greece: the necessity to classify religious resources for their rational valorization. In: Trono, A. (ed.), *Tourism, Religion and Culture. Regional Development through Meaningful Tourism Experiences. Proceedings of the International Conference, University of Salento 27th/30th October 2009*. Mario Congredo Publ, Salento, Italy, pp. 465–480.

Mylonopoulos, D., Moira, P., Nikolaou, E. and Spakouri, A. (2009) Pilgrimage centers of Greece and tourism development. The legal framework of protection. In: Trono, A. (ed.) *Tourism, Religion and Culture. Regional Development through Meaningful Tourism Experiences. Proceedings of the International Conference, University of Salento 27th/30th October 2009*. Mario Congredo Publ., Salento, Italy, pp. 523–537.

North, D.C. (1991) Institutions. *Journal of Economic Perspectives* 5(1), 97–112. DOI: 10.1257/jep.5.1.97.

Novy, J. and Colomb, C. (2019) Urban tourism as a source of contention and social mobilisations: a critical review. *Tourism Planning & Development* 16(4), 358–375. DOI: 10.1080/21568316.2019.1577293.

Olsen, D.H. and Timothy, D.J. (2006) Tourism and religion journeys. In: Timothy, D.J. and Olsen, D.H. (eds) *Tourism, Religion and Spiritual Journeys*. Routledge, London, pp. 1–21. DOI: 10.4324/9780203001073.

O'Neil, P.H. (2021) *Essentials of Comparative Politics*, 7th edn. W.W. Norton and Company, New York.

Pearce, P. (1991) *Fundamentals of Tourist Motivation*. International Academy for the Study of Tourism. University of Calgary, Canada.

Raj, R. and Griffin, K. (2015) *Religious Tourism and Pilgrimage Management: An International Perspective*, 2nd edn. CAB International, Wallingford, UK. DOI: 10.1079/9781780645230.0000.

Raj, R. and Griffin, K. (2017) *Conflicts, Religion and Culture in Tourism*. CAB International, Wallingford, UK. DOI: 10.1079/9781786390646.0000.

Rashid, A.G. (2018) Religious tourism – A review of the literature. *Journal of Hospitality and Tourism Insights* 1(2), 150–167. DOI: 10.1108/JHTI-10-2017-0007.

Reader, I. (2014) *Pilgrimage in the Marketplace*. Routledge, New York. DOI: 10.4324/9781315885704.

Rinschede, G. (1992) Forms of religious tourism. *Annals of Tourism Research* 19(1), 51–67. DOI: 10.1016/0160-7383(92)90106-Y.

Robichaud, P. (1999) *Tourist or Pilgrim?: Rescuing the Jubilee—The Heart of Pilgrimage Is Conversion, Not Travel; The Journey Is Only the Means to the End (Religious Travel to Rome, Italy as the Year 2000 Approaches)*. America Press, Inc, Boston, MA.

Shackley, M. (2001) *Managing Sacred Sites: Service Provision and Visitor Experience*. Continuum Press, London and New York.

Sharpley, R. (2015) Tourism: a vehicle for development? In: Sharpley, R. and Tefler, D. (eds) *Tourism and Development: Concepts and Issues*. Channel View Publications, Bristol, UK, pp. 3–30. DOI: 10.21832/9781845414740.

Smith, V. (1992) The quest in guest. *Annals of Tourism Research* 19(1), 1–17.

Stabler, M.J., Papatheodorou, A. and Sinclair, M.T. (2010) *The Economics of Tourism*. Routledge, London. DOI: 10.4324/9780203864272.

Stausberg, M. (2011) *Religion and Tourism: Crossroads, Destinations and Encounters*. Routledge, London.

Telfer, D.J. (2015) The evolution of development theory and tourism. In: Sharpley, R. and Tefler, D.J. (eds) *Tourism and Development: Concepts and Issues*. Channel View Publications, Bristol, UK, pp. 31–73. DOI: 10.21832/9781845414740.

Timothy, D.J. and Olsen, D.H. (2006) *Tourism, Religion and Spiritual Journeys*. Routledge, London. DOI: 10.4324/9780203001073.

Trono, A. (2015) Politics, policy and the practice of religious tourism. In: Raj, R. and Griffin, K. (eds) *Religious Tourism and Pilgrimage Management: An International Perspective*, 2nd edn. CAB International, Wallingford, UK.

Turner, V. and Turner, E. (1978) *Image and Pilgrimage in Christian Culture: Anthropological Perspectives*. Columbia University Press, New York.

Vukonić, B. (1996) *Tourism and Religion*. Emerald Publishing Limited, London.

WTTC (2022) Economic impact reports. Available at: https://wttc.org/Research/Economic-Impact (accessed 8 August 2022).

Μοίρα, Π. (2009) *Θρησκευτικός Τουρισμός* [Religious Tourism]. Interbooks, Αθήνα [in Greek].

Μοίρα, Π. (2019) *Θρησκευτικός Τουρισμός Και Προσκύνημα. Πολιτικές-Διαχείριση-Αειφορία [Religious Tourism and Pilgrimage. Politics-Management-Sustainability]*. εκδ. Φαίδιμος, Αθήνα [in Greek].

Μοίρα, Π. (2022) *Τουρισμός. Ιστορία, Εξέλιξη, Προοπτικές [Tourism. History, Development, Prospects]*. Εκδ. Τζιόλα, Θεσσαλονίκη [in Greek].

2 Religious and Faith Tourism and the Politicization of Sacred Sites

Daniel H. Olsen*

Department of Geography, Brigham Young University, Provo, USA

Abstract

Sacred sites are centres of 'emotionally charged visions of life' (Friedlander, 2010, p. 125), which mark places where the sacred has manifested itself within mundane space. However, sacred sites are also places that are contested by religious and secular groups in terms of control, maintenance and interpretation. The purpose of this chapter is to examine the politicization of sacred sites in the context of religious and faith tourism. First, the characteristics of sacred spaces and places that lead them to be politicized are noted. Then, three types of politicization of sacred sites are examined, followed by a discussion of how this politicization affects religious and faith tourism before concluding.

2.1 Introduction

On a Sunday afternoon in early 2018, the Church of the Holy Sepulchre closed its doors for several hours to protest a proposed municipal plan to tax religious properties within the city of Jerusalem. This proposal would not tax major religious sites that attracted millions of tourists and pilgrims a year, but rather church-owned businesses (Lewis, 2018). As one of the poorest cities in Israel, the search for additional revenue had led the mayor of Jerusalem to propose this tax plan, which would bring in tens of millions of dollars of revenue. In a statement, the municipality of Jerusalem wrote that '...hotels, halls and businesses cannot be exempt from municipal taxes simply because they are owned by the churches. These are not houses of worship.... We will no longer require Jerusalem's residents to bear the burden of these huge sums.' In response, the Greek Orthodox, Roman Catholic, and Armenian Apostolic leaders who run the Church of the Holy Sepulchre argued that this taxation plan would 'weaken the Christian presence in Jerusalem,' and was akin to a 'systematic campaign of abuse' against them (APNews, 2018, n.p.). The move to close one of the most famous pilgrimage-tourism landmarks in the city, as well as the closure of other major religious sites in other parts of Israel by other Christian groups in solidarity with the Church of the Holy Sepulchre, led to a suspension of the tax plan a couple of days later (Casper, 2018). What made this a historic event was that considering the 'politics of possession' at Jerusalem's Holy Sepulchre – where disputes over sacred space as 'real estate' have led to violent clashes between the three Christian communities that control different sections of the church in the past (see Bowman, 2011) – the threat of taxation of non-sacred religious properties prompted a heretofore unknown degree of unity between them.

*dholsen@byu.edu

© CAB International 2023. *The Politics of Religious Tourism* (eds D. Bozonelos and P. Moira)
DOI: 10.1079/9781800621732.0002

This tension between Christian Church leaders and the municipality of Jerusalem highlights the textured or layered politics that can arise at even the smallest of scales when it involves sacred spaces. Sacred spaces and places at various scales are locations on the earth's surface that are marked and maintained as special, being set apart from the profane or mundane world. They are also centres of 'emotionally charged visions of life' (Friedlander, 2010), repositories of collective memory, receptacles of embodied ritual and ritualized commemoration, storehouses of sacred time, and visible reminders of the sacred in everyday life (Chidester and Linenthal, 1995; Holloway, 2003; Hamilton and Spicer, 2016). As such, sacred spaces and places play an important role in the creation and maintenance of emotional geographies and landscapes. However, these sacred spaces and places do not exist in a sociopolitical and spatial vacuum, but rather are affected by adjacent past and present political and social events and trends (Olsen, 2019a). As such, they are often sites of contestation within or between social, political and religious groups in terms of ownership and narrative control or are utilized to promote and protest – or counter-protest – political or religious ideologies, often in violent terms (see Schramm, 2011).

This dichotomous use of sacred spaces and places has led many scholars to examine the *poetics* and *politics* of sacred space, or what Chidester and Linenthal (1995, p. 6) refer to as the *substantial* and *situational* characteristics of the sacred. The poetic or substantial view of sacred spaces refers to a space or place as having an 'essential character' (Chidester and Linenthal, 1995, p. 5) – that sacred space is an 'ontological given' (della Dora, 2018). In other words, there is some 'thing' that constitutes the 'sacred' – the sacred has a reality – and that reality on occasion manifests itself or 'irrupts' on the earth's surface, making those areas qualitatively different from areas around them (della Dora, 2018). These spaces, then, provide the possibility for people to enter into the presence of the divine (Eliade, 1959). However, other scholars deny that the 'sacred' has inherent mystical or otherworldly qualities. Instead, what constitutes the sacred is based on power relations, and is socially constructed by groups

who seek to claim space based on economic, political, historical, or socio-cultural bases. As such, sacred spaces and places are devoid of meaning until an individual or group gives them meaning – sacred meaning – leading to 'a potentially unlimited number of claims and counterclaims about the significance, boundaries, meanings, symbolism, interpretations and narratives, surveillance, maintenance, importance and use of sacred sites...at multiple scales' (Olsen, 2019b). However, even in cases where the sacred divinely irrupts, individuals and groups seek to control these spaces and places to maintain interpretational purity, to claim legitimacy and to make those locations 'officially sacred' (Kong, 2001).

The purpose of this chapter is to examine the politicization of sacred sites and its relationship to religious and faith tourism. First, the characteristics of sacred spaces and places that lead them to be politicized are noted. Then, three types of politicization of sacred sites are examined, followed by a discussion of how this politicization affects religious and faith tourism before concluding.

2.2 Why Are Sacred Sites Politicized?

If sacred sites are inherently contested – where 'power, identity, meaning and behaviour are constructed, negotiated and renegotiated according to socio-cultural dynamics' (Aitcheson and Reeves, 1998, p. 51; in Pritchard and Morgan, 2001) – then it is right to ask what characteristics of sacred sites lead to their politicization. In other words, what causes disputes involving sacred sites?

First, as noted previously, sacred sites are centres of 'emotionally charged visions of life' (Friedlander, 2010). These 'visions of life' stem from religious beliefs regarding the nature of reality and appropriate living, in which beliefs and ethical living standards are often set and rarely change. Unlike sacred lands that lack clearly defined boundaries, the places from which these 'visions of life' spring are often bounded and demarcated. Sacred sites are thus often the loci of emotional attachment for individuals, groups, communities, and faith and secular organizations. For example, 'A person's religious self can be linked to places and spaces significant to his/her religion' (Mazumdar and Mazumdar, 2004, p. 386), and the same is true for individuals or groups at multiple scales. Sacred places that people are most attached to have certain qualities of place – where a notable religious event occurred or where an important religious person is buried. Religious architecture, objects, icons and art also create a strong sense of symbolic meaning – a 'sense of place' (Shackley, 2001) or 'spiritual magnetism' (Preston, 1992) that fosters emotional attachment to these places. The stronger the emotional attachment people have to a sacred place, the more psychologically 'indivisible' or unshareable it becomes (Sosis, 2011)[1]. As such, religious sites can become politicized when disparate stakeholders or groups within the same stakeholder set seek to claim these sites (Olsen and Timothy, 2002), or when secular authorities attempt to co-opt or interfere with the performative or interpretational practices at these sites. Many sacred sites also serve as centres of religious nationalism, where individual or networks of religious sites symbolize either transnational diasporic nationalism or ethnic homelands which can cause conflict when contested (e.g. Skrbis, 2005; De Silva, 2013; Dubuisson and Genina, 2013; Olsen, 2016; Jaffrelot, 2017).

Second, sacred sites exist within community settings, where, over time, they become important components of community identity, economic development and urban/rural landscapes. These sites often play an important role in organizing community life, such as initiating calls to prayer, being end-points of ritual processions and centres of community activities. Sacred sites can also play an important role in economic development by serving as sites of pilgrimage or 'value-added' sites in the context of broader cultural tourism itineraries. While religious organizations and government officials often collaborate to preserve and utilize these sites for tourism and community purposes (Tilson, 2001, 2005; Olsen, 2003), over-commodification, heritagization or the destruction of sacred sites in the name of tourism or redevelopment can lead to conflict between community decision makers and the general public (Olsen, 2003; Sinha, 2011; Levi

and Kocher, 2013; Thouki, 2019; Barclay and Steele, 2020; Olsen and Timothy, 2021).

Third, ; see Collins-Kreiner, 2008) suggested several geographical elements or criteria related to sacred sites that determine whether they may be contested and politicized. The first two elements are the *physical aspects* of the site, including its shape and size, and its *location*. The more visible or conspicuous a sacred site, the higher the chance that it will become contested, especially if it becomes a symbol related to nationalism and inter-faith conflict. The third element is how local groups *perceive* a sacred site in terms of its fit. In other words, does the site fit naturally into the cultural landscape? Do local residents and religious and secular groups accept the religious group who controls the site? Does the architectural style fit the overall landscape aesthetic? The fourth element is *timing*. When was the sacred site built? Is it old, or new? The newer a sacred site is, the more 'transgressive' or 'deviant' (Cresswell, 1996) it may be viewed by both residents and religious and political stakeholders, which will increase its potential for contestation.

Fourth, Hassner (2013) argues that disputes over sacred sites occur because of contests over legitimacy, security or profit. Hassner argues that *legitimacy* disputes occur when religious movements 'bifurcate,' or split into competing sects, which results in each sect staking claim 'to the sacred sites of the parent movement in order to establish its position as the rightful heir' (p. 325). These claims to legitimacy include not just ownership, but also interpretative authority over the site(s) in question. This is the case with the contestation over the spatial divisions in the Church of the Holy Sepulchre in Jerusalem (Bowman, 2011; Hamilton and Spicer, 2016) or claims to legal ownership of religious historical sites between sects within the Mormon movement (see Olsen and Timothy, 2002; Howlett, 2014). The second category of disputes regards *security*, particularly when groups utilize sacred sites as strongholds during times of war, believing that the other side will not want to destroy important religious heritage sites. The third category of dispute is when secular organizations, whether political or economic in nature, seek ownership over sacred lands for their geological resources for *profit* (e.g. Gottlieb, 2003; Carpenter *et al.*, 2009).

Fifth, similar to the discussion above, Hassner also lists three reasons why sacred sites are indivisible. The first reason is due to the *lack of cohesion*. If sacred spaces represent sacred time and space, then any additions or changes to its material design deprives the site of particular meanings and, at an extreme, amounts to a type of desecration. Second, sacred sites are indivisible because they mark the *boundaries* between sacred and profane space, and as such, sacred site boundaries must be maintained and guarded against the intrusion of secular forces and out-of-place persons or groups. Third, sacred sites are indivisible because of their *value* in the eyes of believers. Sacred sites are irreplaceable, and as such, must be owned and controlled. Losing control and ownership of these sites would represent a great loss to that faith community. As such, religious groups may resort to violent means to secure their religious rights over religious sites. Hassner thus suggests that the intensity of conflict over sacred sites will depend upon their religious significance – their primacy in a ranking of the sacrality of sacred sites – and political vulnerability – their importance in terms of political significance.

2.3 Examples of the Political Nature of Sacred Sites

World history is replete with examples of sacred sites that have been, and continue to be, contested by groups of all secular and religious persuasions. As such, there are hundreds of cases to draw upon regarding instances where sacred sites are the loci of politicization and violence. However, the examples listed below have been chosen to more concretely demonstrate ways in which sacred sites are contested and politicized based on the discussion above.

2.3.1 Sacred sites as sites of protest

Sacred sites become politicized when they become loci for socio-political protests. Often these protests are to contest the influence religious organizations have on secular matters. As a case in point, the Great Jubilee in 2000 was a major celebratory year for the Roman Catholic Church – commemorating two thousand years of Christianity and celebrating God's mercy, grace and forgiveness. Millions of Roman Catholics from around the world were expected to visit Rome and the Vatican throughout the year for special jubilee events. However, in early July of that year, a World Gay Pride event took place in Rome – a LGBT (Lesbian, Gay, Bisexual and Transgender) event whose organizers purposively chose to have the event take place alongside the Jubilee celebrations in Rome because it was the 'nerve centre' of Roman Catholicism. Organizers of the event hoped that the event would 'draw attention both nationally and internationally to discriminatory practices pointed at Rome's gay population' (Mudu, 2002, p. 189) due to the Church's restrictive biblical view on homosexuality (McNeill, 2003). Despite the protests of the Pope and the government of Rome, an estimated 200,000 people participated in the event.

In the same vein, LGBT groups struggle to claim the right to protest in public spaces in Jerusalem due to strong public opposition from the ultra-Orthodox Jewish community, as 'a person exposing their sexuality is considered impure and polluting in Jerusalem' (Misgav and Hartal, 2019, p. 62). Jerusalem is a religious city, and as such, petitions to the local government to hold a pride parade are repeatedly denied due to any potential overt antagonism over any LGBT presence in a public/sacred space. As such, most of the city's LGBT community has moved to Tel Aviv, which is a more secular city (Misgav and Hartal, 2019). If Jerusalem ever allowed an unfettered pride parade to take place, there would be a strong chance that, like in Rome, the parade would past by sites of religious significance to voice dissatisfaction with the religiously conservative nature of the city (Fig. 2.1).

At a much smaller scale, Salt Lake City, Utah, which is the headquarters for The Church of Jesus Christ of Latter-day Saints – an indigenous American Christian church that emerged in the 1830s – has also been a site for LGBT protests. While the Church reserves the right to speak on social issues because of the influence the Church has on city and state policymaking, people who disagree with the Church's views on LGBT issues often march on Temple Square, the Church's holiest site, to protest these views. For example, in 2008, thousands of people marched

Fig. 2.1. Mea Shearim neighbourhood in Jerusalem.
Source: Dino Bozonelos, 2020.

around Temple Square to protest the Church's involvement in California's Proposition 8, a law that, if enacted, would have banned same-sex marriages (KSL.com, 2008). In 2010, protestors walked around Temple Square to protest the words of a Church leader who spoke out against same-sex attraction (Taylor, 2010; Winters, 2010). In addition, in 2020, thousands of people went to Temple Square to protest changes to the honour code at Brigham Young University, sponsored by the Church, in which same-sex romantic behaviour could result in expulsion from the school (Matsuura, 2020). Temple Square is also a place of protest for many evangelical groups and street preachers who travel to Salt Lake City during the Church's semi-annual conference to raise awareness of what they consider the un-Christian nature of the Church (Weenig, 2015; Curtis, 2019).

Sacred sites can also be the epicentre of protests involving nationalism and minorities and subordinate groups in terms of resistance

and identity politics. For example, Luz (2008) pointed to an event in Tel Aviv in 2001 caused by a suicide bomber who blew himself up outside a disco. A street demonstration protesting the bombing the next day eventually became violent, causing local police to break up the protest. This protest, however, took on a nationalistic flavour when a few protesters brought Israeli flags in a spontaneous display of Israeli nationalism. Luz also highlighted the case of the Hassan Bek Mosque conflict in Jaffa, Israel, where Arab Israelis marched on a neglected mosque to protest its imminent destruction to make way for a shopping mall. The real estate deal was eventually rescinded, and the mosque was returned to the Jaffa Muslim Community.

At the same time, religious organizations sometimes use sacred sites to protest decisions by secular authorities. Religious morals and perspectives can be a motivator for social protest (Wood, 1999; Smith, 2014), ranging from peaceful demonstrations to violent activism

(Silberman *et al.*, 2005). This was the case with the closure of the Church of the Holy Sepulchre as noted earlier in this chapter, where religious leaders in Israel used their religious sites to protest the attempt to implement taxation policies in Jerusalem. Another example of this is the use of sacred sites to protest government and medical overreach regarding policies to limit pilgrim mobilities to sacred sites during the COVID-19 pandemic. For some religious leaders, the COVID-19 pandemic became a litmus test of faith – to see if believers would trust God or the medical community when it came to their decision to participate in religious rituals. As a case in point, leaders at the Fatima Masumeh Shrine in Qom, Iran, encouraged pilgrims to ignore government and medical mandates and travel to the shrine for healing (Quadri, 2020). In Brazil, adherents who did not go to church were seen as having a lack of faith in divine power (Capponi, 2020, n.p.), and in India, the closing of temples led one commentator to suggest that 'even the gods are [now] out of bounds' (Chaturvedi, 2020) (see Olsen and Timothy, 2020 for more examples). Many pilgrims chose to visit sacred sites during the pandemic to demonstrate their faith that God would protect them as they performed religious rituals (see Olsen and Shinde, 2023).

2.3.2 Sacred sites as in-place/out-of-place

Transgression, according to Cresswell (1996), occurs when people in authority criticize or fight against a particular group that they believe to be deviant – or out-of-place – in order to solidify their own ideological positions. The act of a new religious group attempting to impress themselves on the religious landscape of an area or become a political influence, causes there to be a 'break... from "normality" and causes a questioning of that which was previously considered "natural", "assumed", and "taken for granted" (Cresswell, 1996, p. 26) by the dominant group(s) in an area. As Sibley (1995, pp. 101–110, 185) argues, the acceptance of rejection of new religious influences by the dominant group(s) will depend upon 'the degree to which a group stereotype matches the place in which it is located.' As such, when

different religious and secular ideological beliefs converge at various scales, questions regarding the (in)appropriateness of the presence of a new religious other and whether they are 'in-place' or 'out-of-place' (Cresswell, 1996) arise as various stakeholders vie for control over maintaining or recreating the natural order of previously taken-for-granted socio-political relations within an area.

Todd (2017) gives the example of the spatial politics of religion within the city of Moscow. In Moscow, both the Russian Orthodox Church and Muslim religious community believe that they lack the necessary religious infrastructure to be visible and influential in the city. As such, both faith communities have made conscious efforts to build religious buildings throughout the city. The Russian Orthodox Church has been more successful in building their churches because of government interest in incorporating Russian Orthodoxy within the everyday lives of the city's inhabitants. However, attempts to build mosques has been more difficult because of vociferous opposition from various groups over concerns regarding potential Muslim influence over public spaces and politics – with mosques being the most visible sign of this influence. At a broader scale, attempts by religious communities to integrate themselves more fully into post-socialist Russia have met with great resistance in the form of what Kormina (2021, p. 574) calls 'passionate secularism', where several publics passionately call for a greater separation of church and state in Russia. This can be seen in the failed move to transfer the ownership of St. Isaac's Cathedral from the state government to the Russian Orthodox Church in 2016 due to opposition from several secular groups (Kormina, 2021).

Another example is the building of the Brigham Young University Jerusalem Center in the 1980s. Like other Christian Churches, The Church of Jesus Christ of Latter-day Saints considers Israel/Palestine to be a holy land, and that the return of the Diaspora Jews to Israel was a sign preceding the millennium. To this end, in 1841, Orson Hyde, a leading elder of the Church, was sent to the land of Palestine to dedicate it for the gathering of Israel and the eventual conversion of the Jews who would 'embrace Christ as their king' (Van Dyke and Berrett, 2008, p. 61). While the building of the

Jerusalem Center was supported by government officials at several scales, the building of the Center in such a visible, prominent location led several Orthodox and ultra-Orthodox Jewish groups to protest its building. The main concern was that the Church would eventually use this educational institution as a hub for missionary efforts among the Jewish population, resulting in a 'spiritual holocaust'. Eventually, the concerns of these groups ended when Church leaders formally signed a document promising not to engage in proselytizing efforts in Israel (Olsen and Guelke, 2004). While the Jerusalem Center is not a religious site per se, the presence of the Church in eastern Jerusalem caused Orthodox and ultra-Orthodox Jewish groups to question the city's religious status quo and argue that the Church's presence in such a visible location in the city was a transgression of the status quo.

2.3.3   Sacred sites as casualties of war and ideology

As noted above, many sacred sites end up being a casualty of politics, particularly during war (see Hassner, 2013). In some cases, sacred sites are destroyed in indiscriminate military offenses. However, historically, sacred sites have often been specifically targeted by opposing forces. One ancient example is the purposeful destruction of sacred sites around the Roman Empire during the Sullan Wars in 69 CE, when the Roman general Lucius Cornelius Sulla marched on Rome to make himself emperor (Rutledge, 2007). Roman armies also destroyed pagan sacred sites, deeming them as not legally 'consecrated' despite the Roman belief in respecting all gods and ancestors (Rutledge, 2007).

Bevan (2006, p. 8) argues that the destruction of architecture, including sacred sites, during times of war is not seen as collateral damage, but rather is a contemporary military strategy, because 'memories, history and identity [are] attached to architecture and place.' As Hoffman (2006, p. 1) notes, 'In the past 50 years, but particularly in the past several decades, it has become apparent that culture matters and that protecting it is the concern not only of local people and of sovereign nations, but of the international community.' As such, the purposeful

destruction of architecture is used as a 'weapon of war' (Bevan, 2006, p. 210), in which one side engages in an 'enforced forgetting' (p. 8) through this destruction to more fully claim victory and remove unwanted populations from an area. The destruction of cultural heritage sites occurs most often in cases when there is an increased or growing polarization between groups (Sørensen and Viejo-Rose, 2015).

For example, while the 1983–2009 civil war between Tamil separatists and the Sri Lankan government 'hardly qualified as a religious war' (Devotta, 2018, p. 281), Tamil separatists targeted Buddhist shrines because the Sri Lankan government privileged Buddhism over their traditional Hindu faith. These attacks against Buddhist sacred sites included indiscriminate shootings at monks and nuns at the Sri Maha Bodhiya complex – a sacred site for Sri Lankan Buddhists that houses a tree grown from a sapling of the Bodhi tree under which the original Buddha sat and became enlightened (Time.com, 1985) – and bombing the Sri Dalada Maligawa complex, believed to hold one of the original Buddha's teeth (Coningham and Lewer, 1999; Beech, 2019). The Tamil separatists also attacked and killed Muslims while they worshipped in their mosques because of their support for the Sri Lankan government during the civil war (Devotta, 2018). These acts of violence against Buddhist shrines and Muslim mosques later led local police to allow Muslims to destroy the Hindu Pathirakali Amman Temple in an act of reprisal after the civil war was over (McGilvray, 1997). During the Kosovo Conflict (1998–1999), 'immovable cultural properties' (Defreese, 2009, p. 258) in the form of Christian and Muslim religious sites were systematically targeted by both sides 'due to their high visibility and association with national identity' (p. 257) and 'ethno-nationalistic ideology' (p. 260). During the Bosnian War (1992–1995), over 1000 mosques, 480 Catholic churches, and 400 Serbian Orthodox churches were destroyed or severely damaged (Mose, 1996).

The destruction of religious sites is also a common occurrence where majority groups seek to remove the presence of deviant minority ethnic groups through the destruction of their sacred sites. This is the case in India, Myanmar and Xinjiang, China, where dominant ethnic communities purposefully seek to remove Muslim religious sites and symbols to both 'literally and symbolically...claim a space for the dominant group' and 'to engage in a historical revisionism that diminishes or vilifies Muslims belonging in the region' (Malji, 2021, p. 50).

In other cases, iconoclasm – 'an attack against and often the destruction of a physical object...that is believed to have some kind of spiritual power or sacred significance and which is worshipped in the place of the "true" God' (Noyes, 2016, pp. 3–4) – often occurs when dominant groups seek to solidify their ideological positions or recapture religious identity within an area. This has been particularly acute in locations where the Islamic State is the dominant religio-political force (Isakhan and González Zarandona, 2017; Ba, 2020). In these locations, non-Islamic icons are often defaced, beheaded, trampled upon, or, at the extreme, destroyed (Campion, 2017). For example, in 2012, Al-Qaeda-linked Islamists destroyed centuries-old mausoleums of saints in Timbuktu, Mali, considering these mausoleums a form of idolatry (Diarra, 2012; Bamidele et al., 2021). Another example that received international attention at the time was the destruction of the Bamiyan Buddhas in Afghanistan – two 6th century statues carved into sandstone cliffs. To justify the destruction of these statues, the Taliban argued that since no Buddhists were living in the area, the statues could not be considered a sacred place. However, there was an international uproar regarding the destruction of these statues (Francioni and Lenzerini, 2003). As Elias (2007, p. 26; Campion, 2017, p. 28) noted: 'Those who condemned the destruction of the statues on the grounds of preservation of global heritage, art, and religious tolerance view the icon smashers as the standard-bearers of an archaic ideology completely out of place in modern society.' One non-Islamic State example of the destruction of the sacred sites of a minority group for ideological purposes is the demolition of the Babri Masjid Mosque in Ayodhya, India in 1992. The destruction of the mosque took place in part to reclaim Hindu sacred space as the mosque was believed to have been built over a former Hindu temple which housed the birthplace of Rama, a Hindu deity (Bernbeck and Pollock, 1996; Bacchetta, 2000).

2.4 Religious and Faith Tourism and the Politics of Sacred Sites

Religious tourism, as a term used to describe a particular tourism niche market, is not easily defined. This is in part because of questions around whether this niche market should be defined from a supply or a demand perspective. The tourism industry normally defines its niche markets by the activities that people do while they travel, not their motivations for travel (Timothy and Olsen, 2006). As such, religious tourism is defined here as 'travel by tourists to religious destinations, cultures and sites regardless of motivation, whether the visits to these sites are of primary or secondary interest' (Olsen, 2008). This is different from the faith or pilgrimage tourism market, which involves 'trips undertaken by people who travel because they are motivated by religion' (Olsen, 2022, p. 284), and the spiritual tourism market, which is a form of tourism 'characterised by a self-conscious project of spiritual betterment' (Norman, 2012, p. 20). At the same time, all three tourism niche markets utilize sacred sites as a part of their itineraries.

Sacred sites have long been a part of travel itineraries and are considered value-added sites for people interested in culture, heritage and educational forms of travel. In many cases, the economic potential of religious tourism and faith tourism is used as a justification for the maintenance and support for sacred sites. Many important and popular sacred sites draw millions of religious and faith tourists a year, making these sites profitable for faith organizations and surrounding communities (Olsen, 2003; Shepherd, 2016). Also, religious tourism and, more particularly, faith tourism, are relatively recession-proof, as in times of crises people travel to religious sites for comfort and healing (Singh, 1998; Olsen and Shinde, 2023). However, the destruction of sacred sites or safety concerns can deter all but the most ardent faith tourists from visiting sacred sites, hurting the destination economically. This was the case during the second Intifada between 2000 and 2004, where economic activity and livelihoods were curtailed due to the lack of tourists to Israel (Farsakh, 2016). This decrease in economic activity also occurred throughout the broader Holy Land due to the sharp decrease in religious and faith tourists (Collins-Kreiner et al., 2006).

Religious and faith tourism can be utilized as a political tool to support various ideologies to sacred homelands. For example, Israeli Birthright tours are designed to take Diasporic Jewish youth on a tour of Israel to strengthen their Jewish identities and support for Israeli nationalism (Kelner, 2010; Sasson et al., 2014; Abramson, 2017). In the case of the longstanding Israeli/Palestinian conflict, American 'Zionist' tourists engage in faith tourism or pilgrimage-like travel to Israel to express solidary with and support for Israel (Belhaussen, 2009; Belhaussen and Ebel, 2009), giving rise to the 'Zionist tourism' niche market (Smith, 1999) that revolves around 'faith-based activism' (Belhaussen, 2009). This has led to the growth of 'Palestinian tourism', which challenges the hegemonic Christian and Israeli views of Israel in favour of the telling of the Palestinian side of the conflict and showing solidary with the Palestinian people (Isaac, 2009, 2010, 2018; Nasser, 2009). Schneider (2020) notes that as a counterbalance of sorts, some tour companies have developed alternative Jewish tourist itineraries that take Jewish youth to sites in the occupied Palestinian Territories to give a more balanced perspective of the conflict.

Even when sacred sites are destroyed, they are often still visited by both religious and faith tourists. For example, many people travel to see the reconstruction efforts of the Bamiyan Buddhas in Afghanistan to commemorate this ancient religious heritage. This increase in tourist visitation has been an economic boon to the region (Wyndham, 2015; Meharry, 2020). This is the same with the present-day faithscapes of Bosnia and Herzegovina, where memorial tours and visits to destroyed churches and mosques are a part of the heritage tourism product (Timothy, 2021, 2022). Also, the destruction of sacred groves and forests can lead to increased religious and faith tourism to these destinations in an attempt to convince government and tourism officials of the importance of preserving these sites for religious and ecotourism purposes (Nyamweru and Kimaru, 2008). Indeed, the economic potential of religious and faith tourism, along with the socio-cultural importance of natural sacred sites, can be a strong force in pressuring government officials

to participate in conservation efforts rather than to pursue resource extractive economic strategies (Verschuuren et al., 2010; Shinde and Olsen, 2020). In this sense, travel to sacred sites that are threatened with or have been destroyed can be considered a form of 'dark pilgrimage' (Olsen and Korstanje, 2020) or 'last chance tourism' (Lemelin et al., 2011).

Sacred sites that are the focus of ethno-religious conflict may also see an increase in visitation by religious and faith tourists. In the case of Medjugorje, one of the most active apparitional sites in the world (Skrbis, 2005), the 'specialness' of Medjugorje as a grassroots religious site for Roman Catholics was appropriated by Croatian nationalist discourse during the Bosnian War and became a symbol of Croatian identity and nationalism. As such, pilgrims and tourists flocked to Medjugorje for religious and/or nationalistic reasons (Skrbiš, 2007; Wiinikka-Lydon, 2010). After the war, the Muslim community in Bosnia and Herzegovina began to reappropriate and rebuild holy sites within the cultural landscape as a form of ethnonationalism (Henig, 2012).

2.5   Conclusion

In all the cases listed above, the politicization of sacred sites can increase religious and faith tourism to these locations. Rome saw a marked increase in the number of people who visited the city for the counter-protest, and the Brigham Young University Center brings hundreds of students (pre-COVID-19) a year from the United States to Jerusalem. Sacred sites are also rallying points for ethnonationalism, and the destruction of sacred sites can promote activism and encourage people to visit these sites after they are gone. While tourism is often viewed as a vehicle for peace and cross-cultural understanding (McIntosh, 2021; Shepherd, 2022), and tourism is generally seen as benefiting from peace (Litvin, 2020), conflict also is a tourism generator. Much of the cultural and heritage tourism market is based on visiting sites of death, atrocity and the commemoration of victors of war (Stone et al., 2018; Vanneste and Winter, 2018; Lischer, 2019). While dissonance, conflict and contestation at religious sacred sites is not good from a socio-cultural perspective, these centres of 'emotionally charged visions of life' (Friedlander, 2010) bring people to a destination, which in turn brings in much needed tourism dollars. As such, it is an irony that religious and faith tourism would benefit from conflict when the sacred sites people visit are designed to promote peace.

Note

[1] However, there are several studies that demonstrate efforts to 'share' sacred spaces and places–albeit at times this sharing is contentious (for example, see Hayden, 2002; Kilde, 2008; Albera and Couroucli, 2012; Hayden and Walker, 2013). Shinde (2015) suggests that many religious groups practice 'religious tolerance' when members of one faith tradition interact with people from other faith/secular traditions at their sacred sites (see also Nyaupane et al., 2015).

References

Abramson, Y. (2017) Making a homeland, constructing a diaspora: the case of Taglit-Birthright Israel. *Political Geography* 58, 14–23.

Aitcheson, C. and Reeves, C. (1998) Gendered (bed)spaces: the culture and commerce of women only tourism. In: Aitchison, C. and Jordan, F. (eds) *Gender, Space and Identity: Leisure, Culture and Commerce*. Leisure Studies Association, Brighton, UK, pp. 47–68. DOI: 10.1080/026143698375150.

Albera, D. and Couroucli, M. (eds) (2012) *Sharing Sacred Spaces in the Mediterranean: Christians, Muslims, and Jews at Shrines and Sanctuaries*. Indiana University Press, Bloomington, IN.

APNews (2018) Christians shutter famous Jerusalem church to protest taxes. Available at: https://apnews.com/article/9af7d38ed96540e5852f5cd6c08ae50a (accessed 20 June 2022).

Ba, O. (2020) Governing the souls and community: Why do Islamists destroy world heritage sites? *Cambridge Review of International Affairs* 35(1), 73–90.

Bacchetta, P. (2000) Sacred space in conflict in India: the Babri Masjid affair. *Growth and Change* 31(2), 255–284. DOI: 10.1111/0017-4815.00128.

Bamidele, S., Idowu, O.O. and Ajisage, D. (2021) Securing world heritage sites: insurgency and the destruction of UNESCO's world heritage sites in Timbuktu, Mali. *GeoJournal* 87(4), 2467–2478. DOI: 10.1007/s10708-021-10383-9.

Barclay, S.H. and Steele, M. (2020) Rethinking protections for Indigenous sacred sites. *Harvard Law Review* 134(4), 1294–1359.

Beech, H. (2019) A new enemy but the same hate: can Sri Lanka heal its divisions? *New York Times*. Available at: https://www.nytimes.com/2019/05/05/world/asia/sri-lanka-attacks-hate.html (accessed 27 April 2022).

Belhaussen, Y. (2009) Fundamentalist Christian pilgrimages as a political and cultural force. *Journal of Heritage Tourism* 4(2), 131–144. DOI: 10.1080/17438730802366516.

Belhaussen, Y. and Ebel, J. (2009) Tourism, faith and politics in the Holy Land: an ideological analysis of evangelical pilgrimage. *Current Issues in Tourism* 12(4), 359–378.

Bernbeck, R. and Pollock, S. (1996) Ayodhya, archaeology, and identity. *Current Anthropology* 37(S1), S138–S142.

Bevan, R. (2006) *The Destruction of Memory: Architecture at War*. Reaktion, London.

Bowman, G. (2011) "In dubious battle on the Plains of Heav'n": the politics of possession in Jerusalem's Holy Sepulchre. *History and Anthropology* 22(3), 371–399.

Campion, K. (2017) Blast through the past: terrorist attacks on art and antiquities as a reconquest of the modern Jihadi identity. *Perspectives on Terrorism* 11(1), 26–39.

Capponi, G. (2020) Overlapping values: religious and scientific conflicts during the COVID-19 crisis in Brazil. *Social Anthropology* 28(2), 236–237. DOI: 10.1111/1469-8676.12795.

Carpenter, K.A., Katyal, S.K. and Riley, A.R. (2009) In defense of property. *Yale Law Journal* 118, 1022–1125.

Casper, J. (2018) Holy Sepulchre will reopen after Jerusalem suspends church tax grab. *Christianity Today.Com*. Available at: https://www.christianitytoday.com/news/2018/february/holy-sepulchre-reopen-jerusalem-suspend-church-tax-property.html (accessed 20 June 2022).

Chaturvedi, A. (2020) COVID-19 puts curbs on religious travel. *India Times*. Available at: https://economictimes.indiatimes.com/news/politics-and-nation/covid-19-puts-curbs-on-religious-travel/articleshow/74742051.cms (accessed 1 June 2020).

Chidester, D. and Linenthal, E.T. (1995) Introduction. In: Chidester, D. and Linenthal, E.T. (eds) *American Sacred Space*. Indiana University Press, Bloomington, IN, pp. 1–42.

Collins-Kreiner, N. (2008) Religion and politics: new religious sites and spatial transgression in Israel. *Geographical Review* 98(2), 197–213.

Collins-Kreiner, N., Kliot, N., Mansfeld, Y. and Sagi, K. (2006) *Christian Tourism to the Holy Land: Pilgrimage during Security Crisis*. Ashgate, Burlington, VT.

Coningham, R. and Lewer, N. (1999) Paradise lost: the bombing of the temple of the tooth—A UNESCO world heritage site in Sri Lanka. *Antiquity* 73(282), 857–866.

Cresswell, T. (1996) *In Place/Out of Place: Geography, Ideology, and Transgression*. University of Minnesota Press, Minneapolis, MN.

Curtis, L.D. (2019) Photos: outside conference center are protests, hymns, tourism. *KJZZ.Com*. Available at: https://kjzz.com/news/local/photos-outside-conference-center-are-protests-hymns-tourism (accessed 28 April 2022).

Defreese, M. (2009) Kosovo: cultural heritage in conflict. *Journal of Conflict Archaeology* 5(1), 257–269. DOI: 10.1163/157407709X12634580640614.

della Dora, V. (2018) Infrasecular geographies: making, unmaking and remaking sacred space. *Progress in Human Geography* 42(1), 44–71. DOI: 10.1177/0309132516666190.

De Silva, P. (2013) Reordering of postcolonial Sri Pāda Temple in Sri Lanka: Buddhism, state and nationalism. *History and Sociology of South Asia* 7(2), 155–176. DOI: 10.1177/2230807513479041.

Devotta, N. (2018) Religious intolerance in post-civil war Sri Lanka. *Asian Affairs* 49(2), 278–300. DOI: 10.1080/03068374.2018.1467660.

Diarra, A. (2012) Mali Islamists destroy holy Timbuktu sites. *Reuters.Com*. Available at: https://www.reuters.com/article/us-mali-crisis/mali-islamists-destroy-holy-timbuktu-sites-idUSBRE85T04E20120630 (accessed 28 April 2022).

Dubuisson, E.M. and Genina, A. (2013) Claiming an ancestral homeland: Kazakh pilgrimage and migration in Inner Asia. In: Reeves, M. (ed.) *Movement, Power and Place in Central Asia and Beyond*. Routledge, London and New York, pp. 119–136. DOI: 10.4324/9780203718360.

Eliade, M. (1959) *The Sacred and the Profane: The Nature of Religion*. Harcourt, Inc, Orlando, FL.

Elias, J.J. (2007) (Un)making idolatry. *Future Anterior* 4(2), 12–29.

Farsakh, L. (2016) Palestinian economic development: paradigm shifts since the first Intifada. *Journal of Palestine Studies* 45(2), 55–71.

Francioni, F. and Lenzerini, F. (2003) The destruction of the Buddhas of Bamiyan and international law. *European Journal of International Law* 14(4), 619–651.

Friedlander, L. (2010) Sacred geographies: myth and ritual in serious games. In: Van Eck, R. (ed.) *Interdisciplinary Models and Tools for Serious Games: Emerging Concepts and Future Directions*. IGI Global, Hershey, PA, pp. 125–145. DOI: 10.4018/978-1-61520-719-0.

Gottlieb, R.S. (2003) *This Sacred Earth: Religion, Nature, Environment*. Routledge, London and New York. DOI: 10.4324/9780203426982.

Hamilton, S. and Spicer, A. (2016) Defining the holy: the delineation of sacred space. In: Spicer, A. (ed.) *Defining the Holy: Sacred Space in Medieval and Early Modern Europe*. Routledge, London and New York, pp. 19–42.

Hassner, R. (2013) Conflicts over sacred ground. In: Kitts, M., Juergensmeyer, M. and Jeeryson, M. (eds) *Oxford Handbook on Religion and Violence*. Oxford University Press, New York, pp. 324–331.

Hayden, R. (2002) Antagonistic tolerance: competitive sharing of religious sites in South Asia and the Balkans. *Current Anthropology* 43(2), 205–231.

Hayden, R.M. and Walker, T.D. (2013) Intersecting religioscapes: a comparative approach to trajectories of change, scale, and competitive sharing of religious spaces. *Journal of the American Academy of Religion* 81(2), 399–426.

Henig, D. (2012) "This is our little hajj": Muslim holy sites and reappropriation of the sacred landscape in contemporary Bosnia. *American Ethnologist* 39(4), 751–765.

Hoffman, B. (2006) *Art and Cultural Heritage: Law, Policy, and Practice*. Cambridge University Press, Cambridge, UK.

Holloway, J. (2003) Make-believe: spiritual practice, embodiment, and sacred space. *Environment and Planning A* 35(11), 1961–1974.

Howlett, D.J. (2014) *Kirtland Temple: The Biography of a Shared Mormon Sacred Space*. University of Illinois Press, Urbana, IL. DOI: 10.5406/illinois/9780252038488.001.0001.

Isaac, R.K. (2009) Alternative tourism: Can the segregation wall in Bethlehem be a tourist attraction? *Tourism and Hospitality Planning & Development* 6(3), 247–254. DOI: 10.1080/14790530903363381.

Isaac, R.K. (2010) Palestinian tourism in transition: hope, aspiration, or reality? *The Journal of Tourism and Peace Research* 1(1), 16–26.

Isaac, R.K. (2018) From pilgrimage to dark tourism? A new kind of tourism in Palestine. In: Gmelch, S.B. and Kaul, A. (eds) *Tourists and Tourism. A Reader*. Waveland Press Inc, Long Grove, IL, pp. 179–186.

Isakhan, B. and González Zarandona, J.A. (2017) Layers of religious and political iconoclasm under the Islamic State: symbolic sectarianism and pre-monotheistic iconoclasm. *International Journal of Heritage Studies* 24(1), 1–16. DOI: 10.1080/13527258.2017.1325769.

Jaffrelot, C. (2017) From holy sites to web sites: Hindu nationalism, from sacred territory to diasporic ethnicity. In: Michel, P., Possamai, A. and Tuner, S. (eds) *Religions, Nations, and Transnationalism in Multiple Modernities*. Palgrave Macmillan, New York, pp. 153–174.

Kelner, S. (2010) *Tours That Bind: Diaspora, Pilgrimage, and Israeli Birthright Tourism*. New York University Press, New York.

Kilde, J.H. (2008) *Sacred Power, Sacred Space: An Introduction to Christian Architecture and Worship*. Oxford University Press, Cambridge, UK. DOI: 10.1093/acprof:oso/9780195314694.001.0001.

Kong, L. (2001) Mapping 'new' geographies of religion: politics and poetics in modernity. *Progress in Human Geography* 25(2), 211–233. DOI: 10.1191/030913201678580485.

Kormina, J. (2021) The church should know its place': the passions and the interests of urban struggle in post-atheist Russia. *History and Anthropology* 32(5), 574–595. DOI: 10.1080/02757206.2020.1848822.

KSL.com (2008) Thousands of prop. 8 opponents protest LDS church at temple square. Available at: https://ksl.com/article/4728411/thousands-of-prop-8-opponents-protest-lds-church-at-temple-square (accessed 18 April 2022).

Lemelin, R.H., Dawson, J. and Stewart, E.J. (eds) (2011) *Last Chance Tourism: Adapting Tourism Opportunities in a Changing World*. Routledge, London and New York.

Levi, D. and Kocher, S. (2013) Perception of sacredness at heritage religious sites. *Environment and Behavior* 45(7), 912–930. DOI: 10.1177/0013916512445803.

Lewis, O. (2018) Christian leaders shutter Jerusalem holy site to protest Israeli tax, land policies. *Huffington Post*. Available at: https://www.huffpost.com/entry/church-leaders-shutter-jerusalem-holy-site-to -protest-israeli-tax-land-policies_n_5a942030e4b03b55731e4a5d (accessed 11 April 2022).

Lischer, S.K. (2019) Narrating atrocity: genocide memorials, dark tourism, and the politics of memory. *Review of International Studies* 45(5), 805–827. DOI: 10.1017/S0260210519000226.

Litvin, S.W. (2020) "Tourism and peace": a review and commentary. Tourism Review International 23(3–4), 173–181.

Luz, N. (2008) The politics of sacred places: Palestinian identity, collective memory, and resistance in the Hassan Bek Mosque conflict. *Environment and Planning D: Society and Space* 26(6), 1036–1052. DOI: 10.1068/d2508.

Malji, A. (2021) People don't want a Mosque here: destruction of minority religious sites as a strategy of nationalism. *Journal of Religion and Violence* 9(1), 50–69. DOI: 10.5840/jrv202142086.

Matsuura, A. (2020) CES letter addresses BYU Honor Code updates. *The Daily Universe*. Available at: https://universe.byu.edu/2020/03/04/ces-letter-addresses-byu-honor-code-updates/ (accessed 18 April 2022).

Mazumdar, S. and Mazumdar, S. (2004) Religion and place attachment: a study of sacred places. *Journal of Environmental Psychology* 24(3), 385–397. DOI: 10.1016/j.jenvp.2004.08.005.

McGilvray, D.B. (1997) Tamils and Muslims in the shadow of war: schism or continuity? *South Asia: Journal of South Asian Studies* 20(s1), 239–253. DOI: 10.1080/00856409708723313.

McIntosh, I.S. (2021) Pilgrimage, tourism, and peace building. In: Olsen, D.H. and Timothy, D.J. (eds) *The Routledge Handbook of Religious and Spiritual Tourism*. Routledge, London and New York, pp. 120–132. DOI: 10.4324/9780429201011.

McNeill, D. (2003) Rome, global city? Church, state and the Jubilee 2000. *Political Geography* 22(5), 535–556. DOI: 10.1016/S0962-6298(03)00034-9.

Meharry, J.E. (2020) Nationalism, politics and the practice of archaeology in Afghanistan: a case study of Bamiyan. In: Peycam, P., Wang, S.-L. and Hsiao, H.-H.M. (eds) *Heritage as Aid and Diplomacy in Asia*. ISEAS Publishing, Singapore, pp. 226–253. DOI: 10.1355/9789814881166.

Misgav, C. and Hartal, G. (2019) Queer urban movements in Tel Aviv and Jerusalem: a comparative discussion. In: Yacobi, H. and Nasasra, M. (eds) *Routledge Handbook on Middle East Cities*. Routledge, London and New York, pp. 57–74.

Mose, G.M. (1996) The destruction of churches and mosques in Bosnia Herzegovina: seeking a rights-based approach to the protection of religious cultural property. *Buffalo Journal of International Law* 3(1), 180–208.

Mudu, P. (2002) Repressive tolerance: the gay movement and the Vatican in Rome. *GeoJournal* 58(2), 189–196. DOI: 10.1023/B:GEJO.0000010838.88923.86.

Nasser, C. (2009) Silenced voices in the development of Palestinian tourism. In: Issac, R., Platenkamp, V. and Protegies, A. (eds) *Voices in Tourism Development: Creating Spaces for Tacit Knowledge and Innovation*. NHTV Expertise Series 8, Amsterdam, pp. 132–150.

Norman, A. (2012) *Spiritual Tourism: Travel and Religious Practice in Western Society*. Bloomsbury, New York.

Noyes, J.R. (2016) *The Politics of Iconoclasm: Religion, Violence and the Culture of Image-Breaking in Christianity and Islam*. I.B. Tauris, London.

Nyamweru, C. and Kimaru, E. (2008) The contribution of ecotourism to the conservation of natural sacred sites: a case study from coastal Kenya. *Journal for the Study of Religion, Nature and Culture* 2(3), 327–350. DOI: 10.1558/jsrnc.v2i3.327.

Nyaupane, G.P., Timothy, D.J. and Poudel, S. (2015) Understanding tourists in religious destinations: a social distance perspective. *Tourism Management* 48, 343–353. DOI: 10.1016/j.tourman.2014.12.009.

Olsen, D.H. (2003) Heritage, tourism, and the commodification of religion. *Tourism Recreation Research* 28(3), 99–104. DOI: 10.1080/02508281.2003.11081422.

Olsen, D.H. (2008) *Contesting Identity, Space and Sacred Site Management at Temple Square in Salt Lake City, Utah*. PhD Dissertation, University of Waterloo, Waterloo, ON, Canada.

Olsen, D.H. (2016) Ritual journeys in North America: opening religious and ritual landscapes and spaces. *International Journal of Religious Tourism and Pilgrimage* 4(1), 34–48.

Olsen, D.H. (2019a) Religion, spirituality, and pilgrimage in a globalizing world. In: Timothy, D.J. (ed.) *Handbook of Globalisation and Tourism*. Edward Elgar, London, pp. 270–283. DOI: 10.4337/9781786431295.

Olsen, D.H. (2019b) The symbolism of sacred space. In: Crous-Costa, N., Aulet, S. and Vidal-Casellas, D. (eds) *Interpreting Sacred Stories: Religious Tourism, Pilgrimage and Intercultural Dialogue*. CAB International, Wallingford, UK, pp. 29–41. DOI: 10.1079/9781789241129.0000.

Olsen, D.H. (2022) Faith, new age spirituality, and religion: negotiating the religious tourism niche market. In: Novelli, M., Cheer, J.M., Dolezal, C., Jones, A. and Milano, C. (eds) *Handbook of Niche Tourism*. Edward Elgar, London, pp. 282–299. DOI: 10.4337/9781839100185.

Olsen, D.H. and Guelke, J.K. (2004) Spatial transgression and the BYU Jerusalem center controversy. *The Professional Geographer* 56(4), 503–515. DOI: 10.1111/j.0033-0124.2004.00444.x.

Olsen, D.H. and Korstanje, M. (eds) (2020) *Dark Tourism and Pilgrimage*. CAB International, Wallingford, UK. DOI: 10.1079/9781789241877.0000.

Olsen, D.H. and Shinde, K.A. (2023) Practicing faith from afar: the impact of the COVID-19 pandemic on pilgrim behaviour. In: Cakmak, E., Isaac, R.K. and Butler, R. (eds) *Changing Practices of Tourism Stakeholders in COVID-19 Affected Destinations*. Channel View, Bristol, UK, pp. 83–99. DOI: 10.21832/9781845418762.

Olsen, D.H. and Timothy, D.J. (2002) Contested religious heritage: differing views of Mormon heritage. *Tourism Recreation Research* 27(2), 7–15. DOI: 10.1080/02508281.2002.11081215.

Olsen, D.H. and Timothy, D.J. (2020) COVID-19 and religious travel: present and future directions. *International Journal of Religious Tourism and Pilgrimage* 8(7), 170–188.

Olsen, D.H. and Timothy, D.J. (2021) Contemporary perspectives of pilgrimage. In: Liutikas, D. (ed.) *Pilgrims: Values and Identities*. CAB International, Wallingford, UK, pp. 224–238. DOI: 10.1079/9781789245653.0000.

Preston, J. (1992) Spiritual magnetism: an organizing principle for the study of pilgrimage. In: Morinis, A. (ed.) *Journeys: The Anthropology of Pilgrimage*. Greenwood Press, Westport, CT, pp. 31–46.

Pritchard, A. and Morgan, N.J. (2001) Culture, identity and tourism representation: marketing Cymru or Wales? *Tourism Management* 22(2), 167–179. DOI: 10.1016/S0261-5177(00)00047-9.

Quadri, S.A. (2020) COVID-19 and religious congregations: implications for spread of novel pathogens. *International Journal of Infectious Diseases* 96, 219–221. DOI: 10.1016/j.ijid.2020.05.007.

Rutledge, S.H. (2007) The Roman destruction of sacred sites. *Historia: Zeitschrift fur Alte Geschichte* 56(2), 179–195. DOI: 10.25162/historia-2007-0014.

Sasson, T., Shain, M., Hecht, S., Wright, G. and Saxe, L. (2014) Does taglit-birth right Israel foster long-distance nationalism? *Nationalism and Ethnic Politics* 20(4), 438–454. DOI: 10.1080/13537113.2014.969149.

Schneider, E. (2020) It changed my sympathy, not my opinion: alternative Jewish tourism to the occupied Palestinian territories. *Sociological Focus* 53(4), 378–398. DOI: 10.1080/00380237.2020.1823286.

Schramm, K. (2011) Introduction: landscapes of violence: memory and sacred space. *History & Memory* 23(1), 5–22.

Shackley, M. (2001) *Managing Sacred Sites: Service Provision and Visitor Experience*. Continuum, London.

Shepherd, R.J. (2016) Faith in Heritage. In: *Faith in Heritage: Displacement, Development, and Religious Tourism in Contemporary China*. Routledge, London and New York. DOI: 10.4324/9781315428659.

Shepherd, J. (2022) Exploring a unifying approach to peacebuilding through tourism: Abraham and Israel/Palestine. *Journal of Sustainable Tourism* 30(2–3), 482–499. DOI: 10.1080/09669582.2021.1891240.

Shinde, K.A. (2015) Religious tourism and religious tolerance: insights from pilgrimage sites in India. *Tourism Review* 70(3), 179–196. DOI: 10.1108/TR-10-2013-0056.

Shinde, K.A. and Olsen, D.H. (eds) (2020) *Religious Tourism and the Environment*. CAB International, Wallingford, UK. DOI: 10.1079/9781789241600.0000.

Sibley, D. (1995) *Geographies of Exclusion: Society and Difference in the West*. Routledge, London.

Silberman, I., Higgins, E.T. and Dweck, C.S. (2005) Religion and world change: violence and terrorism versus peace. *Journal of Social Issues* 61(4), 761–784. DOI: 10.1111/j.1540-4560.2005.00431.x.

Singh, S. (1998) Probing the product life cycle further. *Tourism Recreation Research* 23(2), 61–63. DOI: 10.1080/02508281.1998.11014839.

Sinha, V. (2011) . *Religion and Commodification: 'Merchandizing' Diasporic Hinduism*. Routledge, London and New York. DOI: 10.4324/9780203842799.

Skrbis, Z. (2005) The apparitions of the Virgin Mary of Medjugorje: the convergence of Croatian nationalism and her apparitions. *Nations and Nationalism* 11(3), 443–461. DOI: 10.1111/j.1354-5078.2005.00213.x.

Skrbiš, Z. (2007) From Migrants to pilgrim tourists: diasporic imagining and visits to Medjugorje. *Journal of Ethnic and Migration Studies* 33(2), 313–329. DOI: 10.1080/13691830601154294.

Smith, A.D. (1999) Sacred territories and national conflict. *Israel Affairs* 5(4), 13–31. DOI: 10.1080/13537129908719528.

Smith, C. (2014) Disruptive Religion. In: *Disruptive Religion: The Force of Faith in Social Movement Activism*. Routledge, London and New York. DOI: 10.4324/9781315022147.

Sørensen, M.L.S. and Viejo-Rose, D. (eds) (2015) *War and Cultural Heritage*. University Press, Cambridge, UK. DOI: 10.1017/CBO9781107444911.

Sosis, R. (2011) Why sacred lands are not indivisible: the cognitive foundations of sacralising land. *Journal of Terrorism Research* 2(1), 17–44. DOI: 10.15664/jtr.172.

Stone, P.R., Hartmann, R., Seaton, A.V., Sharpley, R. and White, L. (eds) (2018) *The Palgrave Handbook of Dark Tourism Studies*. Palgrave Macmillan, London.

Taylor, S. (2010) 2,000-3,000 protest for gay rights outside Mormon church offices in Salt Lake city. *Deseret News*. Available at: https://www.deseret.com/2010/10/8/20145588/2-000-3-000-protest-for-gay-rights-outside-mormon-church-offices-in-salt-lake-city (accessed 19 April 2022).

Thouki, A. (2019) The role of ontology in religious tourism education—Exploring the application of the postmodern cultural paradigm in European religious sites. *Religions* 10(12), 649. DOI: 10.3390/rel10120649.

Tilson, D.J. (2001) Religious tourism, public relations and church-state partnerships. *Public Relations Quarterly* 46(3), 35–39.

Tilson, D.J. (2005) Religious-spiritual tourism and promotional campaigning: a church-state partnership for St. James and Spain. *Journal of Hospitality & Leisure Marketing* 12(1–2), 9–40. DOI: 10.1300/J150v12n01_03.

Time.com (1985) Sri Lanka tamil terror: blood flows at a Buddhist shrine. Available at: https://content.time.com/time/subscriber/article/0,33009,957036,00.html (accessed 28 April 2022).

Timothy, D.J. (2022) Sociopolitical and economic implications of religious and spiritual tourism. In: Olsen, D.H. and Timothy, D.J. (eds) *The Routledge Handbook of Religious and Spiritual Tourism*. Routledge, London and New York, pp. 301–314. DOI: 10.4324/9780429201011.

Timothy, D.J. (2021) *Cultural Heritage and Tourism: An Introduction*, 2nd edn. Channel View Publications, Bristol, UK.

Timothy, D.J. and Olsen, D.H. (2006) Conclusion-Whither religion and tourism? In: Timothy, D.J. and Olsen, D.H. (eds) *Tourism, Religion and Spiritual Journeys*. Routledge, London and New York, pp. 271–278. DOI: 10.4324/9780203001073.

Todd, M. (2017) The political geographies of religious sites in Moscow's neighborhoods. *Eurasian Geography and Economics* 58(6), 642–669. DOI: 10.1080/15387216.2018.1457448.

Van Dyke, B.G. and Berrett, L.C. (2008) In the footsteps of Orson Hyde: subsequent dedications of the Holy Land. *Brigham Young University Studies* 47(1), 57–93.

Vanneste, D. and Winter, C. (2018) First World War battlefield tourism: journeys out of the dark and into the light. In: Stone, P.R., Hartmann, R., Seaton, T., Sharpley, R. and White, L. (eds) *The Palgrave Handbook of Dark Tourism Studies*. Palgrave Macmillan, London, pp. 443–467.

Verschuuren, B., Wild, R., McNeely, J.A. and Oviedo, G. (2010) *Sacred Natural Sites: Conserving Nature and Culture*. Earthscan, London.

Weenig, B. (2015) First Amendment freedoms to collide at the conference center. *The Daily Universe*. Available at: https://universe.byu.edu/2015/04/16/first-amendment-freedoms-to-collide-at-the-conference-center/ (accessed 18 April 2022).

Wiinikka-Lydon, J. (2010) The ambivalence of Medjugorje: the dynamics of violence, peace, and nationalism at a Catholic pilgrimage site during the Bosnian war (1992–1995). *Journal of Religion & Society* 12, 1–18.

Winters, R. (2010) Mormon apostle's words about gays spark protest. *Salt Lake Tribune*. Available at: https://archive.sltrib.com/article.php?id=50434583&itype=CMSID (accessed 18 April 2022).

Wood, R.L. (1999) Religious culture and political action. *Sociological Theory* 17(3), 307–332. DOI: 10.1111/0735-2751.00082.

Wyndham, C. (2015) Reconstructing Afghan identity: nation-building, international relations and the safeguarding of Afghanistan's Buddhist heritage. In: Basu, P. and Modest, W. (eds) *Museums, Heritage and International Development*. Routledge, London and New York, pp. 132–152. DOI: 10.4324/9780203069035.

3   Human Rights: The Right to Tourism and Access to Religious Tourism and Pilgrimage Sites

Dimitrios Mylonopoulos*, Polyxeni Moira and Spyridon Parthenis
Department of Tourism Management, University of West Attica, Aigaleo, Greece

Abstract

This chapter examines the concepts of culture and heritage and unravels the ambiguous nature of cultural herit-age and its connection with both the protection of human rights and the conservation of religious heritage. It traces the origin of modern human rights and explores the equivocal character of the right of participation in cultural life as it is enshrined in international law. It also explores the role of international organizations as major actors in safeguarding and promoting cultural–religious heritage and cultural diversity, seeking to reconcile the individual rights with respect for the cultures of different human groups. The chapter highlights tourism both as a human right to travel and an important contributor to reciprocal and respect between peoples and seeks to grasp how restricted access to religious tourism sites by public authorities or local cultures on different grounds might generate tensions and conflicts between the residents' rights and the tourists' rights. The chapter presents the case of Greece's Mount Athos, a UNESCO World Heritage Site, where there is a centuries-old ban on all women.

3.1   Introduction

Heritage is a key element of the particular identity and historical development of societies, as the etymology of the word suggests: 'something transmitted by or acquired from a predecessor' (Merriam-Webster Online Dictionary, n.d.); 'the evidence of the past, such as historical sites, buildings, and the unspoiled natural environ-ment, considered collectively as the inheritance of present-day society' (Collins Online Dictionary, n.d.). Culture and heritage are concepts with a positive value; therefore, they are considered to be the common good of humanity.

It is through tangible and intangible cultural heritage that the personal identity of every individual is shaped, as well as the community and national identity for every nation. The Greeks would not be the same today had they lost the unique cultural works of their ancestors (tangible and intangible). For this reason, the shaping of a strong identity by means of cultural heritage has a positive added value.

Nevertheless, cultural heritage interweaves not only with identity but with space as well. In this case, spatial assertions often emerge between individuals and communities and between ethnic and religious groups. This may lead to rivalry and total conflict and difficult and complex questions may arise. This often leads to conflict over access to religious places. Complexity arises as cultural heritage collides

*Corresponding author: dimilon@uniwa.gr

© CAB International 2023. *The Politics of Religious Tourism* (eds D. Bozonelos and P. Moira)
DOI: 10.1079/9781800621732.0003

with politics. For example, how do international human rights regimes fit in? Who gets to define cultural heritage? Who should have the control over the stewardship of cultural assets and their benefits? Well known examples of conflict over religious places include the holy sites in Jerusalem and Hagia Sofia in modern-day Istanbul. So critical questions arise: Who do Israel's sacred sites and shrines belong to? Who has the legitimate ownership of Jerusalem's religious–cultural heritage? Who has the property rights to Hagia Sophia, and who can manage and regulate its utilization and access to it? This leads us to our central research question: how does a right to tourism lead to a right to access religious tourism sites and pilgrimages?

Cultural heritage may unite and divide at the same time. These disputes could lead to protests, resistance, violence, and even armed conflicts. This is the dilemma of world vs national heritage and individual vs local rights. The concept of 'cultural heritage' is not socially and politically neutral and not necessarily positive. It may allow, in appropriate circumstances, familiarization with identity and patrimony, it may demonstrate common points and may facilitate communication, but it can also turn into a tool for enhancing inequalities and oppression (Logan, 2007, p. 3). These problems may become more intense when culture and heritage are associated with the delicate topic of religion, that is why we refer to religious–cultural heritage.

Therefore, implementing international charters and doctrinal texts developed and adopted by the United Nations, UNESCO, ICOMOS and other international bodies on the protection of human rights and the conservation of world cultural (and religious) heritage is a difficult task, especially when it comes to monuments and sites of religious–spiritual interest.

3.2 The Development of Human Rights

Human rights are ethical principles that define specific standards for human conduct. They are regarded as 'inalienable fundamental rights to which a person is inherently entitled simply because she or he is a human being' (Sepúlveda *et al.*, 2004, p. 3). The term 'human rights' was born in Western Europe in the 18th century and it is the product of turbulent philosophical, political and social development. However, conceptually human rights date back to Classical Antiquity in Ancient Greece. Equality, egalitarianism, and equal right of speech of the free citizens in the Greek cities originated in the ancient political philosophy. The Stoic philosophers elaborated natural rights theories which have influenced political and legal thought up to the present. In addition to this, Christianity and other religions have impacted considerably the historical course of human rights. Through the centuries there have been significant milestones in the philosophical and political thought, which have marked the latent evolution of human rights (Περράκης, 1998, p. 15). Nevertheless, it was only after two millennia that these values re-emerged through the United States Declaration of Independence (US Congress, 1776) and the Declaration of the Rights of Man and of Citizen in (Archives nationales, 1789).

The essence of the emerging principles of human rights is visible in President Franklin D. Roosevelt's State of the Union Address on January 6, 1941:

> [...] we look forward to a world founded upon four essential freedoms. The first is freedom of speech and expression [...] The second is the freedom of every person to worship God in his own way [...] The third is the freedom from want [...] The fourth is freedom from fear [...] (Roosevelt, 1941).

The question of determining and protecting human rights at the international or systemic level starts just after World War II. On 10 December 1948, the Universal Declaration of Human Rights (UDHR) was proclaimed by the United Nations General Assembly in Paris. It is a fundamental document in the history of human rights (Μπάλιας, 2004) as human rights and their protection were considered to be the common goal of the peoples and the nations.

In the framework of the protection of human rights and international cooperation on the respect of fundamental freedoms, any discrimination on race, gender, language or religion is prohibited. Language and religion are structural elements for every cultural environment on a local, national and international level (Σκουλάς and Σκουλά, 2011, p. 34). The General Assembly and the Economic and Social Council have repeatedly referred in their recommendations to the need for respect of the human rights and the right of every person to enjoy whatever is interwoven with their cultural environment (e.g. language, religion, culture).

Article 27 par. 1 of the Universal Declaration of Human Rights specifically states, 'Everyone has the right freely to participate in the cultural life of the community, to enjoy the arts and to share in scientific advancement and its benefits.' (UN, 1948). Thereby the right to culture is introduced as an essential aspect of human rights. However, the Declaration defines neither the cultural relationship and cultural differences between individuals, communities and nations nor the way that potential differences might be resolved.

By virtue of the UN General Assembly resolution 2200A (XXI) of 16 December 1966, three legal instruments, equivalent to multi-lateral treaties, were adopted, which provided for the obligatory ratification or accession by a minimum number of States Parties so that these legal instruments entered into force. These are the following: (a) the International Covenant on Civil and Political Rights (ICCPR) (UN, 1966a); (b) the International Covenant on Economic, Social and Cultural Rights (ICESCR), which establishes the right of everyone to participate in cultural life (UN, 1966b), and (c) the Optional Protocol to the above-mentioned Covenant.

Thus, the freedoms or the rights of participation to cultural life, protection and enjoyment of cultural heritage have come of age as important human rights (Βενιζέλος, 1999). This promotes inter-generational solidarity, as is the case with the right to the environment and its protection. Having connected human rights, human dignity and culture has been a significant step towards the placement of culture on the foreground of international cooperation 'making it constitutive and not only expressive of individual and group identity and independence' (Abdulqawi, 2005, p. 2). Nevertheless, as individuals belong to different cultural groups, it is likely that the wish for cultural self-direction of a group clashes with 'the claim of universal human rights principles on the part of different and competing groups' or a dominant nation-state (Silverman and Fairchild Ruggles, 2007).

3.3 Cultural Heritage and Human Rights

In 1972 the Convention Concerning the Protection of the World Cultural and Natural Heritage was signed in Paris by the State Parties, who noted that cultural heritage and natural heritage are more and more in danger of being destroyed not only by the usual causes of disintegration, but also by changeable social and economic circumstances (UNESCO, 1972). The degree of protection of cultural heritage increases once monuments (including religious heritage monuments) and sites, as defined in Articles 1 and 2 of the Convention, are inscribed on the List of World Heritage in Danger. This happens when cultural properties are faced with specific and imminent proven man-made or natural dangers such as: outbreak or threat of armed conflict, uncontrolled urbanization and tourism development, pollution, big public or private works, serious deterioration of materials, earthquakes, floods, etc. (Mylonopoulos *et al.*, 2017). This protection was extended to the intangible cultural heritage with the signing of the Convention for the Safeguarding of the Intangible Cultural Heritage adopted on 17 October 2003 (UNESCO, 2003). According to the Convention, *religious monuments* are included in cultural heritage, as *religious art* has greatly influenced for a long time the developments in architecture, monumental art and urban planning in many regions of the world. Moreover, the religious monuments and complexes represent important stages in man's history, and they are intricately linked with ideas, live traditions, beliefs, religious landscapes, etc. The intangible cultural heritage also includes oral traditions and forms of expression, social practices, rituals and festive events (e.g. religious ceremonies, pilgrimages, burial rituals), knowledge and practices related with the natural environment and the universe (Moira *et al.*, 2009; Μοίρα, 2009, 2019, p. 308).

UNESCO's goal is to safeguard the freedom of expression for all cultures, particularly in the context of globalization and by extension, the consolidation of world peace. Some of the main thematic axes selected for the promotion of intercultural dialogue are 'The Dialogue Routes', 'Post-conflict Mediation', 'Inter-religious Dialogue', 'Cultural Pluralism', etc. In addition to this, UNESCO seeks to ensure the unimpeded universal access to cultural heritage monuments regardless of gender, race, religion and ethnicity (Moira, 2021, p. 149).

On 2 November 2001, the UNESCO Universal Declaration on Cultural Diversity was adopted (UNESCO, 2001, p. 61). Article 1 states that cultural diversity is 'a source of exchange, innovation and creativity [and] the common heritage of humanity'. The Declaration aims at preserving multiculturalism as an active and inexhaustible asset and as a process which assures the survival of humanity. It also seeks to prevent discrimination and fundamentalism, which in the name of cultural differences, sanctify these differences and clash with the UNESCO Universal Declaration of Human Rights. This Declaration brings an end to the conflict between States that wish to defend 'cultural goods and services which, as vectors of identity, values and meaning, must not be treated as mere commodities or consumer goods.' (Article 8) and between countries which hope to advance cultural rights. The aforementioned approaches come under the UNESCO Universal Declaration on Cultural Diversity, which has underscored the causal relationship connecting these two complementary stances (UNESCO, 2002).

3.4   Tourism and Human Rights

In 1980, during the World Tourism Conference in Manila, Philippines, the main debate was the responsibility of the States to develop tourism in modern societies, as something more than a mere economic activity for the States and the peoples. According to the Manila Declaration on World Tourism, 'tourism is considered an activity essential to the life of nations' and a factor of economic development and prosperity. Tourism is also considered to bring various social, cultural, educational and economic effects. The Manila Declaration was an innovative and pioneering legal text at that

time because it refers to modern tourism as 'a fundamental right of the human being to rest and leisure' through annual paid holidays. In fact, the Manila Declaration reflects the provision of Article 24 of the UDHR: 'Everyone has the right to rest and leisure, including reasonable limitation of working hours and periodic holidays with pay.' It is the government's duty to take all the necessary measures to ensure that these rights are exercised seamlessly and fulfilled. For the above reasons, the Manila Declaration could be called 'Magna Carta of Tourism'. Although researchers argue that Article 24 of the UDHR endorses an individual's right to holiday (Hashimoto, 2021, p. 213) the Convention on the Rights of Persons with Disabilities (CRPD), Article 30 emphasizes that each State Party ensures persons with disabilities, '...[enjoy] access to places for cultural performances or services, such as theatres, museums, cinemas, libraries and tourism services, and, as far as possible, enjoy access to monuments and sites of national cultural importance', and must take measures to 'ensure that persons with disabilities have access to sporting, recreational and tourism venues' (UN, 2007).

The significant benefits of participation in tourism have led to the discussion about the nature of tourism as a human need (according to Maslow's hierarchy of needs), therefore as an entitlement, as a right for the rich and wealthy, or as a luxury (Minnaert *et al.*, 2006). This brings into question whether a right to tourism exists and, if so, what is the legal basis for this right. Even though some researchers regard that the right to tourism has been recognized by international organizations (UNWTO, ICOMOS, UNESCO, etc.) and by many countries (mostly developed ones) there is lack of evidence about the legitimacy of tourism as a right.

However, the huge expansion of the tourism phenomenon along with the particular emphasis placed on tourism by national governments and international organizations over the recent years leads us inescapably to the conclusion that not only tourism as a right exists but it is a new human right, the *human right to tourism* has already started to shape. In the framework of globalization and the international organizations' action in tackling global crises, e.g.

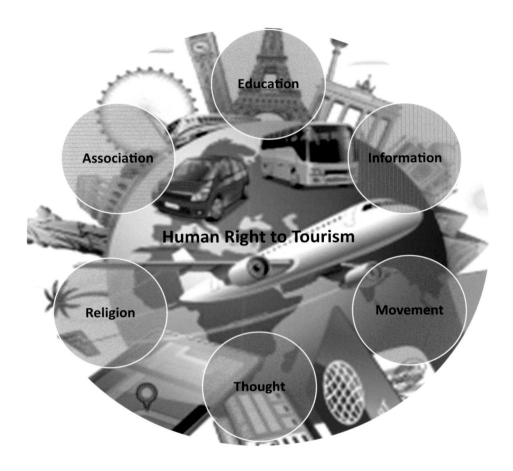

Fig. 3.1. The human right to tourism encompasses all human rights.

climate change, we believe that the *right to tourism* is being transformed into an *autonomous* fundamental universal right. The human right to tourism encompasses fundamental human rights derived from the Universal Declarationof Human Rights(UN, 1948), the UNWTO Manila Declaration on World Tourism (UNWTO, 1980) and the UNWTO Framework Convention on Tourism Ethics, adopted in 2019 (Fig. 3.1). In the light of the above typical universal rights coexist: the right to freedom of movement, the right to personal liberty and security, the right to respect for private and family life, the prohibition of discrimination, the right to freedom of expression, and the right to freedom of thought, conscience and religion.

The human right to tourism has emerged from this discourse. This right seems 'autonomous' and distinct from the original human rights, which include the need to travel, to get to know other cultures, to communicate, to express themselves, to learn, to develop, to improve their physical and mental health, to achieve well-being, happiness and quality of life (Gilbert and Abdullah, 2004; Dolnicar *et al.*, 2012), without physical, mental or other obstacles. Contrary to some scholars (McCabe and Diekmann, 2015) who claim that tourism cannot be included as a human right to the remaining indivisible and interdependent UN rights because of the unequal economic development and poverty, we believe that the right to tourism can stand on its own as a means for individual and collective fulfilment.

Nevertheless, it is necessary to exercise this human right by respecting the common moral values of mankind, while displaying tolerance towards religious differences and moral beliefs, thus, avoiding a clash with the remaining human rights. National governments are, therefore, obliged and committed to lifting any barriers to freedom of movement and facilitating tourist travel.

Given this, we can define the Human Right to Tourism:

..as the right to travel anywhere with no limits, no barriers and regardless of social or ethnic group, religion, gender, race, language or income level.

3.5 The Clash Over the Human Right to Tourism and Access to Religious Sites

Cultural rights are based on ethical codes, that is rules (social ethics) that prescribe what is ethically correct for individuals. Nevertheless, what is considered to be acceptable by social ethics may not be ethically correct from the perspective of human rights (e.g. gender inequality, honour crimes). For instance, in Afghanistan under the Taliban government (1992–2001) married women accused of *zina* (non-marital sex), usually translated as 'adultery' were subject to death by stoning or flogging (Hodgkinson, 2016, pp. 256–257). Even though these actions were ethically justified and acceptable for the country, they are unacceptable from the point of view of human rights. In addition to this, many practices are justified based on religious beliefs. For example, Logan (2007, p. 37) has asserted that in Northern India it is thought that burning girls to death for various reasons is a sacrifice to the Hindu goddess of destruction, Kali, which will bring the perpetrators a better life in this world. These cultural rights are interwoven with the culture of a human community and usually derive from religious creeds and traditions.

In tourism things are more complicated, as people from countries with a different 'ethical philosophy' and different perceptions of human rights come into contact and interact. In this case the differences with regard to ethical codes and respect for human rights may cause problems. For instance, celibate partners or friends of the opposite sex travelling together to specific countries should always be discreet in public. In a few Muslim countries (e.g. Iran, Saudi Arabia) where Islamic law is strictly enforced unmarried couples are not allowed to share a double room in a hotel (GOV.UK, 2020). Couples should take extra care in their public behaviour as fines may be imposed on them or they may get arrested (Campbell, 2022), or may be sentenced to be whipped (OSAC, 2019).

Now that we have defined a human right to tourism, how does this right work with access to religious sites? The questions of human rights and ethics regarding tourism may be examined from two perspectives: *from the perspective of the rights of the locals and from the perspectives of the rights of visitors/tourists.* As mentioned before, the human right to tourism is linked with the right to free mobility and directly or indirectly to other human rights. For this reason, tourists and public and private tourism sectors are alarmed when direct or indirect restrictions or banning of free travel of any kind are put in place. The reactions do not only touch on human rights issues but also economic, social consequences emanating from these restrictions which are necessary when the physical-ecological carrying capacity and/or social-psychological carrying capacity is exceeded (Joshi and Dahal, 2019).

Spatial and time restrictions in visiting monuments and sites could be enforced. For instance, tourists are allowed to visit the historical sanctuary of Machu Picchu, Peru, at particular times of the day; there is restricted access through entrance tickets to Antoni Gaudí's monuments at the Park Güell in the southern area in Barcelona (Catalan News, 2013; DW, 2019); a Green Tax was introduced in 2016 by the Maldives government for tourists who stay in tourist resorts, hotels, tourist vessels and guest houses (The Edition, 2020); each day, 100 Orthodox male pilgrims and 10 non-Orthodox, are admitted for a three-night stay in one of the 20 monasteries on the peninsula of Mount Athos, Greece (BBC, 2016); wishing to avoid the participation of tourists and the media during the Romería of the Pentecost, local pilgrims undertake pilgrimages to the shrine of

Nuestra Señora del Rocío (Our Lady of the Dew), Spain, with family members throughout the year (Crain, 1996); female believers entering churches, monasteries or mosques have to cover their heads with a headscarf, a chador or a hijab.

These bans and restrictions of human rights often take place in religious–cultural monuments and sites, which is dictated by religious norms. *However, it could be argued that these restrictions violate and suppress human rights.* For instance, there is a 400-year-old tradition of banning entry to the women of age group 10–50 to the Sabarimala Temple, because women of menstruating age are regarded as being impure (Gupta, 2016, p. 7). Another example of restriction of access to a religious site is Mount Athos, Greece, where all women without any exception, are forbidden entry. Konidaris (2003) argues that 'a first superficial approach might lead to the conclusion that the prohibition of women's entry into the Mount Athos territory contravenes the principle of equality and/or constitutes a restriction of personal freedom' but for him this is not the case because 'various special reasons, social, economic, religious etc., fully justify different treatment, provided that such different treatment is objective and is based on general and impersonal criteria.' These restrictions cause a clash between travellers'/ tourists' rights and the local people's rights.

3.6   The (Human) Right to Tourism and Gender Based Restrictions to Religious Sites

Most religions establish female gender based restrictions to access holy/religious sites and monuments, e.g. the ban on vising Mount Athos for all women (Kapilevich and Karvounis, 2015), a female under 45 cannot perform Hajj without being accompanied by a mahram (Zamani-Farahani and Eid, 2016, p. 146), etc.

The religious perception of woman's inferiority and the lowering of her dignity emanates from the sacred texts which talk about her origins. For instance, Eve is a female figure in the Book of Genesis in the Hebrew Bible as well as a female figure in the Quran and is thought to have been created because Adam was alone and felt sad. Therefore, woman is portrayed in the

sacred texts of various religions as being inferior to man, because she was created from Adam's rib, so she is submitted to him. This perception of woman's inferior position is depicted in permanent or temporary restrictions of access to holy places (e.g. dress code for women). Women are banned from entering, sojourning and praying at specific places of worship: the Sabarimala Ayyappa Hindu temple in Kerala, India (Kapur, 2016), the Sufi shrine of Haji Ali Dargah in Mumbai, India (Saigal, 2016), the sacred Mount Ōmine in Japan and Mount Athos, Greece, both UNESCO World Heritage sites (Iefimerida, 2016). Also, the Western Wall in Jerusalem's Old City, Israel, which has distinct sections where men and women are allowed permitted to pray (BBC, 2019), while women who travel to Saudi Arabia to perform Hajj must be accompanied by a male relative in order to be granted a tourist visa (Bachelor, 2015).

3.7   Ban on Entry of Women to Sites of Religious–Cultural Heritage. Case Study: Mount Athos, Greece

3.7.1   Historical background

The Peninsula of Athos is the easternmost and most mountainous of the three peninsulas which make the peninsula of Chalcidice and reach out into the Aegean Sea in northern Greece. From the 7th to the 9th centuries a large number of hermits and orthodox monks decided for reasons of safety to flee from Egypt and Palestine to Mount Athos and establish their hermitages there. In the 10th century the first monastic settlements, known as 'lavras', along with the first coenobiac groups (living in the community) started to emerge (Axiotis, 1995, p. 519). In 963 CE the monastery of Agia Lavra was founded after St. Athanasius had received a *chrysobull* (imperial document) from the emperor Nicephorus Phocas. In the 11th century entry to the monastery was officially banned for all women by the rule '*Avaton*' established by the Byzantine emperor.

In 1045, Mount Athos was named 'Agion Oros' (Holy Mountain) according to a chrysobull of Emperor Konstantinos I Monomachos, while in 1046 the Second Typikon (Charter on the organization of the monastic way of life) was written. In 1406 by virtue of a chrysobull of the emperor Manuel II Paleologos (Fourth Typikon), the monks were given the right of property and possession and entry of women to Mount Athos was prohibited. In 1453 Mount Athos was conquered by the Ottomans, but it remained a spiritual centre through the 17th and 18th centuries.

There are 20 monasteries and subsidiary establishments on Mount Athos, where about 1400 monks reside. Seventeen of them are Greek, one monastery is Russian, one is Serbian, and one is Bulgarian.

In 1923 the Treaty of Lausanne recognized Greek sovereignty in all Mount Athos. In 1924 the Charter and the Statute of Mount Athos was drafted while in 1926 it was ratified by the Greek State by virtue of a Legislative Decree. By virtue of Article 105 par. 1 of the Greek Constitution (2008) 'the Athos peninsula extending beyond Megali Vigla and constituting the region of Agion

Oros' (Mount Athos) is 'a self-governed part of the Greek State, whose sovereignty thereon shall remain intact', so it enjoys an autonomous statute (Μυλωνόπουλος, 2001). The administration of Agion Oros is exercised by representatives of the twenty Holy Monasteries constituting the Holy Community (Assembly) which meets at Karyes, the seat of the civil governor, who reports to the Ministry of Foreign Affairs in Athens. The executive organ of the Holy Community is the four-member Holy Superintendence, which rotates every 5 years. Paragraph 4 of Article 105 of the Greek Constitution (2008) states that 'the regimes of the Mount Athos entities shall in the spiritual field be under the supreme supervision of the Ecumenical Patriarchate of Constantinople', and, 'in the administrative, under the supervision of the Greek State, which shall also be exclusively responsible for safeguarding public order and security'.

The peninsula of Athos has an exceptional natural landscape (Fig. 3.2). The monasteries

Macedonia, Ag. Oros, Mon. Ag. Grigoriou © GNTO/H. Kakarouhas

Fig. 3.2. Mount Athos, St Gregory Monastery.
Source: Greek National Tourism Organization © H_Kakarouhas.

built in it are edifices and architectural complexes of a unique archaeological and historical significance which host cultural treasures and artistic collections, such as Byzantine and post-Byzantine icons, historical manuscripts, codices, old Gospels, rare editions, heirlooms, etc. (Μοίρα, 2018, p. 192). Mount Athos was inscribed in 1988 on the UNESCO World Heritage List because of its Outstanding Universal Value as a Mixed Natural/Cultural World Heritage Site on the basis of six criteria. Apart from its rich tangible cultural heritage, Mount Athos is a custodian of traditions of the intangible cultural heritage as the brotherhoods that have existed there for the last twelve centuries have been preserving the unique Orthodox tradition and way of life (Kadas, 1991). It is a religious spatial complex where the natural and the man-made environment interact harmoniously, culminating in a rich spiritual and cultural centuries-long tradition and demarcating a sacred enclosure, where the monastic ideal sent by God thrives (Δωρής, 1994, p. 21). This is the key to the interpretation of the term 'treasure of Mount Athos', which refers to both the tangible and the intangible cultural heritage, in the sense of spiritual patrimony (Alexopoulos and Fouseki, 2016).

The ancient monastic principle of 'Avaton' in Greek means the prohibition of entry for women, 'impassible and untrodden by females', which was proclaimed by emperor Constantine IX Monomachos in 1046, to make living in celibacy easier for the monks who live there. This ban dates back to St. Anthony's Canon 10 which addressed the young hermits or monks and asked them not to let women approach them and not to tolerate that she set foot in their house, because wrath supervenes from those walking behind (Monastic Institutions).

The first charter (which set rules and disciplines of the Athonite monastic life) of the Monastery of the Great Lavra (970 CE), issued by the emperor John I Tsimiskis, commonly known as 'Tragos' because it was written on a goat skin, states: 'You will not own any animal of the female sex, for the purpose of doing any work which you require, because you have absolutely renounced all female being' (Sanidopoulos, 2016; Iellada, 2018). Therefore, 'Avaton' is part of a living intangible cultural tradition and heritage. Ban of entry

is reciprocal. By virtue of Canon 47 of the Ecumenical Council by the Eastern Orthodox Church in Trullo in 692 CE 'No woman may sleep in a monastery of men, nor any man in a monastery of women.' Later on, this prohibition was further confirmed by virtue of Canon 18 of the Seventh Ecumenical Council of Nicaea in 787 AD which states: 'Now for women to live in the houses of bishops or in monasteries is a cause for every sort of scandal'.

3.7.2 Claims and requests for lifting of ban

Nowadays the question of prohibiting the access of women to Mount Athos has caused various discussions and reactions on a European level. By virtue of Legislative Decree no. 2623/1953 those who breach the 'Avaton' get one-year imprisonment. When Greece joined the European Community (precursor of the European Union) in 1981 its membership status contained provisions for Mount Athos to maintain its administrative autonomy.

More than thirty years ago, when Mount Athos was inscribed in the UNESCO World Heritage List, the ethical issue of the ban on women entering Mount Athos (Avaton) was raised. How can the monastic community of Mount Athos with a huge significance for the cultural heritage of the Greek nation and Orthodox Christianity, which goes beyond the national borders, both maintain this special status and be granted aid by both the Greek State and the EU structural funds to restore and renovate monasteries and preserve cultural treasures, which belong to both men and women? How is the restriction of access of women to Mount Athos ethically justifiable and why is the breach of human rights (sex segregation) tolerated since Greek women are included in the Greek taxpayers who fund these restoration projects? (Alexopoulos and Fouseki, 2016).

The conflict emerges between the human right of a monastic community to determine freely its rules of procedure and the way it is managed and the rights of women (human and cultural) to have access to a World Heritage Site. The biggest question is derived from the inherent contradiction of how a World Heritage Site of universal value can exclude access and impede the enjoyment of its resources to half the global population. Considering that access to culture and works of cultural heritage is an inalienable human right, the restriction of access of women to Mount Athos could be regarded as a violation of the basic principles of management of a UNESCO World Heritage listed monument, such as universal access, social inclusion and gender equality.

Nevertheless, 'Avaton' could be considered to fall under the fundamental principle of respect for the local communities, the minorities, the different cultural groups and religions, goods which are protected by UNESCO. The centuries-old ban on all female visitors to Mount Athos is a major principle of the Autonomous Monastic State of the Holy Mountain. Lifting the ban would lead to a change in the traditional way of life of the monks and would alter the defining features of Mount Athos, which would not meet the selection criteria for its inclusion on the UNESCO World Heritage List and its protection.

On the part of the Athonite monks, 'Avaton' could be seen as a fundamental human right of a group of people (monks) to religious freedom, to the right of freedom of worship, and to the right of management of their property (Τσιβόλας, 2013, pp. 234, 259). All the above rights are protected by both the Greek Constitutional Law and international law.

In early 2000 the European Parliament Members started to challenge this special status of Mount Athos and submit written requests to the European Commission to lift the ban of women on entry to Mount Athos on the grounds of violation of the principle of the freedom of movement for persons in the EU and breach of human rights (individual rights of women). See for instance the written question of the Italian MP Gianni Vattimo from the Party of European Socialists on 26 June 2001 to the Commission (European Parliament, 2001a).

On 15 January 2003 the European Parliament (2003) by virtue of its resolution on the situation concerning basic rights in the European Union requested:

> The lifting of the ban on women entering Mount Athos in Greece, a geographical area of 400 km², where women's access is prohibited in accordance with a decision taken in 1045 by monks living in the twenty monasteries in the area, a decision which nowadays violates

the universally recognised principle of gender equality, Community non-discrimination and equality legislation and the provisions relating to free movement of persons within the EU.

The answers given to the above parliamentary questions on behalf of the Commission highlight the special legal status of Mount Athos mentioned in the Joint Declaration concerning Mount Athos, attached to the Final Act of 29 May 1979 concerning the accession of Greece to the European Economic Community. This Declaration recognizes 'that the special status granted to Mount Athos [...] is justified exclusively on grounds of a spiritual and religious nature' (European Communities, 1979). In addition to this, a similar Declaration was made at the time of the signing of the Accession Agreement of Greece to the Convention implementing the Schengen Agreement, part of the Schengen acquis, which has been integrated into European Union law (European Parliament, 2001b, 2013).

3.8   Conclusion

A human right to tourism can help better situate some of the debates in religious tourism. The religious element is respected on a global level with regard to the protection of human rights. The human right to tourism, and by extension to religious tourism as a special interest tourism form, is shaped under the restrictions set by any religion. In many tourist destinations a conflict is likely to emerge between different human rights. This is the case in religiously active sites or monuments. On the one hand, there is the right of access to, and enjoyment of, culture and to works of cultural heritage and on the other hand, there is the right of everyone to take part in cultural life including culture and religion as well as the right to cultural identity and protection of cultural heritage. Reasonable questions might arise from this clash with regard to the ranking of human rights. However, international and supranational entities, e.g. European Union, claim that there is no human rights ranking.

The right of access to religious sites and monuments relates to ethics and, in many cases, it is resolved legally through ban of entry to the sacred site. The different treatment of tourist visitors, based on religious grounds, is justifiable if it is done objectively, and it is generic and impersonal. This question is not addressed on the basis of the 'one world-one global ethics' logic.

References

Abdulqawi, A.Y. (2005) *Toward a Convention on Cultural Diversity: Background and Evolution*. Presentation in the Third Forum on Human Development, Paris. Available at: https://www.iprsonline.org/unctadictsd/dialogue/docs/Abdulqawi_2005-01-17.pdf (accessed 15 August 2022).

Alexopoulos, G. and Fouseki, K. (2016) Gender exclusion and local values versus universal cultural heritage significance: the Avaton debate on the monastic community of Mount Athos. *European Journal of Post-Classical Archaeologies* 6, 235–254.

Archives nationales (France) (1789) 30 Septembre 1789, AE/II/1129, Déclaration des droits de l'homme et du citoyen, at Elyssee Declaration of the Rights of Man and of Citizen. Available at: https://www.elysee.fr/en/french-presidency/the-declaration-of-the-rights-of-man-and-of-the-citizen (accessed 26 April 2023).

Axiotis, G.N.C. (1995) Pilgrimage. The native architecture of Mount Athos. *Θεολογία* 66(3), 511–561.

Bachelor, B. (2015) No women allowed: tourist destinations where females are forbidden. *FoxNews*. Available at: https://www.foxnews.com/travel/no-women-allowed-tourist-destinations-where-females-are-forbidden (accessed 9 June 2022).

BBC (2016) Why are women banned from Mount Athos? *BBC*. Available at: https://www.bbc.com/news/magazine-36378690 (accessed 9 June 2022).

BBC (2019) Western wall: Jewish women clash over prayer rights. *BBC*. Available at: https://www.bbc.com/news/world-middle-east-47496456 (accessed 9 June 2022).

Βενιζέλος, Ε. (1999) Το δικαίωμα στον πολιτισμό ως "σύνθετο ανθρώπινο δικαίωμα" την περίοδο της μεταβιομηχανικής κοινωνίας [The right to culture as a "complex human right" in the post-industrial society]. In: στο Κούφα, Κ. (ed.) *(Διεύθυνση Έκδοσης) 50 Χρόνια Της Οικουμενικής Διακήρυξης Των Δικαιωμάτων Του Ανθρώπου 1948–1998, Εκδ. Σάκκουλα, Αθήνα-Θεσσαλονίκη, Σσ.* 13–19. [in Greek].

Campbell, F. (2022) The complexities of traveling to Saudi Arabia. *Condé Nast Traveler*. Available at: https://www.cntraveler.com/story/the-complexities-of-traveling-to-saudi-arabia (accessed 1 June 2022).

Catalan News (2013) Barcelona's park Güell will have an entrance fee from Friday. *Catalan News*. Available at: https://www.catalannews.com/life-style/item/barcelona-s-park-gueell-will-have-an-entrance-fee-from-friday (accessed 7 June 2022).

Collins Online Dictionary (n.d.) *Heritage*. Available at: https://www.collinsdictionary.com/dictionary/english/heritage (accessed 9 June 2022).

Crain, M.M. (1996) Contested territories. The politics of touristic development at the Shrine of El Rocío in Southwestern Andalucia. In: Boissevain, J. (ed.) *Coping with Tourists. European Reactions to Mass Tourism*. Providence, RI and Berghahn Books, Oxford, UK, pp. 27–55.

Dolnicar, S., Yanamandram, V. and Cliff, K. (2012) The contribution of vacations to quality of life. *Annals of Tourism Research* 39(1), 59–83. DOI: 10.1016/j.annals.2011.04.015.

DW (2019) Peru restricts access to Machu Picchu Inca city to prevent damage. *Deutsche Welle*. Available at: https://www.dw.com/en/peru-restricts-access-to-machu-picchu-inca-city-to-prevent-damage/a-48700956 (accessed 7 June 2022).

European Communities (1979) *Documents Concerning the Accession of the Hellenic Republic to the European Communities*. Final Act, Joint Declaration Concerning Mount Athos, OJ L 291, 19.11.1979. p. 186. Available at: https://eur-lex.europa.eu/legal-content/EN/TXT/?uri=OJ:L:1979:291:TOC (accessed 9 June 2022).

European Parliament (2001a) *Written question by Gianni Vattimo (PSE) to the Commission, Violation of the Principle of Equality of Access to Mount Athos*, P-1954/01, June 26. Available at: https://www.europarl.europa.eu/sides/getDoc.do?pubRef=-//EP//TEXT+WQ+P-2001-1954+0+DOC+XML+V0//EN&language=EN (accessed 9 June 2022).

European Parliament (2001b) *Parliamentary questions, Answer given by Mr Vitorino on behalf of the Commission*, E1055/2001, June 11. Available at: https://www.europarl.europa.eu/sides/getAllAnswers.do?reference=E-2001-1055&language=EN (accessed 9 June 2022).

European Parliament (2003) P5_TA(2003)0012. *Basic Rights in the EU*(2001). European Parliament resolution on the situation concerning basic rights in the European Union (2001) (2001/2014(INI)), January 15. Available at: http://www.europarl.europa.eu/sides/getDoc.do?pubRef=-//EP//TEXT+TA+P5-TA-2003-0012+0+DOC+XML+V0//EN (accessed 9 June 2022).

European Parliament (2013) *Parliamentary questions, Answer given by Mrs Reding on behalf of the Commission*, E-003271/2013, May 14. Available at: https://www.europarl.europa.eu/sides/getAllAnswers.do?reference=E-2013-003271&language=EL (accessed 9 June 2022).

Gilbert, D. and Abdullah, J. (2004) Holidaytaking and the sense of well-being. *Annals of Tourism Research* 31(1), 103–121.

GOV.UK (2020) *Iran. Foreign Travel Advice*. Available at: https://www.gov.uk/foreign-travel-advice/iran/local-laws-and-customs (accessed 9 June 2022).

Greek Constitution (2008) *As Revised by the Parliamentary Resolution of May 27, 2008 of the VIIIth Revisionary Parliament*. Hellenic Parliament, Athens. Available at: https://www.hellenicparliament.gr/UserFiles/f3c70a23-7696-49db-9148-f24dce6a27c8/001-156%20aggliko.pdf (accessed 9 June 2022).

Gupta, K. (2016) *Gender Equality in Relation to Access to Worship Places*. 1st National University of Study and Research in Law (NUSRL)-CLAP National Socio-Legal Essay Writing Competition, Ranchi, India. Available at: https://www.academia.edu/27462847/_GENDER_EQUALITY_IN_RELATION_TO_ACCESS_TO_WORSHIP_PLACES_ (accessed 9 June 2022).

Hashimoto, A. (2021) Rights to freedom of movement and tourism. In: Hashimoto, A., Härkönen, E. and Nkyi, E. (eds) *Human Rights Issues in Tourism. Routledge*. New York, pp. 208–235. DOI: 10.4324/9781351033862.

Hodgkinson, P. (2016) *Capital Punishment: New Perspectives*. Routledge, London and New York. DOI: 10.4324/9781315570815.

Iefimerida (2016) Γιατί απαγορεύεται η είσοδος γυναικών στο άγιον όρος [Why is it forbidden for women to enter Mount Athos?]. *Iefimerida*. Available at: https://www.iefimerida.gr/news/269123/giati-apagoreyetai-i-eisodos-ton-gynaikon-sto-agio-oros-poies-kataferan-na-mpoyn (accessed 9 June 2022).

Iellada (2018) Πως δημιουργήθηκε το Άβατο στο Άγιο Όρος—Η μοναδική ιστορία [The creation of the Avaton in Mount Athos. The unique story]. *Iellada*. Available at: https://www.iellada.gr/thriskeia/pos-dimioyrgithike-avato-sto-agio-oros-i-monadiki-istoria-deite-ta-vinteo (accessed 9 June 2022).

Joshi, S. and Dahal, R. (2019) Relationship between social carrying capacity and tourism carrying capacity: a case of Annapurna conservation area, Nepal. *Journal of Tourism and Hospitality Education* 9, 9–29. DOI: 10.3126/jthe.v9i0.23677.

Kadas, S. (1991) *Mount Athos: An Illustrated Guide to the Monasteries and Their History*. Ekdotiki Athenon, Athens.

Kapilevich, L.V. and Karvounis, Y.A. (2015) Gender-based restrictions in tourism: an example of the phenomenon of Avaton in the modern socio-cultural expanse. *Procedia - Social and Behavioral Sciences* 166, 7–11. DOI: 10.1016/j.sbspro.2014.12.474.

Kapur, R. (2016) Supreme Court: Indian temple can't stop women from entering. *The Diplomat*. Available at: https://thediplomat.com/2016/05/supreme-court-indian-temple-cant-stop-women-from-entering/ (accessed 9 June 2022).

Konidaris, I.M. (2003) *Mount Athos Avaton. Bilingual edition in Greek and English*. Αντ. Ν. Σάκκουλας, Athens.

Logan, W.S. (2007) Closing Pandora's box: human rights conundrums in cultural heritage protection. In: Silverman, H. and Fairchild Ruggles, D. (eds) *Cultural Heritage and Human Rights*. Springer, New York, pp. 33–52.

McCabe, S. and Diekmann, A. (2015) The rights to tourism: reflections on social tourism and human rights. *Tourism Recreation Research* 40(2), 194–204. DOI: 10.1080/02508281.2015.1049022.

Merriam-Webster Online Dictionary (n.d.) *Heritage*. Available at: https://www.merriam-webster.com/dictionary/heritage (accessed 11 January 2023).

Minnaert, L., Maitland, R. and Miller, G. (2006) Social tourism and its ethical foundations. *Tourism Culture & Communication* 7(1), 7–17. DOI: 10.3727/109830406778493533.

Moira, P. (2021) Cultural-religious routes and their tourism valorization. In the footsteps of the Apostle Paul in Greece. In: Bielo, J.S. and Wijnia, L. (eds) *The Bible and Global Tourism, The Bible in Contemporary Culture series*. T&T Clark, London.

Moira, P., Parthenis, S., Kontoudaki, A. and Katsoula, O. (2009) Religious tourism in Greece: the necessity to classify religious resources for their rational valorization. In: Trono, A. (ed.) *Proceedings of the International Conference "Tourism, Religion and Culture"*, University of Salento and Mario Congedo Publishing, Lecce, Italy, pp. 465–480.

Mylonopoulos, D., Moira, P. and Kikilia, A. (2017) War and cultural heritage. The case of religious monuments. In: Raj, R. and Griffin, K. (eds) *Conflicts, Religion and Culture in Tourism*. CAB International, Wallingford, UK, pp. 155–166.

OSAC (2019) *Sharia Law and Western Travelers in Southeast Asia*. Research and Information Support Center (RISC). Available at: https://www.pacom.mil/Portals/55/Documents/pdf/J34-OSAC_Sharia_Law_in_Southeast_Asia.pdf%3Fver%3D2017-03-31-171632-753 (accessed 9 June 2022).

Roosevelt, F.D. (1941) Using Human Rights Here and Now. State of the Union Address. In: Flowers, N. (ed.) Human Rights Resource Center, University of Minnesota. Available at: http://hrlibrary.umn.edu/edumat/hreduseries/hereandnow/Intro/using.htm (accessed June 2022).

Saigal, S. (2016) Women can enter Haji Ali sanctum, rules HC. *The Hindu*. Available at: https://www.thehindu.com/news/cities/mumbai/Women-can-enter-Haji-Ali-sanctum-rules-HC/article14593111.ece (accessed 9 June 2022).

Sanidopoulos, J. (2016) Are female animals forbidden in Mount Athos? Available at: https://www.johnsanidopoulos.com/2016/01/are-female-animals-forbidden-in-mount.html (accessed 9 June 2022).

Sepúlveda, M., Van Banning, T., Gudmundsdóttir, G., Chamoun, C. and Van Genugten, W.J.M. (2004) *Human Rights Reference Handbook*, 3rd edn. University of Peace, Ciudad Colon, Costa Rica.

Silverman, H. and Fairchild Ruggles, D. (eds) (2007) *Cultural Heritage and Human Rights*. Springer, New York, pp. 3–29. DOI: 10.1007/978-0-387-71313-7.

The Edition (2020) Maldives collects MVR 35.7 MLN in April as green tax. Available at: https://edition.mv/news/17717 (accessed 7 June 2022).

UN (1948) *Universal Declaration of Human Rights*. Available at: https://www.un.org/en/about-us/universal-declaration-of-human-rights (accessed 26 April 2023).

UN (1966a) *International Covenant on Civil and Political Rights* (ICCPR). Adopted and opened for signature, ratification and accession by General Assembly resolution 2200A (XXI) of 16 December 1966, entry into force 23 March 1976, in accordance with Article 49. Available at: https://www.ohchr.org/Documents/ProfessionalInterest/ccpr.pdf (accessed 9 June 2022).

UN (1966b) *International Covenant on Economic, Social and Cultural Rights* (ICESCR). Adopted and opened for signature, ratification and accession by General Assembly resolution 2200A (XXI) of 16 December 1966 entry into force 3 January 1976, in accordance with article 27. Available at: https://www.ohchr.org/en/professionalinterest/pages/cescr.aspx (accessed 9 June 2022).

UN (2007) Convention on the Rights of Persons with Disabilities and Optional Protocol. Available at: https://treaties.un.org/doc/Publication/CTC/Ch_IV_15.pdf (accessed 10 June 2022).

UNESCO (1972) *Convention concerning the Protection of the World Cultural and Natural Heritage 1972*. Paris. Available at: http://portal.unesco.org/en/ev.php-URL_ID=13055&URL_DO=DO_TOPIC&URL_SECTION=201.html (accessed 9 June 2022).

UNESCO (2001) *Universal Declaration on Cultural Diversity*. Resolution adopted on the report of Commission IV at the 20th plenary meeting, November 2. p. 3. Available at: https://unesdoc.unesco.org/in/documentViewer.xhtml?v=2.1.196&id=p::usmarcdef_0000124687&file=/in/rest/annotationSVC/DownloadWatermarkedAttachment/attach_import_ff876097-f321-419d-81ab-1b67fcd29032%3F_%3D124687eng.pdf&locale=en&multi=true&ark=/ark:/48223/pf0000124687/PDF/124687eng.pdf#25 (accessed 9 June 2022).

UNESCO (2002) *Declaration on Cultural Diversity*. 31 C/Resolution 25, Resolutions (Volume 1), 31st session, Paris, 15 October to 3 November 2001. Paris: UNESCO. Available at: https://unesdoc.unesco.org/in/documentViewer.xhtml?v=2.1.196&id=p::usmarcdef_0000124687&file=/in/rest/annotationSVC/DownloadWatermarkedAttachment/attach_import_ff876097-f321-419d-81ab-1b67fcd29032%3F_%3D124687eng.pdf&locale=en&multi=true&ark=/ark:/48223/pf0000124687/PDF/124687eng.pdf#25 (accessed 9 June 2022).

UNESCO (2003) *Convention for the Safeguarding of the Intangible Cultural Heritage*. MISC/2003/CLT/CH/14, October 17, Paris, article 21. pp. 8–9. Available at: http://unesdoc.unesco.org/images/0013/001325/132540e.pdf (accessed 9 June 2022).

UNWTO (1980) Manila Declaration on World Tourism, UNWTO Declarations, UNWTO, Madrid, Spain 1(1). DOI: 10.18111/unwtodeclarations.1980.01.01.

US Congress (1776) Declaration of Independence: A Transcription, Americas Founding Documents. Available at: https://www.archives.gov/founding-docs/declaration-transcript (accessed 26 April 2023).

Zamani-Farahani, H. and Eid, R. (2016) Muslim world: a study of tourism and pilgrimage among OIC member states. *Tourism Management Perspectives* 19, 144–149. DOI: 10.1016/j.tmp.2015.12.009.

Δωρής, Ε. (1994) *Το Δίκαιον Του Αγίου Όρους, [The Law of Mount Athos]*. τ. Β', Πηγαί του Αγιορείτικου Δικαίου, Αντ. Ν. Σάκκουλας, Αθήνα-Κομοτηνή [in Greek].

Μοίρα, Π. (2009) *Θρησκευτικός Τουρισμός [Religious Tourism]*. Interbooks, Αθήνα [in Greek].

Μοίρα, Π. (2018) *Τουριστική Γεωγραφία Της Ελλάδας. Γεωγραφικές Προσεγγίσεις Στον Τουρισμό. [Tourism Geography of Greece. Geographical Approaches to Tourism]*. Φαίδιμος, Αθήνα [in Greek].

Μοίρα, Π. (2019) *Θρησκευτικός Τουρισμός Και Προσκύνημα. Πολιτικές-Διαχείριση-Αειφορία [Religious Tourism and Pilgrimage. Politics-Management-Sustainability]*. Φαίδιμος, Αθήνα [in Greek].

Μπάλιας, Στ. (2004) *Τα Ανθρώπινα Δικαιώματα Στην Εποχή Της Δημοκρατίας [Human Rights in the Age of Democracy]*. Παπαζήσης, Αθήνα [in Greek].

Μυλωνόπουλος, Δ. (2001) *Το Σύνταγμα 1975/1986/2001. Νομοτεχνική Προσέγγιση Της Αναθεώρησης Του 2001 [The (Greek) Constitution 1975/1986/2001. Legal Approach to the 2001 Review]*. Σταμούλης, Αθήνα [in Greek].

Περράκης, Σ. (1998) *Διαστάσεις Της Διεθνούς Προστασίας Των Δικαιωμάτων Του Ανθρώπου [Dimensions of International Protection of Human Rights]*. Β' έκδοση. Σάκκουλας, Αθήνα-Κομοτηνή [in Greek].

Σκουλάς, Γ. and Σκουλά, Δ. (2011) Το δικαίωμα του πολίτη στο πολιτιστικό περιβάλλον: η συνταγματική και νομική του διάσταση στην παιδεία και στον πολιτισμό. [The citizen's right to the cultural environment: the constitutional and legal dimension in education and culture]. *Το Βήμα Των Κοινωνικών Επιστημών* 15(60). Available at: https://journals.lib.uth.gr/index.php/tovima/article/view/303/282 (accessed 9 June 2022).

Τσιβόλας, Θ.Χ. (2013) *Η Έννομη Προστασία Των Θρησκευτικών Πολιτιστικών Αγαθών [The Legal Protection of Religious Cultural Property]*. Βιβλιοθήκη Εκκλησιαστικού Δικαίου, Σάκκουλας, Αθήνα-Θεσσαλονίκη [in Greek].

4 Soft Power and Sacred Sites: The Geopolitics of Prayer

Dino Bozonelos*

Departments of Political Science and Global Studies, California State University, San Marcos, USA

Abstract

This chapter explores the concept of religious soft disempowerment, where religious actions and, the incorporation of religious principles of a sacred site into cultural diplomatic efforts offends and alienates others, leading to a loss of credibility and attractiveness. The soft power discourse within international relations, which implies that cultural attraction, values or ideology function as key elements within a country's efforts to exert power. Religious soft power and religious diplomacy can be vital tools in a country's relations with the world. The author highlights, through a case study of the 2020 conversion of Hagia Sophia into a mosque, how a strategy of religious soft power through sacred sites can generate negative geopolitical implications that could potentially offset any positive soft power benefits.

4.1 Introduction

Sacred sites are levers for geopolitical goals, where their status as destination locations are important to a country's overall strategic discourse. Destinations are defined as geographical spaces with a set of resources that are of value to someone. Not only are these spaces of value in international relations, but they are also important for internal popular discourse, helping to shape national and local policy agendas. This is especially evident when religious tourism and pilgrimage are part of a country's soft power approach. Soft power, a term coined by scholar Joseph Nye, Jr. (Nye, 1990, 2004, 2008, 2011; Fan, 2008), refers to a state's ability to attract allies through the legitimacy of its policies and their underlying cultural and political values. As soft power emanates from two sources, domestic policies and from international policies, pilgrimage and religious tourism sites better serve a country's interest. These sites are coveted not just by domestic pilgrims and tourists, but often also by international visitors as well. A good example is the soft power wielded by Saudi Arabia. The country is referred to as the Land of Two Holy Shrines, which refer to the two holiest sites in Islam. al-Masjid al-Nabawi in Medina, or the Prophet's Mosque, and al-Masjid al-Haram, or the Great Mosque in Mecca are the two major pilgrimage sites in Islam (Gallarotti and al-Filali, 2012). This status gives the country a particular advantage when it comes to influence in the larger Muslim world.

Soft power differs from its conceptual opposite, hard power. Soft power tends to imply cultural attraction, values or ideology as key elements. It does not imply a physical resource. Physical resources, such as geographic size

*dbozonelos@csusm.edu

DOI: 10.1079/9781800621732.0004

and position, natural resources and size of population are critical sources of hard power for states. Sacred sites ostensibly represent a physical resource. Consecrated spaces are often highly sought-after locations for tourists and pilgrims alike. States can develop this resource into tangible sources of power, such as industrial development, economic diversification and improved infrastructure. Yet, while sacred sites are important economic engines, and have been for centuries, the value of such locations is in their appeal to the faithful, which by definition is cultural, and in its essence, a soft power resource. For many, pilgrimage to a consecrated space represents a culmination of their faith. They may be required to attend, as in one of the five pillars of Islam, or as a matter of honour, such as a visit to the holy sites in Jerusalem for Orthodox Christians.

This connection to the geography transforms sacred sites into more than just an important physical location. Such sites are thick with meaning and have intimate appeal to believers. Even more important, Jobani and Perez (2020) comment that these believers, 'tend to view the meanings and activities attributed by others (even those that do not physically impede their own activities) as injurious or offensive to their own beliefs and religious activities' (p. 21). Thus, how these sites are incorporated as part of its cultural diplomacy, and a country's soft power approach, is important. Sovereignty over a site allows for how the site can be interpreted.

This chapter explores the implications of sacred site incorporation in the foreign relations of countries, in light of the growing importance of geopolitics. This chapter presents a brief case study of the conversion of Hagia Sofia into a mosque and religious destination site by the Erdoğan administration in Turkey. Building on Brannagan and Giulianotti (2018), *religious soft disempowerment* explains how a strategy of religious soft power through sacred sites can generate negative geopolitical implications that could potentially offset any positive soft power benefits. As globalization and its neoliberal context decelerates or even recedes, geopolitics will figure more in the success of a religious soft power strategy.

4.2 Religious Soft Power

Mandaville and Hamid (2018) conceptualize religious soft power as 'the phenomenon whereby states incorporate the promotion of religion into their broader foreign policy conduct' (p. 6). It is when 'states see value – and, seemingly, results – in using religion to engage and influence populations in other countries' (p. 7). This builds on Haynes's (2012) discussion of religious soft power where, through shared religious beliefs, the author argued that certain religious actors can exert influence on a state's foreign policies. These actors, often domestic in their origin but transnational in their approach, encourage a state's foreign policy establishment to adopt the religious values, practices and norms that they promote. For example, Haynes looks at how the Religious Right in the US affects American foreign policy, particularly towards Israel and the broader Middle East. The author also investigates the role of Hindutva in Indian foreign policy and the impacts of messianic Mahdi groups in Iran on foreign policy towards its neighbour Iraq. The difference is that Mandaville and Hamid see the state as the initiator in the process, whereas Haynes sees outside actors taking the initiative.

Mostly, religious soft power has been discussed in a positive tone. A common interpretation explains how religious soft power can co-opt rather than force cooperation with other countries by making its culture more attractive or appealing, although Steiner (2011) early on referenced both the positive and negative roles in faith-based diplomacy. Indeed, Mandaville's recent project, the *Geopolitics of Soft Power*, chronicles the 'varying motivations, strategies, and practices associated with the deployment of religious soft power' (Berkley Center for Religion, Peace and World Affairs, 2022). The positive benefits of soft power rest on attraction and persuasion, where a country can attain the outcomes that it wants without having to resort to hard power. In this friendly and attractive approach to foreign policy, soft power is considered to be more effective in certain relationships and thus preferable to the 'carrots and sticks' approach found in hard power (Nye, 2004). Religious soft power is potentially more influential as religion is leveraged to further the goals and produce favourable outcomes. As religion has returned to the public realm domestically, it has created a space where religion and religious beliefs, practices, and interpretations can influence international relations as well (Haynes, 2014). Indeed, Voll (2008) writes that part of the appeal of militant transnational movements has been their use of soft power to gain support and recruit new members.

For example, Mandaville and Hamid (2018) discuss how Saudi Arabia's support for transnational Wahhabism/Salafism teaching and Iran's exportation of its Shi'a Islamic Revolution have largely benefitted the two countries. Each country has extended its influence through religious soft power. Saudi Arabian trained scholars lead congregations and proselytize throughout Sunni majority countries, most notably in the South Asian continent. Iranian revolutionary rhetoric, where the Shi'a see themselves as a historically oppressed minority group within Islam is driving politics in Shi'a dominated societies such as Lebanon, Yemen and Iraq, and to a lesser extent in Bahrain and Azerbaijan. Blitt (2021) discusses how the Putin administration has legally incorporated the Russian Orthodox Church (ROC) into its constitution. Russian foreign policy makers see the ROC as an extension of Russian global influence and expect church officials to promote Russian interests abroad. Finally, Ashiwa and Wank (2020) conceptualize sharp power, a form of soft power where religion is under official state control and is used to promote the diplomatic aims of the government. In their analysis, they illustrate how Xi Jinping, the leader of the People's Republic of China, has incorporated Buddhism into the Belt and Road Initiative. The routes used by Buddhist monks to transmit their philosophy and thought approximate some of the corridors used in the Initiative. Xi has recognized the global promotion of Chinese Buddhism as an important segment of Chinese soft power, public diplomacy and person-to-person diplomacy.

However, less discussed are the possible negative implications that can come from the use of religious soft power. Or, that soft power has diminished in favour of hard power (Li, 2018). Nye (2004) discusses the limitations of soft power, but not that it could lead to potentially negative policy outcomes. Such limitations include the conditions that could fail to

produce the desired outcomes. In addition, soft power is diffuse, where Nye posits that the benefits are more general than specific. More importantly, Nye conceptualized soft power when the world was accelerating towards globalization, a process where worldwide interconnectivity intensifies over time and space (Steger, 2020). In this context, the author contended that the United States would be able to maximize its soft power, given the dominant role of the US in the global economic system. Indeed, often one of the major critiques of soft power is its American-centric understandings and applications, as Nye wrote his volumes primarily with the US as his example (Brooks and Wohlforth, 2002; Lee, 2009; Brannagan and Giulianotti, 2018). One could consider his original work more of a manifesto, as a set of directions for the US in a post-Cold War era. The extension of soft power dynamics and the use of soft power tools by other countries is largely the work of other scholars (see Shambaugh, 2015 on Chinese soft power; Feklyunina, 2016 on Russian identity and soft power; and Kugiel, 2012 for Indian soft power in South Asia).

A good discussion of negative impact of soft power is what Brannagan and Giulianotti (2018) call *soft disempowerment*, defined as 'actions, inactions and/or policies of states that ultimately upset, offend or alienate others, leading to a loss of credibility and attractiveness' (p. 1152). Steiner (2018) echoes a similar sentiment, where if the values incorporated as part of the soft power approach are seen as hypocritical, then any soft power 'will detract rather than attract' (p. 52). Soft power is better understood as a capacity, rather than an actuality. As such, the attempt to exercise soft power can lead to unanticipated outcomes. Brannagan and Guilianotti posit that soft disempowerment can happen in three processes: (1) the contravention of international laws and rules; (2) failing to uphold international conventions or standards on global development, including, but not limited to, environmental and humanitarian norms; and (3) direct and negative impacts on other individual nations or communities of nations. Using Qatar as an example, Brannagan and Guilianotti chronicle how in the process to acquire the 2022 World Cup, Qatar's attempt to redefine itself as a global tourist attraction backfired, leading to a scrutiny of their human rights record and their support of various militant groups in the region. Qatar experienced soft disempowerment and a reversal of any generated goodwill, an unintended outcome of their World Cup bid.

The increasing importance of geopolitics in foreign affairs reflects a shift in the international environment. Ohnesorge (2020) writes that soft power reached its peak under the era of globalization. As power diffused and shifted away from nation states to non–state actors, including multinational corporations, non-governmental organizations and transnational networks, there was a corresponding decline in the utility of hard power. According to this perspective, as the world becomes more interconnected, ideas rather than artillery become more relevant. Attraction is a key variable in the growth of soft power. Attraction is a complex concept, though Solomon (2014) posits that attraction consists of affect and emotion, important elements of identity and language, which allow for an idea, concept, place or activity to be rendered attractive in the first place. Nye (2004) mentions, 'if I can get you to want what I want, then I do not have to use carrots or sticks to make you do it' (Nye, 2004).

Finally, it is important to recognize the possibility that soft power, as a general concept, may be entering into a decline, and has passed its peak utility. A series of events in the last two decades, rooted in geopolitics or with geopolitical consequences, has rocked the international system and has questioned the effectiveness of soft power. The Global Financial Crisis of 2008, the European Union (EU) migration crisis of 2015, the COVID-19 pandemic of 2020 and the Russian invasion of Ukraine in 2022 have made a desire to be 'attractive', for lack of a better phrase, *less* attractive. Hard power and power conversion, important for protecting a country's health system, economy, and for some, territorial integrity, has proven invaluable. Economic protectionist measures, social restrictions and outright bans on travel brought on by the COVID-19 pandemic have curbed what soft power can accomplish. While some of these measures have been reversed post-pandemic, others have not. Indeed, the number of protectionist policies are on the rise.

Likewise, the conflict in Ukraine has forced quite a few countries to rearm, or at least build up their defence capabilities.

Still, within the family of soft power, religious soft power may prove to be the most resilient. As Ganiel et al. (2014) write, 'religion is a common and valid response to the crisis of modernity' (p. 6). In addition, Roose (2021) states that organized religion is an 'important part of the globalist populist surge' (p. 53). Indeed, religious leaders are competing with secular political leaders for influence and are finding success. The Global Financial Crisis left a void in many societies. The failures that neoliberalism produced cracked the confidence that many had in the system. When capitalism fails, other 'isms' rush in, including nationalism, populism and various religionisms. Thus, the rise in geopolitics and the decline in neoliberalism may mean that soft power as understood by Nye and rooted in neoliberalist economic interdependence, has become less attractive. Yet *religious* soft power, rooted in the power of religious ideas, institutions and interests may continue to have broad appeal, particularly among national leaders and foreign policy makers.

4.3 Geopolitics and Tourism

What is geopolitics? Geopolitics is defined by Caldara and Iacoviello (2022) as the 'study of how geography affects politics and the relations among states' (p. 1197). Geopolitics is shaped by a number of factors, including geographic location, resources (both natural and man-made), demographic and people factors, and relationships with other countries (Dodds, 2019). The key variable that separates out geopolitics from other types of politics, is the focus on geography. Classical geopolitics involved the analysis of 'invasions, battles and the deployment of military force' (Ó Tuathail and Agnew, 1992, p. 191). Since World War II, geopolitics has also been referred to as political geography, especially after the term geopolitics was appropriated by Fascists in the 1930s to explain their expansionist visions. This association with Nazi and Italian fascism led geopolitics as a term to fall out of use, particularly after the defeat of the Nazis. Geopolitics, however, has roared back this past decade, particularly in the aftermath of the 2008 Global Financial Crisis, when it became clear that our global interconnectedness exposed vulnerabilities in the global political economy.

The increased use of the term has been documented in a number of disciplines, primarily in international business. Munoz's (2013) handbook on the geopolitics of business chronicles how the global business environment has shifted in light of the consequences of the Global Financial Crisis. Bozonelos and Tsagdis (2023) (have shown a four-fold increase in the number of academic articles referencing geopolitics/geopolitical over the past 10 years. Indeed, numerous scholars, including Suder (2004), Bremmer and Keat (2010), Rice and Zegart (2018) and Caldara and Iacoviello (2022) have focused on geopolitical risk, which covers a diverse range of geopolitical phenomena, from terrorism to bank crises, that can adversely impact the ability of international firms to compete. Munoz and Pettus (2013) provide a Geopolitical Preparedness Index for contemporary corporations to assess their challenges. Likewise, Blackrock, 2022, the world's largest fixed income institutional asset manager, has created a geopolitical risk dashboard, which informs investors of the probability of a geopolitical event taking place, and its impact. As the neoliberal foundations of the global market give way to different understandings of capitalism, including statist and patrimonial, geopolitics will become more salient.

It is not a coincidence then that there has also been an increase in the application of the term in tourism as well, particularly as tourism is often researched by management scholars and practitioners. Hall (2017b) highlights how geopolitics has always been an element of tourism, considering the geographical dimension of tourism spaces. Hall also sees tourism as an instrument of soft power, where cultural heritage has immense propaganda value. In addition, the interconnectedness of tourism activities leaves the industry exposed to political and economic volatility. Hall (2017a) notes that quite a few tourism scholars have not only incorporated geopolitical themes in their analyses, but more recently *critical* geopolitics, which largely views tourism as exercises of power through physical spaces (Ó Tuathail, 1994). Tourism sites are arenas for several

geopolitical themes, including identity, hospitality, events and gateways.

A good example is the previous conversation on geopolitical risks. Recently, geopolitical risk has been applied to tourism in a more general approach. In previous articles, scholars were more concerned about the effect of terrorism on tourism, which is a specific kind of geopolitical risk (Enders *et al.*, 1992; Araña and León, 2008; Thompson, 2011). Balli *et al.* (2019) explore the impact of geopolitical risk on tourism demand, ultimately concluding that the effect is heterogenous. Some countries appear to be relatively resistant to geopolitical events, whereas other countries are more affected. Demiralay and Kilincarslan (2019) provide evidence that geopolitical risks impact the stock performance of leisure and tourism companies. Their analysis suggests that European and North American stocks are more susceptible than stocks in the Asian markets. In addition, Demir *et al.* (2019) found that geopolitical risk negatively impacts inbound tourism, particularly for countries that are much more dependent on tourism. Finally, Gozgor *et al.* (2022) systematically studied the impact of geopolitical risk and capital investment in tourism, defined as tourism supply. They conclude that geopolitical risks are generally harmful, and that tourism policy makers should be cognizant of the potential negative effects.

Mostafanezhad and Norum (2016) proposed four complimentary themes from which to approach the geopolitics of tourism: '(1) popular geopolitics; (2) embodied geopolitics; (3) environmental geopolitics; and (4) geopolitical imaginaries' (p. 226). The authors suggest approaching tourism geopolitics as an assemblage, as geopolitics is more than just international relations events as suggested in classical geopolitics. Indeed, geopolitics can be viewed as a discourse, where geopolitical identities are formed and can be thrust upon tourism, often with little control or input by the tourist (Gillen, 2021). Gillen and Mostafanezhad (2019) explain how the tourism encounter itself can be geopolitical. Encounters are not ahistorical or apolitical, as suggested in a neoliberal paradigm, but 'part of the coproduction of political, economic, cultural, social and/or geopolitical assemblages' (p. 71).

Mostafanezhad *et al.* (2021) provided what will be become a seminal work on the geopolitics of tourism. The authors discuss various frameworks from which to analyse the geopolitics of tourism. These include feminist and everyday geopolitics, popular geopolitics, mobility geopolitics, environmental geopolitics and security geopolitics. Each potential framework has been drawn from the existing geopolitics literature and each provides a way forward in tourism research. However, religious tourism does not fall neatly into any one of these frameworks. At some level, elements of all five frameworks manifest themselves at sacred sites. More so than other forms of tourism, religious tourism and specifically pilgrimage, can be more phenomenologically based. Lived experiences and how such experiences are consumed and interpreted are the basis for what gives religious destinations their value (Pernecky and Jamal, 2010). This value is in turn harnessed by various entities to power project and promote national interests.

4.4   Geopolitics, Soft Power and Religious Tourism

Surprisingly, there has been little research on the soft power of religious tourism, even though it is an important intersection of diplomacy and tourism. The use of cultural diplomacy as soft power is well documented, particularly through tourism (e.g. Ooi, 2015; Chen and Duggan, 2016; Ohnesorge, 2020; Xu *et al.*, 2020). As a form of 'public diplomacy' (Nye, 2004), tourism is a critical part of what Davidson and Montville (1981–1982) refer to as 'two track diplomacy', where track one entails the official channels of communication between governments and track two involves informal, unofficial communication channels between the same countries but through person-to-person contact through, say, tourism. As an important force for peace, tourism facilitates the interaction of people on an informal level, which interaction may 'trickle-up' and lead to a decrease in the political tensions that are inherent in track one diplomacy (D'Amore, 1988; Kim and Crompton, 1990; Kim *et al.*, 2007). Since culture is considered 'among the key foundations of soft power' (Hayden, 2012,

p. 29), cultural tourism is viewed as an effective and cost-effective strategy in public diplomacy efforts, most notably in the context of nation branding (e.g. Hollinshead and Chun, 2012; Hurn, 2016; Nye and Kim, 2019).

Parallel to cultural diplomacy, or part of it, depending on the author, is religious diplomacy. *Religious diplomacy* may be defined as the incorporation of religious values as core interests in a country's foreign policy. This is similar to the concept of sharp power discussed by Ashiwa and Wank (2020), where religious history, symbols and heritage are harnessed by a country to promote its foreign policy agenda. It differs in that religious diplomacy is a two-way process, where religious leaders have real influence in the cultivation of state interests, both vital and less-than vital. In addition, it varies from faith-based diplomacy, which is more focused on the use of religion as a method for conflict resolution (Sandal, 2016). In the Chinese example provided by Ashiwa and Wank, the Chinese government maintains a strict control over the Buddhist clergy. Essentially, the process is a one-way street, with little room for religious leaders to impact Chinese diplomacy. A good example of religious diplomacy is Hall's (2019) discussion of Indian foreign policy, where Indian Prime Minister Narendra Modi has explicitly engaged with the Hindutva community regarding diplomacy. Modi has referenced Indian religious ideas and religious texts in his foreign policy speeches and has invited religious leaders to important conferences and symposiums (Bhonsale, 2019).

Religious tourism, where governments promote religious views at religious destination sites that align with their interests, is a natural extension in this discourse. In addition, leaders will co-opt religion to promote their interests abroad. This desire to 'export the religion' is relevant for quite a few states, especially for states that compete for leadership and have competing views on a religion, such as Iran and Saudi Arabia. Their regional rivalry makes extensive use of religious soft power to engage other governments and actors (Haynes, 2012). Religious tourism as soft power can be understood through the concept of sacred capital. Sacred capital is understood by Bettiza (2020) as 'religious characteristics and dynamics [that] generate particular power resources for such states'. The author notes that this list includes, but is not limited to 'holy sites, sacred artifacts, spiritual leaders, places of religious learning and knowledge production, [and] official institutions' (p. 2). Bettiza divides sacred capital into three types: *sacred symbolic capital*, which occurs when a state leader can make a claim about a religious status, identity or role, and is seen as authoritative; *sacred cultural capital*, which is based on ideas and norms promoted by the country's own religious population, giving leaders clout in reaching out to co-religionists; and *sacred network capital*, which draws on the strength of networked religious institutions to promote their interests abroad. All three types of sacred capital are potential sources for religious soft power.

4.5   Case Study: Hagia Sofia, Religious Soft Disempowerment and the Geopolitics of Prayer

This chapter contends that when it comes to the incorporation of religious tourism destination sites into a country's soft power strategy, the negative *geopolitical* implications may potentially outweigh the benefits. Brannagan and Guilianotti's concept of soft disempowerment is adapted and relabelled *as religious soft disempowerment*, where the religious actions and the incorporation of religious principles of a sacred site into cultural diplomatic efforts offends and alienates others, leading to a loss of credibility and attractiveness. This mimics Steiner's (2011) and Haynes (2012) pattern of applying 'religious' as an adjective to soft power to describe a particular version of it. Sacred sites become spaces for geopolitical competition and strategy. Naniopoulos and Tsalis (2015) discuss how 'heritage spaces' have been increasingly used as 'social asset(s)' (p. 241). Governance of these spaces is about preserving heritage, and for protecting the country and fellow kin against possible encroachment. Such sites are important for 'their connection with the social, economic, political, religious and cultural context of the place and time of their creation' (p. 241).

A good example of religious soft power involves the recent conversion of Hagia Sofia into a mosque by Turkish court authorities in 2020. Turkey's founder, Mustafa Kemal Ataturk turned the mosque, which before its capture by the Sultan Mehmet in 1453 was the seat of Christianity in the Byzantine empire, into a museum in 1934. It was part of his administrative effort to secularize the republic, through the conversion of both Byzantine and Ottoman religious buildings into museums. The current Turkish President, Recep Tayyip Erdoğan sees the conversion as a cornerstone for a neo-Ottomanist policy and seeks to reverse Ataturk's legacy. Turkey sees itself as the leader of a geopolitical world of Turkic-speaking communities spread out across Central Asia, the Caucuses, and the Middle East (Jamaleddine, 2020).

Turkey also sees itself as a potential rival to Iran and Saudi Arabia for influence within Islam as well. Öztürk (2020) writes that Turkey desires to 'establish itself as a leader of the Muslim world and to compete directly with other countries that have traditionally claimed this status' (p. 1). Yilmaz (2020) echoes this by stating, 'Erdoğan highlighted his claim to leadership of the Muslim world once more in a soft power move'. Indeed, Erdoğan directly tied the conversion of Hagia Sophia to Israeli–Palestinian struggles over the Temple Mount/al-Aqsa. He was directly quoted in saying that the 'resurrection of Hagia Sophia was the harbinger of the liberation of Masjid al-Aqsa, and footsteps of Muslims' will to leave hard days behind' (Hürriyet Daily News, 2020a). The first khutbah or sermon given after the conversion took place, strategically mentioned the suffering and oppression of Muslims worldwide (Akcan, 2020). Kuru (2020) worries that the conversion of Hagia Sophia into a mosque will galvanize populists throughout the world to mobilize religiously conservative forces. Instead, the author suggests that Turkey and other Muslim-majority countries should promote 'interreligious dialogue, multicultural coexistence, and minority rights, rather than provoking interreligious tensions'.

Neo-Ottomanism deftly incorporates sacred sites as part of Turkey's geopolitical code. Yavuz, 1998 Yavuz, 2016 contends that neo-Ottomanism is about constructing a new 'national' (milli) identity and translating it into foreign policy by using historical, cultural and religious ties to former Ottoman territories. With the rise to prominence of the AKP, or Justice and Development Party, under Erdoğan in the late 1990s and 2000s, neo-Ottomanism has been increasingly used to portray Turkey as an heir to Ottoman tradition and thus legitimate in its attempt to play a leading role in Islam. Perhaps most important, in pointing to the heritage of the Ottomans, the AKP decisively moved the focus of Turkish political discourse from a secular, republican perspective to a religious one (Murariu and Anglițoiu, 2020). Yavan's discussion can be contextualized in a speech Erdoğan gave at his palace in 2016. In that speech, Erdoğan revealed a picture of Turkey constrained by external forces that 'aim to make us forget our history of Ottoman and Seljuk', when the ancestors of Turkey occupied territories spanning Central Asia and the Middle East. Converting Hagia Sofia back into a mosque is seen as an essential step in promoting neo-Ottomanism, both at home and abroad.

Yet, as mentioned in the introduction, less is discussed regarding the unfavourable geopolitical consequences of religious soft power and religious tourism. For example, while many AKP supporters and general admirers

of Erdoğan abroad may applaud his recent action, the conversion of Hagia Sofia created a storm of criticism (Fig. 4.1). There has been strong global criticism of this action. One of the most poignant rebuttals was from the United Nations Educational, Scientific and Cultural Organization, more commonly referred to as UNESCO. In July 2020, UNESCO issued a statement that called the Turkish decision regrettable. The UNESCO Director-General Audrey Azoulay wrote,

> Hagia Sophia is an architectural masterpiece and a unique testimony to interactions between Europe and Asia over the centuries. Its status as a museum reflects the universal nature of its heritage and makes it a powerful symbol for dialogue.... Such measures could constitute breaches of the rules derived from the 1972 World Heritage Convention. (UNESCO, 2020)

The UNESCO World Heritage Committee added that it was 'regrettable that the Turkish decision was not the subject of dialog nor notification beforehand' and calls on:

Fig. 4.1. Hagia Sophia is an architectural masterpiece (interior).
Source: Polyxeni Moira, personal archive.

...the Turkish authorities to open a dialog without delay in order to avoid a step back from the universal value of this exceptional heritage whose preservation will be reviewed by the World Heritage Committee in its next session (al Jazeera, 2020).

Condemnation of the Turkish government's actions has come from a chorus of political and religious actors. Josep Borrell, the European Union's foreign policy chief called the action regrettable (European Union External Action, 2020). The Council of Europe also criticized the decision, calling it 'a discriminatory step backward, that clearly undermines Turkey's secular identity and multicultural legacy' (Council of Europe, 2020). The US added to the criticism with the US Department of State mentioning their disappointment given the rich multicultural history of the sacred site (Smith et al., 2020). In contrast, the Russian government avoided using strong language, with a spokesperson for President Putin stating 'the decision to change the status of St. Sophia Cathedral in Istanbul is Turkey's own internal affair' (Suchkov, 2020). Suchkov suggests that this reflects the rearranging geopolitical relationship between the two countries, which plays to Turkey's favour.

Orthodox Christian religious authorities have been the most vociferous in their rejection of the Turkish decision. Ecumenical Patriarch Bartholomew, the spiritual head of some 300 million Orthodox Christians worldwide, who is located in Istanbul, has condemned the conversion. He noted that altering its status as a museum will 'fracture these two worlds' (Dikmen and Usta, 2020). The Russian Orthodox Church (ROC) has called the action unacceptable and labelled it as going back to the Middle Ages. Metropolitan Hilarion, who was at that time the chairman of the ROC's external relations, stated 'we live in a multipolar world, we live in a multiconfessional world and we need to respect the feelings of believers' (Reuters, 2020). The Greek Orthodox Archdiocese of North America has been the most critical, referencing the actions as 'deliberate policies to erase the cultural heritage of Orthodox Christians' (Ekathimerini, 2020) and has pressed the UN to stop Turkey from going 'down a path toward [the] denial of history, a path that denies the future as well' (AP News, 2020).

Additional condemnation has also come from other religious leaders as well. The Interim General Secretary of the World Council of Churches, the Reverend Professor Ioan Sauca asked for different churches to 'join in prayer and sorrow with millions of Christians around the world marking this sad day in history of Christianity and of inter-religious relations' (World Council of Churches, 2020). Pope Francis, the leader of the global Catholic Church, also expressed displeasure 'I think of Hagia Sophia, and I am very saddened' (Catholic News Agency, 2020). Likewise, the Conference of Presidents of Major American Jewish Organizations also strongly condemned the move. The umbrella group representing 53 American Jewish organizations worried that the conversion of Hagia Sophia into a mosque would be a 'precursor to the "liberation" of the Al-Aqsa Mosque in Jerusalem' (Times of Israel, 2020)

A number of Islamic religious scholars and leaders also criticized the decision. For example, the Grand Mufti of Egypt, Shawky Allam, heavily criticized the decision. He maintains that churches and other religious buildings are part of the 'earth's architecture in Islam' and that the Prophet Muhammad and his Companions were careful with cultural heritage (The New Arab, 2020). Dr al-Drees, former Saudi permanent representative to UNESCO, found the move to be hypocritical. Islamic scholars, supported by Turkish officials, condemned Spain's decision to convert the mosque in Cordoba into a Catholic cathedral. Dr al-Drees asked, 'How will I as an individual criminalize the Spanish decision and support the Turkish decision [to convert Hagia Sofia into a mosque]?' (Holtmeier, 2020). Probably one of the most stinging condemnations came from Dr Syeed, the President of the Board of Directors of the Islamic Society of North America (ISNA). Publishing on the website of the Greek Orthodox Archdiocese of America, Dr Syeed specifically writes, 'it is clear that our Islamic texts and the practice of the Prophet and his rightly guided Califs define the role of Islam as the protector of other's holy places' and adds 'that such an act is not giving glory to Islam which strongly forbids Muslims from such a sacrilegious act' (Syeed, 2020).

Surprisingly, the main opposition party in Turkey, the Republican People's Party (CHP) has remained largely silent. Part of neo-Ottomanist thought is the forging of a new civic nationalism at home, one that attempts to fuse religious interests with political interests. Ostensibly, the expectation is that the CHP would have opposed the move, seeing it as an affront to its Kemalist heritage of laïcité and promotion of secularism. However, Çevik (2020) notes that the opening of Hagia Sophia as a mosque was a tactical move by Erdoğan to box in the CHP. If they oppose the move, it would paint the CHP as being anti-Turkish. If they supported the move, it would move the CHP closer to the AKP neo-Ottomanist position. This is seen in the quasi-ambivalent stance taken by the current mayor of Istanbul, Ekrem İmamoğlu, who has largely supported the decision by the Turkish courts but is cautious in how it will be perceived. He questions the motives behind the push and suggests that '...such a decision to convert Hagia Sophia into a mosque could have consequences and its price would be heavy', especially if the decision is simply to distract from economic issues in Turkey (Hürriyet Daily News, 2020b).

Finally, Kilinç (2020) writes that the fallout from the conversion will affect Turkish foreign policy and tarnish Turkey's brand in several ways. First, the author suggests that the decision by the Turkish courts will damage Turkey's promotion of Istanbul's multicultural heritage. Second, it may fuel Islamophobia in other countries, particularly in India and China where large Muslim minorities already face stiffening persecution. Turkey's adamant argument that it has the sovereign right to act as it pleases with Hagia Sophia, can easily be adapted by other countries in their mistreatment of their Muslim populations. Finally, Kilinç posits that the heavy use of religion in politics will eventually backfire on the AKP. As the economy falters and corruption and injustice are more associated with the ruling party, younger members will exhibit less trust in religious–political figures and possibly see a decline in their piety.

4.6 Conclusion

If soft power refers to a state's ability to attract allies through the legitimacy of its policies and their underlying cultural and political values,

the push by the Erdoğan administration and the decision by the Turkish courts to reinstate Hagia Sofia as a mosque could be viewed as a case of *religious soft disempowerment*. While the Turkish government expected some pushback, particularly among Orthodox Christians, the strong condemnation by European leaders, UNESCO and World Council of Churches, plus the critiques by some American Jewish and American Muslim leaders, was not expected. Also, Erdoğan viewed this action as a matter for both internal domestic Turkish political consumption and for soft power projection in the Muslim world. In doing so, he may have overlooked the potential geopolitical implications of this decision.

A good example includes how President Biden has differed regarding the US relationship with Turkey. Consistently framing the relationship with Turkey as one of geopolitical necessity, US political leaders have long refrained from criticizing Turkish decisions and positions. Indeed, Erdoğan had a strong working relationship with former US President Trump, who even though they clashed occasionally over issues, called Erdoğan 'a friend' and a 'hell of a leader' (Pamuk and Coskun, 2019). It has become clear though that under President Biden, the US is seeking greater leverage in its relationship with Turkey, primarily through the language of human rights, tolerance and democracy (Danforth, 2021). Biden has used this frame from which to pressure Erdoğan to moderate his behaviour, both at home and abroad.

This shift away from US unequivocal support for Turkey under Biden first became visible with the conversion of Hagia Sofia. As the Democratic candidate for US President, Biden was especially critical of Erdoğan's efforts. Using strong words not typical for a US politician, he wrote in a statement posted to Medium in 2020

> I deeply regret the Turkish government's decision to convert the Hagia Sophia into a mosque and urge Turkish President Recep Erdoğan to reverse his decision and instead keep this treasured place in its current status as a museum, ensuring equal access for all. (Biden, 2020).

President Biden followed up on the criticism of Turkish politics the next year, when he became the first American president to recognize the Armenian genocide. The White House released an official statement on Armenian Holocaust Remembrance Day, where Biden stated, 'we remember the lives of all those who died in the Ottoman-era Armenian genocide and recommit ourselves to preventing such an atrocity from ever again occurring' (Biden, 2021). This is quite monumental, as official Turkish policy has for decades deliberately denied Ottoman genocide against Christian minorities and instead posits that both Turks and Armenians died in large numbers. Later that year, Biden specifically excluded Erdoğan from the US sponsored Summit for Democracy, a clear rebuke of Turkey's democratic decline (Kirişci, 2021).

Finally, what have been the geopolitical considerations of US President Biden's rebuke of Turkey under Erdoğan? Recently, in 2022, the US and Greece signed the US–Greece Mutual Defense Cooperation Agreement (MDCA). This agreement allows for the port of Alexandroupolis, which is near the border with Turkey, to be transformed into an American naval base. This has angered the Erdoğan administration and officials have come to openly question US intentions in the region (Daily Sabah, 2022). What is clear then is that the decision by the Turkish courts and governments to turn Hagia Sophia into a mosque, has simply provided additional justification for countries such as the US to become critical of Turkish policies. While it would be naïve to suggest that the conversion is the sole factor in explaining the nadir of Turkish–American relations, what can be discussed is how the action led to an opportunity for the current US president to frame American antipathy towards Turkey. This is the essence of religious soft disempowerment.

References

Akcan, E. (2020) *Erasing History at the Hagia Sophia*. Berkley Center for Religion, Peace and World Affairs, Washington, DC.

al Jazeera (2020) World reacts to Turkey reconverting Hagia Sophia into a mosque. *al Jazeera*. Available at: https://www.aljazeera.com/features/2020/7/11/world-reacts-to-turkey-reconverting-hagia-sophia-into-a-mosque (accessed 25 October 2022).

AP News (2020) Orthodox church petitions UN over Istanbul's Hagia Sophia. *AP News*. Available at: https://apnews.com/article/turkey-freedom-of-religion-istanbul-recep-tayyip-erdogan-christianity-e41979352205ab10fe56ee780cd6a949 (accessed 25 October 2022).

Araña, J.E. and León, C.J. (2008) The impact of terrorism on tourism demand. *Annals of Tourism Research* 35(2), 299–315. DOI: 10.1016/j.annals.2007.08.003.

Ashiwa, Y. and Wank, D.L. (2020) *The Chinese State's Global Promotion of Buddhism*. Berkley Center for Religion, Peace and World Affairs, Washington, DC.

Balli, F., Uddin, G.S. and Shahzad, S.J.H. (2019) Geopolitical risk and tourism demand in emerging economies. *Tourism Economics* 25(6), 997–1005. DOI: 10.1177/1354816619831824.

Berkley Center for Religion, Peace and World Affairs (2022) *The Geopolitics of Religious Soft Power*. Available at: https://berkleycenter.georgetown.edu/projects/the-geopolitics-of-religious-soft-power (accessed 25 October 2022).

Bettiza, G. (2020) *States, Religions, and Power: Highlighting the Role of Sacred Capital in World Politics*. Berkley Center for Religion, Peace and World Affairs, Washington, DC.

Bhonsale, M. (2019) Religious tourism as soft power: strengthening India's outreach to Southeast Asia. In: *ORF Special Report No.97*. Observer Research Foundation, New Delhi, India.

Biden, J.R. (2020) My statement on the status of the Hagia Sophia. *Medium.Com*. Available at: https://medium.com/@JoeBiden/my-statement-on-the-status-of-the-hagia-sophia-9e9d16dd5f07 (accessed 25 October 2022).

Biden, J.R. (2021) Statement by president Joe Biden on Armenian remembrance day. *The White House*. Available at: https://www.whitehouse.gov/briefing-room/statements-releases/2021/04/24/statement-by-president-joe-biden-on-armenian-remembrance-day/ (accessed 25 October 2022).

Blackrock (2022) Geopolitical risk dashboard. *Blackrock*. Available at: https://www.blackrock.com/corporate/insights/blackrock-investment-institute/interactive-charts/geopolitical-risk-dashboard (accessed 25 October 2022).

Blitt, R.C. (2021) *Religious Soft Power in Russian Foreign Policy: Constitutional Change and the Russian Orthodox Church*. Berkley Center for Religion, Peace and World Affairs, Washington, DC.

Bozonelos, D. and Tsagdis, D. (2023) From fragmented geopolitics to geopolitical resilience in international Business. *Academy of International Business Insights* 23(2). Available at: https://doi.org/10.46697/001c.73803

Brannagan, P.M. and Giulianotti, R. (2018) The soft power–soft disempowerment nexus: the case of Qatar. *International Affairs* 94(5), 1139–1157. DOI: 10.1093/ia/iiy125.

Bremmer, I. and Keat, P. (2010) *The Fat Tail: The Power of Political Knowledge in an Uncertain World*. Oxford University Press, Oxford, UK.

Brooks, S.G. and Wohlforth, W.C. (2002) American primacy in perspective. *Foreign Affairs* 81(4), 20–33. DOI: 10.2307/20033237.

Caldara, D. and Iacoviello, M. (2022) Measuring geopolitical risk. *American Economic Review* 112(4), 1194–1225. DOI: 10.1257/aer.20191823.

Catholic News Agency (2020) Pope Francis expresses sadness after Hagia Sophia is declared a mosque. *Catholic News Agency*. Available at: https://www.catholicnewsagency.com/news/45142/pope-francis-expresses-sadness-after-hagia-sophia-is-declared-a-mosque (accessed 25 October 2022).

Çevik, S. (2020) Political implications of the Hagia Sophia reconversion. *Stiftung Wissenschaft Und Politik*. Available at: https://www.swp-berlin.org/en/publication/political-implications-of-the-hagia-sophia-reconversion (accessed 25 October 2022).

Chen, Y.W. and Duggan, N. (2016) Soft power and tourism: a study of Chinese outbound tourism to Africa. *Journal of China and International Relations* 4(1), 45–66.

Council of Europe (2020) Written declaration on Hagia Sofia. Parliamentary Assembly of the Council of Europe (PACE). Available at: https://rm.coe.int/0900001680a6f03f (accessed 25 October 2022).

Daily Sabah (2022) Greece upgrades military base deal with US despite opposition. *Daily Sabah*. Available at: https://www.dailysabah.com/world/europe/greece-upgrades-military-base-deal-with-us-despite-opposition (accessed 25 October 2022).

D'Amore, L.J. (1988) Tourism — A vital force for peace. *Tourism Management* 9(2), 151–154. DOI: 10.1016/0261-5177(88)90025-8.

Danforth, N. (2021) A cool, cautious calm: US-Turkey relations six months into the Biden administration. *The Brookings Institution*. Available at: https://www.brookings.edu/research/a-cool-cautious-calm-us-turkey-relations-six-months-into-the-biden-administration/ (accessed 25 October 2022).

Demiralay, S. and Kilincarslan, E. (2019) The impact of geopolitical risks on travel and leisure stocks. *Tourism Management* 75, 460–476. DOI: 10.1016/j.tourman.2019.06.013.

Demir, E., Gozgor, G. and Paramati, S.R. (2019) Do geopolitical risks matter for inbound tourism? *Eurasian Business Review* 9(2), 183–191. DOI: 10.1007/s40821-019-00118-9.

Dikmen, Y. and Usta, B. (2020) Orthodox patriarch says turning Istanbul's Hagia Sophia into mosque would be divisive. *Reuters*. Available at: https://www.reuters.com/article/us-turkey-museum-preview/orthodox-patriarch-says-turning-istanbuls-hagia-sophia-into-mosque-would-be-divisive-idUSKBN24130F (accessed 25 October 2022).

Dodds, K. (2019) *Geopolitics: A Very Short Introduction*. Oxford University Press, Oxford, UK. DOI: 10.1093/actrade/9780198830764.001.0001.

Ekathimerini (2020) Orthodox church petitions UN over Istanbul's Hagia Sophia, 30 october. *Ekathimerini.Com*. Available at: https://www.ekathimerini.com/news/257540/orthodox-church-petitions-un-over-istanbul-s-hagia-sophia/ (accessed 25 October 2022).

Enders, W., Sandler, T. and Parise, G.F. (1992) An econometric analysis of the impact of terrorism on tourism. *Kyklos* 45(4), 531–554. DOI: 10.1111/j.1467-6435.1992.tb02758.x.

European Union External Action (2020) Turkey: statement by the high representative/vice-president Josep Borrell on the decision regarding Hagia Sophia. *European Union*. Available at: https://www.eeas.europa.eu/eeas/turkey-statement-high-representativevice-president-josep-borrell-decision-regarding-hagia_en (accessed 25 October 2022).

Fan, Y. (2008) Soft power: power of attraction or confusion? *Place Branding and Public Diplomacy* 4(2), 147–158. DOI: 10.1057/pb.2008.4.

Feklyunina, V. (2016) Soft power and identity: Russia, Ukraine and the Russian world(s). *European Journal of International Relations* 22(4), 773–796. DOI: 10.1177/1354066115601200.

Gallarotti, G. and al-Filali, I.Y. (2012) Saudi Arabia's soft power. *International Studies* 49(3–4), 233–261. DOI: 10.1177/0020881714532707.

Gillen, J. (2021) Troubling self and other at the Hanoi Hilton: recasting geopolitical identity in tourism. In: Mostafanezhad, M., Cordoba Azcarate, M. and Norum, R. (eds) *Tourism Geopolitics: Assemblages of Infrastructure, Affect, and Imagination*. University of Arizona Press, Tucson, AZ, pp. 167–184.

Gillen, J. and Mostafanezhad, M. (2019) Geopolitical encounters of tourism: a conceptual approach. *Annals of Tourism Research* 75, 70–78. DOI: 10.1016/j.annals.2018.12.015.

Ganiel, G., Winkel, H. and Monnot, C. (2014) Introduction. In: Ganiel, G., Winkel, H. and Monnot, C. (eds) *Religion in Times of Crisis*. Brill, Leiden, Netherlands, pp. 1–7. DOI: 10.1163/9789004277793.

Gozgor, G., Lau, M.C.K., Zeng, Y., Yan, C. and Lin, Z. (2022) The Impact of geopolitical risks on tourism supply in developing economies: the moderating role of social globalization. *Journal of Travel Research* 61(4), 872–886. DOI: 10.1177/00472875211004760.

Hall, C.M. (2017a) Tourism and geopolitics: the political imaginary of territory, tourism and space. In: Hall, D. (ed.) *Tourism and Geopolitics: Issues and Concepts from Central and Eastern Europe*. CAB International, Wallingford, UK, pp. 15–24.

Hall, D. (2017b) Bringing geopolitics to tourism. In: Hall, D. (ed.) *Tourism and Geopolitics: Issues and Concepts from Central and Eastern Europe*. CAB International, Wallingford, UK, pp. 3–14. DOI: 10.1079/9781780647616.0000.

Hall, I. (2019) Narendra Modi's new religious diplomacy. In: Gupta, S., Mullen, R.D., Basrur, R., Hall, I., Blarel, N., *et al.* (eds) *Indian Foreign Policy under Modi: A New Brand or Just Repackaging?*, Vol. 20. International Studies Perspectives, pp. 1–45. DOI: 10.1093/isp/eky008.

Hayden, C. (2012) *The Rhetoric of Soft Power: Public Diplomacy in Global Contexts*. Lexington Books, Lanham, MD.

Haynes, J. (2012) *Religious Transnational Actors and Soft Power*. Routledge, New York.

Haynes, J. (2014) *Religion in Global Politics*. Routledge, New York. DOI: 10.4324/9781315841700.

Hollinshead, K. and Chun, X.H. (2012) The seductions of "soft power": the call for multifronted research into the articulative reach of tourism in China. *Journal of China Tourism Research* 8(3), 227–247. DOI: 10.1080/19388160.2012.703923.

Holtmeier, L. (2020) Arab media calls Erdogan hypocrite, says he supports extremism on Hagia Sophia move. *al-Arabiya News*. Available at: https://english.alarabiya.net/features/2020/07/16/Arab-media-calls-Erdogan-hypocrite-says-he-supports-extremism-after-move-to-convert (accessed 25 October 2022).

Hurn, B.J. (2016) The role of cultural diplomacy in nation branding. *Industrial and Commercial Training* 48(2), 80–85. DOI: 10.1108/ICT-06-2015-0043.

Hürriyet Daily News (2020a) Hagia Sophia to be open for all, says Erdoğan after conversion into mosque. *Hürriyet Daily News*. Available at: https://www.hurriyetdailynews.com/hagia-sophia-to-be-open-for-all-says-erdogan-as-it-is-converted-into-mosque-156457 (accessed 25 October 2022).

Hürriyet Daily News (2020b) Istanbul Mayor supports Hagia Sophia conversion move 'as long as it benefits Turkey'. *Hürriyet Daily News*. Available at: https://www.hurriyetdailynews.com/istanbul-mayor-supports-hagia-sophia-conversion-move-as-long-as-it-benefits-turkey-156527 (accessed 25 October 2022).

Jamaleddine, Z. (2020) Hagia Sophia past and future. *Places Journal*. DOI: 10.22269/200811.

Jobani, Y. and Perez, N. (2020) *Governing the Sacred: Political Toleration in Five Contested Sacred Sites*. Oxford University Press, Oxford, UK. DOI: 10.1093/oso/9780190932381.001.0001.

Kilinç, R. (2020) *Why Is Hagia Sophia's (Re)Conversion into a Mosque Bad for Muslims?* Berkley Center for Religion, Peace and World Affairs, Washington, DC.

Kim, Y.K. and Crompton, J.L. (1990) Role of tourism in unifying the two Koreas. *Annals of Tourism Research* 17(3), 353–366. DOI: 10.1016/0160-7383(90)90003-A.

Kim, S.S., Prideaux, B. and Prideaux, J. (2007) Using tourism to promote peace on the Korean Peninsula. *Annals of Tourism Research* 34(2), 291–309. DOI: 10.1016/j.annals.2006.09.002.

Kirişci, K. (2021) Biden's exclusion of Erdoğan from the democracy summit may be a blessing in disguise for Turkey. *The Brookings Institution*. Available at: https://www.brookings.edu/opinions/bidens-exclusion-of-erdogan-from-the-democracy-summit-may-be-a-blessing-in-disguise-for-turkey/ (accessed 25 October 2022).

Kugiel, P. (2012) India's soft power in South Asia. *International Studies* 49(3–4), 351–376. DOI: 10.1177/0020881714534033.

Kuru, A.T. (2020) *Hagia Sophia, Islamism, and Secularism in Turkey*. Berkley Center for Religion, Peace and World Affairs, Washington, DC.

Lee, G. (2009) A theory of soft power and Korea's soft power strategy. *Korean Journal of Defense Analysis* 21(2), 205–219. DOI: 10.1080/10163270902913962.

Li, E. (2018) The rise and fall of soft power. *Foreign Policy*. Available at: https://foreignpolicy.com/2018/08/20/the-rise-and-fall-of-soft-power/# (accessed 25 October 2022).

Mostafanezhad, M. and Norum, R. (2016) Towards a geopolitics of tourism. *Annals of Tourism Research* 61, 226–228. DOI: 10.1016/j.annals.2016.08.003.

Mandaville, P. and Hamid, S. (2018) *Islam as Statecraft: How Governments Use Religion in Foreign Policy*. Berkley Center for Religion, Peace and World Affairs, Washington, DC.

Mostafanezhad, M., Cordoba Azcarate, M. and Norum, R. (2021) *Tourism Geopolitics: Assemblages of Infrastructure, Affect, and Imagination*. University of Arizona Press, Tucson, AZ.

Munoz, J.M.S. (2013) *Handbook on the Geopolitics of Business*. Edward Elgar, Cheltenham, UK. DOI: 10.4337/9780857939753.

Munoz, J.M.S. and Pettus, M. (2013) Geopolitical forces and strategic approaches for the contemporary corporation. In: Munoz, J.M.S. (ed.) *Handbook on the Geopolitics of Business*. Edward Elgar, Cheltenham, UK.

Murariu, M. and Anglițoiu, G. (2020) Anatolian security and neo-Ottomanism: Turkey's intervention in Syria. *Middle East Policy* 27(2), 132–147. DOI: 10.1111/mepo.12500.

Naniopoulos, A. and Tsalis, P. (2015) A methodology for facing the accessibility of monuments developed and realised in Thessaloniki, Greece. *Journal of Tourism Futures* 1(3), 240–253. DOI: 10.1108/JTF-03-2015-0007.

Nye, J.S. (1990) *Bound to Lead: The Changing Nature of American Power*. Basic Books, New York.

Nye, J.S. (2004) *Soft Power: The Means of Success in World Politics*. Public Affairs, New York.

Nye, J.S. (2008) Public diplomacy and soft power. *Annals of the American Academy of Political and Social Science* 616(1), 94–109. DOI: 10.1177/0002716207311699.

Nye, J.S. (2011) *The Future of Power*. Public Affairs, New York.

Nye, J.S. and Kim, Y. (2019) Soft power and the Korean wave. In: Kim, Y. (ed.) *South Korean Popular Culture and North Korea*. Routledge, New York, pp. 41–53. DOI: 10.4324/9781351104128.

Ohnesorge, H.W. (2020) Soft power. In: *Soft Power: The Forces of Attraction in International Relations*. Springer, Cham. DOI: 10.1007/978-3-030-29922-4.

Ooi, C. (2015) Soft power, tourism. In: Jafari, J. and Xiao, H. (eds) *Encyclopedia of Tourism (pp. 878)*. Springer, Cham, Switzerland, pp. 1–2.

Ó Tuathail, G. (1994) The critical reading/writing of geopolitics: re-reading/writing Wittfogel, Bowman and Lacoste. *Progress in Human Geography* 18(3), 313–332. DOI: 10.1177/030913259401800303.

Ó Tuathail, G. and Agnew, J. (1992) Geopolitics and discourse: practical geopolitical reasoning in American foreign policy. *Political Geography* 11(2), 190–204.

Öztürk, A.E. (2020) *The Many Faces of Turkey's Religious Soft Power*. Berkley Center for Religion, Peace and World Affairs, Washington, DC.

Pamuk, H. and Coskun, O. (2019) Behind Trump-Erdogan 'Bromance', A White House meeting to repair U.S.-Turkey ties. *Reuters*. Available at: https://www.reuters.com/article/us-turkey-usa-trump-erdogan/behind-trump-erdogan-bromance-a-white-house-meeting-to-repair-u-s-turkey-ties-idUSKBN1XM0F0 (accessed 25 October 2022).

Pernecky, T. and Jamal, T. (2010) (Hermeneutic) Phenomenology in tourism studies. *Annals of Tourism Research* 37(4), 1055–1075. DOI: 10.1016/j.annals.2010.04.002.

Reuters (2020) Russian orthodox church says 'unacceptable' to turn Hagia Sophia into a mosque—Ifax. *Reuters*. Available at: https://www.reuters.com/article/uk-turkey-museum-russia-idAFKBN2450HN (accessed 25 October 2022).

Rice, C. and Zegart, A. (2018) *Political Risk: How Businesses and Organizations Can Anticipate Global Insecurity*. Twelve, New York.

Roose, J.M. (2021) *The New Demagogues: Religion, Masculinity and the Populist Epoch*. Routledge, New York. DOI: 10.4324/9780429431197.

Sandal, N.A. (2016) Religion and foreign policy. In: Haynes, J. (ed.) *Handbook of Religion and Politics*, 2nd edn. Routledge, New York, pp. 284–298.

Shambaugh, D. (2015) China's soft-power push: the search for respect. *Foreign Affairs* 94(4), 99–107.

Smith, S., Jovanoski, K. and Akyavas, A. (2020) Turkey's Erdogan re-converts Istanbul's Hagia Sophia into mosque. *NBC News*. Available at: https://www.nbcnews.com/news/world/istanbul-s-hagia-sophia-set-be-converted-mosque-top-court-n1233310 (accessed 25 October 2022).

Solomon, T. (2014) The affective underpinnings of soft power. *European Journal of International Relations* 20(3), 720–749. DOI: 10.1177/1354066113503479.

Steger, M.B. (2020) *Globalization: A Very Short Introduction*, 5th edn. Oxford University Press, Oxford, UK. DOI: 10.1093/actrade/9780198849452.001.0001.

Steiner, S.M. (2011) Religious soft power as accountability mechanism for power in world politics. *SAGE Open* 1(3). DOI: 10.1177/2158244011428085.

Steiner, S.M. (2018) *Globalization: Religious Diplomacy in the Age of Anthropocene*. Brill, Leiden, Netherlands.

Suchkov, M.A. (2020) Why did Moscow call Ankara's Hagia Sophia decision 'Turkey's Internal Affair'? *Middle East Institute*. Available at: https://www.mei.edu/publications/why-did-moscow-call-ankaras-hagia-sophia-decision-turkeys-internal-affair (accessed 25 October 2022).

Suder, G.G.S. (2004) The complexity of the geopolitics dimension in risk assessment for international business. In: Suder, G.G.S. (ed.) *Terrorism and the International Business Environment: The Security–Business Nexus*. Edward Elger, Cheltenham, UK.

Syeed, S.M. (2020) Official statement of the Islamic Society of North America (ISNA). *Greek Orthodox Archdiocese of America*. Available at: https://www.goarch.org/-/official-statement-isna (accessed 25 October 2022).

The New Arab (2020) Mufti of Egypt says Turkey's Hagia Sophia mosque conversion is 'Forbidden'. *The New Arab*. Available at: https://english.alaraby.co.uk/news/turkeys-hagia-sophia-mosque-conversion-forbidden-egypt-mufti (accessed 25 October 2022).

Thompson, A. (2011) Terrorism and tourism in developed versus developing countries. *Tourism Economics* 17(3), 693–700. DOI: 10.5367/te.2011.0064.

Times of Israel (2020) Jewish umbrella group slams Erdogan for vowing to liberate al-Aqsa. *Times of Israel*. Available at: https://www.timesofisrael.com/jewish-umbrella-group-slams-erdogan-for-vowing-to-liberate-al-aqsa/ (accessed 25 October 2022).

UNESCO (2020) UNESCO statement on Hagia Sophia, Istanbul. *World Heritage Convention. UNESCO*. Available at: https://whc.unesco.org/en/news/2156 (accessed 25 October 2022).

Voll, J.O. (2008) Trans-state Muslim movements and militant extremists in an era of soft power. In: Banchoff, T. (ed.) *Religious Pluralism, Globalization, and World Politics*. Oxford University Press, Oxford, UK, pp. 253–274. DOI: 10.1093/acprof:oso/9780195323405.001.0001.

World Council of Churches (2020) WCC statement on Hagia Sofia. *World Council of Churches*. Available at: https://www.oikoumene.org/resources/documents/wcc-statement-on-hagia-sophia (accessed 25 October 2022).

Xu, H., Wang, K. and Song, Y.M. (2020) Chinese outbound tourism and soft power. *Journal of Policy Research in Tourism, Leisure and Events* 12(1), 34–49. DOI: 10.1080/19407963.2018.1505105.

Yavuz, M.H. (1998) Turkish identity and foreign policy in flux: the rise of neo-Ottomanism. *Critique* 7(12), 19–41. DOI: 10.1080/10669929808720119.

Yavuz, M.H. (2016) Social and intellectual origins of neo-Ottomanism: searching for a post-national vision. *Die Welt Des Islams* 56(3–4), 438–465. DOI: 10.1163/15700607-05634p08.

Yilmaz, I. (2020) *Hagia Sophia and Turkish Anxiety to Lead the Muslim World*. Berkley Center for Religion, Peace and World Affairs, Washington, DC.

5 Bringing the State Back Into Religious Tourism: Institutional Logics and Religious Tourism Governance

Dino Bozonelos*

Departments of Political Science and Global Studies, California State University, San Marcos, USA

Abstract

In this chapter, Bozonelos discusses religious tourism governance. This is where various institutions at different levels of analysis, both inside and outside the government, come together to produce positive outcomes, usually in the form of public policy. This necessitates a discussion on the role of the state in religious tourism, an ignored concept within the dominant discourse of neoliberalism, which assigns a primary role to market pre-eminence. The author discusses the impact of formal religious tourism governance and distinguishes between governance and management. The chapter wraps up with a discussion of institutional logics and how they can help guide future research on religious tourism and pilgrimage.

5.1 Introduction: Bringing the State Back Into Religious Tourism

Chapter 1, in this book has led to the development of a more updated category of analysis, *religious tourism governance*. This reconceptualization better reflects what actually occurs and provides for a definition of religious tourism governance – *various institutions at different levels of analysis, both inside and outside the government, coming together to produce positive outcomes, usually in the form of public policy*. In the modern context, religious tourism governance involves the relationships between state institutions, market actors and religious authorities, both formal and informal. However, unlike *religious tourism policy studies*, religious tourism governance places an emphasis on the role, or sometimes the lack thereof, of state

institutions and how their behaviour impacts religious tourism and pilgrimage. The state is given a pre-eminent role and its actions are often the major variables in analyses regarding governance.

Governance has been the domain of the state since its modern inception in the 1648 Treaty of Westphalia. For many political scientists, state governance and state institutions are the hallmark of what makes a state. What differentiates a state from other governing entities is that the state has the *sovereignty* to internally govern as it sees fit (Sørensen, 2006). Jenkins *et al.* (2014, p. 658) draw a distinction between governance and government. Governance consists of the 'ways in which the decisions are made'. Government in contrast provides the steering mechanisms, often organized in a hierarchical way, for when the decisions are

*dbozonelos@csusm.edu

© CAB International 2023. *The Politics of Religious Tourism* (eds D. Bozonelos and P. Moira)
DOI: 10.1079/9781800621732.0005

made. Governance explains the decision-making process, whereas government is how the decisions are executed. Thus, governance analyses the interrelationships between private individuals, civic society and government institutions.

Quite a few scholars (Bramwell and Lane, 2012; Hall, 2012; Jamal and Camargo, 2018; Piva et al., 2019) have outlined that there has been a 'gradual shift in approach to tourism policy literature from the notion of government to that of governance' (Hall, 2012, p. 27). Governance has become a way for scholars to bring back the state in policy research, particularly when the state intervenes in an economy, ostensibly for social or political reasons. The dominance of neoliberal thought since the collapse of the Soviet Union in the early 1990s led some to think that the state should mostly withdraw from the growing global economy. Referred to as neoliberalism, it is the ideology that a self-regulating market should emerge as the governing framework for a global economy (Steger, 2020). Neoliberalism has been the driving force behind globalization, where the goal of removing the state from major macroeconomic decisions would bring the benefits of market liberalization to other countries. Of course, Steger correctly points out that the core message of liberalizing and integrating markets is only realizable through the political project of engineering free markets. Thus, even for the 'free market' to work globally, it required for the state to make it so.

Telfer (2015) notes that an expectation has developed that tourists and tour companies should be free to operate as they see fit across international borders. Any state intervention is seen as onerous and should be either minimized or eliminated altogether. If state involvement exists, it should only be to promote tourism growth. Indeed, almost all states have invested in the infrastructure to facilitate the economic development that comes with global tourism (Hall, 2017). This neoliberal management approach has led to a fractured approach to governance in tourism, and more specifically in religious tourism. Mosedale (2016) writes that privatization of former national assets, such as transportation and in some countries, hotel infrastructure, has increased tourist access. Similarly, liberalization of health care access has led to a boom in medical tourism. One of the more impactful trends has been the creation of new tourism markets where none existed before. Mosedale (2016) notes, 'neoliberal ideology views unrestrained markets as the best organization of exchange, this form of organization is to be expanded into all sphere of society' (p. 6). Neoliberalism has similarly affected religious tourism and pilgrimage. Reader (2014) comments how 'pilgrimages are embedded in a context of markets, consumer activity, publicity and promotion, and how they operate not just in the marketplace but through it' (p. 8).

This problem has become acute, especially regarding issues of sustainability in tourism. Moscardo (2012) is highly critical of this deregulated approach, arguing that a business approach to tourism is completely disconnected from issues of sustainability, as tourists often stretch the resource capacity of destination locations. Bramwell (2012) contends that any governance of sustainable tourism would require the direct intervention of the state as there are competing actors and governance cuts across policy areas. Sustainability problems in transportation, lodging and other infrastructure require collective action to solve the issues of a fractured approach to governance. Without state involvement, the market will set the priorities and sustainability will take a back seat. Finally, Hall (2013) points out that non-market interventions are often marginalized and/or ignored in the policy process. The author suggests that an effort must be made to change this thinking and better incorporate varying modes of intervention by state institutions and ultimately modify sustainable tourism policy.

Globalization and neoliberal thinking have also certainly influenced tourism governance between countries, where multinational firms have come to dominate international tourism. Airlines, hotels, tour companies and other tourism affiliated industries pursue horizontal integration, often seeking consolidation and routinized experiences, applying what Cornelissen (2011) describes as a Fordist approach to tourism. Dwyer (2015) notes that this can lead to abuse by larger international firms, where anti-competitive practices significantly affect the political economies of developing countries. For example, Dredge and Whitford (2012) point out that corporate interests often take advantage of liberalization and privations to take control of local conditions. Local resistance is often accused of upsetting the 'government-business-civil society' complex, which ostensibly favours the larger multinational corporations.

Fractured governance has also affected religious tourism and pilgrimage. A good example includes studies by Shinde (2012, 2018) where the author notes an 'institutional vacuum' when it comes to religious tourism policymaking in India. India has adopted a more neoliberal approach to religious tourism governance, with a marked absence of regulation as state-established governing bodies have taken the place of formal regulatory agencies. Even though these bodies have been successful in a few locations, most of the governance is informal and the local municipalities and resident communities often do not have their problems addressed. Likewise, the role of religious service providers, ritual priests and pilgrims has not been formally incorporated. In response, they have formed religious trusts, both public and private, to fill the void created by minimal state involvement. Finally, there has been a rise in 'religious entrepreneurship where businesses cater to the needs of the pilgrims or provide services such as entertainment. Shinde (2012, p. 285) notes that this has created a 'free-for-all market'.

5.2   The Importance of Formal Religious Tourism Governance

A good to question to ask is why *should* governments be involved in the governance of religious tourism sites? Why not just leave governance to either market-driven entities or to at least non-governmental entities that operate within market forces? Globalization and neoliberalist policies have led to significant growth in religious tourism and pilgrimage. This growth can be measured economically, where the faith-based global tourism market is predicted to be worth $13.7 billion in 2022. Despite the recent pandemic, this market is expected to grow even more, reaching an estimated market valuation of $37 billion in ten years (Future Market Insight, 2022). In addition, religious tourism and pilgrimage is positively correlated with population growth, job creation and the development of infrastructure (Terzidou *et al.*, 2008). Finally, the religious tourism infrastructure

development that has accompanied this growth is directly correlated with meeting the demands of those who travel. Kim *et al.* (2020) discusses how the reputation of the travel agent, the expertise of the tour guide, the schedule of events, and the overall program of the tour itself are fundamental aspects of a successful religious tourism and pilgrimage experience.

However, a rising number of religious tourism scholars have argued that the state not only needs but *must* take a more active role in the governance of these sacred sites. The economic importance of religious tourism and pilgrimage has prompted calls for intervention (Vukonic, 1998, 2002; Olsen, 2003; Collins-Kreiner, 2009; Shepherd, 2013; Tobón Perilla and Tobón Perilla, 2013; Álvarez-García *et al.*, 2018; Hvizdová, 2018). Timothy (2022) highlights that 'billions of dollars are spent each year on pilgrimages and or other religious journeys', leading to a high degree of commercialization at sacred destination sites (p. 305), which in turn has led to significant employment growth in this sector. In addition to the jobs normally created through tourism – lodging, transportation, food services, retail, tour operations, entertainment, construction – there are jobs specific to sacred sites, particularly those that cater to pilgrims. These include clergy and religious officials, religious guides that are there to assist pilgrims, and medical staff trained in the practices of the religion, especially for the larger religious festivals and events.

In other words, a desire exists for *formal religious tourism governance* as opposed to informal approaches. Formal rules in politics allow for stability. Examples include determining to whom in the government a religious official may turn when the need arises for infrastructure improvement. Trono (2015) points in a case study of the Church of San Pio in Italy that all stakeholders, from non-profit organizations managing accommodations, to supranational organizations that manage the site itself, benefited from Italian government initiatives. Trono points to a 'certain kind of synergy between the Church, the state and private enterprises leads to better experience and better management of religious tourism' (p. 33).

Formal religious tourism governance could also manage the growing problems associated with religious tourism of which there are plenty. Olsen (2006) discusses how sacred spaces have overlapping goals, serving both the religious/

spiritual needs of the visitors and the tourist expectations. This convergence of activities often leaves one aspect less fulfilled. Allowing for a greater number of tourists into hallowed spaces may make for better revenue streams but it can also lead to the degradation of the site itself (Shackley, 2001; Woodward, 2004; Olsen, 2006). In addition to the sustainability issues discussed earlier, additional strains include the destructive impact of increased tourist arrivals on traditional communities, culture and religious practices, and infrastructure.

Religious tourism governance could also be more democratic as effective governance structures can include officials at all levels of elected government, including national, provincial/state and local. It can also incorporate important public organizations such as national civil service bodies, government ministries, statutory authorities, and officials of religious organizations and religious institutions. Clarke and Raffay (2015) refer to this as co-creation, where producers and consumers are taken into account. In their conceptual framework, the power position matters. In their case study of a sacred destination site in Hungary, the Catholic Church is considered the most powerful stakeholder, yet it is far from the only one. In addition, formal governance can involve entities outside of traditional government. For example, in a pluralistic democratic political system, space is made available for interest groups, nongovernmental organizations (NGOs) at all levels, industry associations, international governmental organizations (IGOs), political parties, public opinion and mass media.

This push for formal religious tourism governance is not meant for the supremacy of national level institutions over provincial and local institutions. Indeed, local governance may be preferable, particularly when it comes to sites of interreligious significance, as it is sometimes considered more democratic (Zarb, 2020). Indeed, Griffiths and Wiltshier (2019) point out that decentralization could lead to better outcomes regarding the preservation of a site and several studies have noted that bottom-up strategies can be more effective (Shepherd, 2013; Shoup *et al.*, 2015). In addition, it is not meant to ignore the concept of global religious governance, where international organizations, intergovernmental organizations and non-governmental

organizations work together to solve cross-national and global coordination problems regarding religious tourism (see Chapter 6).

5.3   Religious Tourism Governance vs. Religious Tourism Management

Governance is not management, even though management could be considered a subset within governance. For many academics, policy makers and practitioners, governance and management are often interchangeable terms. In many instances, a state entity will often both govern and manage a sacred site. Or, the government may delegate or designate a private entity, such as charitable trust, to run and maintain the location. At the minimum, such private entities will often have a stake in the governing process, generally representing the interests of the religious group, which makes any clear delineation between governance and management futile (Rodrigues *et al.*, 2019). A good example is by Shinde (2018), where the author contextualizes the intertwining of governance and management in religious tourism through two cases, Vrindavan and Shirdi, both important sites within the Indian religious tourism market. Shinde does not differentiate between the two terms, and nor does the author really need to. In the case studies, they are one and the same.

Yet despite the interchangeability of the two terms, governance does differ from management. Using neoliberal discourse, management refers to the *business* of running a sacred site. Management activities include the typical challenges associated with operating any business in the tourism sector, including but not limited to lodging, dining, parking, security, tours and labour considerations (Olsen, 2003). Management focuses on the customer experience, whether the client is a pilgrim or a religious tourist (Blackwell, 2007; Raj *et al.*, 2015). Managers need to 'supervise and mediate the interactions between people in both the natural and built environment' (Olsen, 2006, p. 106). Given the dominance of neoliberal language in schools of business management, this perspective has been the most utilized for understanding the supervision of sacred locations (Reader, 2014; Coleman and Eade, 2018).

The Global Financial Crisis and more recently, the COVID-19 pandemic, has shown that government and governance institutions must play a vital role in maintaining macroeconomic and macropolitical stability. The deregulated marketplace lacked solutions for these shocks. It took direct, forceful government intervention, sometimes against the national popular will, for countries and systems to survive (Danielli *et al.*, 2021). This has been the case with religious tourism as well, where numerous scholars have either lauded direct government involvement or have recommended it (Manhas and Balakrishnan Nair, 2020; Haq and Medhekar, 2022).

One of the more developed writings on religious tourism management and governance can be found in Piva *et al.* (2019). The authors note the mutual dependency that exists between various actors, including governmental agencies and private tourism actors, such as tour companies, hotels and other entities. The integration of these processes is referred to as 'destination governance', which is useful when conceptualizing the complexity and dynamic settings of religious destination sites. However, the authors use the terms destination management and destination governance interchangeably. While they note that the tourism discourse has moved in the general direction of adopting the concept of governance, their use is more reflective of the neoliberalist views found in many studies on religious tourism and pilgrimage. For example, they reference how different models of destination governance affect the creation of the tourist experience, which is indicative of the reductivist focus found in most studies.

Piva *et al.* (2019) do correctly point out that understanding the governance of religious tourism means understanding the internal context of contemporary arrangements. Through the development of a matrix diagram and using axes of spatial concentration of religious sites and the level of connection among their actors, they describe four variants of destination religious governance. Where there is a low number of sacred sites and low level of connections, the result is *fragmentation*. The next variant combines a high spatial concentration of religious sites, coupled with a low level of connections among the stakeholders. This leads to *conflict* as different stakeholders will contest

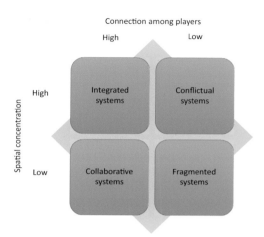

Fig. 5.1. Religious tourism destination governance (from Piva *et al.*, 2019).

the limited resources given the high number of sites. The third variant involves a high level of connectivity among interested players, but a low spatial concentration of sacred sites. Here, sites are spread out in a territory and often *collaboration* is the end result. There is less competition among stakeholders and the authors note that a unitary management plan can develop. The final variant is one of *integration*, a high spatial concentration of religious sites and strong connections among the major players. This leads to a synergistic effect, where the dynamics allow for strong management and governance, often resulting in the growth of the religious destination site. Fig. 5.1 shows the religious tourism destination governance found in Piva *et al.* (2019).

5.4 The Complex Role of Religious Institutions in Religious Tourism

Central to religious tourism governance are the roles of religious institutions. Institutions can be defined as:

> a relatively stable collection of rules and practices, embedded in structures of resources that make action possible – organizational, financial and staff capabilities, and structures of meaning that explain and justify behavior – roles, identities and belongings, common

purposes, and causal and normative beliefs (March and Olsen, 1989, 2011, p. 480).

Decisions are structured as the resources that are available allow that action to be possible. March and Olsen note that the capabilities of the institution, and the meanings that clarify and rationalize behaviour are what give institutions their worth and their longevity. From democratic institutions in a society, to industry associations, to churches, individuals and businesses find value in institutions as they provide the 'roles, identities and belonging, common purposes, and causal and normative beliefs for actors. Given this, religious institutions are not easily removed from governance. Religious arrangements in a society, such as concordats, established state religions, or tax and regulatory arrangements, directly affect sacred sites (Bozonelos, 2021).

With institutional complexity comes governance complexity. Governance involves direction and control, often through an institution, or in the case of religious tourism, multiple overlapping institutions. Governance is then contested, even if the institutions governing the site are all from the same religion or sect/denomination. Governance does not necessarily refer to government institutions, though that is usually the case. It can also involve quasi-governmental entities, such as national tourism organizations. As Coleman and Eade (2018, pp. 3–4) write, 'pilgrimage is not only a source of popular religious activity but is also subject to varied forms of control on the part of national churches, denominations, social movements, commercial enterprises and regional and national governments, not to mention transnational organizations, such as UNESCO.'

The obvious issue then in religious tourism is that sometimes there are no clear lines of demarcation between differing levels of governance and the various actors involved. Sacred sites compete for scarce resources and demanding the attention of one of the more powerful actors can sometimes require needing to build political alliances or forge relationships with stronger actors. Stausberg (2011) writes that many religious organizations publish opinions and instructions regarding tourism at their sites. For example, the Catholic Church created a Pontifical Commission on Migration and Tourism in 1970 as a way to address the concerns of religious tourists. These strategic responses are often in response to the lack of coordination by national governments on religious tourist and pilgrim mobility. This is especially more acute in countries with secularized societies.

Given this, the religious tourism industry often finds itself cooperating with governments and governing bodies out of necessity. Policy implications matter for religious officials managing sacred destination sites, particularly as 'explicit religious needs, religious preferences, and values have an impact on tourism' (Stausberg, 2011, p. 44). Conversely, tourism to sacred sites has a secularizing effect on the location itself. As more people visit, religious authorities will have less control over the impact. As the touristification of religious travel increases, the boundaries between what is a sacred experience, and what is a secular tourist experience will blur.

5.5 The Importance of Institutionalism Logics for Religious Tourism Governance

Schmidt (2009, p. 517) writes that, 'as a polity, the state constitutes the political institutions that frame the interactions between political and economic actors'. Government drives the political discourse that is essentialized through public policy. When discussing the role of government in society and the economy, institutions are key. Institutions are the working mechanisms of governance. When it comes to governance, we generally include political institutions, such as executive agencies or commissions. Similarly, religious institutions are central to effective state governance of faith-based tourism sites. Thus, understanding how and why institutions, including political, economic and religious, function is important for the governance of sacred destination sites.

This is where institutional theory can help us. Piva *et al.* (2019) do a great job of describing what these arrangements may look like, yet they do not explain how these institutions *behave*. Institutions have their own logics, or logic of decision making. Searing (1991, p. 1241) refers to 'rules, roles, and reasons' and categorizes three approaches: structural, interactional, motivational, which describe how these three elements come together. The structural approach emphasizes institutions over individuals, where individuals fulfil a role already described by the institution. In a structural institution, the governance of a sacred site would be set by the 'rules', and a clear hierarchy exists. In an interactional approach, roles are negotiated and renegotiated based on the informal rules of the institutions. In this approach, religious tourism governance is not set, and religious, political and economic actors interact to eventually develop particular 'roles' regarding the sacred site. Finally, the motivational approach tries to understand the motivations or 'reasons' that actors bring to the institution. For religious tourism governance, it could involve asking why a particular actor chose a particular role. This can include understanding why a religious authority may choose not to actively govern a sacred site.

The recent discourses in institutionalism is better referred to as neoinsitutionalism, which itself is a grounded response to behaviouralism. Beginning in the 1950s, behaviouralists were able to shift the focus of analysis away from institutions and to individual human behaviour instead. Any discussion of the potential moderating effect that institutions could have on behaviour were assumed away. This reductivist approach was at first used to simply describe the political behaviour of voters, but over time it was extended to include the behaviour of politicians and policy makers. Hull (1999) points out that when behaviouralists shifted from description to explanation, they discarded any variable that could not be operationalized. This included the rejection of formal institutions as quantifying their effects on individual level behaviour was seen as less than scientific. Neoinsitutionalism attempts to bring the institutions back into the analysis.

For example, one of the more recent undertakings involves analyzing the *logics* of the institutions themselves. Institutional logic is defined as 'a set of material practices and symbolic constructions [that] constitute organizing principles' (Friedland and Alford, 1991, p. 248). March and Olsen (2011) explain that the logic for democratic governance requires stability and a *logic of appropriateness* influences behaviour in democratic political institutions. This logic understands

decision making by politicians and policy makers as being driven by rules. Rules are followed by actors because 'they are seen as natural, rightful, expected, and legitimate.' The obligations of upholding the norms and values of an institution is what justifies an actor's place within the institution. This then reinforces rules of appropriate behaviour and can justify the norms that undergird the institutions themselves. This is also referred to as *homo sociologicus*, where appropriateness reflects the role of informal rules in the process (Searing, 1991).

Often contrasted with the logic of appropriateness, is the *logic of consequentiality*. In this approach, it is less about whether an actor's decisions conform to the rules and expected norms, and more about what the consequences will be for these decisions (Schulz, 2016). March and Olsen (2011) discuss that the focus is on a set of shared objectives, whereas in the logic of appropriateness, the focus is on shared rules, principles and regulations. This is also referred to as *homo economicus*, which is considered instrumentalist in nature. The focus is on motivations (Searing, 1991). The goal is to maximize utility by analysing and understanding the consequences of various actions, within the context of the institution itself (March and Olsen, 1994).

The logics of appropriateness and consequentiality are the two major dimensions of understanding decision making in the fields of political science, public administration and public policy. However, other logics have been proposed in the social sciences, particularly in environmental policy and management. For example, Dewulf *et al.* (2020) recently proposed a *logic of meaningfulness*. In this logic, the authors describe how decision makers interpret the meaning of a decision problem. Behaviour here is guided by how people understand complicated circumstances, and how decision makers seek to understand the meaning of what the decision is all about. The authors refer to this as *homo semioticus*, which represents the interpretivist approach of how meaning matters in the process.

Finally, we see a *logic of interaction* between different stakeholders in society. This logic is almost exclusively used in political science where authors refer to it as *homo politicus*. Buchanan (2008) suggests that this occurs when an

Table 5.1. Theories of institutionalism in political science.

Institutional theory	Focus/emphasis	Logic of	Assumptions
Normative	Norms of the institution	Appropriateness	*homo sociologicus*
Rational choice	Maximizing utility of institutional members	Consequentiality	*homo economicus*
Historical	Early choices lead to path dependence	Appropriateness	*homo sociologicus*
Empirical	Structure and design of the institution	Appropriateness	*homo sociologicus*
Discursive/constructivist	Internal discourses within the institution	Meaningfulness	*homo semioticus*
Sociological/societal	Structured interactions between state and society	Appropriateness	*homo sociologicus*
International (regime theory)	Structured interactions between states and international institutions	Social interaction	*homo politicus*

actor, 'acts in the interest of the community' (Buchanan, 2008). In each of the previous three logics, the focus is on the individual and how the individual behaves, either on the maximization of interests (rational-choice), norms and values (sociological), or on meaning (semiotics). In this approach, the individual looks beyond their own interest, and instead considers the interest of the community, however that community may be defined (Boda, 2013). Thus, institutions reflect the collective action decisions that are negotiated between leaders. These institutions promote the common or public good.

Out of these discussions, Peters (2019) developed a typology of institutional theories. These theories are in Table 5.1, correlated to both logics and assumptions. In each type, Peters outlines the distinction between each theory and how 'individuals will make conscious choices, but [that] those choices will remain within the parameters established by the dominant institutional values.' Most of the theories incorporate a logic of appropriateness, where the norms and values matter in decision making. In these theories, structures matter greatly and allow for routines to develop, which are then imbued with certain values. This may explain why institutions exist for so long.

This is not to say that institutions lack the ability to change. It is simply that institutional change varies conditionally on the structures in place. For example, if an institution is designed

to maximize an actor's utility, then change can occur rather quickly. Indeed, the reshaping and adaption of preferences is considered a natural part of the norms and value of the institution. Markets as institutions often fit the description, where equilibria can be altered when preferences shift. However, change is less likely with institutions built on the logic of appropriateness, particularly in institutions where the effects of path dependency are stronger. Or, depending on the strength of the institution, they might try to shape its environment. Manipulation of outside actors and changes in policies can be effective. Ironically, change in institutions based on a logic of social interaction, are more mutable. At first glance, one would assume that political institutions would be incentivized not to change. However, as is the case with many regimes, particularly in the international arena, they are often quite fragile, thus making them quite exposed to both external and internal pressures.

A more detailed discussion of each theory by Peters (2019) follows. In *normative institutionalism*, emphasis is placed on the norms and values and how they establish, or at least bind, the behaviour of individuals. In this approach, the rules are prescriptive. They describe how decisions should be made given the particular context. In *rational-choice institutionalism*, institutions are designed by actors as an avenue to maximize utility. In this approach, actors have a given set of preferences and make decisions based on the expected consequences. In *histori-cal institutionalism*, the early decisions become set in stone, where actions are path-dependent and actors are unable to navigate away from these proscribed actions.

In *empirical institutionalism*, the formal structure can explain differences in behaviour. In this approach, structure comes first, then norms and values. This differs from normative institutionalism, where norms and values come first, then the structure. Indeed, structuralists argue that when appropriate institutions are put in place, then appropriate values and norms will follow. In *discursive institutionalism*, what matters is how the ideas are communicated within the structures. Normative and discursive institutionalism are similar in that the theories both posit that institutions are defined by their ideas and norms. The difference is that in the discursive approach, the norms are not inherent within the structure, but emerge from the discussions held between actors.

Sociological institutionalism, as the name portends, has its roots in sociological literature. Given this, Peters (2019) cites that there are numerous models within this strand. The more traditional variant is that of functionalism. In functionalism, society is seen as consisting of various functions that must be performed if they are to survive and succeed (Parsons, 1960). Society is an organism, where constituent elements need to work in unison. Out of this tradition have come the newer population ecology models of organization. In these approaches, an analogy is made with the populations of biological organisms. For example, limited resources lead to competition among members of species within an ecosystem. Peters notes that markets act in a similar fashion, where only so much capital exists for businesses. Finally, there is *international institutionalism*, where the actors are not individuals, but states and organizations. Interaction is at the global level, where leaders represent the interests of their national communities, to promote a common global good. Out of this comes regime theory, where scholars discuss that institutionalization of norms and values at the systemic or global level can help produce positive outcomes for the world (Keohane, 1988).

5.6 The State, Institutional Logics, and Religious Tourism Governance: Future Research

This chapter responds to a call for a deeper understanding of religious tourism governance. If the state is to take a more prominent role in religious tourism and pilgrimage, then discussing how governing institutions behave is relevant. Given this, the various institutional logics can give us a framework from which to better understand religious tourism governance. The next steps are two-fold. The first step is to further discuss how institutionalist theory can help explain religious tourism phenomena. This has already occurred in the general tourism literature, where Falaster *et al.* (2017) note that over 130 articles in the top tourism journals reference institutionalism. They identify three major strands within their bibliometric analysis: ecotourism and sustainability, social and economic issues, and culture and its effects on tourism. This trend should quickly develop in religious tourism and pilgrimage studies as well.

The second step is to apply the listed institutional logics through a number of in-depth case studies in religious tourism governance, where each logic can be thoroughly developed. Falaster *et al.* (2017) notes that tourist destinations develop their legitimacy under institutional logics, which can explain how governments and businesses determine and develop the image of the destination. The authors also note that tourism destinations will often mimic each other, leading to the homogenization of tourism sites. As religious sites have undergone touristification, there has been a similar effect in these sacred spaces (Olsen, 2006). Similar application of institutional logics can also help disaggregate how touristification develops in religious destinations.

Religious tourism governance is an underresearched and understudied dimension of religious tourism and pilgrimage. Governance is the vehicle from which the state has entered the religious tourism industry. As neoliberal governance recedes in certain countries, in its wake comes statism, or state-led economics. This is not a return to the nationalization of industries or the expropriation of privately owned production. Instead, it often involves the state either becoming the primary source of investment or at least directing how inward foreign direct investment will take form. Braunstein (2019) notes how state-led foreign investment has also become a method for projecting state power, a part of a country's geopolitical toolbox. States have a major role to play in the development of religious tourist and pilgrimage destination sites and that role will only continue to grow in the future.

References

Álvarez-García, J., del Río Rama, M. and Gómez-Ullate, M. (2018) *Handbook of Research on Socio-Economic Impacts of Religious Tourism and Pilgrimage*. IGI Global, Hersey, PA. DOI: 10.4018/978-1-5225-5730-2.

Blackwell, R. (2007) Motivations for religious tourism, pilgrimage, festivals and events. In: Raj, R. and Morpeth, N.D. (eds) *Religious Tourism and Pilgrimage Management: An International Perspective*. CAB International, Wallingford, UK, pp. 103–117.

Boda, Z. (2013) Towards a theory of political action and motivation. *World Political Science Review* 9(1), 71–96. DOI: 10.1515/wpsr-2013-0004.

Bozonelos, D. (2021) The political economy of religious and spiritual tourism. In: Olsen, D. and Timothy, D. (eds) *The Routledge Handbook of Religious and Spiritual Tourism*. Routledge, New York, pp. 36–52.

Bramwell, B. (2012) Governance, the state and sustainable tourism: a political economy approach. In: Bramwell, B. and Lane, B. (eds) *Tourism Governance: Critical Perspectives on Governance and Sustainability*. Routledge, New York, pp. 459–477.

Bramwell, B. and Lane, B. (2012) Introduction: critical research on the governance of tourism and sustainability. In: Bramwell, B. and Lane, B. (eds) *Tourism Governance: Critical Perspectives on Governance and Sustainability*. Routledge, New York, pp. 411–421.

Braunstein, J. (2019) Domestic sources of twenty-first-century geopolitics: domestic politics and sovereign wealth funds in GCC economies. *New Political Economy* 24(2), 197–217. DOI: 10.1080/13563467.2018.1431619.

Buchanan, J.M. (2008) In search of homunculus politicus. *Public Choice* 137(3–4), 469–474. DOI: 10.1007/s11127-008-9351-5.

Clarke, A. and Raffay, A. (2015) Stakeholders and co-creation in religious tourism and pilgrimage. In: Raj, R. and Griffin, K. (eds) *Religious Tourism and Pilgrimage Management: An International Perspective*, 2nd edn. CAB International, Wallingford, UK, pp. 160–172.

Coleman, S. and Eade, J. (eds) (2018) *Pilgrimage and the Political Economy: Translation of the Sacred*. Berghahn Books, New York. DOI: 10.2307/j.ctvw04k6c.

Collins-Kreiner, N. (2009) Researching pilgrimage: continuity and transformations. *Annals of Tourism Research* 37(2), 440–456. DOI: 10.1016/j.annals.2009.10.016.

Cornelissen, S. (2011) Regulation theory and its evolution and limitations in tourism studies. In: Mosedale, J. (ed.) *Political Economy of Tourism: A Critical Perspective*. Routledge, London and New York, pp. 39–54.

Danielli, S., Patria, R., Donnelly, P., Ashrafian, H. and Darzi, A. (2021) Economic interventions to ameliorate the impact of COVID-19 on the economy and health: an international comparison. *Journal of Public Health* 43(1), 42–46. DOI: 10.1093/pubmed/fdaa104.

Dewulf, A., Klenk, N., Wyborn, C. and Lemos, M.C. (2020) Usable environmental knowledge from the perspective of decision-making: the logics of consequentiality, appropriateness, and meaningfulness. *Current Opinion in Environmental Sustainability* (42), 1–6. DOI: 10.1016/j.cosust.2019.10.003.

Dredge, D. and Whitford, M. (2012) Event tourism governance and the public sphere. In: Bramwell, B. and Lane, B. (eds) *Tourism Governance: Critical Perspectives on Governance and Sustainability*. Routledge, New York, pp. 1–21.

Dwyer, L. (2015) Globalization of tourism: drivers and outcomes. *Tourism Recreation Research* 40(3), 326–339. DOI: 10.1080/02508281.2015.1075723.

Falaster, C., Zanin, L.M. and Guerrazzi, L.A. (2017) Institutional theory in tourism research: new opportunities from an evolving theory. *Brazilian Journal of Tourism Research* 11(2), 270–293. DOI: 10.7784/rbtur.v11i2.1310.

Friedland, R. and Alford, R. (1991) Bringing society back in: symbols, practices and institutional contradictions. In: Powell, W. and Dimaggio, P. (eds) *The New Institutionalism in Organizational Analysis*. University of Chicago Press, Chicago, IL, pp. 232–263.

Future Market Insight (2022) *Faith Based Tourism: Overview, Highlights, and Industry Outlook Overview, Faith Based Tourism Market*. Available at: https://www.futuremarketinsights.com/reports/faith-based-tourism-sector-overview (accessed 27 August 2022).

Griffiths, M. and Wiltshier, P. (2019) Introduction. In: Griffiths, M. and Wiltshier, P. (eds) *Managing Religious Tourism*. CAB International, Wallingford, UK, pp. 1–9.

Hall, C.M. (2012) A typology of governance and its implications for tourism analysis. In: Bramwell, B. and Lane, B. (eds) *Tourism Governance: Critical Perspectives on Governance and Sustainability*. Routledge, New York, pp. 27–47.

Hall, C.M (2013) Framing behavioural approaches to understanding and governing sustainable tourism consumption: beyond neoliberalism, "nudging" and "green growth"? *Journal of Sustainable Tourism* 21(7), 1091–1109. DOI: 10.1080/09669582.2013.815764.

Hall, C.M. (2017) Tourism and geopolitics: the political imaginary of territory, tourism, and space. In: Hall, D. (ed.) *Tourism and Geopolitics: Issues and Concepts from Central and Eastern Europe*. CAB International, Wallingford, UK, pp. 15–24.

Haq, F. and Medhekar, A. (2022) The economic impact of COVID-19 on religious tourism to the Kartarpur corridor. *International Journal of Religious Tourism and Pilgrimage* 10(2), 36–46.

Hull, A.P. (1999) Comparative political science: an inventory and assessment since the 1980s. *PS: Political Science and Politics* 32(1), 117–124. DOI: 10.2307/420760.

Hvizdová, E. (2018) Religious tourism and its socio-economic dimensions. *European Journal of Science and Theology* 14(2), 89–98.

Jamal, T. and Camargo, B.A. (2018) Tourism governance and policy: whither justice? *Tourism Management Perspectives* 25, 205–208. DOI: 10.1016/j.tmp.2017.11.009.

Jenkins, J.M., Hall, C.M. and Mkono, M. (2014) Tourism and public policy: contemporary debates and future directions. In: Lew, A.A., Hall, C.M. and Williams, A.M. (eds) *The Wiley Blackwell Companion to Tourism*. John Wiley & Sons, Malden, MA, pp. 542–556.

Keohane, R.O. (1988) International institutions: two approaches. *International Studies Quarterly* 32(4), 379–396. DOI: 10.2307/2600589.

Kim, B., Kim, S. and King, B. (2020) Religious tourism studies: evolution, progress, and future prospects. *Tourism Recreation Research* 45(2), 185–203. DOI: 10.1080/02508281.2019.1664084.

Manhas, P.S. and Balakrishnan Nair, B. (2020) Strategic role of religious tourism in recuperating the Indian tourism sector post COVID-19. *International Journal of Religious Tourism and Pilgrimage* 8(7), 52–66.

March, J.G. and Olsen, J.P. (1989) *Rediscovering Institutions*. Free Press, New York.

March, J.G. and Olsen, J.P. (1994) *Democratic Governance*. Free Press, New York.

March, J.G. and Olsen, J.P. (2011) The logic of appropriateness. In: Goodin, R.E. (ed.) *Oxford Handbook of Political Science*. Oxford University Press, Oxford, UK, pp. 478–497.

Moscardo, D. (2012) Exploring social representations of tourism planning. In: Bramwell, B. and Lane, B. (eds) *Tourism Governance: Critical Perspectives on Governance and Sustainability*. Routledge, New York, pp. 13–26.

Mosedale, J. (2016) *Neoliberalism and the Political Economy of Tourism*. Routledge, New York. DOI: 10.4324/9781315597782.

Olsen, D.H. (2003) Heritage, tourism, and the commodification of religion. *Tourism Recreation Research* 28(3), 99–104. DOI: 10.1080/02508281.2003.11081422.

Olsen, D.H. (2006) Management issues for religious heritage attractions. In: Timothy, D.J. and Olsen, D.H. (eds) *Tourism, Religion and Spiritual Journeys*. Routledge, London and New York, pp. 104–118.

Parsons, T. (1960) A sociological approach to the theory of organizations. In: Parsons, T. (ed.) *Structure and Process in Modern Societies*. Free Press, New York, pp. 16–59.

Peters, B.G. (2019) *Institutional Theory in Political Science*, 4th edn. Edward Elgar Publishing, Northampton, MA.

Piva, E., Cerutti, S. and Raj, R. (2019) Managing the sacred: a governing perspective for religious tourism destinations. In: Griffiths, M. and Wiltshier, P. (eds) *Managing Religious Tourism*. CAB International, Wallingford, UK, pp. 10–21.

Raj, R., Griffin, K.A. and Blackwell, R. (2015) Motivations for religious tourism, pilgrimage, festivals and events. In: Raj, R. and Griffin, K.A. (eds) *Religious Tourism and Pilgrimage Management: An International Perspective*, 2nd edn. Elsevier, Boston, MA, pp. 16–36.

Reader, I. (2014) *Pilgrimage in the Marketplace*. Routledge, New York.

Rodrigues, A.P., Vieira, I., Ferreira, L. and Madeira, R. (2019) Stakeholder perceptions of religious tourism and local development: evidence from Lamego (Portugal) historic town. *International Journal of Religious Tourism and Pilgrimage* 7(4), 41–53.

Schmidt, V.A. (2009) Putting the political back into political economy by bringing the state back in yet again. *World Politics* 61(3), 516–546. DOI: 10.1017/S0043887109000173.

Schulz, M. (2016) Logic of consequences and logic of appropriateness. In: Augier, M. and Teece, D. (eds) *The Palgrave Encyclopedia of Strategic Management*. Palgrave Macmillan, London.

Searing, D.D. (1991) Roles, rules, and rationality in the new institutionalism. *American Political Science Review* 85(4), 1239–1255. DOI: 10.2307/1963944.

Shackley, M. (2001) *Managing Sacred Sites: Service Provision and Visitor Experience*. Continuum Press, London and New York.

Shepherd, R.J. (2013) *Faith in Heritage: Displacement, Development, and Religious Tourism in Contemporary China*. Left Coast Press, Walnut Creek, CA.

Shinde, K. (2012) Policy, planning, and management for religious tourism in Indian pilgrimage sites. *Journal of Policy Research in Tourism, Leisure and Events* 4(3), 277–301. DOI: 10.1080/19407963.2012.726107.

Shinde, K. (2018) Governance and management of religious tourism in India. *International Journal of Religious Tourism and Pilgrimage* 6(1), 58–71.

Shoup, D., Bonini Baraldi, S. and Zan, L. (2015) The Turkish model of decentralization in cultural heritage. In: Zan, L., Bonini Baraldi, S., Lusiani, M., Shoup, D., Ferri, P., *et al.* (eds) *Managing Cultural Heritage: An International Research Perspective*. Routledge, New York, pp. 47–64.

Sørensen, E. (2006) Metagovernance: the changing role of politicians in processes of democratic governance. *The American Review of Public Administration* 36(1), 98–114.

Stausberg, M. (2011) *Religion and Tourism: Crossroads, Destinations and Encounters*. Routledge, New York.

Steger, M.B. (2020) *Globalization: A Very Short Introduction*. Oxford University Press, Oxford, UK. DOI: 10.1093/actrade/9780198849452.001.0001.

Telfer, D.J. (2015) The evolution of development theory and tourism. In: Sharpley, R. and Tefler, D.J. (eds) *Tourism & Development: Concepts and Issues*. Channel View Publications, Tonawanda, New York, pp. 31–73.

Terzidou, M., Stylidis, D. and Szivas, E.M. (2008) Residents' perceptions of religious tourism and its socio-economic impacts on the Island of Tinos. *Tourism and Hospitality Planning & Development* 5(2), 113–129. DOI: 10.1080/14790530802252784.

Timothy, D.J. (2022) Sociopolitical and economic implications of religious and spiritual tourism. In: Olsen, D. and Timothy, D. (eds) *The Routledge Handbook of Religious and Spiritual Tourism*. Routledge, New York, pp. 301–314.

Tobón Perilla, S. and Tobón Perilla, N. (2013) Turismo religioso: fenómeno social y económico. *Anuario Turismo y Sociedad* 14, 237–249.

Trono, A. (2015) Politics, policy and the practice of religious tourism. In: Raj, R. and Griffin, K.A. (eds) *Religious Tourism and Pilgrimage Management: An International Perspective*, 2nd edn. Elsevier, Boston, MA, pp. 16–36.

Vukonic, B. (1998) Religious tourism: economic value or an empty box? *Zagreb International Review of Economics & Business* 1(1), 83–94.

Vukonic, B. (2002) Religion, tourism and economics: a convenient symbiosis. *Tourism Recreation Research* 27(2), 59–64. DOI: 10.1080/02508281.2002.11081221.

Woodward, S.C. (2004) Faith and tourism: planning tourism in relation to places of worship. *Tourism and Hospitality Planning & Development* 1(2), 173–186. DOI: 10.1080/1479053042000251089.

Zarb, J.C. (2020) How religious tourism and pilgrimages can be beneficial to communities. *International Journal of Religious Tourism and Pilgrimage* 8(2), 13–19.

6 Global Governance and Religious Tourism: The Role of International Organizations

Panagiota Manoli*

Department of Political Science and International Relations, University of the Peloponnese, Greece

Abstract

This chapter attempts to fill a gap in the literature by placing the study of religious tourism within the context of global governance, nuancing the role of international organizations in shaping the development of religious tourism globally. In doing so, the chapter investigates the performance of the UNWTO, UNESCO, ICOMOS and the Council of Europe as the primary shapers of a global framework for the development of religious tourism through their work on framing and norms setting, stakeholders pooling and networking, capacity building, information sharing, and in monitoring and assessment measures.

6.1 Introduction

Tourism is a significant global industry and a source of growth for many economies in the world. One of the oldest types of tourism, pilgrimage or religious tourism, is still developing at a significant pace spurred by factors varying from the search for authenticity and personal belief to the increasing investment in mass transportation and the internet (Griffin and Raj, 2017, p. iii). Literature has also pointed to factors such as the rise of fundamentalism (Riesebrodt, 2000), the retreat of religions into historic forms of spirituality and religious ritual (Post *et al.*, 1998), modernization and the role of mass media in the globalization of local cultures (Vásquez and Marquandt, 2000; Koskansky, 2002). Global politics especially since 2001 have witnessed a resurgence of religion (Dawson, 2015, pp. 23–29) which has been a contributing factor to

raising the importance of religious tourism and its academic study. Although 'religious tourist' is a notion used to refer to, in modern times, a 'pilgrim', the two notions are often defined differently with 'pilgrim' viewed as a religious traveller while 'religious tourist' as a vacationer. In this work, an inclusive approach is used in defining religious tourism.

The market size of religious tourism was estimated at US\$1071 million in 2020 (heavily affected downwards by the COVID-19 pandemic) and it is projected to reach US\$1704.2 million by 2028, growing at a compound annual growth rate (CAGR) of 6% from 2021 to 2028 (Verified Market Research, 2021). Indicative of its importance for national economies is the estimation that in Saudi Arabia the pilgrims visiting the holy cities of Mecca and Madinah (Medina) generate an annual income of US\$16 billion (Trono, 2015, p. 28). It is difficult to estimate the exact size of

*manoli@uop.gr

© CAB International 2023. *The Politics of Religious Tourism* (eds D. Bozonelos and P. Moira)
DOI: 10.1079/9781800621732.0006

the religious tourism market as reliable statistical data are difficult to compile (Rawlinson, 2012). Religious tourism cannot be easily separated from other historical and cultural tourism flows, so statistical surveys cannot adequately assess its benefits and beneficiaries separately (Trono, 2015, p. 29). In 2017, it was anticipated that approximately 300 to 330 million tourists visited the world's top religious sites annually (Griffin and Raj, 2017, p. viii) while other estimates indicate that approximately 600 million people travel internationally for religious reasons (UNWTO, 2011). Beyond its economic significance, travelling, especially for visiting cultural and religious sites, is valued as a means of fostering intercultural understanding, tolerance and inclusive societies. Religious tourism may be domestic (i.e. travel by residents within their own country) or international, with the first one weighing significantly more. For the whole OECD area, domestic tourism consumption accounts for about 75% of tourism consumption within it, with the remainder representing inbound tourism (OECD, 2010, p. 22). At the national level, the role of the state institutions is central in promoting religious tourism as part of cultural tourism and for boosting the local and national economy. Private actors (tour operators, travel agents and the hotel industry) also play a key role in providing means including rituals and events and ensuring availability of transport services.

Although travel for faith reasons has long been a motive for peoples' mobility worldwide, its global governance perspective has been only recently studied. One aspect of the global governance of religious tourism is that of the role of international organizations (IOs). International organizations that have been established and are involved, directly or indirectly, in religious tourism vary and include governmental agencies such as the United Nations World Tourism Organization (UNWTO) and the United Nations Educational, Scientific and Cultural Organization (UNESCO) or non-governmental organizations such as the International Council of Monuments and Sites (ICOMOS). There are also several regional organizations such as the Council of Europe (CoE) whose activities bear an impact on the normative aspects of religious tourism, while international networks of private actors such as the Faith Travel Association (FTA) shape the global market of religious tourism. The confluence of actors,

policies and resources, both from the local and the global levels makes religious tourism difficult to study systemically. Given the complexity of religious tourism, an important question arises: is there a global governance of religious tourism? In addition, are there any inferences that can be developed through this research?

This chapter attempts to address the above question and shed light on the ways and processes of the involvement of international organizations in shaping the development of religious tourism and building an international regime to govern religious tourism.

6.2 Nuancing Religious Tourism

One of the difficulties in discussing religious tourism and its institutional setting is to agree on a common definition. There are various definitions of religious tourism. Whereas some scholars (Rinschede, 1992) point to the exclusive or partial existence of religious motivations for tourism to be labelled as 'religious', others do not stress the existence of personal motivations arguing that religious tourism refers to visiting religious sites without necessarily religious or existential engagement (Geybels, 2014). Of course, as travellers for sightseeing may also participate in a pilgrimage, the above defining lines are usually blurred. Therefore, manifestations of religious tourism are mainly visits to and worship in sanctuaries and places, visits to religiously important UNESCO World Heritage Sites, religious events and festivals.

As religious monuments constitute an important part of civilization, religious events constitute also cultural events (Σφακιανάκης, 2000). Thus, as a key expression of cultural tourism, religious tourism comprises not only pilgrimages but also visiting sacred sites, churches, mosques, temples and travel for the purpose of worship (CBI, 2020). In this chapter, in defining religious tourism we use the approach of the Council of Europe according to which religious tourism refers to 'visitors to religious locations and buildings, sites of relics and pilgrimage routes, including visitors who are interested in religious sites for their architectural and cultural importance' (Council of Europe, 2020, p. 23) and thus it is a manifestation of cultural tourism. Μοίρα (2009) constructed a framework of positions, showing the changing motives of a traveller, at the ends of which are the sanctuary (pilgrim) and the secular (cosmic tourism), and between the two extremes there are unlimited numbers of possible combinations of sacred and secular where religious tourism is placed in the centre. Vukonić (1996) argues that after meeting religious needs, religious tourists will behave like other tourists because they have the same needs. Bremer (2005), considering the intersections of religion and tourism, notes three broader dimensions on which researchers have focused: the spatial dimension (different behaviours towards the same sites), the historical dimension (evolution of religious travel and tourism) and the cultural dimension (modern practices of pilgrimage and tourism).

The socio-economic impact of the development of religious tourism is another aspect that has been researched (Álvarez-García et al., 2018; Hvizdová, 2018). In addition to increasing cultural diversity, religious tourism brings socio-economic benefits and positively affects the development of infrastructure projects, medical services, and thus living standards in tourist destinations. Religious tourism is increasingly discussed within the sustainable development context which implies a balance between the environment, the economy and the social dimensions of tourism and respect of local cultures. Though religious tourism does not inherently guarantee sustainability it is often considered as an alternative to mass tourism.

6.3   The (Global) Governance Perspective

Tourism literature has increasingly focused on governance issues and the study of relevant policy-making processes which encompass public and private authorities (Dredge, 2006; Griffiths and Wiltshier, 2019). While some researchers have discussed governance in tourism given the interdependency between public and the private actors (Nordin and Svensson, 2007), others have focused on the identification of varieties of governance models of destinations ranging from community-focused to corporate-run types (Flagestad and

Hope, 2001). The concept of governance in tourism literature has been introduced with reference to the local and national policy level implying 'setting and developing rules for a policy as well as business strategies involving together all the institutions (municipalities and government districts) and their products and services supplier in order to create an effective strategy at all levels (planning, promotion, monitoring, and control)' (Beritelli et al., 2007, p. 96). As responsibility for tourism policy primarily lies at the national level, it is institutionally positioned within an economic ministry or some countries prioritize tourism with a separate ministry (e.g. Greece and Israel). Growing inter-connection of the world as reflected in the expanding mobility of people, ideas, technologies and services has resulted in the need for international, cross-country and multilevel cooperation also in the field of tourism which constitutes another manifestation of globalized societies.

As Bramwell and Lane (2011, pp. 411–412) argue in the tourism literature, the term governance is not used frequently especially when compared to other terms such as those of tourism politics, policy, planning and destination management. Governance as a term has a wide scope encompassing elements of actorness, norms, principles and processes through which social action is shaped. It is thus better understood as 'a process (or a complex of processes), its principal modes including markets, hierarchies and networks' (Heywood, 2011, p. 125) and as such it refers to 'a variety of cooperative problem-solving arrangements' (Heywood, 2011, p. 455). Literature on governance brings in the role of regimes (Krasner, 1983), networks (Rhodes, 1997), associations (Streeck and Schmitter, 1985), and processes of 'negotiated co-ordination' (Scharpf, 1994) in the management of social activity (Hall, 2011).

Numerous transnational forms of governance have arisen from changing relationships between public and private international actors. Thus, global governance has emerged as a framework for the study of the interaction of multiple interest groups which engage in the regulation of the tourism industry across borders (Duffy and Moore, 2011). Accordingly, global governance can be defined as a 'collection of governance-related activities, rules and mechanisms, formal and informal, existing at a variety of levels in the world today' (Karns and Mingst, 2009), which is characterized by a prevailing intergovernmentalism, but also by polycentrism, multi-actor engagement, multilevel processes and deformalization (Heywood, 2011, p. 458). The concept includes formal institutions with the power to impose compliance, and informal arrangements and institutions based on voluntary consent. Especially in the post-war period, international organizations (IOs) were established at a global or regional level and of a different content depending on the field of activity (such as politics, security, economy, culture). They have acted both as 'spaces' that facilitate communication and collective action to address global problems, but also as 'actors' that allow state and non-state entities to coordinate their actions, build trust and socialize or familiarize themselves with common rules and standards (Goodwin and Painter, 1996).

Religious tourism studies have relatively recently incorporated the literature on governance but still the international aspect is at the margins. According to Amore and Hall (2016, pp. 5–6), by 2015 more than 75% of publications on tourism and governance were written after 2008, reflecting a plethora of approaches. Approximately 72 different aspects of governance are identified in tourism studies, deriving from political sciences, business and health studies (Ruhanen *et al.*, 2010). Most of the governance literature on religious tourism has a national or regional scope or refers to case studies, weak in comparative analysis and global elements. However, in the last decade, issues such as financial and economic crises (Hall, 2010; Giovanelli *et al.*, 2015), uneven development and justice, climate and environmental change, migrant and refugee flows and, more recently, pandemics, have had a considerable impact on tourism, underscoring the need for collective international action.

6.4 International Organizations and Religious Tourism

The rise of international organizations is often cited as a key expression of global governance. International organizations – including intergovernmental organizations, non-governmental organizations and multi-actor (private and sub-state actor) arrangements – are central to global governance in today's interrelated societies. This is because organizations have agency, influence or set the policy agenda and bear important socializing effects (Simmons and Martin, 2002, p. 258). They are viewed as actors that provide global, collective or redistributive goods (Kindleberger, 1951) and increasingly, IOs transcend national borders and govern many aspects of the social, political and economic life that traditionally fell within the exclusive authority of the nation-state (Smouts, 1993).

IOs are viewed through primarily two competing approaches. The realists put state competition at the centre of their analysis and they argue that IOs play a marginal, coordinating role in international affairs which is delegated to them by states. Accordingly, world politics is an arena where states, perceived as rational, unitary actors, prefer to ignore IOs whenever they clash with the pursuit of their own national interests (Krasner, 1991; Mearsheimer, 1994). On the opposite side stand the liberalists who recognize the centrality of IOs in global affairs and consider states as non-unitary actors embedded in domestic and international contexts which shape and constrain their action. In that respect, IOs facilitate interaction between states, reducing the transaction costs, developing shared norms and solving common problems. Their role is important in disseminating information, monitoring and correcting behaviour, disciplining defectors, and facilitating transparency at a reduced cost to actors especially with regard to collective action (Keohane and Martin, 1995). Today, issues of legitimacy and authority have fed contemporary discussion on the role of IOs, as public policy at the domestic level (i.e. in finance, trade, environment, labour, migration, etc.) is considerably shaped by IOs.

The international organization literature gave rise to other notions such as that of 'regimes' and 'institutions'. Regimes are defined for specific issue-areas and focal points around which actors' expectations converge (Krasner, 1983; Haggard and Simmons, 1987), focusing on rules and norms rather than states to influence governmental behaviour. The word 'institution' has largely replaced 'regime' in the literature, the latter being often criticized as a vague notion that blurs real power relationships. Institutions are widely defined as 'persistent and connected sets of rules (formal and informal) that prescribe behavioral roles, constrain activity, and shape expectations' (Keohane, 1989, p. 3). Accordingly, this chapter refers to institutions as sets of rules while making the distinction between institutions and organizations, with the latter being of a formal nature. While international organizations and global governance literature cover a broad range of issues, including trade, finance, security, environment and human rights, they have only marginally addressed the field of tourism, especially religious tourism. There are two main categories of IOs that are active in the field of religious tourism (Μοίρα, 2019, pp. 291–316). In the first category belong intergovernmental organizations (IGOs) which are formed by governments and are established by legally binding, international, intergovernmental agreements. At the global level, the main intergovernmental organization established specifically to address international tourism policy issues is the United Nations World Tourism Organization (UNWTO). Tourism policy is also in the agenda of the World Trade Organization as a service sector activity. Tourism commitments have been undertaken by over 133 members of the World Trade Organization, more than in any other service sector, indicating the intention of countries to develop their tourism sectors as a vehicle of economic growth. Another global organization which addresses specifically the cultural dimensions of tourism is the United Nations Educational, Scientific and Cultural Organization (UNESCO). At the regional level, there are also various regional organizations that affect tourism policy but are not exclusively designed to address tourism issues such as the Council of Europe, the Organization for Economic Cooperation and Development (OECD), the Organization of American States (OAS), the Asia-Pacific Economic Cooperation (APEC) and the European Union (EU). Tourism specific, regional intergovernmental organizations include the Caribbean Tourism Organization (CTO). Within the policy agenda of the above IOs the handling of religious tourism tends to be rather instrumental, linked to the primary, usually wider in scope, purpose of the organization in question.

The second category includes international non-governmental organizations (NGOs) whose members are individuals, groups or associations.

There are various groupings which represent mainly private sector stakeholders in the field of tourism such as the World Travel and Tourism Council (WTTC) which includes all stakeholders in the travel and tourism industry – varying from tour operators, hotels, retail travel agents and airlines, to insurance groups and the technology industry – the Faith Travel Association (FTA) and regional organizations such as the Pacific Asia Travel Association. Other leading IOs in the field of tourism are: the United Federation of Travel Agents' Associations, the Travel and Tourism Research Association, the Association for Tourism and Leisure Education and Research (ATLAS), and the World Federation of Tourist Guides Associations. There are also organizations of a hybrid type, with members from both inside and outside of government whose agenda touches upon tourism policy. An example is the International Labour Organization (ILO), the first specialized agency of the UN, with a Governing Body that consists of members that represent the government, employer and employee sectors, which carries out sectorial activities in the tourism sector. In a way, one can notice the emergence of an international issue-network in the field of religious tourism in terms of 'a set of organizations bound by shared values and by dense exchanges of information and services, working internationally on an issue' (Sikkink, 1993, pp. 411–442).

Beyond the above-mentioned international organizations, religious tourism has fallen under the policy radar of institutions and networks directly linked to this type of tourism (such as the defunct World Religious Travel Association) or to culture and heritage (such as the International Council on Monuments and Sites) and it is promoted by religion-linked activities such as in the Religious Youth Music Festivals tourism (Caton et al., 2013). Actually, multi-stakeholder associations rather than intergovernmental bodies are the most common international tourism structures, especially in the sector of religious tourism. Such associations and transnational institutions constitute a voluntary union of actors and horizontal forms of cooperation, lacking strong authoritative powers and producing 'soft law' agreements.

An international regime on religious tourism is, however, yet to emerge. But there

Table 6.1. Key international institutions on religious tourism.

Type of institution	Institutions
Intergovernmental organizations	United Nations World Tourism Organization (UNWTO), United Nations Educational, Scientific and Cultural Organization (UNESCO), Council of Europe (CoE)
International non-governmental organizations	International Council of Monuments and Sites (ICOMOS), World Travel and Tourism Council (WTTC), World Religious Travel Association (defunct), Faith Travel Association (FTA), United Federation of Travel Agents' Associations (UFTA), International Association of Scientific Experts in Tourism (AIEST)
Hybrid multi-stakeholders	European Cultural Tourism Network (ECTN), Association for Tourism and Leisure Education and Research (ATLAS)

Source: Author's own work.

has been an expansion of IOs, international networks and non-governmental organizations that have been set up to inform policy, shape the global agenda, mobilize stakeholders and provide practical input – management trainers, educators, etc. (Table 6.1). IOs have, in particular, been promoting religious tourism while linking it to heritage conservation, cultural expression and economic development and they have played a role in: setting strategic frameworks for the development of religious tourism; providing guidance for cooperation between stakeholders; spreading information; developing monitoring and assessment measures; and networking.

6.4.1 Drivers of IOs engagement in religious tourism

What drives the engagement of IOs in the field of religious tourism? Globalization has contributed to the growth of religious tourism (Tanahashi, 2008, p. 110) while posing new challenges for the sector that need to be addressed collectively at the international level. The expansion of human interaction across regions and cultures raises people's interest in foreign traditions and religions. Globalization has raised people's curiosity in acquainting themselves with cultural heritage, inclusive of religions, because it represents an epitome of human ties. In response, the tourism industry

has begun to redirect its activities at catering for such interests. The expansion of religious tourism activities worldwide raises collective policy challenges. Thus, the main driver of IOs is the need to form global responses and regimes to address common challenges such as destination management and meeting the sustainable development goals (SDGs) and ensure some degree of compliance to common rules and principles. The need for access to information to support science informed policy is another key driver. Acting as common spaces, IOs allow for regular interaction and communication, the sharing of information and best practices. IOs bring together the expert community and policy makers to disseminate, exchange and make new knowledge, drive policies, and shape rules while monitoring the outcomes of these actions (Gutner, 2017, p. 25). IOs in the field of religious tourism are also formed to pool stakeholders' power. The heterogeneity of religious tourism stakeholders varying from the pilgrim to travel agencies and ministries make even more necessary the coordination of their actions at a transnational context given the globalization of the tourism product. Still, IOs may also emerge as symbolic acts. States and other actors' support to IOs may have little to do with the actual response to common problems and more with concerns on actors' prestige. Support and membership of IOs is thus often viewed as a means to show commitment to values such as cooperation and a way to possibly gain leverage over others.

6.4.2 United Nations World Tourism Organization (UNWTO)

The right to tourism, holidays and to the use of leisure is a modern attainment. The right to holidays was first recognized by the Universal Declaration of Human Rights of 1948 (article 24) and the right to tourism and the use of leisure as part of the fulfilment of a human being was mentioned at the 1980 Manila Declaration adopted by the WTO's World Tourism Conference. A few years later, the WTO's Bali Declaration 1996 reiterated that tourism had become an important human need and 'not just a leisure activity'. No special reference to religious tourism is however made there.

The United Nations World Tourism Organization (UNWTO) has been a key player in the international recognition of religious tourism being the leading organization overseeing the development of responsible and sustainable tourism globally. According to the UNWTO its mission is to promote 'tourism as a driver of economic growth, inclusive development and environmental sustainability', offer 'leadership and support to the sector in advancing knowledge and tourism policies worldwide' (UNWTO, 2022), and incorporate socially responsible actions (UNWTO, 2011).

A landmark document in the governance of global tourism was the Global Code of Ethics for Tourism (GCET) adopted in 1999 by the General Assembly of the UNWTO which, although not legally binding, outlined the principles to guide tourism development and serves as a reference for key stakeholders in the tourism sector. The GCET constituted a synthesis of previously elaborated documents, codes, and declarations which were complemented with new approaches and considerations reflecting modern developments. The Code was converted to an international convention namely the UNWTO Convention on Tourism Ethics approved by the 23rd General Assembly held in Saint Petersburg in September 2019.

The convention mentions that '[t]ravel for purposes of health, education and spiritual, cultural or linguistic exchanges is particularly beneficial and deserve encouragement' (UNWTO, 2020, article 5, para. 4). The World Committee on Tourism Ethics was also established in 2001 to resolve issues resulting from the implementation of the GCET.

The various UNWTO-sponsored Conferences and their Declarations have contributed to global governance of religious tourism. The first international conference on religious tourism organized by the UNWTO took place in Cordoba (Spain) in 2007 entitled 'Tourism and Religions: A Contribution to the Dialogue of Cultures, Religions, and Civilizations' and highlighted the sociology of religions in world tourism (UNWTO, 2011). Since then, numerous conferences have been held under the auspices of the UNWTO and in cooperation with national authorities (Olsen and Timothy, 2021). UNWTO Declarations adopted at those gatherings have set the guidelines for religious tourism development globally, namely, the Ninh Binh Declaration on Spiritual Tourism for Sustainable Development of 2013, the Santiago de Compostela Declaration on Tourism and Pilgrimages of 2014, the Elche Declaration on Religious Heritage and Tourism of 2014, and the Bethlehem Declaration on Religious Tourism as a Means of Fostering Socio-Economic Development of Host Communities of 2015 (Table 6.2).

6.4.3 UNESCO and ICOMOS

Religious tourism is treated within the context of the protection of cultural and natural heritage in the work of the United Nations Educational, Scientific and Cultural Organization (UNESCO). UNESCO's work is complemented by that of the International Council on Monuments and Sites (ICOMOS) which is its advisory body responsible for the management of cultural heritage. ICOMOS constitutes an international network of key stakeholders in the field which enables information and expertise sharing, defines preservation principles and standards and promotes relevant research and practice (Smith, 2003, p. 102).

Table 6.2. UNWTO Declarations on Religious Tourism

Declaration/event	Place	Date
Bethlehem Declaration on Religious Tourism as a Means of Fostering Socio-Economic Development of Host Communities, adopted at the UNWTO International Conference on 'Religious Tourism: Fostering Socio-Economic Development of Host Communities'	Bethlehem, Palestine	15–16 June 2015
Elche Declaration on Religious Heritage and Tourism, adopted at the UNWTO Conference on 'Religious Heritage and Tourism: Types, Trends and Challenges'	Elche, Spain	27–28 November 2014
Santiago de Compostela Declaration on Tourism and Pilgrimages, adopted at the First UNWTO International Congress on 'Tourism and Pilgrimage'	Santiago de Compostela, Spain	17–20 September 2014
The Ninh Binh Declaration on Spiritual Tourism adopted at the First UNWTO International Conference on 'Spiritual Tourism for Sustainable Development'	Ninh Bihn, Vietnam	21–22 November 2013

Source: Based on UNWTO Declarations. Available at https://www.e-unwto.org/loi/unwtodeclarations.

UNESCO and ICOMOS have a leading role in supporting normative action related to heritage of religious importance. This is done through a body of standard-setting documents including agreements, recommendations and policy decisions on the protection of cultural and natural heritage. By 1972, UNESCO adopted the World Heritage Convention in order to provide organized international protection of and support for world heritage sites. UNESCO (2008, p. 86) defines three main types of cultural landscape: (i) one designed and created intentionally by man, (ii) organically evolved landscape which falls into two sub-categories, a relic (or fossil) landscape and a continuing landscape, and (iii) an associative landscape which is often linked with intangible heritage of a spiritual nature.

There are a number of policy recommendations drawn from UNESCO/ICOMOS activities on religious and sacred heritage, such as the ICOMOS 15th General Assembly Resolution calling for the 'establishment of an International Thematic Programme for Religious Heritage' in 2005, the ICOMOS General Assembly Resolution on 'Protection and Enhancement of Sacred Heritage Sites, Buildings and Landscapes', and the UNESCO MAB/IUCN 'Guidelines for the Conservation and Management of Sacred

Natural Sites' (Table 6.3.). Several recommendations directly or indirectly concern the safeguarding of the spirit of place, in particular the Nara Document on Authenticity of 1994 and the Quebec Declaration on the Preservation of the Spirit of Place of 2008.

ICOMOS provides a comprehensive set of universal guidelines for the management of World Heritage Sites. The ICOMOS International Cultural Tourism Charter adopted in 1999 recognizes that heritage management should primarily communicate the importance of heritage preservation to the host community and tourists. According to the normative framework of religious tourism policy as reflected in ICOMOS policy instruments, tourism should empower and benefit the local communities, serve sustainable development, and balance conservation of and access to heritage (Smith, 2003, pp. 111–112). The ICOMOS International Cultural Tourism Charter (ICOMOS, 1999) sets the normative basis for global management of tourism in the context of religious heritage and supports activities which facilitate:

The accessibility of key actors involved in heritage management to the host communities;

Table 6.3. UNESCO/ICOMOS international instruments on religious tourism.

Instrument	Event/organization	Date
Agreements:		
ICOMOS International Cultural Tourism Charter: Managing Tourism at Places of Heritage Significance	12th General Assembly of ICOMOS, Mexico	17–23 October 1999
International Charter for the Conservation and Restoration of Monuments and Sites (The Venice Charter)	ICOMOS, Venice, Italy	31 May 1964
ICOMOS Charter on Cultural Routes	16th General Assembly of ICOMOS, Québec, Canada	4 October 2008
Guidelines		
Guidelines for the Conservation and Management of Sacred Natural Sites	UNESCO MAB/IUCN, Paris, France	2008
Declarations		
Siem Reap Declaration on Tourism and Culture – Building a New Partnership Model	UNWTO/UNESCO World Conference on Tourism and Culture – Building a New Partnership, Siem Reap, Cambodia	4–5 February 2015
The Paris Declaration on heritage as a driver of development	17th General Assembly of ICOMOS, Paris, France	1 December 2011
Kyiv Statement on the protection of religious properties within the framework of the World Heritage Convention	International Seminar on the role of religious communities in the management of World Heritage Sites, Kyiv, Ukraine	5 November 2010
Quebec Declaration on the Preservation of the Spirit of Place	16th General Assembly of ICOMOS and International Scientific Symposium, Quebec, Canada	4 October 2008
Xi'an Declaration on the Conservation of the Setting of Heritage Structures, Sites and Areas	15th General Assembly of ICOMOS, Xi'an, China	21 October 2005
Nara Document on Authenticity	Nara Conference on Authenticity in relation to the World Heritage Convention, ICOMOS, Nara, Japan	6 November 1994

Source: Based on ICOMOS Charters and other Doctrinal Texts. Available at: https://www.icomos.org/en/resources/charters-and-texts.

The promotion of responsible tourism that respects the heritage and living cultures of host communities;

Dialogue among stakeholders about sustainability and the significance of heritage.

In parallel to developing the normative framework in cooperation with ICOMOS, UNESCO has developed specific activities in support of religious tourism (see Table 6.1). The Initiative on Heritage of Religious Interest is the centrepiece of UNESCO's work in providing guidelines in religious heritage governance while implementing the World Heritage Convention of 1972 aiming to integrate guiding principles into cultural policies at all levels, from the local to the national, regional and international levels. Heritage assets, such as active religious and sacred sites, constitute one of the main categories on the World Heritage List as approximately 20% of the properties inscribed on it have a religious or spiritual connection (UNESCO, 2020). Within the framework of the Initiative,

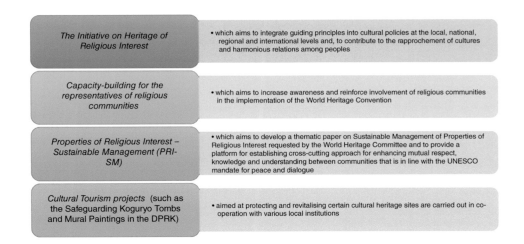

Fig. 6.1. UNESCO activities in religious tourism.
Source: based on World Heritage Convention, UNESCO activities. Available at: https://whc.unesco.org/en/activities/search_theme=43&action=list.

a specific action called 'Properties of Religious Interest – Sustainable Management (PRI-SM)' has brought together UNESCO's World Heritage Center and the UNESCO Advisory Bodies to elaborate a paper formulating general guidelines to states on the management of religious heritage, considering also national specificities. The action includes preparatory activities, inventory, research and data analysis (Fig. 6.1.).

6.4.4   The Council of Europe (CoE)

The Council of Europe has also approached religious tourism as a dimension of cultural tourism and cultural heritage management. There are various levels at which matters relating to tourism are discussed within the Council of Europe: at the intergovernmental level (the Committee of Ministers and the Council for Cultural Cooperation), at the parliamentary level (Committees of the Parliamentary Assembly), at the local and regional level (the Standing Conference of Local and Regional Authorities of Europe), and at specialized ministers level.

The policy tools of the Council of Europe in dealing with tourism, directly or indirectly, are its recommendations, resolutions, agreements and conventions such as the CoE Assembly's

Resolution on 'The Need for Stronger Political Support in Favour of Tapping Europe's Tourism Potential' (8720/2000) and the Resolution on the 'Need to Accelerate the Development of Tourism in Central and Eastern Europe' (1148/1998). Key documents that frame religious tourism originate in the 1950s such as the European Cultural Convention (Paris, 19 December 1954) and include the Santiago de Compostela Declaration (23 October 1987), the Council of Europe Framework Convention on the Value of Cultural Heritage for Society (Faro, 27 October 2005) and the European Cultural Heritage Strategy for the 21st Century, adopted in April 2017. Throughout the years, the principles of tourism policy as reflected in various CoE documents include the freedom of travel, protection of the environment, preservation of the architectural heritage, protection of culture, the legal and social protection of tourists, and promoting regional development in economically disadvantaged areas.

Beyond the above-mentioned policy instruments, the main actions of the Council of Europe (Fig. 6.2.) regarding religious tourism develop through specific thematic programmes (Council of Europe, 2020, p. 18):

European heritage days: this programme, launched in 1985, engages all levels of state

Fig. 6.2. Actions of the Council of Europe regarding religious tourism.
Source: Author's own work.

authorities, civil society, the private sector and volunteers in organizing events under a shared European theme (e.g. the 2022 European heritage days focus on sustainable heritage).

The technical co-operation and consultancy programme: this programme, launched in 1977, provides tailor made technical assistance and sets standards for policy making to governments with regard to problems of heritage protection, rehabilitation, management and conservation at local, national and regional levels.

The European Cultural Heritage Information Network (HEREIN): this programme, launched in 1999, is an information system which brings together public authorities from the member states that are responsible for national cultural heritage policies. The network monitors national legislation, policies and practices relating to cultural heritage.

Cultural Routes of the Council of Europe: this programme, launched in 1987, builds networks of shared heritage and history under common themes (which vary from gastronomy to literature).

The programme of European Cultural Routes – previously called the European Pilgrim Routes – constitutes the cornerstone of the activities of the Council of Europe in religious tourism (Council of Europe, 2015). The programme was launched with the Declaration of Santiago de Compostela, reflecting the values of the Council of Europe: human rights, cultural diversity and intercultural dialogue. By 2021, 45 cultural routes were established, out of which 11 link to religious routes: the Santiago de Compostela Pilgrim Routes (1987), the European Route of Jewish

Heritage (2004), the Saint Martin of Tours Route (2005), the Via Regia (2005), the Cluniac sites in Europe (2005), the TRANSROMANICA – The Romanesque Routes of European Heritage (2007), the European Route of Cistercian Abbeys (2010), the European Cemeteries Route (2010), the Route of Saint Olav Ways (2010), the Via Romea Germanica (2020), and the Cyril and Methodious Route (2021). The implementation of the Cultural Routes programme came as a result of Recommendation 987 of the Parliamentary Assembly of the Council of Europe in 1984 which recommended that the Committee of Ministers set up pilgrim routes and the framework of pilgrim tourism along the following guidelines (PACE, 1984):

Co-operation of member states in preserving the international pilgrim routes;

Encouragement of the authorities of towns situated on specific pilgrim routes to cooperate in joint activities for the conservation and promotion of sites of architectural heritage;

Promotion of cultural tourism along these routes in collaboration with European tourist organizations;

Granting a special emblem of the Council of Europe to towns and institutions active in the conservation and promotion of pilgrim routes.

6.5 Conclusion: Tracing Global Governance Elements of Religious Tourism

All four international institutions (UNWTO, UNESCO, ICOMOS and the Council of Europe)

have worked complementarily in crafting a framework for the development of religious tourism. The main contribution of IOs in global governance of religious tourism can be seen in issue framing and norm setting, stakeholder pooling and networking, capacity building, information sharing, and in monitoring and assessment measures.

Issue framing and norm setting. IOs have framed religious tourism in the global policy level through a corpus of agreements but primarily through non-legally binding declarations. In framing religious tourism, the UNWTO, UNESCO/ICOMOS and the Council of Europe have shaped policies and perceptions on tourist needs and protection, destination management and site preservation. The main global principles and norms enshrined in IOs policy instruments act as guidelines for stakeholders' action and refer to the freedom of tourist movement and travel, inclusive and sustainable development, heritage protection and preservation, and intercultural dialogue.

Stakeholder pooling and networking. One of the key aspects of the work of IOs is cooperation between the various stakeholders. ICOMOS is par excellence a hybrid network of experts (architects, engineers and town planners, historians, archaeologists, art historians, etc.) who jointly interact with public authorities. UNWTO offers also national tourism administrations and organizations a machinery to interact through the UNWTO International Network of Sustainable Tourism Observatories (INSTO). Conferences, seminars and networks have become the drivers of agenda setting in religious tourism and they have produced key policy instruments such as declarations. UNESCO scientific studies and policy related work on religious heritage relies heavily on the input of its Advisory Bodies – ICCROM, ICOMOS and IUCN – which engage public and private stakeholders.

Capacity building. IOs in religious tourism provide support to their members in strengthening their tourism policy frameworks, strategies and product development. Both the UNWTO and the Council of Europe have developed technical cooperation programmes (i.e. the UNWTO Technical Cooperation and Services) to meet primarily governments' demands with regard to addressing problems of heritage conservation and developing the tourism industry.

Information access and sharing. Access to information and information sharing is important for a science-based policy in any field and in this regard the UNWTO has played a role through its publications, research (i.e. UNWTO, 2011, 2020) and as a source of statistics on global tourism. A key challenge is how to address the difficulty of including religious tourism data separately in tourism statistics, as even the statistics like the Tourism Satellite Accounts do not distinguish religious tourism. With regard to information sharing at the European level, the Council of Europe has, among others, developed the European Cultural Heritage Information Network (HEREIN) whose mission is exactly to support information sharing among public authorities. The Tourism Resilience Committee (TRC) of the WTO has also been formed as a platform for its members to receive and share information on the impact on the tourism sector of global economic shifts. Furthermore, the websites of IOs provide resources for informed decision making and promote the exchange of good practices showcasing management systems and innovative religious tourism experiences.

Developing monitoring and assessment measures. Developing assessment measures in religious tourism is probably the most challenging task for IOs given the numerous actors engaged. The UNWTO in particular has formulated the Private Sector Commitment to the Global Code of Ethics for Tourism (launched in 2011) according to which the signatories report to the World Commission on Tourism Ethics on the implementation of the principles of norms in tourism corporate governance.

Despite numerous organizations that have developed some sort of activities in the field of tourism policy, just a handful of them have systematically focused on religious tourism. The UNWTO, the Council of Europe, UNESCO and ICOMOS have been the pioneers in shaping a strategic framework for religious tourism development.

A global regime in the development of religious tourism is yet to emergence. However, IOs have been concerned with setting structures, processes and ethics in religious tourism development, and in framing it as a distinct type of tourism. In this regard, one of the most obvious results of IOs actorness is that they have framed religious tourism as a global policy issue raising its importance from the local and national to the international level while shaping the way we perceive it.

References

Álvarez-García, J.M., del Río Rama, M. and Gómez-Ullate, M. (2018) *Handbook of Research on Socio-Economic Impacts of Religious Tourism and Pilgrimage*. IGI Global, Hersey, PA. DOI: 10.4018/978-1-5225-5730-2.

Amore, A. and Hall, C.M. (2016) From governance to meta-governance in tourism? Re-incorporating politics, interests and values in the analysis of tourism governance. *Tourism Recreation Research* 41(2), 109–122. DOI: 10.1080/02508281.2016.1151162.

Beritelli, P., Bieger, T. and Laesser, C. (2007) Destination governance: using corporate governance theories as a foundation for effective destination management. *Journal of Travel Research* 46(1), 96–107. DOI: 10.1177/0047287507302385.

Bramwell, B. and Lane, B. (2011) Critical research on the governance of tourism and sustainability. *Journal of Sustainable Tourism* 19(4–5), 411–421. DOI: 10.1080/09669582.2011.580586.

Bremer, T.S. (2005) Tourism and religion. In: Jones, L. (ed.) *Encyclopedia of Religion*. Thomas Gale, Macmillan Reference, Detroit, MI, pp. 9260–9264.

Caton, K., Pastoor, C., Belhassen, Y., Collins, B. and Wallin, M. (2013) Christian music festival tourism and positive peace. *The Journal of Tourism and Peace Research* 3(2), 21–42.

CBI (2020) *The European Market Potential for Religious Tourism*. Center for the Promotion of Imports from Developing Countries (CBI), Ministry of Foreign Affairs of the Netherlands. Available at: https://www.cbi.eu/market-information/tourism/religious-tourism/market-potential (accessed 27 December 2021).

Council of Europe (2015) *Cultural Routes Management: From Theory to Practice*. Council of Europe, Strasburg.

Council of Europe (2020) *Cultural Tourism in the EU Macro-Regions: Cultural Routes to Increase the Attractiveness of Remote Destinations Routes4U|7*. European Commission and Council of Europe. Available at: https://rm.coe.int/09000016809ef75a (accessed 1 February 2022).

Dawson, S. (2015) The religious resurgence: problems and opportunities for international relations theory. In: Herrington, L.M., McKay, A. and Haynes, J. (eds) *Nations under God: The Geopolitics of Faith in the Twenty-First Century*. E-International Relations, Bristol, UK.

Dredge, D. (2006) Networks, conflict and collaborative communities. *Journal of Sustainable Tourism* 14(6), 562–581. DOI: 10.2167/jost567.0.

Duffy, R. and Moore, L. (2011) Global regulations and local practices: the politics and governance of animal welfare in elephant tourism. *Journal of Sustainable Tourism* 19(4–5), 589–604. DOI: 10.1080/09669582.2011.566927.

Flagestad, A. and Hope, C.A. (2001) Strategic success in winter sports destinations: a sustainable value creation perspective. *Tourism Management* 22(5), 445–461. DOI: 10.1016/S0261-5177(01)00010-3.

Geybels, H. (2014) Religious common culture and religion tourism. *Yearbook for Ritual and Liturgical Studies/Jaarboek voor Liturgie-onderzoek* 30, 39–50.

Giovanelli, L., Rotondo, F. and Fadda, N. (2015) The evolution of governance networks in a time of crisis. Evidence from the Italian tourism sector. *Journal of Public Administration and Policy Research* 7(4), 76–88. DOI: 10.5897/JPAPR2015.0317.

Goodwin, M. and Painter, J. (1996) Local governance, the crises of Fordism and the changing geographies of regulation. *Transactions of the Institute of British Geographers* 21(4), 635–648. DOI: 10.2307/622391.

Griffin, K. and Raj, R. (2017) The importance of religious tourism and pilgrimage: reflecting on definitions, motives and data. *International Journal of Religious Tourism and Pilgrimage* 5(3), article 2, n.p.

Griffiths, M. and Wiltshier, P. (eds) (2019) *Managing Religious Tourism*. CAB International, Wallingford, UK and Boston, MA.

Gutner, T. (2017) *International Organizations in World Politics*. Sage, London and New Delhi.

Haggard, S. and Simmons, B. (1987) Theories of international regimes. *International Organization* 41(03), 491–517.

Hall, C.M. (2010) Crisis events in tourism: subjects of crisis in tourism. *Current Issues in Tourism* 13(5), 401–417. DOI: 10.1080/13683500.2010.491900.

Hall, C.M. (2011) A typology of governance and its implications for tourism policy analysis. *Journal of Sustainable Tourism* 19(4–5), 437–457. DOI: 10.1080/09669582.2011.570346.

Heywood, A. (2011) *Global Politics*. Palgrave Macmillan, New York.

Hvizdová, E. (2018) Religious tourism and its socio-economic dimensions. *European Journal of Science and Theology* 14(2), 89–98.

ICOMOS (1999) *International Cultural Tourism Charter. Managing Tourism at Places of Heritage Significance*. Available at: icomos.org/charters/tourism_e.pdf (accessed 2 August 2022).

Karns, M. and Mingst, K. (2009) *International Organizations: The Politics and Processes of Global Governance*. Lynne Rienner Publishers, Boulder, CO.

Keohane, R. (1989) *International Institutions and State Power. Essays in International Relations Theory*. Westview Press, Boulder, CO.

Keohane, R.O. and Martin, L.L. (1995) The promise of institutionalist theory. *International Security* 20(1), 39–51. DOI: 10.2307/2539214.

Kindleberger, C.P. (1951) Group behavior and international trade. *Journal of Political Economy* 59(1), 30–46. DOI: 10.1086/257026.

Koskansky, O. (2002) Tourism, charity, and profit: the movement of money in Moroccan Jewish pilgrimage. *Cultural Anthropology* 17(3), 359–400. DOI: 10.1525/can.2002.17.3.359.

Krasner, S.D. (ed.) (1983) *International Regimes*. Cornell University Press, Ithaca, NY.

Krasner, S.D. (1991) Global communications and national power: life on the Pareto Frontier. *World Politics* 43(3), 336–366. DOI: 10.2307/2010398.

Mearsheimer, J.J. (1994) The false promise of international institutions. *International Security* 19(3), 5–49. DOI: 10.2307/2539078.

Nordin, S. and Svensson, S. (2007) Innovative destination governance: the Swedish ski resort of Are. *Entrepreneurship and Innovation* 8, 53–66.

OECD (2010) *OECD Tourism Trends and Policies 2010*. OECD, Paris. DOI: 10.1787/tour-2010-en.

Olsen, D.H. and Timothy, D.J. (2021) *The Routledge Handbook of Religious and Spiritual Tourism*. Taylor and Francis, London and New York. DOI: 10.4324/9780429201011.

PACE (1984) *European Pilgrim Roots*. Recommendation 987 (1984) 36th session, Parliamentary Assembly of the Council of Europe, Strasburg. Available at: http://assembly.coe.int/nw/xml/XRef/Xref-XML2HTML-en.asp?fileid=15021&lang=en (accessed 8 June 2022).

Post, P.G.J., Pieper, J.Z.T. and Van Uden, M.H.F. (1998) The modern pilgrim: multidisciplinary explorations of Christian pilgrimage. *Liturgia Condenda*, no.8 Peeters, Leuven.

Rawlinson, J. (2012) *Religious and Pilgrimage Tourism*. Report. Mintel Group Ltd, London.

Rhodes, R. (1997) *Understanding Governance: Policy Networks, Governance, Reflexivity, and Accountability*. Open University Press, Philadelphia, PA.

Riesebrodt, M. (2000) Fundamentalism and the resurgence of religion. *Numen* 47(3), 266–287. DOI: 10.1163/156852700511559.

Rinschede, G. (1992) Forms of religious tourism. *Annals of Tourism Research* 19(1), 51–67. DOI: 10.1016/0160-7383(92)90106-Y.

Ruhanen, L., Scott, N., Ritchie, B. and Tkaczynski, A. (2010) Governance: a review and synthesis of the literature. *Tourism Review* 65(4), 4–16. DOI: 10.1108/16605371011093836.

Scharpf, F.W. (1994) Games real actors could play: positive and negative coordination in embedded negotiations. *Journal of Theoretical Politics* 6(1), 27–53.

Sikkink, K. (1993) Human rights, principled issue-networks, and sovereignty in Latin America. *International Organization* 47(3), 411–442. DOI: 10.1017/S0020818300028010.

Simmons, B. and Martin, L. (2002) International organizations and institutions. In: *Handbook of International Relations*. SAGE Publications, London. DOI: 10.4135/9781848608290.

Smith, M.K. (2003). *Issues in Cultural Tourism Studies*. Routledge, London and Taylor and Francis Group, London. DOI: 10.4324/9780203402825.

Smouts, M.C. (1993) Some thoughts on international organizations and theories of regulation. *International Social Science Journal* 45(4), 443–452.

Streeck, W. and Schmitter, P.C. (1985) Community, market, state—and associations? *European Sociological Review* 1(2), 119–138. DOI: 10.1093/oxfordjournals.esr.a036381.

Tanahashi, K. (2008) Globalization and emerging roles of cultural tourism. *Journal of Tokyo Keinzai University* 260, 101–114.

Trono, A. (2015) Politics, policy and the practice of religious tourism. In: Raj, R. and K. Griffin (eds) *Religious Tourism and Pilgrimage Management an International Perspective*. CAB International, Wallingford, UK, pp. 16–36.

UNESCO (2008) *Guidelines on the Inscription of Specific Types of Properties on the World Heritage List.* Annex 3. Available at: https://whc.unesco.org/archive/opguide08-en.pdf#annex3 (accessed 25 July 2022).

UNESCO (2020) *World Heritage List.* Available at: https://whc.unesco.org/en/list/ (accessed 10 January 2022).

UNWTO (2011) *Religious Tourism in Asia and the Pacific.* UNWTO, Madrid.

UNWTO (2020) *Framework Convention on Tourism Ethics.* Resolution A/RES/722, XXIII General Assembly of UNWTO, Madrid.

UNWTO (2022) *About Us.* Available at: https://www.unwto.org/about-us (accessed 9 January 2022).

Vásquez, M.A. and Marquandt, M.F. (2000) Globalizing the rainbow Madonna: old time religion in the present age. *Theory, Culture and Society* 19(4), 119–142.

Verified Market Research (2021) *"Religious Tourism Market Size, Share, Scope, Opportunities and Forecast"* (Report no 54665, July). Available at: https://www.verifiedmarketresearch.com/product/religious-tourism-market/ (accessed 8 June 2022).

Vukonić, B. (1996) *Tourism and Religion.* Emerald, Menomonie, WI.

Μοίρα, Π. (2009) *Θρησκευτικός Τουρισμός [Religious Tourism].* Interbooks, Αθήνα [in Greek].

Μοίρα, Π. (2019) *Θρησκευτικός Τουρισμός Και Προσκύνημα [Religious Tourism and Pilgrimage].* Φαίδιμος, Αθήνα [in Greek].

Σφακιανάκης, Μ. (2000) *Εναλλακτικές Μορφές [Alternative Types of Tourism].* Έλλην, Αθήνα [in Greek].

7 Blurring the Lines: Governance and Management in the Promotion of Religious and Spiritual Sites

Spyridon Parthenis*, Polyxeni Moira and Dimitrios Mylonopoulos
Department of Tourism Management, University of West Attica, Greece

Abstract

This chapter seeks to describe the relevance of National Tourism Administrations (NTAs) and National Tourism Organizations (NTOs) in the governance of religious and spiritual sites and answer some crucial questions: What is the contemporary role of NTAs/NTOs as public institutions and what is their mission? Where does governance stop and when does management start? Are the boundaries between governance and management blurred? What does the marketing and promotion of religious and spiritual sites and places as part of the national cultural heritage of a country consist of? This chapter also seeks to outline the public sector and civil society actors as well as the private travel and tourism industry stakeholders involved in the management, conservation and promotion of religious and sacred sites.

7.1 Introduction

Governments all over the world may not disburse considerable sums of money from their budget on tourism policy compared with their spending on other public policies, yet the public sector has an essential role to play in tourism (Devine and Devine, 2011, p. 1254) despite the fact that tourism is predominantly an activity controlled by the private sector. This is because only governments have the power to guarantee the political stability, security, safety and the legal and financial framework which is indispensable for tourism to survive (Elliott, 1997, p. 2). Politics and tourism politics in particular require governance, including 'allocating resources, deciding on policy and goals, delivering services, regulating and facilitating social action and social order' (Jamal and Camargo, 2018,

p. 206). Governance in tourism in particular refers to 'coordination, planning, legislation, regulation and entrepreneur stimulation', which have always been the core responsibilities and tasks of the tourism public sector (IUOTO, 1974). In the context of the promotion of religious and spiritual sites, effective tourism governance, seen through a functionalist lens, means that the public tourism sector is in charge of providing effectual steering and guidance to the other institutions and it involves meeting the following four criteria outlined by Peters (2012, pp. 21–22):

1. Developing collective policy choices, taking decisions and selecting broad and operational goals, incorporated across all levels of government.

*Corresponding author: spyrosparth@gmail.com

DOI: 10.1079/9781800621732.0007

2. Setting priorities through goal reconciliation and coordinating the actions taken in line with those priorities.
3. Carrying out central government's policies and decisions through subnational government and social, cultural and religious actors and institutions.
4. Establishing feedback mechanisms, which allows the adaptation of the design and the implementation of policies and the improvement of the quality of the decisions made, which leads to democratic accountability.

Nevertheless, in the light of the increasing trends for the transition from government to governance, manifested in the loss, concession or delegation of tourism functions, such as management, by central and local government tourism departments to substitute tourism service delivery agencies and the loss, concession or delegation of functions by modern governments to supranational or international organizations (e.g. European Union, UNESCO), tourism public intervention needs to be redefined. This is because of the complexity of the modern world, the plethora of policy problems, the scarcity of resources, which means that the state can no longer do everything effectively and has to delegate duties, responsibilities and power to other institutions so that they can act on its behalf. Therefore, state or non-state actors and institutions are entrusted with the day-to-day management and running of the religious and spiritual sites.

However, the central government retains the authority and state power and maintains the privilege of steering, overseeing and controlling the local cultural, religious institutions, custodians and other social actors. This transfer of power inevitably generates a power struggle, a fight for control. This shift of state functions considerably affects the way that religious and spiritual sites are promoted throughout the world, which means a re-allocation of power among state and non-state actors involved in the governance and management of religious and spiritual sites as tourist attractions. Borrowing the terminology used by IT and applying it to tourism literature, the governance function of a National Tourism Authority (NTA)/National Tourism Organization (NTO) is responsible for defining strategic direction, leading and steering,

whereas the management function transforms this strategic direction into actions, which will enable NTAs/NTOs to attain their strategic goals (Magowan, 2020). This leads us inevitably to some crucial questions: Who are the real power holders in the governance and management of religious and spiritual sites? How are governance and management of religious and spiritual sites conducted? How are policies regarding the governance and management of religious and spiritual sites formulated, carried out and managed? How are goals achieved and by what means?

This chapter seeks to describe the relevance of NTAs/NTOs in the governance of religious and spiritual sites. Where does governance stop and when does management start? Are the boundaries between governance and management blurred? Does this blurring affect the relevance of NTAs/NTOs? Does governance involve activities such as promotion, an important part of management? We will show that occasional blurring between governance and management duties is counterproductive and could lead to bad governance and bad management. Both functions would be more effective when those in charge of governance and management comprehend their roles distinctly and stay inside their lines.

7.2 The Role of NTAs/NTOs as Public Institutions

Some scholars view that the role of government, understood as institutions of a state which are controlled directly by the central state authority, has been on a wane since the 1980s, due to the gradual 'hollowing-out of the state' (Rhodes, 1994), that is the shift from the hierarchical control of the government to governance, scattered among a number of distinct, non-governmental entities (Hall, 2000, p. 144). Some other scholars (Elliott, 1997; Boin et al., 2021) do not share this view. They think that powerful and robust public administration all over the world has always been crucial for effectively tackling the crises and ever-increasing complexity, uncertainty and ambiguity in these challenging times. Hence, an institutionalist approach will be adopted throughout this chapter. 'Trust is the foundation upon which the legitimacy of public institutions is built and is crucial for maintaining social cohesion.' (OECD, 2020). Despite the increasing mistrust of citizens in their national governments and public institutions and services in the wake of the 2007 global financial crisis, which exposed the incompetence of national governments 'to manage public finance in a sensible and sustainable way' (OECD, 2017, p. 101), governments were able to exploit public trust as a force out of another crisis, the COVID-19 pandemic, responding rapidly and effectively, planning and implementing an inclusive rebound (Rieger and Wang, 2021). Thus, in this era of the dominance of neoliberal values and marketization of tourism, citizens in many countries all over the world have started to regain their confidence in public administration, which can contribute to a successful and sustainable economic recovery and social welfare.

Institutionalists suppose that institutions are of importance as they help explain public policy choices and policy choices in their turn define institutions; therefore, public policies are embedded in institutions (Peters, 2016, p. 58). Institutions draw much of 'their structure of meaning' from the society from which they are shaped (Peters, 2019, p. 40), because it depends on how the things governments do are understood and appreciated by the members of a community (Hughes, 2018, p. 81). That said individual political behaviour and preferences are always present in institutions because they are largely shaped by their involvement with institutions (endogenous to the institutions). In other words, institutions transfer their dominant values to the individuals who have become members of these institutions and could possibly impose sanctions when the individuals' behaviour is not aligned with the institutions' expectations, that is when individuals do not follow institutional guidelines and values and do not act appropriately. Studying institutions, therefore, involves the interaction of structure and agency in producing policy outcomes. Institutions have a few significant features in common (Boin *et al.*, 2021): they are acknowledged for their ability to tackle serious public problems; they proclaim their history and hire staff who are eager to safeguard their values; and they stimulate learning, adaptation, and innovation.

Although there has been an increased interest in tourism research for more than 40 years, little research has been conducted on the connection between politics and (religious) tourism, and few studies have examined the political nature of tourism. Tourism is a very controversial policy area, which has almost totally been ignored by political science (Mathews, 1975; Richter, 1983; Hall, 1994; Kerr, 2003; Richter, 2009). Hollinshead and Suleman (2017, p. 961) underline the inherent political nature of tourism which involves conflict: 'Since it fundamentally deals with the promotion and development of local sites and sights and with the harnessing of local, regional, and national inheritances, tourism is inevitably a conflictual phenomenon at each of those levels.' Lennon *et al.* (2006, p. 5) underscore that governments have traditionally been involved in tourism development and in 'the promotion of their countries as tourism destinations' and claiming that, although tourism is an economic activity largely driven by the private sector, government intervention in the tourism sector is crucial as it can contribute to 'improvements in the balance of payments, regional development and regeneration, diversification of the national economy, co-ordination of a fragmented industry, employment opportunities and increased revenue' and that for tourism to flourish, a suitable legal, 'physical, regulatory, fiscal and social framework' is necessary (Lennon *et al.*, 2006, p. 5).

There is also limited public and academic interest in public organizations and institutions such as NTAs/NTOs and to what degree they can adapt and innovate in the face of global constant unexpected crises (e.g. natural disasters, pandemics, terrorist attacks) and thus perform a *mission mystique* (Goodsell, 2011). Some scholars do not share the view that 'there have been increasing signs of a disengagement from tourism by the public sector – notably, at national, or central government level' and that 'governments' traditional responsibilities and activities in the field of tourism' have been delegated to 'both local authorities and the private sector.' (Lennon *et al.*, 2006, p. 5). For example, Hall (2000, p. 143) underlines that the role of government in tourism has long since moved away from the traditional bureaucratic model of public administration towards a market-based corporatist model. This is partially true for the core countries of the Anglosphere: UK, Australia, USA, Canada and New Zealand, the Nordic countries (Denmark, Finland, Iceland, Sweden and Norway) and some of the Baltic States (Estonia, Latvia). Most governments worldwide still maintain the tourism portfolio at national level, without excluding partnerships with the private travel and tourism sector.

By 2021 the United Nations World Tourism Organization (UNWTO) comprised of 159 Full Member NTAs/NTOs, out of the 193 Member States of the United Nations. It is an international organization of intergovernmental character which was established in 1975 to provide public goods and 'address specific problems and may therefore be comprised in the category of special organizations' (Droesse, 2020, pp. 58–59). It became a UN specialized agency in 2004, which means it is an organization created for special purposes. 'UN specialized agencies (...) were created in response to the need to enhance coordination and cooperation at the international level', where functional, not political, 'neutrality' is feasible. The functional approach 'should help to shift the emphasis from political issues which divide, to the social issues [tourism in this case] in which the interest of the peoples is plainly akin and collective; to shift the emphasis from power to problem and purpose' (Mitrany 1948, cited in Droesse, 2020, p. 59). Higgins-Desbiolles (2006, p. 1193) reminds us that 'tourism is much more than just an 'industry'; it is a social force, which if freed from the fetters of 'market ideology' can achieve vital aims for all of humanity'.

There has been sustained political interest and will for most governments to join the UNWTO and maintain membership, with the exception of the Anglosphere, Nordic and Baltic countries which have either not joined or have also withdrawn membership of the UNWTO 'due to budgetary considerations and disagreements with the Organization's priorities' (RIDEA, 2019, p. 28). What is noteworthy is the fact that since 2004, when the World Tourism Organization became a specialized agency of the United Nations, the UNWTO Framework Convention on Tourism Ethics, approved in September 2019, was the first international convention of UNWTO ever. Although this is a UN Convention legally binding for the countries which will ratify it, it has not entered into force yet. This means that notwithstanding the advent of neoliberalism and hollowing of the state, tourism governance functions of national tourism authorities have not shifted to the global level yet. Still, for other countries, culture governance functions of national cultural and religious authorities have been delegated to international organizations. A good example is the Council of Europe.

International tourism has grown exponentially within the last fifty years with significant large-scale economic and social impacts. Being aware of the dynamics of tourism and its direct, indirect and induced effects, a growing number of governments around the world are seeking to increase their share of this boosting market and foreign tourism revenue, by integrating tourism in their national development and economic strategies (O'Brien, 2011, p. 4). To this end, government tourism administrations are established known as 'National Tourist Organizations or Administrations [which] are country-level organizations established to foster or guide the development of tourism' (Pearce, 2016, p. 651).

Many and different administrative bodies (e.g. ministries, public entities and local government organizations are responsible for the management and supervision of the tourism sector (Airey, 1984; Elliott, 1997; Mylonopoulos et al., 2012). Following Baum's (1994) early categorization, there have been three prevailing forms of NTAs/NTOs, operating under different names, if any (Gee et al., 1997, p. 102; Kotler et al., 2017, p. 539): (i) a central government department (e.g. ministry, state commission, national council or agency), or state, or province, together with local government officials; (ii) semi-governmental, reporting to a government agency (usually a tourist board reporting to a ministry), (iii) quasi-public, a national Destination Management Organization (DMO), which is often quasi-governmental and cooperates with the private sector.

In some countries, the term NTA refers to national organizations that are usually assigned the task of advising the governments on how to improve productivity and growth across the tourism sector and formulating and implementing national tourism policies and programmes while NTO applies to those having other national-level tasks, especially international marketing, research and destination development with a view to enhancing a country's reputation and popularity as a tourism destination. This type of NTO usually has its own chairman and board of directors. Some examples of DMOs are the South Africa National Convention Bureau, Melbourne Convention Bureau, Tokyo Convention and Visitors Bureau, Destination Toronto, Las Vegas Convention and Visitors Authority. Their main mission is to attract and support major meetings, conventions and business events.

In some countries National Tourism Authorities are exclusively in charge of both national tourism policies and promotion of a country's tourism industry but hierarchically they are under another national administrative structure, usually a ministry (e.g. the Federal Agency for Tourism of the Russian Federation operates under the supervision of the Ministry of Economic Development). In some instances, all or most of the above functions are undertaken by a single national organization (e.g. Deputy Ministry of Tourism of Cyprus, Mexican Secretariat of Tourism [SECTUR]), Ministry of Finance and Economy of Monaco [Tourist and Convention Authority]).

Almost every country has established an NTA/NTO/DMO with various tasks and functions (Μυλωνόπουλος and Κοντουδάκη, 2011, pp. 13–17). An NTA/NTO is the executive arm of government policy as agreed by the ministry and public money provides the main or the exclusive source of funds for most NTAs/NTOs (Μυλωνόπουλος and Κοντουδάκη, 2011, p. 15; Fletcher *et al.*, 2018, p. 454). The specific structure of an NTA/NTO/DMO will depend upon the objectives set for it by government and the tasks it must undertake in order to embrace and pursue its vision and mission (see Table 7.1 for the distribution of tourism portfolio in the national governments of the 159 UNWTO Full Members). Where tourism is a significant component of economic activity, it is standard practice to have a Ministry of Tourism (Μυλωνόπουλος and Κοντουδάκη, 2011, p. 14; Fletcher *et al.*, 2018, p. 455). In 56 out of 159 UNWTO full Member States (35%) there is a Ministry, State Commission, State Agency or National Council dedicated exclusively to tourism. In 34 UNWTO Member States (21%) a Ministry of Tourism and Culture, Antiquities or Arts is established whose mission is to promote

tourism activities that contribute to increasing public awareness and support for the protection and conservation of cultural heritage. In 20 UNWTO Member States (13%) the portfolio of tourism is combined with that of the environment, wildlife, natural resources or sustainability, because the natural environment of an area is one of the fundamental 'ingredients' of the tourist product offered and, obviously, the quality of this product depends crucially on the quality of its basic component (Briassoulis and van der Straaten, 1992, p. 1). In 18 UNWTO Member States (11%) the competence for formulating and implementing tourism policies is integrated into the responsibilities of the ministries of economy, economic development, regional development and energy, as the tourism sector is seen as the main economic activity and instrument for economic and regional development, generating both employment and income through its direct, indirect and induced impacts, and thus contributing to national economies and GDP. In 12 UNWTO Member States (8%) there is a Ministry of Tourism and Commerce, Trade or Industry as '[e]xport earnings from tourism are an important source of foreign revenue for many destinations around the world' (United Nations, 2020, p. 29). International tourism accounts for 30% of the world's services export and 7% of overall exports of goods and services, while '[f]or around one-third of developing countries, tourism is their principal export' (ITC and UNWTO, 2015, p. vii). In nine UNWTO Member States (6%), tourism and sport come under the same national central administration because they 'can be described as cultural phenomena [and] their common feature is that they all include voluntarily performed activities, deriving from people's somatic and psychological needs with the aim of renewing and restoring their own physical and intellectual energies, which are typically done in people's free time and which contribute to the development of human personality' (Győri and Balogh, 2017, pp. 122–123). In eight UNWTO Member States (5%) the portfolio of tourism is joined by that of infrastructure, transport and civil aviation because there is a strong interrelationship between the air transport sector and the tourism industry (Papatheodorou and Zenelis, 2013) with significant interdependencies

Table 7.1. Typology of religious heritage, sacred and spiritual sites, and experiences

Type of religious heritage, sacred and spiritual site	Examples	Promoted by the public sector (NTAs/NTOs)	Promoted by the private tourism sector
1. UNESCO World Heritage Sites	San Antonio Missions National Historical Park (TX, USA), Writing-on-Stone / Áísínai'pi Provincial Park (Canada), Bagan (Myanmar), Seowon (Korea)	✓	✓
2. Single nodal feature (e.g. buildings, structures, places of worship, monument)	Salt Cathedral of Zipaquirá (Colombia), Baháʼí House of Worship in Wilmette (IL, USA), Gloria dei Church National Historic Site (PA, USA)	✓	✓
3. Buildings and monuments built in fulfilment of vows or out of gratitude for miracles that have occurred, but not used for religious purposes	The statue of Christ the Redeemer (Rio de Janeiro, Brazil)	✓	✓
4. Archaeological sites and heritage: 'any form of archaeological site or individual monument, including earthworks, burial mounds, cave dwellings, settlements (towns, villages, farms, villas), temples and other public buildings, defensive works, cemeteries, routes, etc., that are not in use or occupied' (Jokilehto et al., 2005)	Baalbek (Lebanon), Temple of Apollo, (Delphi, Greece)	✓	✓
5. Burial monuments and sites: (e.g. burial mounds, cairns, mausolea, tombs, cenotaphs, cemeteries) (Jokilehto et al., 2005)	Catacombs of Milos (Greece), Basilica of the Holy Sepulchre (Israel), Catacombs of Rome (Italy)	✓	✓
6. Whole sacred towns/cities	Vatican City (Italy), Lalibela (Ethiopia)	✓	✓
7. Shrine/temple complexes, sacred landscapes (Moira, 2009, 2019)	Angkor Wat (Cambodia), Lumbini (Nepal), Tiruchirappalli Rockfort (India)	✓	✓

Continued

Table 7.1. Continued

Type of religious heritage, sacred and spiritual site	Examples	Promoted by the public sector (NTAs/NTOs)	Promoted by the private tourism sector
8. 'New Age' or 'Earth energy' sites, spiritual retreats, landscapes and camps, ashrams, Kibbutzes, meditation retreats (inclusive view of the world, quest for spirituality, meaning, engagement and peace, personal discovery, self-improvement, and spiritual enlightenment through experimentation with other religious faiths, alternative spiritual schools of thought and philosophies that stress upon 'the sanctity of nature [...] and self-improvement in the realms of spirit, mind, and body' (Timothy and Conover, 2006, p. 139), participating in holistic well-being activities and practices through healing, meditation, yoga, music, chanting, breathing, Chinese medicine, martial arts)	Wiltshire (England, UK), Gaia Tree Healing Center (Peru), Templestay (Republic of Korea), Sedona (AZ, USA)	✓	✓
9. Sacred natural sites: 'areas of land or water having special spiritual significance to peoples and communities' (Wild and McLeod, 2008) (e.g. sacred mountains, sacred lakes, sacred springs, sacred rivers, sacred natural rock formations and rock-art sites)	Mount Yasumandake (Japan), Golden Mountains of Altai (Russia), Taos Blue Lake (NM, USA), Ganges River (India), Quitobaquito Springs (AZ ,USA), Eagle Point, Grand Canyon West (AZ, USA), Devil's Tower National Monument (WY, USA)	✓	✓
10. Sacred islands	Nakaenoshima (Japan), Patmos (Greece), Isla del Sol (Bolivia)	✓	✓
11. Pilgrimage foci-pilgrimage trails/circuits	Char Dham (India), Holy Land (Israel, Palestine), Sri Pada or Adam's Peak (Sri Lanka), Via Francigena (England, France, Switzerland, Italy)	✓	✓
12. Faith-based or themed cruises or denominational conferences on a cruise ship	Christian cruises, Jewish cruises, Mormon cruises		✓

Continued

Table 7.1. Continued

Type of religious heritage, sacred and spiritual site	Examples	Promoted by the public sector (NTAs/NTOs)	Promoted by the private tourism sector
13. Sacred and secular pilgrimage or dark tourism (e.g. visits to war graves, memorials, cemeteries, churchyards and funerary sites, graves and residences of deceased celebrities and sites of loss)	Canberra War Memorial (Australia), Gallipoli battlefields (Turkey), República de Cromañón (Buenos Aires, Argentina), Pont d' Alma and Père Lachaise cemetery (Paris, France), Graceland (TN, USA), Auschwitz–Birkenau concentration Camp (Oświęcim, Poland)	✓	✓
14. Religious or spiritual events and festivals (Μοίρα, 2009, 2019)	Timkat (Ethiopian Epiphany), Diwali (India) Tumpek Uduh (Bali, Indonesia), Kannamesai rite and festival (Japan), Oberammergau Passion Play (Germany)	✓	✓
15. Religious theme parks or contrived attractions	The Holy Land Experience (FL, USA), Tierra Santa, Buenos Aires (Argentina), Creation Museum, (KY, USA), Haw Par Villa (Singapore)		✓
16. Religious/spiritual national parks	US National Parks (e.g. Yellowstone National Park, WY; San Antonio Missions National Historical Park, TX) as pilgrimage sites	✓	✓
17. Volunteer tourism (e.g. evangelism: spreading of the Christian gospel by public preaching, humanitarian missions/tours and humanitarian aid projects: serving the poor, building orphanages, providing medical assistance, teaching in schools)	Missionaries of Charity by Mother Teresa (Kolkata, India)		✓
18. Religious routes (UNESCO, CoE)	Santiago de Compostela Pilgrim Route, Saint Martin of Tours Route, Saints Cyril and Methodius Route	✓	✓
19. Religious objects in exhibition venues, religious art museums, ecclesiastical museums	Museum of the Bible (Washington, DC, USA), Vatican Museums (Vatican City) Shree Swaminarayan Museum (Ahmedabad, India)	✓	✓
20. Religious symbols (Μοίρα, 2009, 2019)	Christ the Redeemer (Rio de Janeiro, Brazil), Virgin of El Panecillo (Quito, Equador)	✓	✓

Source: Authors' own compilation based on Shackley (2001); Bumbaru (2008); Μοίρα, 2009, 2019

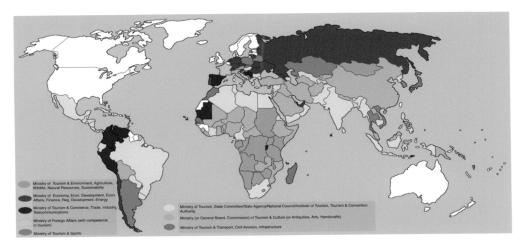

Fig. 7.1. Distribution of Tourism Portfolio in the National Governments of the 159 UNWTO Full Members (as of August 2021).
Source: Authors' own compilation.

impacting destinations, regional development, tourist traffic and airlines. ICAO and UNWTO have recognized that tourism and air transport can play a pivotal role in creating employment opportunities and are committed to ensuring the sustainable development of both sectors (UNWTO/ICAO, 2015). In just two UNWTO Member States (1%) tourism is an integral part of the foreign policy of a country (see Fig. 7.1).

Edgell (1983) has underscored '[t]ourism's ability to shape the political views of individuals and to influence the foreign policies of nations'. For example, on the BBC (2020) website there was an article entitled 'Colombian army rescues abducted Swiss and Brazilian tourists', which has to do with two foreign tourists kidnapped in March 2020 in the Cauca Department, Colombia, by armed dissidents from the former rebel Farc movement. Such an act has both political and foreign policy consequences. Furthermore, the UNWTO (2013, p. 4) has stressed that 'visa policies are among the most important governmental formalities influencing international tourism [and are] acknowledged to be an obstacle to tourism growth'.

In 2021 the New Zealand Tourism Board celebrated 120 years of public service to tourists, being the first nation in the world to formally conduct promotion and marketing campaigns overseas to attract international visitors. It was in 1901 when the New Zealand government founded the New Zealand Tourist and Health Resort/THR (Page and Connell, 2006), the predecessor of Tourism New Zealand.

In the light of the above, a question is emerging: Do these NTAs/NTOs/DMOs have a mission creep, understood as 'the widening of the mission, adopting new ambitions and tasks that distract from the original aims' (Boin *et al.*, 2021)? Can NTAs/NTOs/DMOs no longer be a trusted source of marketing information and services for citizens and tourists because they pursue different ideals through generic and impersonal destination marketing campaigns? Smeral (2006) pinpoints that state tourism marketing is essential to boost international tourism demand because of market failures, which must be remedied, and transaction costs, which must be reduced. On the contrary, Hay (2020) challenges the necessity of NTOs in that they can no longer live up to the expectations and personalized interests, preferences and needs of an increasing number of independent travellers globally whose travel patterns and motivations change incessantly and who have instantaneous access to a plethora of information on tourist destinations and services while searching the internet before making any travel decisions. In addition to this, research results often show that 'state expenditures to promote tourism' through advertising by NTAs/NTOs/DMOs are sure to be disputable because of ineffective marketing strategies (Kotler *et al.*, 2017, p. 537).

The WTO (1983, pp. 4–10) has early on underscored the obligation of national governments to get involved in tourism management in terms of four basic functions: coordinating, legislative, planning and financing. The major task of an NTA/NTO/DMO is 'destination branding', which consists of 'creating a differentiated destination image that influences travelers' decision to visit a destination and conveys the promise of a memorable experience that is uniquely associated with the destination' (Kotler *et al.*, 2017), building up an image, a brand of the country as a tourist destination. This entails two main marketing tasks: (1) formulating and developing the tourist product or products of the destination and (2) promoting them in appropriate markets (Kotler *et al.*, 2017). Other common tasks and objectives assumed by NTAs/NTOs/DMOs (Gee *et al.*, 1997; Borzyszkowski and Marszac, 2011; Kotler *et al.*, 2017; Fletcher *et al.*, 2018) include: monitoring the quality of tourism products and services, regulating the travel and tourism market to protect consumers and prevent unfair competition, careful coordination of government agencies, collecting, analysing and publishing tourism statistics and market reports, providing support for international conventions and incentive events. However, the most important task, which encapsulates all the others, is that of 'nation branding', defined as 'the application of corporate marketing concepts and techniques to countries, in the interests of enhancing their reputation in international relations' (Kerr and Wiseman, 2013, p. 354).

Governments around the world in usual times aim at informing the public on different issues through different channels (e.g. government websites). Robinson *et al.* (2020) underline the fact that public managers encounter more uncertainty and complexity as they attempt to spread information during events featuring controversy such as the COVID-19 pandemic. Under these extraordinary circumstances, NTAs/NTOs as government institutions assumed an extra function which consisted of convincing the public that the travel safety information they provide to domestic and international travellers is reliable and conducive (Mylonopoulos *et al.*, 2016a).

What is paradoxical is that official, formally stated, national policies for tourism are not always advertised and accessible via the websites of NTAs/NTOs, which impedes researchers from evaluating and comparing the components of the different national tourism policies or programmes. Moreover, the functions and roles of NTAs/NTOs differ significantly across countries and destinations. Despite that it seems that some of these NTAs/NTOs remain publicly prized over relatively long periods of time. This is because these institutions functioned as beacons of tourism diplomacy, national and cultural identity, and managed to guard public policy values, understood as 'valued ends embodied in, and implemented through, the collective choices we make through policy processes' (Stewart, 2009, p. 14).

Nevertheless, although most NTAs/NTOs declare their intention to build a country branding, they fail to do this because they rarely promote their tourism products and services and manage their reputation in a coordinated way, which results in a cognitive dissonance in the target markets and audiences (Anholt, 2007, p. 2). Consequently, they fail to develop a competitive identity, which consists of brand management and public diplomacy, coupled with trade, tourism and export promotion (Anholt, 2007, p. 3).

7.3 Marketing and Promotion of Religious and Spiritual Sites and Places by NTAs/NTOs

The travel and tourism industry consists of numerous interconnected actors and forces. In Fig. 7.2 we can see that travellers or individual tourists are at the core of the system while NTAs/NTOs/DMOs or Tourist boards are situated in the second band, the so-called tourism promoters, along with tour operators and travel agents.

NTAs/NTOs/DMOs, apart from their institutional tasks described above, also have responsibilities emanating from countries' (State Parties') accession to/ratification of international conventions or treaties (e.g. UNESCO World Heritage Convention (UNESCO, 1972), Council of Europe Granada Convention for the Protection of the Architectural Heritage

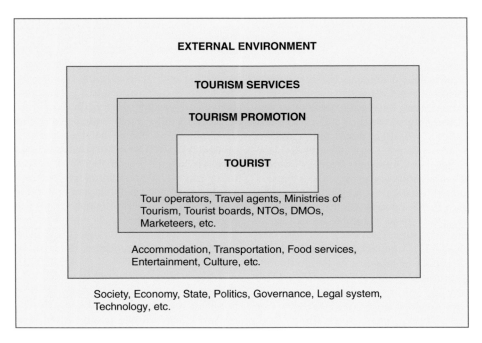

Fig. 7.2. The Tourism System.
Source: adapted from Cook *et al.* (2018, p. 21).

of Europe (Council of Europe, 1985); ICOMOS Nara Document on Authenticity (ICOMOS, 1994)), other international documents adopted by UNESCO Advisory Bodies (IUCN, ICOMOS, ICCROM) and countries' membership to special committees and initiatives (e.g. UNESCO Initiative on Heritage of Religious Interest (UNESCO, 2011); UNESCO/IUCN Guidelines for the Conservation and Management of Sacred Natural Sites [Wild and McLeod, 2008]). These responsibilities include:

- The conservation of spiritual, religious and cultural values and heritage in the context of tourism.
- The development, management, promotion and interpretation of religious and spiritual tourist attractions.
- The preservation of the spirit of a place which is made up of tangible (sites, buildings, landscapes, routes, objects) as well as intangible elements (memories, narratives, written documents, festivals, commemorations, rituals, traditional knowledge, values, textures, colours, odours, etc.) (ICOMOS, 2008).

- The preservation and protection of religious property, sacred sites and natural sacred sites so as to satisfy the spiritual ambitions of the local community and visitors.

It is only over the last two decades that international organizations, national governments and the travel and tourism industry have started to realize and recognize the potential of religious and spiritual tourism and take notice of the rising numbers of travellers who visit different types of religious property and sacred sites. Faith-based tourism, religious tourism and pilgrimage were given high visibility after the UNWTO established a series of international conferences and congresses on both religious tourism and spiritual tourism, advocating their relevance worldwide. These events provide an opportunity for NTAs and NTOs, delegates of religious communities, the private travel and tourism sector and academia to debate and express their views and experiences on the best ways to promote religious and spiritual tourism as an instrument for comprehensive socio-economic development.

Moreover, it is only recently that the global academic community took interest in the systematic study of the religious and spiritual tourism and pilgrimage. For instance, the International Religious Tourism and Pilgrimage (IRTP) Group was launched in 2003 by a lively and research-active group, which organizes annual international conferences, gathering scholars from all over the world, while 10 years later the *International Journal of Religious Tourism and Pilgrimage* (IJRTP) was founded by an international group of researchers (the Institute for Religious Tourism and Pilgrimage).

UNWTO (2019b, p. 7) estimated that in 2018 there were 1.4 billion tourists globally. Travel for other purposes (visiting friends and relatives, religious reasons/pilgrimages, health treatment, etc.) accounted for 27%, less than a third of all international arrivals. This increased interest of the NTAs/NTOs/DMOs emerged mainly due to the increasing purchase power and expenditure of religious tourists and because 'faith-based tourism is quite resistant to financial and economic turbulence' (MTA, 2017). As a result, places of worship and other religious sites have been converted into tourism assets that can be commercialized for cultural and religious heritage travellers. Tombs, monasteries, cathedrals, pilgrimage routes, sacred natural landforms and meditation retreats are used to a large extent in tourism promotion and advertising. Intense marketing of cultural and religious sites coupled with growing liberalization in air transport, has resulted in increasing visitation in religious and cultural sites more by spiritually oriented and curious tourists than by pilgrims (Shackley, 2001; Olsen, 2003). The final product of this commodification of religious/sacred sites superimposes religious space on tourist/secular space, generating a 'duality of place' (Bremer, 2001, p. 3). This inevitably complicates the traditional management practices at sacred sites where the emphasis has been on the special requests of pilgrims rather than other visitors (Olsen, 2006, p. 104). In Fig. 7.3, the various actors involved in the governance, management, protection and promotion of religious, sacred and spiritual sites are identified.

Questions are also raised with regard to the conservation, interpretation and assignment of meaning to kaleidoscopic religious sites, which perform multiple functions simultaneously, as places of rituals and worship, leisure, education and escapism. One of the governments' main tasks is to augment tourism receipts, turning physical and socio-cultural resources which lose their original use into tourism and secular commodities. Tourism promotion becomes crucial in transforming religious/holy/sacred sites destined for worship and contemplation into tourist recreational places for consumption (Olsen, 2006, p. 112).

In order to gain a competitive advantage in an increasingly globalized travel and tourism market, many national, regional and local governments, due to NTAs/NTOs/DMOs' sustained marketing efforts, utilize religious (heritage) and spiritual sites as emblematic tourist attractions to lure travelers from all over the world regardless of whether they are affiliated to a religion or not. Therefore, religious site guardians, government agencies and private-sector businesses, which provide visitor services, must deal with both internal management issues and external factors and stakeholders that play an important role in the complexity of management that is required to keep the spiritual or religious sense of place and the physical structure intact and not distort the original symbolic meaning of the religious/holy site (Olsen, 2006; Amara, 2017). Diverse religious sites and places of worship usually must fulfil competitive and operational strategies to adapt to differing organizational objectives. This could potentially generate conflict among the actors involved. In Fig. 7.4, the different components of the private travel and tourism industry developed around a religious property and sacred (natural) site are described.

In addition to this, the pilgrimage and religious tourism market is fragmented and diversified as there is no agreement among scholars and researchers and international organizations over a universal or commonly accepted definition of this niche tourism market. For example, the World Tourism Organization gives the operational definition of fourteen types of tourism; nevertheless, no definition is provided for religious, pilgrimage, spiritual or faith-based tourism (UNWTO, 2019a). NTAs/NTOs/DMOs can choose whether this form of tourism will be included in their national tourism strategy and the tourist product they offer, how they are going to present and promote their cultural and religious heritage resources domestically and

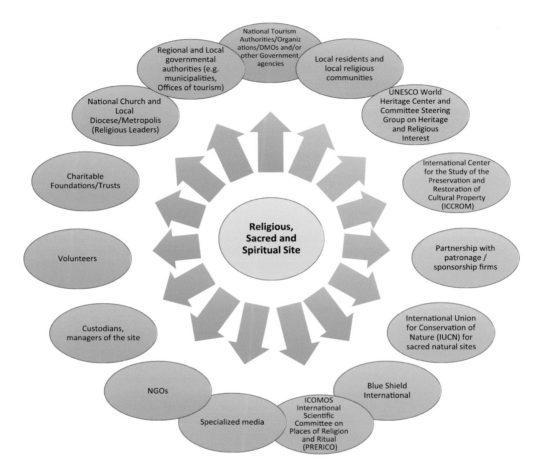

Fig. 7.3. The blurring of governance and management actors involved in the management, protection and promotion of religious, sacred and spiritual sites.
Source: Author's own compilation.

internationally, and thus define religious and spiritual tourism accordingly. Cook *et al.* (2018, pp. 73–74) do not incorporate pilgrimage/religious/spiritual tourism into 'niche tourism' or 'special-interest tourism' (SIT), which is 'defined as a form of tourism which involves consumers whose holiday choice is inspired by specific motivations and whose level of satisfaction is determined by the experience they pursue' (Robinson and Novelli, 2005, p. 13). Smith *et al.*, 2010 classify pilgrimage tourism and religious heritage tourism as subcategories of religious tourism while Robinson and Novelli, 2005, p. 3) places religious tourism and spiritual tourism under the cultural tourism micro-niche.

Rinschede (1992, p. 52) identifies religious tourism as 'that type of tourism whose participants are motivated either in part or exclusively for religious reasons', which is closely linked to cultural tourism. For Μοίρα (2019), culture and tourism create a 'symbiotic' or 'complementary' relationship between two social phenomena: (a) the pilgrimage, where the spiritual element of faith is dominant, and which emerges under appropriate conditions: spirituality, austerity, abstinence, observing the rituals, ongoing interior soul searching, and (b) religious tourism as a subcategory of cultural tourism, whereby the religious element of the site or the event is valorized under tourism criteria as cultural heritage.

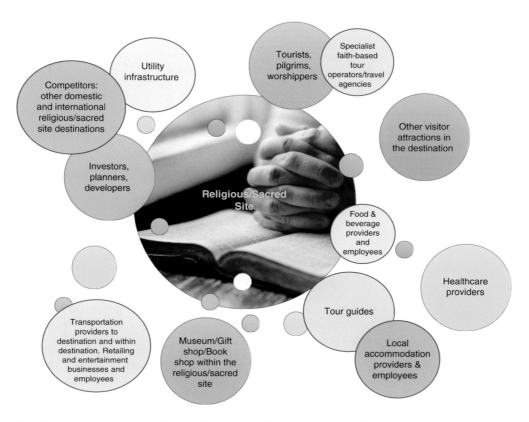

Fig. 7.4. The private travel and tourism industry developed around a religious and a sacred site. Source: Authors' own compilation.

Culture is the joint component of tourism and religion.

Peterson and Seligman (2004) acknowledge six fundamental moral virtues that appear consistently across cultures and throughout time. One of them is 'transcendence', defined as 'strengths that forge connections to the larger universe and provide meaning' (Peterson and Seligman, 2004, p. 30). One of the character strengths under this virtue is 'spirituality', which is composed of religiousness, faith and purpose. Therefore, 'spirituality' is an overarching concept, which encompasses all aspects of religious, spiritual and faith-based tourism, defined as 'having coherent beliefs about the higher purpose and meaning of the universe; knowing where one fits within the larger scheme; having beliefs about the meaning of life that shape conduct and provide comfort' (Peterson and Seligman, 2004, p. 30).

An updated broadened typology of the vast array of religious property, sacred and spiritual sites and experiences, promoted globally by NTAs/NTOs/DMOs and the private travel and tourism sector is suggested in Table 7.1.

The history of attractions is strongly associated with the development of the tourism industry. This is because an attraction is generated when a tourism system is established to designate and upgrade it to an attraction (Benckendorff, 2014). This means that religious and spiritual sites have always existed before they were converted by national governments and international organizations into commercialized tourist attractions. Spiritual experiences on these sites are usually given context and meaning by religious leaders. The particularity of places of religious pilgrimages and spiritual centres is that they 'defy the process of decline' (Singh, 1998, p. 62), suggested by Butler's

Tourism Area Life Cycle Model, which describes the different stages in tourism development over time. Such places with holy shrines (Mecca, Saudi Arabia, Jerusalem's Old City and the Wailing Wall, Israel, Senso-Ji Temple and Meiji Shrine, Tokyo, Japan, Vatican City, Italy) have always been must-visit destinations and continue to attract visitors who crowd into them all year-round or during the celebration of pilgrimages and religious festivals.

According to Collins-Kreiner and Wall 'no place is intrinsically sacred' (2015, p. 695) and that holy/sacred/religious sites are socially constructed, accommodating both pilgrims and tourists, and, therefore, should be perceived as 'simultaneously sacred and secular', that is as 'third spaces', a concept coined by Edward Soja. In Thirdspace 'everything comes together (..) subjectivity and objectivity, the abstract and the concrete, the real and the imagined, the knowable and the unimaginable' (Soja, 1996, p. 57). Thus, these sites can serve multiple contemporary tourism functions and are promoted by NTAs/NTOs and destination planners as tourism attractions, which have been sacralized, that is those that have been signalled as significant, quasi-religious sanctuaries. The role of NTAs/NTOs/DMOs in the promotion of religious and sacred sites as part of the national cultural heritage of a country is very important and there are numerous stakeholders involved in the management, conservation and promotion of these sites, which requires a coordination of their actions (Table 7.2).

7.4 Conclusion

Contemporary National Tourism Administrations/National Tourism Organizations have a very specific role to play and should be reminded that '[i]t is imperative that the concern for tourism development and promotion is returned to its purposes for fulfilling human values and human needs and is not simply left to the goodwill of the market'; therefore, they should not yield 'to the effects of 'marketisation', which has been effected by the dominance of 'neo-liberal' values in much of the global community' (Higgins-Desbiolles, 2006). Nowadays tourism's potential and promise to promote "a cosmopolitan

awareness" that fosters the feelings of respect and interdependency' is more than ever necessary (Higgins-Desbiolles, 2006, p. 1205). Most NTAs/NTOs have realized that religious tourism, pilgrimages and spiritual tourism, apart from their economic benefits, are a significant source of processes which create public value within local communities by allowing regions and local economies to reinforce collaborative processes and rethink human–environment relationships for sustainable tourism development (Romanelli *et al.*, 2021, p. 394).

Despite the global sub-micro trends detected and the individual tourists' tendency to turn away from conventional sources of tourism information, which could potentially compromise the long-standing tourism marketing tasks of NTOs (Hay, 2021, p. 180), we do not agree with the suggestion that an NTO should suspend its global marketing campaigns or that a state should close its NTO on the grounds that NTOs care more about their own survival and rely more on the paragons of nationhood and international visibility, instead of providing services to both tourists and local residents (Hay, 2021, p. 182). On the contrary, NTAs/NTOs are public institutions whose mission is not profit-making but to serve, safeguard and defend the public interest, which has multiple aspects.

The public interest includes protecting, preserving and promoting national natural and cultural heritage attractions (of religious interest) of a country/destination and managing them accordingly. This is a core state responsibility emanating from national law as well as international law or other legally binding or non-binding international texts (e.g. UNESCO World Heritage Convention, Principles of the Cultural Tourism Charter, established by the International Council on Monuments and Sites (ICOMOS, 1999).

Moore's Public Value Framework (1995) focuses on three facets of public management: delivering actual services, achieving social outcomes, and maintaining trust and legitimacy (cited in Mintrom and Luetjens, 2017, p. 171). Many NTAs/NTOs continue to gain recognition for creating public value for considerable periods of time and have built themselves into global brands (e.g. New Zealand Tourism Board since 1901, ENIT-Agenzia nazionale del turismo

Table 7.2. The role of NTAs/NTOs in the promotion of religious and sacred sites in selected destinations. Source: Authors' own compilation.

Country	National tourism authority and role	National tourism organization and role	National promotion of religious tourism and pilgrimage	Stakeholders involved in the management, conservation, and promotion of selected religious and sacred sites
France	Ministry of Europe and Foreign Affairs/ State Secretary in charge of Tourism It promotes and supports the tourism sector through innovative measures suited to the industry's needs. Tourism Sector Committee (CFT) was established in January 2020. Its aim is to jointly design effective tourism policies, working on four themes: – jobs and training, – sustainable development, – digitalization, and regulations and competitiveness	ATOUT FRANCE: It is responsible for reinforcing the country's position as an international destination. It contributes to strengthening the appeal of France as a destination and the competitiveness of its companies, sectors and destinations through various additional actions: promoting France and its destinations internationally in order to increase visitor numbers, championing global French destination brands as a point of entry into France's regions, to encourage a broader distribution of visitor flows, supporting the development of the regions by facilitating the implementation of investment projects, developing a business intelligence platform providing useful information to stakeholders on demand and supply.	Atout France: – Tourism and Spirituality in France (Press Kit 2020) – Tourism and Spirituality in France (Sales Manual 2020) http://www.atout-france.fr/content/tourisme-et-spiritualite	The Sanctuary of Our Lady of Lourdes is managed by: – The Order of Missionnaries of the Immaculate Conception – The Roman Catholic Diocese of Tarbes et Lourdes – Lourdes Sanctuaire-EURL Basilique du Rosaire www.lourdes-france.org Capital: 1.134.990€ – Tourism Office of Lourdes www.lourdes-infotourisme.com
Spain	Ministry of Industry, Trade and Tourism It is in charge of defining the major guidelines of the national tourism policy, in cooperation with the Regional Governments, Local Authorities and the private sector The Secretariat for Tourism co-ordinates three entities at national level: Turespaña, Paradores de Turismo S.A. and SEGITTUR (a state-owned company responsible for promoting research and development for innovation in the Spanish tourism industry).	Spain Tourist Institute (TURESPAÑA) It is in charge of promoting Spain abroad as a tourism destination. It also has the mission of establishing the strategy, action plan and investments for new establishments of 'Paradores de Turismo de España', a network of state-owned hotels mostly placed on protected national heritage locations	Spain's official tourism website Pilgrimage is promoted under the rubric: Routes https://www.spain.info/en/routes/	The Santiago de Compostela Cathedral is managed by the Santiago Cathedral Foundation, presided by the Archbishop. The Foundation runs a Patronage Plan with businesses from the private sector. Examples: – *Hierros Añón*, a company dedicated to the sale of steel products – Compostela Association of Restaurant and Hospitality Businesses – Abanca Bank (Galicia)

Continued

Table 7.2. Continued

Country	National tourism authority and role	National tourism organization and role	National promotion of religious tourism and pilgrimage	Stakeholders involved in the management, conservation, and promotion of selected religious and sacred sites
Greece	Ministry of Tourism It is responsible for tourism policy making and development in Greece. It introduces legislation on tourism, agrees the strategic marketing plan, stimulates investment and works to improve the quality and competitiveness of Greek tourism.	– Greek National Tourism Organization It develops and promotes Greek tourism, within the country and worldwide and implements the Marketing Strategy. – Ministry of Culture and Sports The Ministry is entrusted with preserving the national cultural heritage, including religious sites (e.g. churches, monasteries). – The Synodical Committee of the Holy Synod of the Church of Greece for Pilgrimage Tourism was set up in 2001 with the aim of creating appropriate conditions for the rapprochement and familiarizing people with the holy sites. The Synodical Office for Pilgrimage Tours of the Holy Synod of the Church of Greece is responsible for the promotion of pilgrimage tours in Greece, the development and valorization of religious monuments, the facilitation of the visits, the practices followed and heads delegations of Greek tour operators and travel agencies abroad to promote Greece as a religious tourism destination (Katramados, 2017, p. 223). An MoU has been signed between the Church of Greece and the Greek Ministry of Tourism and a Joint Committee has been established to implement this MoU.	Visit Greece (GNTO's website) Religious tourism and pilgrimage are promoted under the rubric: Religion http://www.visitgreece.gr/en/religion Monuments of religious significance http://www.visitgreece.gr/en/religion/religious_sites Pilgrim's Map http://www.visitgreece.gr/en/downloads/maps/pilgrim_s_map/pilgrims_map – Ministry of Culture and Sports 391 Places of worship in total are presented on its website http://odysseus.culture.gr	Our Lady of Tinos is managed by the Panhellenic Holy *Foundation of Evangelistria of Tinos, which is supervised by the Ministry of Education and Religious Affairs and presided by the Bishop of Syros.* http://www.panagiatinou.gr/eng/ Gross revenue is divided as follows: 10%: Municipality of Tinos 3%: Foundation of Tinos Culture 5%: Apostolic Diakonia of the Church of Greece 2%: Holy Metropolis of Syros The remaining 80% is State revenue. The revenue covers the cost of maintenance of the nursing home of Tinos island.

[Italian Tourist Board] since 1919, Greek National Tourism Organization since 1929, Brazilian Tourist Board [EMBRATUR] since 1966, British Tourist Authority [Visit Britain] since 1969, Atout France [formerly Maison de la France] since 1987). They have also managed to adapt successfully to transformations in both their operating setting (e.g. social media, competing NTAs/NTOs) as well as their authorizing setting (e.g. political power hierarchies) (Boin *et al.*, 2021). These NTAs/NTOs have turned to guardians of public value, that is nationhood, country image and nation branding. During the Covid-19 pandemic, NTAs/NTOs showed that they were adequately prepared for tackling crises and, thus, passed successfully 'the "stress test" of their adaptive capacity' (Boin *et al.*, 2021). They responded timely to the demands of potential inbound and outbound (religious and spiritual) travellers, constantly providing them, through their websites, with official, respected, reliable, accurate and updated information on travel regulations and restrictions and the measures being taken to address the coronavirus, consequently making the case for NTAs'/NTOs' raison d'être.

References

Airey, D. (1984) Tourism administration in the USA. *Tourism Management* 5(4), 269–279. DOI: 10.1016/0261-5177(84)90023-2.

Amara, D. (2017) Responsible marketing for tourism destinations: Saint Catherine Protectorate, South Sinai, Egypt. *Journal of Business & Retail Management Research (JBRMR)* 11(4), 184–191. DOI: 10.24052/JBRMR/V11IS04/RMFTDSCPSSE.

Anholt, S. (2007) *Competitive Identity: The New Brand Management for Nations, Cities and Regions*. Palgrave Macmillan, Basingstoke, UK. DOI: 10.1057/9780230627727.

Baum, T. (1994) The development and implementation of national tourism policies. *Tourism Management* 15(3), 185–192. DOI: 10.1016/0261-5177(94)90103-1.

BBC (2020) *Colombian Army Rescues Abducted Swiss and Brazilian Tourists*. Available at: https://www.bbc.com/news/world-latin-america-53102819 (accessed 13 June 2022).

Benckendorff, P. (2014) Attraction. In: Jafari, J. and Xiao, H. (eds) *Encyclopedia of Tourism*. Springer, Cham, Switzerland, pp. 62–65.

Boin, A., Fahy, L. and 't Hart, P. (2021) Guardians of public value: how public organizations become and remain institutions. In: Boin, A., Fahy, L. and 't Hart, P. (eds) *Guardians of Public Value: How Public Organisations Become and Remain Institutions*. Palgrave Macmillan, Cham, Switzerland, pp. 1–35.

Borzyszkowski, J. and Marszac, M. (2011) Objectives and tasks of national tourism organizations (NTOs): examples of selected European post-communist countries. *e-Review of Tourism Research* 9(2), 47–64.

Bremer, T.S. (2001) *Religion on Display: Tourists, Sacred Place, and Identity at the San Antonio Missions*. Princeton University Press, Princeton, NJ.

Briassoulis, H. and van der Straaten, J. (1992) Tourism and the Environment. In: Briassoulis, H. and van der Straaten, J. (eds) *Tourism and the Environment. Regional, Economic and Policy Issues*. Springer, Dordrecht, pp. 1–10. DOI: 10.1007/978-94-011-2696-0.

Bumbaru, D. (2008) Conserving religious heritage sites: respect for the spirit of the place. In: UNWTO (ed.), *International Conference on Tourism, Religions and Dialogue of Cultures, Córdoba, Spain, 29–31 October 2007 (Documents in English, French and Spanish)*, UNWTO, Madrid, pp. 147–152.

Collins-Kreiner, N. and Wall, G. (2015) Spiritual journeys and their consequences. In: Brunn, S.D. (ed.) *The Changing World Religion Map: Sacred Places, Identities, Practices and Politics*. Springer, Dordrecht, Netherlands, pp. 689–707.

Cook, R.A., Hsu, C.H.C. and Taylor, L.L. (2018) *Tourism: The Business of Hospitality and Travel*, 6th edn, Global Edition. Pearson Education, New York.

Council of Europe (1985) *Convention for the Protection of the Architectural Heritage of Europe, 3 October*, Granada, Spain.

Devine, A. and Devine, F. (2011) Planning and developing tourism within a public sector quagmire: lessons from and for small countries. *Tourism Management* 32(6), 1253–1261. DOI: 10.1016/j.tourman.2010.11.004.

Droesse, G. (2020) *Membership in International Organizations Paradigms of Membership Structures, Legal Implications of Membership and the Concept of International Organization*. Asser Press, The Hague, Netherlands. DOI: 10.1007/978-94-6265-327-6.

Edgell, D.L. (1983) Foreign policy implications for tourism. *Visions in Leisure and Business* 1(4), Article 2, 5–9.

Elliott, J. (1997) *Tourism. Politics and Public Sector Management*. Routledge, London and New York.

Fletcher, J., Fyall, A., Gilbert, D. and Wanhill, S. (2018) *Tourism: Principles and Practice*, 6th edn. Pearson Education, Harlow, UK.

Gee, C.Y., Makens, J.C. and Choy, D. (1997) *The Travel Industry*, 3rd edn. John Wiley and Sons, New York.

Goodsell, C.T. (2011) *Mission Mystique. Belief Systems in Public Agencies*. CQ Press, Washington, DC.

Győri, F. and Balogh, L. (2017) Rethinking the relationship between sport, recreation and tourism. In: Benkő, Z., Modi, I. and Tarkó, K. (eds) *Leisure, Health and Well-Being. A Holistic Approach*. Palgrave Macmillan, Cham, Switzerland, pp. 121–133.

Hall, C.M. (1994) *Tourism and Politics. Policy, Power and Place*. John Wiley and Sons Ltd, Chichester, UK.

Hall, C.M. (2000) Rethinking collaboration and partnership: a public policy perspective. In: Bramwell, B. and Lane, B. (eds) *Tourism Collaboration and Partnerships. Politics, Practice, and Sustainability*. Channel View Publications, Clevedon, UK, pp. 143–158. DOI: 10.21832/9780585354224.

Hay, B. (2020) Are national tourism organisations past their sell-by date? A perspective article. *Tourism Review* 75(1), 170–173. DOI: 10.1108/TR-03-2019-0107.

Hay, B. (2021) The future of national tourism organisations marketing functions – there is no future? *Journal of Tourism Futures* 7(2), 179–183. DOI: 10.1108/JTF-08-2019-0075.

Higgins-Desbiolles, F. (2006) More than an "industry": the forgotten power of tourism as a social force. *Tourism Management* 27(6), 1192–1208. DOI: 10.1016/j.tourman.2005.05.020.

Hollinshead, K. and Suleman, R. (2017) Politics and tourism. In: Lowry, L.L. (ed.) *The SAGE International Encyclopedia of Travel and Tourism*. Sage, Los Angeles, CA, pp. 961–964.

Hughes, O.E. (2018) *Public Management and Administration. An Introduction*, 5th edn. Red Globe Press, London. DOI: 10.1057/978-1-137-56010-0.

ICOMOS (1994) The Nara Document on Authenticity, 1-6 November. Nara, Japan.

ICOMOS (1999) *International Cultural Tourism Charter. Managing Tourism at Places of Cultural Significance, Mexico*. Available at: https://www.icomos.org/charters/tourism_e.pdf (accessed 10 June 2022).

ICOMOS (2008) *Québec Declaration on the Preservation of the Spirit of Place*. Adopted at Québec, Canada, 4 October. Available at: https://whc.unesco.org/uploads/activities/documents/activity-646-2.pdf (accessed 10 June 2022).

ITC and UNWTO (2015) *Tourism and Trade: A Global Agenda for Sustainable Development*. ITC, Geneva, Switzerland.

IUOTO (1974) The role of the state in tourism. *Annals of Tourism Research* 1(3), 66–72. DOI: 10.1016/0160-7383(74)90033-4.

Jamal, T. and Camargo, B.A. (2018) Tourism governance and policy: whither justice? *Tourism Management Perspectives* 25(1), 205–208. DOI: 10.1016/j.tmp.2017.11.009.

Jokilehto, J., Cleere, H., Denyer, S. and Petzet, M. (2005) *The World Heritage List: Filling the Gaps - An Action Plan for the Future Documentation*. ICOMOS, München, Germany.

Katramados, S. (Archimadrite) (2017) Activities of the synodical office for pilgrimage tours of the holy synod of the church of Greece, religious tourism and the contemporary tourism market, *SITCON*. Available at: https://singipedia.singidunum.ac.rs/preuzmi/42792-activities-of-the-synodical-office-for-pilgrimage-tours-of-the-holy-synod-of-the-church-of-greece/3201 (accessed 15 January 2022).

Kerr, W.R. (2003) *Tourism Public Policy, and the Strategic Management of Failure*. Pergamon Press, Oxford, UK.

Kerr, P. and Wiseman, G. (2013) *Diplomacy in a Globalizing World: Theories and Practices*. Oxford University Press, New York.

Kotler, P., Bowen, J.T., Makens, J.C. and Baloglu, S. (2017) *Marketing for Hospitality and Tourism*, 7th edn, Global edition. Pearson Education, Boston, MA.

Lennon, J., Smith, H., Cockerell, N. and Trew, J. (2006) *Benchmarking National Tourism Organisations and Agencies. Understanding Best Practices*. Elsevier, Oxford, UK. DOI: 10.4324/9780080458786.

Magowan, K. (2020) IT governance vs IT management: mastering the differences. *BMC*. Available at: https://www.bmc.com/blogs/governance-vs-management/ (accessed 14 June 2022).

Mathews, H.G. (1975) International tourism and political science research. *Annals of Tourism Research* 2(4), 195–203. DOI: 10.1016/0160-7383(75)90032-8.

Mintrom, M. and Luetjens, J. (2017) Creating public value: tightening connections between policy design and public management. *Policy Studies Journal* 45(1), 170–190. DOI: 10.1111/psj.12116.

Moore, M. (1995) *Creating Public Value*. Harvard University Press, Cambridge, MA.

MTA (2017) Faith-based tourism: scholars and Stakeholders meet in Malta to discuss a 'new' niche market. *Media Release, Malta Tourism Authority October* 17. Available at: https://www.mta.com.mt/en/file.aspx?f=29098 (accessed 10 May 2023).

Mylonopoulos, D., Moira, P. and Aivaliotou, E. (2012) Public tourism management. Case study of the Greek tourism office in Moscow. *Revista Encontros Científicos-Tourism and Management Studies* 1, 160–168.

Mylonopoulos, D., Moira, P. and Kikilia, A. (2016a) The travel advice as an inhibiting factor of tourist movement. *TIMS. Acta: naučni časopis za sport,turizam i velnes* 10(1), 13–26. DOI: 10.5937/timsact10-9902.

Mylonopoulos, D., Moira, P. and Papagrigoriou, A. (2016b) The Travel Advisory as an Obstacle to travel and tourism. Case Study – The Greek Economic Crisis. *International Journal of Research in Tourism and Hospitality* 2(2), 1–13. DOI: 10.20431/2455-0043.0202001.

O'Brien, A. (2011) *The Politics of Tourism Development. Booms and Busts in Ireland*. Palgrave Macmillan, Basingstoke, UK. DOI: 10.1057/9780230348943.

OECD (2017) *Trust and Public Policy: How Better Governance Can Help Rebuild Public Trust. OECD Public Governance Reviews*. OECD Publishing, Paris. DOI: 10.1787/9789264268920-en.

OECD (2020) *Trust in Government*. Available at: https://www.oecd.org/gov/trust-in-government.htm (accessed 14 June 2022).

Olsen, D.H. (2003) Heritage, tourism, and the commodification of religion. *Tourism Recreation Research* 28(3), 99–104. DOI: 10.1080/02508281.2003.11081422.

Olsen, D.H. (2006) Management issues for religious heritage attractions. In: Timothy, D.J. and Olsen, D.H. (eds) *Tourism, Religion and Spiritual Journeys*. Routledge, Abingdon, UK, pp. 104–118.

Page, S. and Connell, J. (2006) *Tourism: A Modern Synthesis*. Learning. Web Case Studies, Case study 2.3W, 2nd edn. Thomson, London. Available at: http://cws.cengage.co.uk/page2/students/cases/2-3.pdf (accessed 16 June 2022).

Papatheodorou, A. and Zenelis, P. (2013) The importance of air transport sector for tourism. In: Tisdell, C.A. (ed.) *Handbook of Tourism Economics. Analysis, New Applications and Case Studies*. World Scientific, Singapore, pp. 207–224.

Pearce, D.G. (2016) National tourism organization and administration. In: Jafari, J. and Xiao, H. (eds) *Encyclopedia of Tourism*. Springer Nature Switzerland AG, Cham, Switzerland, pp. 651–652.

Peters, B.G. (2012) Governance as a political theory. In: Yu, J. and Guo, S. (eds) *Civil Society and Governance in China*. Palgrave MacMillan, New York, pp. 17–38. DOI: 10.1057/9781137092496.

Peters, B.G. (2016) Institutionalism and public policy. In: Peters, B.G. and Zittoun, P. (eds) *Contemporary Approaches to Public Policy. Theories, Controversies and Perspectives*. Palgrave Macmillan, London, pp. 57–72.

Peters, B.G. (2019) *Institutional Theory in Political Science. The New Institutionalism*, 4th edn. Edward Elgar Publishing, Cheltenham, UK and Northampton, MA.

Peterson, C. and Seligman, M.E.P. (2004) *Character Strengths and Virtues. A Handbook and Classification*. American Psychological Association, Washington, DC and Oxford University Press, New York.

Rhodes, R.A.W. (1994) The hollowing out of the state: the changing nature of the public service in Britain. *The Political Quarterly* 65(2), 138–151. DOI: 10.1111/j.1467-923X.1994.tb00441.x.

Richter, L.K. (1983) Tourism politics and the political science. A case of not so benign neglect. *Annals of Tourism Research* 10(3), 313–335.

Richter, L.K. (2009) Power, politics, and political science: the politicization of tourism. In: Jamal, T. and Robinson, M. (eds) *The SAGE Handbook of Tourism Studies*. Sage, London, pp. 188–202.

RIDEA (2019) *The Eventual Accession of Kosovo to the United Nations Specialized Agencies: Procedures and Prospects*. Research Institute of Development and European Affairs, Prishtinë.

Rieger, M.O. and Wang, M. (2021) Trust in government actions during the COVID-19 crisis. *Social Indicators Research* 159, 967–989.

Rinschede, G. (1992) Forms of religious tourism. *Annals of Tourism Research* 19(1), 50–67.

Robinson, M. and Novelli, M. (2005) Niche tourism: an introduction. In: Novelli, M. (ed.) *Niche Tourism: Contemporary Issues, Trends and Cases. Elsevier Butterworth-Heinemann*, Oxford, UK, pp. 1–13.

Robinson, S.E., Ripberger, J.T., Gupta, K., Ross, J.A., Fox, A.S. *et al.* (2020) The relevance and operations of political trust in the COVID-19 pandemic. *Public Administration Review* 81(6), 1110–1119. DOI: 10.1111/puar.13333.

Romanelli, M., Gazzola, P., Grechi, D. and Pollice, F. (2021) Towards a sustainability-oriented religious tourism. *Systems Research and Behavioral Science* 38(3), 386–396. DOI: 10.1002/sres.2791.

Shackley, M. (2001) *Managing Sacred Sites. Service Provision and Visitor Experience.* Continuum, London and New York.

Singh, S. (1998) Probing the produce life cycle further. *Tourism Recreation Research* 23(2), 61–63.

Smeral, E. (2006) Aspects to justify public tourism promotion: an economic perspective. *Tourism Review* 61(3), 6–14.

Smith, M., Macleod, N. and Robertson, M. (2010) *Key Concepts in Tourist Studies.* Sage, London. DOI: 10.4135/9781446251027.

Soja, E.W. (1996) *Thirdspace: Journeys to Los Angeles and Other Real-and-Imagined Places.* Blackwell Publishers, Malden, MA and Oxford, UK.

Stewart, J. (2009) *Public Policy Values.* Palgrave Macmillan, Basingstoke, UK.

Timothy, D.J. and Conover, P.J. (2006) Nature religion, self-spirituality and new age tourism. In: Timothy, D.J. and Olsen, D.H. (eds) *Tourism, Religion and Spiritual Journeys.* Routledge, London, pp. 139–155.

United Nations (2020) *World Economic Situation and Prospects 2020.* UN, New York.

UNESCO (1972) Convention Concerning the Protection of the World Cultural and Natural Heritage. In: *adopted by the General Conference at its seventeenth session* (16 November, Paris, France).

UNESCO (2011) *Thematic Initiative on Heritage of Religious Interest.* World Heritage Centre, Paris, France.

UNWTO (2013) *Tourism Visa Openness Report: Visa Facilitation as Means to Stimulate Tourism Growth,* 2nd edn. UNWTO, Madrid.

UNWTO (2019a) *UNWTO Tourism Definitions.* UNWTO, Madrid.

UNWTO (2019b) *International Tourism Highlights (2019 Edition).* UNWTO, Madrid.

UNWTO/ICAO (2015) *Medellín Statement on Tourism and Air Transport for Development.* Medellín, Colombia. Available at: https://www.icao.int/sustainability/Documents/Declarations%20and%20 Statements/UNWTO_ICAO_medellin_statement.pdf (accessed 10 June 2022).

Wild, R. and McLeod, C. (eds) (2008) *Sacred Natural Sites: Guidelines for Protected Area Managers.* IUCN, Gland, Switzerland.

WTO (1983) Report of the Secretary General on the Execution of the General Programme of Work for the Period 1982–1983: "The Framework of the State's Responsibility for the Management of Tourism". In: *Addendum (B.1.4.), General Assembly, Fifth Session, 13–14 October.* New Delhi, India.

Μοίρα, Π. (2009) *Θρησκευτικός Τουρισμός [Religious Tourism].* Interbooks, Αθήνα [in Greek].

Μοίρα, Π. (2019) *Θρησκευτικός Τουρισμός Και Προσκύνημα [Religious Tourism and Pilgrimage].* Φαίδιμος, Αθήνα [in Greek].

Μυλωνόπουλος, Δ. and Κοντουδάκη, Α. (2011) In: *Επικοινωνιακή Πολιτική Στο Δημόσιο Τομέα Του Τουρισμού. Στρατηγικές Και Τεχνικές Στα Κράτη-Μέλη Της Ευρωπαϊκής Ένωσης, [Communication Policy in the Public Tourism Sector. Strategies and Techniques in the Member States of the European Union].* Π. Μοίρα (επιμ). Ανοικτή Βιβλιοθήκη, Αθήνα [in Greek].

8 'Ministries of Religion' in Western Democracies: Model of Fragmented Religious Tourism Governance

Dino Bozonelos[1]*, Elisa Piva[2] and Stephania Cerutti[3]
[1]*Department of Political Science, California State University, San Marcos, USA;*
[2]*Department of Economics and Business Studies, University of Piemonte Orientale, Vercelli, Italy;* [3]*Department of Sustainable Development and Ecological Transition of the University of Eastern Piedmont, Vercelli, Italy*

Abstract

Even though religious activities are still an important aspect of society in Western style democracies, the surprising fact remains that for most Western democracies, 'affairs of the church' are largely subsumed under the regulatory authority of other ministries. For most democracies, the needs of religious communities are tied to the ministries of interior, justice or culture. Regarding religious tourism governance, it is tied to the ministries of economics or tourism authorities. This contrasts with other countries, particularly less secular Muslim-majority countries, where specific ministries of religion exist for explicit government action and intervention. This chapter discusses a model of fragmented religious tourism governance where governmental authority for EU countries is fragmented for religious activities and largely separated for religious tourism. Finally, we include a case study of Italy to contextualize the path developmental process of 'ministries of religion'. The New Concordat regulates relations between the state and church in Italy, including access to religious sites for tourists and pilgrims. Italy largely illustrates how most EU governments manage religious activities and religious tourism.

8.1 Introduction

Religious activities are still an important aspect of society in European democracies. Despite the decrease in individual religious practice and a turn towards secularism, a large majority of Europeans still claim a religious identity. 70% of Europeans self-identify as Christian according to Sägesser *et al.* (2018), though recent Eurobarometer surveys suggest that this number is close to 50%, with wide variances among Member States (European Commission, 2021). Still, Sägesser *et al.* (2018) note that a growing number of Europeans now see their religion more as part of their cultural identity, rather than as a practicing faith. Europeans may not attend church or pray on a regular basis, or even profess a belief in God, but they still celebrate major religious holidays, and incorporate religious ideals in their daily lives.

In addition, religious freedom, religious association and financial support of organized religion are encoded in EU law. All three European institutions, the EU, the Council of Europe (CoE) and the Organization for the Cooperation and Security in Europe (OSCE)

*Corresponding author: dbozonelos@csusm.edu

© CAB International 2023. *The Politics of Religious Tourism* (eds D. Bozonelos and P. Moira)
DOI: 10.1079/9781800621732.0008

recognize the relevance of religion in Europe, given the historical and cultural dimensions discussed above. A good example is Article 10 of the EU Charter of Fundamental Rights, which states (EU Charter of Fundamental Rights, 2007),

> ...Everyone has the right to freedom of thought, conscience and religion. This right includes freedom to change religion or belief and freedom, either alone or in community with others and in public or in private, to manifest religion or belief, in worship, teaching, practice and observance. (Official Journal of the European Union C 303/17)

Doe (2011) suggests that the EU has developed seven distinct perspectives on religion: (1) the value of religion and of non-religion; (2) subsidiarity, or the principle that national religious affairs are primarily the concern of each Member State; (3) religious freedom; (4) religious equality and non-discrimination; (5) the autonomy of religious associations; (6) cooperation with religion; and (7) the special protection of religion by means of privileges and exemptions – principles that may be induced from their laws and other regulatory instruments. These perspectives are considered a foundation for a common legal foundation for religion in the EU and are considered an integral part of any democratic state.

Finally, there has been a trend worldwide towards increased religiosity. Religiosity is defined by Macaluso and Wanat (1979) as '... the strength of a person's attachment to organized religion'. Juergensmeyer (1993) first wrote about how this rise would affect countries in the early 1990s. The author claimed that the rise of religion, and specifically religious nationalism, is a direct response to the perceived failure of 'Western, secular nationalist movements'. This trend has become much more evident in regions such as the Middle East, India and in sub-Saharan Africa. This trend is also evident in Eastern European countries, especially in the Visegrad countries of Hungary, Poland, Czech Republic and Slovakia, which are Member States of the EU. Bakke and Sitter (2022) note that populist parties in these countries, such as Fidesz in Hungary and the Law and Justice Party in Poland (PiS), intentionally incorporate Christian nationalism into their electoral platforms. They promote policies that are antithetical to religious pluralism and are often cited as evidence for democratic backsliding.

8.2 'Ministries of Religion'

Despite the continued importance of religion in European policy and society, and ostensibly the development of principles of religious freedom and autonomy, 'affairs of the church' are often treated as third order concerns. First order concerns include security, foreign policy and military readiness. Second order concerns involve economic issues, such as trade, central bank decisions and structural features, such as unemployment. Third order concerns contain everything else, from culture to religion to sports to art. These levels of concern are born out of theories in international relations, such as realism and liberalism. Realists focus on power politics, or the desire by states to attain and preserve power, with a right to exercise power when needed. For realists, religion is mostly understood as a potential resource for power (Mingst and McKibben, 2021). For liberalists, economics, political, social and environmental topics are also first order issues. Economic interdependence is the key, where cooperation will lead to mutual gains (Matthews and Callaway, 2017). Religion is not considered one of the primary issues of concern.

McCrea (2010) bluntly states, 'religion has not generally been seen as a central concern of the European Union' (p. 1). This is somewhat puzzling as most Europeans still identify with a religion, and about a third indicate that religion is important in their lives. These numbers are highest in Cyprus, Italy, Slovakia, Bulgaria, Poland and Romania, and lowest in Sweden, Luxembourg, Denmark, Germany, Finland, France, Belgium and Ireland (European Commission, 2021). Lastly, there has been a general trend of using religion as a vehicle for nationalism, especially in Eastern Europe. The evidence that religious affairs are third order or non-central concerns is easily observable in the European context. For example, we see that authority of religious affairs within EU Member States is scattered, with some governance tied to ministries of the interior, whereas others are tied to ministries of culture. More often, governance is fragmented, with multiple ministries retaining authority over religious affairs.

Table 8.1 breaks down the EU Member State governance over religious affairs. The table is based on the 2020 U.S. Department of State Report on Religious Freedom, particularly Section II that described the legal framework for each country. Sometimes, the report would list several ministries for one country. This problem was solved by looking up the ministries, websites and searching specifically for lower-level entities that directly governed or addressed religious affairs. Table 8.1. shows that religious governance is fragmented in Europe. Some countries assign religious affairs to the ministry of interior, whereas other countries locate this authority in their ministries of justice. Still others are in the ministry of culture. Another grouping of countries has sub-ministry bodies, such as commissions, offices, and/or registries that manage religious affairs.

Only Denmark and Greece have religious affairs at ministry level importance. For example, Greece has a Ministry of Education and Religious Affairs. All recognized religious groups in the country fall under the jurisdiction of the ministry. They are required to register with the ministry and all permits to operate a place of worship must be approved by ministry officials. This includes the dominant religion, Orthodox Christianity, which is enshrined in the Greek Constitution as the 'prevailing religion' (Mylonopoulos *et al.*, 2009). The ministry may also appoint members to the board of directors of a religious site, as they did with the planned construction of a mosque in Athens. The ministry is organized into two directorates: a Directorate of Religion Administration and a Directorate of Religion Education and Inter-religion Relations. There is also a Department of Muslim Affairs, which has jurisdiction over the affairs of the Muslim minority in Thrace. The minority group is protected under the 1923 Treaty of Lausanne (Gemi, 2019).

Denmark locates its religious governance in the Ministry of Ecclesiastical Affairs. The ministry historically has the right to recognize and approve the status of religious communities, though there is no national registration system (Doe, 2011). Ministry officials also retain the authority to approve religious clergy (Kirkeministeriet, 2022). A three-tier system

of recognition of a religious group existed for decades, with 11 groups formally recognized through royal decree consisting of the top tier. Within this tier, the Evangelical Lutheran Church in Denmark, more commonly referred to as the Church of Denmark, is considered the 'state' church. This designation affords the Church an exclusive place in Danish society, which is in recognition of the over 1200 year history of the Church in the country. The Church enjoys special privileges, and the Danish Constitution details the relationship between the Church and the state, specifically regarding its autonomy and the state Church tax (Christensen, 2017).

In 2018, the three-tier system was reformed. A single process for recognition now exists. However, a group must still be recognized through ministerial decree. A more contentious change is the introduction of a legal framework that allows the ministry to revoke the status of a religious community. In essence, the ministry can deregister a group through decree as well. For example, in the new single process, the religious group must not 'encourage or do anything that violates the provisions of the law or regulations laid down by the law' (Vinding, 2019, p. 93).

This rather convoluted approach to domestic religious affairs contrasts with other countries, particularly with Muslim-majority countries. Most Muslim-majority countries have dedicated Ministries of Religious Affairs, or Ministries of Awqaf or endowments. In Islamic tradition, believers can donate a fixed asset, such as a building or real estate, in perpetuity for religious use. These are referred to as waqfs and have an important role in maintaining religion within society. The exception appears to be former Soviet countries, where state commissions on religious affairs appear to be the main governing entities. In addition, there are two notable non-Muslim countries with dedicated ministries. The first is India, which has a Ministry of Minority Affairs. Created in 2006, this entity manages the affairs of religious minorities such as Muslims, Christians, Sikhs, Buddhists, Parsis and Jains. Finally, Israel has a Ministry of Religious Services, which supervises Jewish religious affairs. These include religious facilities and services, educational institutions including yeshivas and management of Jewish holy places.

Table 8.1. Ministries of religion.

Country	Ministry	Country	Ministry
Austria	Office of Religious Affairs – Federal Chancellery	Italy	Ministry of Interior
Belgium	Ministry of Justice	Latvia	Ministry of Justice, Ecclesiastical Council[1]
Bulgaria	Directorate for Religious Affairs under the Council of Ministers	Lithuania	Ministry of Justice (Commission for the Activities of Religious, Esoteric and Spiritual Groups)
Croatia	Ministry of Justice and Administration (Register of Religious Communities)	Luxembourg	Ministry of State Ministry for Religious Affairs (position currently held by the PM)
Cyprus	Ministry of Interior	Malta	Ministry for Inclusion and Social Wellbeing (Office of the Commissioner for Voluntary Organizations)
Czech Republic	Ministry of Culture (Department of Churches)	Netherlands	Ministry of Justice and Security[2]
Denmark	Ministry of Ecclesiastical Affairs	Poland	Ministry of Interior and Administration
Estonia	Ministry of Interior	Portugal	Ministry of Justice (Religious Freedom Commission)
Finland	Ministry of Education and Culture	Romania	Ministry of Interior, State Secretariat for Religious Affairs, under the Office of the Prime Minister
France	Ministry of Interior	Slovakia	Ministry of Culture (Department of Church Affairs)
Germany	Federal Ministry of the Interior (Building and Community)	Slovenia	Ministry of Culture (Office for Religious Communities)
Greece	Ministry of Education and Religious Affairs	Spain	Registry of Religious Entities, Ministry of the Presidency[3]
Hungary	Ministry of Human Capacities (The Minister of State for Church, Minority and Non-Governmental Relations)	Sweden	Ministry of Culture
Ireland	Department of Foreign Affairs, Department of Justice, Department of Education and Skills		

Source: Authors' own work.
[1]An advisory body established by law and chaired by the Prime Minister that meets on an ad hoc basis to comment and provide recommendations on religious issues.
[2]There is no official body, agency or department in the state that deals with religion with the exclusion of others. Every government minister and their department will need to take religion into account in the area of its competence.
[3]In January, the government moved responsibility for religious issues from the Ministry of Justice to the Ministry of the Presidency, Relations with Parliament, and Democratic Memory (Ministry of the Presidency).

If religious activities are a third order concern for EU governments, then where does governance of religious tourism fit in? For this chapter, religious tourism is used as an encompassing term to describe all forms of religious travel, including pilgrimage. An argument can be made that religious tourism could be a fourth order concern by policy makers. Even less attention is paid to an important and growing industry. Again, this is somewhat puzzling as tourism has an important role for many European countries. Countries long ago developed National Tourism Organizations, which included religious tourism (Hall, 1994). Tourism is also a major driver of economic development, and brings much needed infrastructure to areas in need. This might be more relevant with religious tourism, where sacred sites are sometimes located outside of city centres and/or coastlines (Trono, 2015). Before the COVID-19 pandemic, tourism was the third largest economic activity in the European Union, right behind trade and construction (European Parliament, 2015). For some countries, it is seen as the engine that will restart their economies.

The above discussion presents a puzzle. There is clearly a continuing importance of religion in EU countries. In addition, there is a recognized importance of tourism, including religious tourism, as an industry in the EU. This has led us to our main research question: *Why is religious tourism not more prominent in EU member-state governance structures?* This question has practical implications for European countries, particularly the poorer countries and regions on the periphery that are more dependent on tourism.

8.2.1 Model of fragmented religious tourism governance

Government oversight of religion and religious tourism sites in Europe is fragmented. Sägesser *et al.* (2018) states:

> ...the institutional role assigned to religions in EU countries, comes in many shapes and forms, whether in matters of financing or status (recognition, registration, different kinds of conventions, etc.). The weight of each country's individual history plays a key role here, based on the evolution of the nation building process.

Consequently, no dominant model can be singled out, and Europe remains characterized by a patchwork of solutions that are often all but compatible and comparable.

Does it matter? We argue that a fragmented 'model' of religious tourism governance can hinder solutions addressing both supply and demand issues. We use the term 'model' here to denote an underlying theoretical argument and not necessarily opportunities for experimentation. The growth in global tourism has directly contributed to an increasing demand for visits to churches and cathedrals, shrines, festivals and other religious events. In addition, there has been an effort to better develop and market sacred sites, with an increase in the supply of both religious sites and pilgrimage routes. Table 8.2 documents the fragmented governance of religious tourism in the EU.

8.2.2 Secularism and its effect on governance

What can explain the fragmented approach to governance and religious affairs? The potential causal mechanism is the institutionalization of secularization principles within Europe (Doe, 2011). Secularism generally means the exclusion of religion from society. Taylor (2007) describes three broad but interconnected phenomena that have led to secularism. The first trend is the steady decline of religion in the public square, or its fading from civil society. The second trend is the waning of church attendance. The third is a reconceptualization of belief, which is disconnected from established understandings. This background allows for secular policy to develop through indifference, which appears to be the case in Northern Europe, where citizens are the least likely to identify or practice their religion. Or it can happen more forcefully where governments specifically seek to minimize or reject religion altogether, such as what is seen in France, Belgium, Albania, and in Turkey before 2003.

Still, there is no doubt that secularization has largely succeeded in formally separating church and state in Europe. There were three historical developments that have ensconced secularism in Europe. The first has been France's policy of laïcité, where in 1905 the

D. Bozonelos *et al.*

Table 8.2. 'Ministries' of Religious Tourism?

Country	Ministry	Country	Ministry
Austria	Federal Ministry of Agriculture, Regions and Tourism	Italy	Ministry of Cultural Heritage, Activities and Tourism
Belgium	Ministry of Justice and Enforcement, Environment and Spatial Development, Energy and Tourism	Latvia	Ministry of Economics
Bulgaria	Ministry of Tourism (National Tourism Council)	Lithuania	Ministry of Economy and Innovation (Tourism Policy Division)
Croatia	Ministry of Tourism	Luxembourg	Ministry of Tourism
Cyprus	Deputy Ministry of Tourism	Malta	Ministry for Tourism and Consumer Protection
Czech Republic	Ministry of Regional Development (Tourism Dept)	Netherlands	Ministry of Economic Affairs and Climate Policy (Netherlands Board of Tourism and Conventions (NBTC) Holland Marketing)
Denmark	Ministry of Industry, Business and Financial Affairs	Poland	Ministry of Economic Development (Polish Tourism Organization)
Estonia	Ministry of Economic Affairs and Communications	Portugal	Ministry of Economy *(Turismo de Portugal)*
Finland	Ministry of Economic Affairs and Employment	Romania	Ministry of Economy, Energy and Business Environment (Consultative Council for Tourism)
France	Ministry of Europe and Foreign Affairs	Slovakia	Ministry of Transport and Construction
Germany	Federal Ministry for Economic Affairs and Energy	Slovenia	Ministry of Economic Development and Technology
Greece	Ministry of Tourism	Spain	Ministry of Industry, Trade and Tourism (State Secretariat for Tourism)
Hungary	Cabinet Office of the Prime Minister (Hungarian Tourism Agency)	Sweden	Swedish Agency for Economic and Regional Growth – *Tillväxtverket*
Ireland	Department of Transport, Tourism and Sport (Tourism Division)		

Source: The authors.

government removed religion from the public square. Laïcité affirms that France is a secular republic and that there is a strict separation between the government and all religious denominations (Zwilling, 2017). In countries that practice laïcité, religion does not receive any legal establishment, the state must be neutral in religious matters, the church is located entirely within the private sector and the principle of secularism must be respected within all public spheres (Sinno, 2008; Soper *et al.*, 2017; Messner, 2019).

France's strict separation of church and state has influenced the development of EU policy towards religious governance. Willaime (2010) writes about a consistent tension between religion and politics within Europe. He contends that 'the separation of politics and law from religion, is at the heart of Europe's identity' (p. 18). Laïcité is thought of as the embodiment of secularism and as an eventual model for state–church governance in Europe. For some scholars, laïcité is not just a French value, but a European value and that should frame the role of religion in the public square. It has become a governing principle in international relations where privatization of religion is the normative expectation (Hurd, 2008). This can help explain the diversity of approaches to governance. As each EU member state has a different relationship with its religious past, there will continue to be a lack of a unified EU approach.

The second historical development was the proclamation of atheism as official policy in Communist Eastern Europe after WWII. Communist governments often repressed religious worship. Educational facilities taught religion was an artefact of the past. Marx, Engels and Lenin were frequently cited, 'Man creates religion, and not vice-versa', and 'religion presents a distorted consciousness of the world' (Marx, 1978). In addition, modernization policies were designed to enhance the power of secular forces, such as the government, over the old social order (Zrinščak, 2004). Repression,

education and urbanization led to a different form of secularism in Eastern Europe. Unlike France where a distinction existed between public and private, Communist governments chose not to respect a person's privacy and autonomy. This led to situation where secularism was considered a largely successful endeavour by the fall of the Berlin Wall in 1989.

The third historical development was the advent of international legal standards regarding religious freedom in the age of globalization. This is evident in the adoption of instruments from the Council of Europe, particularly the Convention for the Protection of Human Rights and Fundamental Freedoms. This eventually led to the approval of an EU Charter on Fundamental Rights in 2010, which incorporated religious rights into the EU's legislative process (Caceres, 2017). Again, this deregulation of believing does not mean that Europeans have become irreligious, more that Europe accepts a more pluralistic future, where deconfessionalism and dechristianization is accompanied by a rise in the number of minority faiths, such as Islam and Hinduism. This push for pluralism through religious freedom has added to the contemporary fragmentation of governance.

All three developments have led to the current mosaic of church–state relations in the European Union. Doe (2011) provides several models that we summarize in Table 8.3. This typology could be construed as on a continuum, even though Doe does not specify as such. On one

Table 8.3. Doe's models of church–state relations.

State–church model	Cooperation model: concordat (Catholic Church)	Cooperation model: formal legal agreement with church	Cooperation model: separation with cooperation	Separation model
Denmark	Italy	Austria	Bulgaria**	France
Finland	Portugal	Belgium	Czechia	Ireland
Greece	Spain	Germany	Estonia	Netherlands
Iceland (non-EU)	Cyprus	Luxembourg	Hungary	Slovenia
Lichtenstein (non-EU)	(Greek Orthodox		Latvia	
Norway (non-EU)	Church)		Lithuania	
Sweden*			Poland	
UK (non-EU)			Romania	
			Slovakia	
			Slovenia	

*Church of Sweden was disestablished in 2000.
**Eastern Orthodoxy shall be considered the traditional religion.

end of the spectrum, there is the state–church model, where the church is provided a special position, either through a constitutional provision or through favourable treatment. In some countries with state–church models, the state exercises a high degree of control, whereas in other countries, state control is at a minimum.

8.3 Case Study

Italy is a great case study from which to understand fragmented religious tourism governance. Italy is a country with a strong dominant religion, as its capital Rome has always been the heart of the Roman Empire and the Holy See of the Catholic Church. Yet, secularism has affected church–state relations, which in turn affect the ways that religious tourism sites are governed. Religious policy rarely evolves in a consistent manner. Rather, it tends to be characterized by long periods of stability, coupled with short bursts of quick transformations (Baumgartner and Jones, 1991, 1993). These rapid changes are often the results of punctured equilibria where the institutional setting changes. These changes can occur from the result of accumulated friction within the institution itself, which is often the result of instabilities within the institution (Flink, 2017). Alternatively, policy change may stem from exogenous shocks. Often a focusing event (Kingdon, 1984), such as a change in government, or a military conflict, may lead to a critical juncture. These junctures provide an opportunity for institutions to change.

Since religious tourism governance in Italy is historically tied to church–state relations, changes in the institutional setting matter. Italian church–state relations can be punctuated through a series of both exogenous shocks and accumulated friction (Mugnaini, 2003). These shocks include the development of a constitution for a unified Italy in the 1800s, when Mussolini assumed power in 1922, the end of World War II in 1945, the 1962 Second Vatican Council, and the negotiation of a new Concordato in 1984. Each of these events was a critical juncture in the secularization of Italy and church–state relations. Each focusing event was an opportunity to incorporate different secularistic conceptions, from removing the Papacy

from territorial and civil power, to the governance of non-Catholic religious organizations in contemporary Italian society (Melloni, 2004). In addition, each juncture permits for modern Italian church–state relations to be divided into five phases, each of which is outlined below.

8.3.1 Catholicism in Italy, the Concordato and the Ministry of Interior

The first phase of modern church–state relations began before the constitution of the unified Kingdom of Italy (Savarino, 2017). In 1848, the Statute of the Monarchy of Savoy (known as the Albertine Statute, from the name of the king who promulgated it, Charles Albert of Savoy) stated that the King must be Catholic (Article 1). This originally applied in the Kingdom of Sardinia, though it was then extended to the nascent Kingdom of Italy during the *Risorgimento*, or the unification of Italy in the 1800s. This 'Roman Question', where popes attempted to retain territorial political and civil power in the new Italian republic took decades to resolve. The papal policy of *non expedit* (i.e. policy of the Roman Catholic Church that prohibited its Italian members from participating in elections) did not prevent Catholics from participating in local elections, or from even having a role in the social life of the country. Italian citizens developed powerful associations, and networks of cooperatives, newspapers and banks. The successors of Pius IX (Leo XIII, Pius X, Benedict XV) continued to maintain the policy of *non expedit*, with some exceptions. In the 1913 election, the papacy feared a Socialist win and Catholics were permitted by the Holy See to vote for the Liberal candidates. However, it was not until 1919 that Benedict XV formally cancelled the *non expedit*. This then led to the Popular Party, recently founded by a Sicilian priest, Don Luigi Sturzo, that had 100 members elected to the Chamber.

The second phase began when Mussolini came to power in 1922. Confidential negotiations between the Holy See and the fascist government culminated in the Lateran Pacts (Margiotta Broglio, 2004). This international treaty led to the creation of the Vatican City State (the world's smallest at 44 hectares), defined Catholicism as the official religion of

Italy, and provided financial compensation for the loss of the Papal States. The Papacy retained temporal power, even if it was only symbolic in some areas. Many considered this a temporary agreement as Italy was a totalitarian state. There was quite a bit of criticism as some Catholics questioned the need for the Church to retain temporal power at all. In the following years, Pope Pius XI's attitude toward Mussolini shifted. He became critical of Italian fascism and the adoption of Nazi racial policies in Italy. Despite this opposition, Mussolini continually sought rapprochement with the Vatican, seeing any effort to unite 'the Tiber with the Basilica of San Pietro' as a success.

The end of World War II led to the third phase of Italian church–state relations. The deputies of the new Italian Constituent Assembly were tasked with reconceptualizing the relations between the newly democratic Italian republic. Many viewed the Lateran Pacts, which came under the fascist Mussolini, as not modern enough and sought changes that were distinct from the previous authoritarian regime. For example, Article Three of the 1948 Republican Constitution guarantees the equality of individuals regardless of their religion. Article Seven formally regulates the relations between the Catholic Church and the Italian state on the basis of two principles: the principle of distinction of orders and the principle of bilateralism (Astorri, 2013).

In addition, Article Eight recognizes that all religious denominations are equally free before the law and have the right to organize without government interference. This article prohibits the government from imposing regulatory restrictions on ecclesiastical bodies, provided that their statutes do not conflict with Italian law. Article Eight also mandates that all relations with the state are regulated by law, based on agreements reached with each respective religious organization. These relations between the Italian government and religious denominations, including Catholic organizations, but excluding the Vatican State, are to be handled by the Ministry of the Interior. The Ministry has the authority to recognize the legal personality of ecclesiastical bodies, the stipulation of agreements and supervision, and to ensure compliance with constitutional guarantees. Article 19 also adds the right to freely profess one's religious faith and practice it, except for 'rites contrary to morality'. Still, despite these changes in the 1948 Constitution, the 1929 Law has never formally been repealed. Even though religious freedom is the norm in Italian society, the Catholic Church and her conservative allies have fought hard to prevent its repeal.

The fourth phase began in October 1962 when Rome announced the Second Vatican Council. The Council represents the most ambitious attempt at modernization in Church history. It led to a rethinking of the Church's place in world relations. For example, the pastoral constitution, *Gaudium et Spes* (GS), or 'The Church in the Modern World', outlines the contemporary social and political teaching of the Church. First, the Church and the political community are independent and autonomous in their own field, and second, both sides must collaborate with each other for the benefit of everyone (Ferrari, 2004). This pastoral constitution reflects the incorporation of the official discourse of laicism in the Catholic Church, even if the document itself did not specifically use this term.

The latest and fifth phase began when the Italian Government and the Holy See subscribed to a new agreement, or New Concordato, signed by the Italian Republic (a government led by the Socialist Bettino Craxi) and the Holy See on 18 February 1984 and ratified by the Italian Parliament on 25 March 1985 (Governo Italiano, n.d.). The New Concordato reflects a revision of the Covenants of 1929, with 'consensual modifications of the Lateran Concordat' agreed to under the Italian Constitution. The document was inspired by the principles of equality and neutrality as expressed in the 1948 Republican Constitution. At the same time, it also incorporated the reformist values expressed by the Second Vatican Council. The New Concordato introduced significant changes in the relations between State and Church, most notably reaffirming the principle of laicism of the state (Rodelli, 1984; Ferrari, 2008). The Catholic Church definitively renounces its status as a state religion and accesses a new system of state funding, based on the division of the so-called 'eight per thousand' of the IRPEF (personal income tax) aimed to guarantee the sustenance of the Catholic clergy (Governo Italiano, 2002).

The new Concordat is best understood as a 'framework agreement' of fundamental principles that regulate the independence of the respective orders of the State and of the Church. The agreement identifies the specific constitutional cornerstones on which to reconstruct the system of their relations and include articulated references to further agreements on specific issues. Each issue can be subsequently stipulated between competent state and ecclesiastical authorities. For example, the first of these agreements involved reform of ecclesiastical entities and assets and of the support system for the clergy. Subsequent agreements included: the appointment of holders of ecclesiastical offices; religious holidays recognized for civil purposes; the teaching of Catholicism in schools; the recognition of academic qualifications of the faculties approved by the Holy See; spiritual assistance to the state police; and the protection of cultural assets of religious interest and of ecclesiastical archives and libraries.

As mentioned previously, the Ministry of the Interior has been tasked with recognizing the legal personality of all Catholic ecclesiastical entities through the requisites established by law (Marano, 2007). Among ecclesiastical bodies, brotherhoods are among the oldest expressions of lay associations, with religious, social and charitable purposes. In ancient times, the vestry boards (*fabbricerie*) were foundations (*fabbrica ecclesiae*) or associations (*Consilium Fabricae*), which dealt with the maintenance and restoration of the churches they were responsible for, often with proceeds from ecclesiastical patrimony.

The Ministry of the Interior carries out its religious functions within the Department of Civil Liberties and Immigration and, internally, with the Central Directorate for Religious Affairs and the Administration of the Religious Buildings Fund. The Central Directorate for Religious Affairs (*Direzione Centrale per gli Affari dei Culti*) monitors the concrete observance of the principles contained in Articles 3, 8 and 19 of the Constitution and the regulations in force, ordinary and special, on religious freedom and regulation of state–religious confessions relations, In turn, this allows for an effective right to religious freedom (Ministero dell'Interno, n.d.).

Conservation and restorations are ensured by numerous interventions, carried out in collaboration with the Ministry for Cultural Heritage and Activities. These activities are financed directly or indirectly through sponsorships. Management is divided into two large areas, one dedicated to the care of the Affairs of Catholic Worship and the other of the Affairs of Non-Catholic Cults. For Catholic worship, relations with the 'Church' are of particular importance, not only for the role it plays in the historical–religious culture of Italy, but also because they are the subject to the guarantee provided for in Article 7 of the Constitution.

The Fund for Religious Buildings (FEC) is a governing body legally represented by the *pro tempore* Minister of the Interior. It is administered by the directorate and supported by a Board of Directors, and at the provincial level by prefectures. The origin of its heritage derives from the laws of the second half of the 1800s with which the Italian state suppressed some ecclesiastical bodies. The Fund's mission is to ensure the protection, enhancement, conservation and restoration of assets. With this aim, publications and exhibitions are organized annually, and are dedicated to the most important architectural and artistic works. The FEC also loans works of art to exhibitions and cultural promotion events of national and international importance.

Vestry boards have the tasks of maintenance and restoration of the churches they manage. This occurs without interference in worship services and accomplished with the proceeds from the heritage administration. Therefore, there is a close correlation between the maintenance and redevelopment of the historical–architectural heritage, widespread and of great value throughout Italy, and its enhancement for tourist use. Within the New Concordato, management of 'ecclesiastical bodies' is legally recognized, as well as any changes (transformations and extinctions) that may take place. Of particular interest are the provisions for the appointment of the Directors of the vestry boards. The 28 existing vestry boards are all connected to churches of significant historical or artistic interest.

Finally, the Ministry has broad power to approve the appointment of ministers of Interior worship in organizations that do not necessarily belong to a denomination that has entered into agreements with the State. Government approval is not aimed at providing legitimacy to the appointment of clergy, but in allowing the ministers to carry out religious services that have legal consequences, such as marriage or baptism. In the Office of Religious Policies and External Relations is incardinated the Observatory on Religious Policies which has the task of examining and investigating the varied realities of non-Catholic cults in the country. Among the aims of the Observatory is a 'consultancy' service both for the interpretation and possible solution of the problems represented by the various Confessions, and for the evaluation of observations and proposals aimed at promoting dialogue with religions. The Observatory carries out other activities as well including, the survey of religious bodies other than Catholic and of new religious movements; interventions to guarantee the right of religious freedom; and issues relating to residence permits and entry visas for religious reasons (Nanni, 2014).

8.4 Conclusions

Our case study of Italy traces the development of church–state governance to better understand contemporary religious tourism governance in Italy. Italy is a country with a strong religious identity, the seat of the Catholic Church. It is reasonable to assume that Italy should have a model of *unified religious tourism governance*, where the State and the Church have a symbiotic relationship. While the country may not have an official 'ministry of religion', it should have something that closely resembles one, particularly given the importance of religious sites as tourist destinations. Tourism is an important segment of the Italian economy, making up 13% of the country's GDP and 14.7% of the workforce (OECD, 2020). Religious tourism is a major sector of the Italian tourism market. There are over 1500 shrines, 30,000 churches, and hundreds of museums, monasteries and convents (Alen, 2017). St. Peter's Basilica is one of the most visited religious destination sites in the world.

However, the governance of religious affairs, and by extension governance of religious tourism is fragmented. As noted in the case study, religious recognition and registration of religious organizations is through the Ministry of Interior, which in turn is divided among several additional governing bodies. Direct religious governance is through the Department of Civil Liberties and Immigration & Central Directorate for Religious Affairs, which itself is understood through the prism of 'religious freedom'. Religious sites are managed through Vestry Boards, whereas the maintenance of these destinations is located in the Ministry for Cultural Heritage and Activities and Tourism.

Italy does a great job of maintaining and developing religious sites and promoting religious tourism despite the fragmented approach to governance. Still, would religious tourism governance benefit from a more unified approach to governing religious affairs and sites? On the one hand, the consolidation of all aspects of religious governance, including religious tourism governance, under one ministry would create a synergistic effect, harmonize policies and reduce friction, particularly the maintenance of religious sites. Ideally, this would require moving much of the governance to the Ministry of Culture, where a Directorate of Religious Governance could be established. Within the Directorate, a Commission on Religious Affairs would replace the regulatory aspects of religious governance, including the confirmation of clerical and religious officials. A separate Commission on Heritage & Tourism would directly regulate religious tourism destination sites.

On the other hand, the inherited politics of Italy may not allow such reforms to occur. Italian politics is strongly regionalized, where regional governments have power of policy implementation. For example, each region is responsible for economic development, a power that is assigned to a central ministry in most EU countries. It is unlikely that the recent reforms of devolution would be welcomed. In addition, the papacy may view a centralized governance authority over religious affairs as a potential threat. While some may presume that Catholic Church interests would dominate a proposed Directorate of Religious Governance, the continued push towards secularization might lead to outcomes that may not favour the

Church. Indeed, Catholic heritage sites may be better served through the various organizations affiliated with both the Ministries of Interior and Culture. In the end, a fragmented approach to religious tourism governance might be the best governance framework for Italy.

References

Alen, B. (2017) Italy: religious tourism on the rise. *Tourism Review*. Available at: https://www.tourism-review.com/religious-tourism-in-italy-is-growing-news5398 (accessed 27 August 2022).

Astorri, R. (2013) Politica ecclesiastica e Chiesa Cattolica. *Quaderni Di Diritto e Politica Ecclesiastica* 16(2), 331–341.

Bakke, E. and Sitter, N. (2022) The EU's enfants terribles: democratic backsliding in central Europe since 2010. *Perspectives on Politics* 20(1), 22–37. DOI: 10.1017/S1537592720001292.

Baumgartner, F.R. and Jones, B.D. (1991) Agenda dynamics and policy subsystems. *The Journal of Politics* 53(4), 1044–1074. DOI: 10.2307/2131866.

Baumgartner, F.R. and Jones, B.D. (1993) *Agendas and Instability in American Politics*. University of Chicago Press, Chicago, IL.

Caceres, G. (2017) Religion as seen by the European authorities, liberty, equality and non-discrimination within the Council of Europe and the European Union. In: Nelis, J., Sägeser, C. and Schreiber, J.P. (eds) *Religion and Secularism in the European Union: State of Affairs and Current Debates*. P.I.E. Peter Lang, Brussels, pp. 51–56.

Christensen, H.R. (2017) Denmark: the still prominent role of the national church and religious traditions. In: Nelis, J., Sägeser, C. and Schreiber, J.P. (eds) *Religion and Secularism in the European Union: State of Affairs and Current Debates*. P.I.E. Peter Lang, Brussels, pp. 193–210.

Doe, N. (2011) *Law and Religion in Europe: A Comparative Introduction*. Oxford University Press, Oxford, UK. DOI: 10.1093/acprof:oso/9780199604005.001.0001.

EU Charter of Fundamental Rights (2007) Official Journal of the European Union C 303/17. Available at: https://fra.europa.eu/en/eu-charter/article/0-preamble (accessed 27 August 2022).

European Commission (2021) Values and identities of EU citizens. *Special Eurobarometer 508 October-November 2020*. Publications Office of the European Union, Brussels. Available at: https://europa.eu/eurobarometer/surveys/detail/2230 (accessed 27 August 2022).

European Parliament (2015) *Tourism and the European Union: Recent Trends and Policy Developments*. European Parliamentary Research Service. Available at: https://www.europarl.europa.eu/RegData/etudes/IDAN/2015/568343/EPRS_IDA(2015)568343_EN.pdf (accessed 27 August 2022).

Ferrari, S. (2004) Il modello concordatario post-conciliare. *Osservatorio Delle Libertà Ed Istituzioni Religiose* 6, 1–11.

Ferrari, S. (2008) Stati e religioni in Europa: un nuovo baricentro per la politica ecclesiastica europea? *Quaderni Di Diritto e Politica Ecclesiastica* 16(1), 3–14.

Flink, C.M. (2017) Rethinking punctuated equilibrium theory: a public administration approach to budgetary changes. *Policy Studies Journal* 45(1), 101–120. DOI: 10.1111/psj.12114.

Gemi, E. (2019) Country report: Greece. In: *GREASE: Religion, Diversity and Radicalisation*. European University Institute. Available at: http://grease.eui.eu/publications/country-reports-and-profiles/#Greece (accessed 27 August 2022).

Governo Italiano (2002) *Servizio per i rapporti con le confessioni religiose e per le relazioni istituzionali*, May 8. Available at: https://presidenza.governo.it/USRI/confessioni/norme/85L222.html (accessed 27 August 2022).

Governo Italiano (n.d.) *Servizio per i rapporti con le confessioni religiose e per le relazioni istituzionali*. Available at: https://presidenza.governo.it/USRI/confessioni/accordo_indice.html (accessed 27 August 2022).

Hall, C.M. (1994) *Tourism and Politics: Policy, Power and Place*. Wiley & Sons, New York.

Hurd, E.S. (2008) *The Politics of Secularism in International Relations*. Princeton University Press, Princeton, NJ.

Juergensmeyer, M. (1993) *The New Cold War? Religious Nationalism Confronts the Secular State*. University of California Press, Berkeley, CA. DOI: 10.1525/9780520915015.

Kingdon, J.W. (1984) *Agendas, Alternatives, and Public Policies*. Little, Brown and Company, Boston, MA.

Kirkeministeriet (2022) *Kirkeministeriet* (The Minister of Church Affairs). Available at: https://www.km.dk/ministeren/ (accessed 27 August 2022).

Macaluso, T.F. and Wanat, J. (1979) Voter turnout and religiosity. *Polity* 12(1), 158–169.

Marano, V. (2007) La personalità giuridica degli enti ecclesiastici e in particolare delle associazioni di fedeli. In: Arrieta, J.I. (ed.) *Enti Ecclesiastici e Controllo Dello Stato: Studi Sull'istruzione CEI in Materia Amministrativa*. Marcianum Press, Venezia, Italy, pp. 175–190.

Margiotta Broglio, F. (2004) La riforma dei patti lateranensi dopo vent'anni. *Quaderni Di Diritto e Politica Ecclesiastica* 12(1), 5–8.

Marx, K. (1978) A contribution to the critique of Hegel's philosophy of right: introduction. In: Tucker, R.C. (ed.) *Marx-Engels Reader*. W.W. Norton & Company, New York, pp. 53–54.

Matthews, E.G. and Callaway, R.L. (2017) *International Relations Theory*. Oxford University Press, Oxford, UK.

McCrea, R. (2010) Religion and the Public Order of the European Union. In: *Religion and the Public Order of the European Union*. Oxford University Press, Oxford, UK. DOI: 10.1093/acprof: oso/9780199595358.001.0001.

Melloni, A. (2004) Il Concordato con l'Italia e gli ultimi vent'anni di rapporti tra Stato e Chiesa. *Quaderni Di Diritto e Politica Ecclesiastica* 12(1), 9–16.

Messner, F. (2019) State and church in France. In: Robbers, G. (ed.) *State and Church in the European Union*, 3rd edn. Nomos Verlagsgesellschaft, Baden-Baden, Germany, pp. 213–238.

Mingst, K.A. and McKibben, H.E. (2021) *Essentials of International Relations*, 9th edn. W.W. Norton & Company, New York.

Ministero dell'Interno (n.d.) *Direzione Centrale Degli Affari Dei Culti e per l'Amministrazione Del Fondo Edifici Di Culto*. Available at: http://www.libertaciviliimmigrazione.dlci.interno.gov.it/it/direzione-centrale-degli-affari-dei-culti-e-lamministrazione-del-fondo-edifici-culto (accessed 27 August 2022).

Mugnaini, M. (2003) *Stato, Chiesa e Relazioni Internazionali*. Franco Angeli, Milano, Italy.

Mylonopoulos, D., Moira, P., Nikolaou, E. and Spakouri, A. (2009) Pilgrimage centers of Greece and tourism development. The legal framework of protection. In: Trono, A. (ed.) *Proceedings of the International Conference 'Tourism, Religion and Culture',* University of Salento and Mario Congedo, Salento, Italy. October 27–30, 2009, pp. 523–537.

Nanni, M.P. (2014) Il pluralismo religioso e la promozione del dialogo: bergamo, a metà del guado. *Critica Sociologica* 190(2), 79–90.

OECD (2020) *OECD Tourism Trends and Policies 2020*. OECD Publishing, Paris. DOI: 10.1787/6b47b985-en.

Rodelli, L. (1984) Il Concordato storico. *Belfagor* 39(6), 721–726.

Sägesser, C., Nelis, J., Schreiber, J.-P. and Vanderpelen-Diagre, C. (2018) *"Religion and Secularism in the European Union Report"*. Centre Interdisciplinaire d'Étude des Religions et de la Laïcité, Brussels. Available at: https://o-re-la.ulb.be/images/stories/RAPPORTS_ISSN_alternative/2397_ORELAZEUZ reportZ2018-09.pdf (accessed 27 August 2022).

Savarino, F. (2017) Riforme e Reforma. Secolarizzazione e chiesa cattolica in Italia e in Messico nel XIX secolo. In: Longhitano, S. (ed.) *La Italia Del Siglo XIX al XXI: Literatura, Crítica, Historia, Cultura*. Universidad Nacional Autónoma de México, Facultad de Filosofía y Letras, México, pp. 135–145.

Sinno, A.H. (2008) *Muslims in Western Politics*. Indiana University Press, Bloomington, IN.

Soper, J.S., den Dulk, K.R. and Monsma, S.V. (2017) *The Challenge of Pluralism: Church and State in Six Democracies*, 3rd edn. Rowman and Littlefield, Washington, DC.

Taylor, C. (2007) *A Secular Age*. Harvard University Press, Cambridge, MA.

Trono, A. (2015) Politics, policy and the practice of religious tourism. In: Raj, R. and Griffin, K. (eds) *Religious Tourism and Pilgrimage Management: An International Perspective*, 2nd edn. CAB International, Wallingford, UK, pp. 16–36.

Vinding, N.V. (2019) State and church in Denmark. In: Robbers, G. (ed.) *State and Church in the European Union*, 3rd edn. Nomos Verlagsgesellschaft, Baden-Baden, Germany, pp. 87–108.

Willaime, J.P. (2010) European integration, *Laïcité* and religion. In: Leustan, L.N. and Madeley, J.T.S. (eds) *Religion, Politics and Law in the European Union*. Routledge, New York, pp. 17–30.

Zrinščak, S. (2004) Generations and Atheism: patterns of response to communist rule among different generations and countries. *Social Compass* 51(2), 221–234. DOI: 10.1177/0037768604043008.

Zwilling, A.L. (2017) France. The struggle for laïcité. In: Nelis, J., Sägesser, C. and Schreiber, J.P. (eds) *Religion and Secularism in the European Union: State of Affairs and Current Debates*. P.I.E. Peter Lang, Brussels, pp. 69–74.

9 The Multiple Scales in the Governance of the Way of Saint James

Xosé M. Santos[1]* and Jorge Olleros-Rodríguez[2]
[1]*Department of Geography, University of Santiago de Compostela, Santiago, Spain;*
[2]*University of Santiago de Compostela, Santiago, Spain*

Abstract

As a cultural itinerary, the Way of St James is formed by a wide network of routes that from different places in Europe head towards the final goal in the city of Compostela. Along thousands of kilometres the Way crosses different countries, regions and municipalities with responsibilities in the management of the route. These public administrations involved in the management of the Way of St James are joined by other actors who, from different spheres, have an outstanding role in the management and handling of the routes. These are international agencies, such as UNESCO or the Council of Europe, associations such as the Friends of the Way and, of course, the Church. This chapter explores the role of these actors, especially the less powerful ones, such as municipalities and associations of Friends of the Camino.

9.1 Introduction

The Camino de Santiago has emerged in recent decades as one of the most important cultural routes. Along its many routes it crosses very diverse territories in which the different states, regions or municipalities have their respective administrative competences. In addition, the church and private associations are also involved, in one way or another, in the decision making and management of the Camino. It is important to be aware of the complexity of actors and scales involved in the governance of the route in order to understand and assess the success of the Camino, but also the challenges it faces. This paper will explore how institutional governance affects the Way of St James.

Since the Middle Ages, Santiago de Compostela has been the final destination of a set of itineraries along which, over the centuries, pilgrims have walked to reach the tomb of the apostle (Fig. 9.1). There is an exhaustive historical bibliography (Stone, 1927; Vázquez de Parga *et al.*, 1948) that helps us understand the character and meaning of these pilgrimages, which became an authentic mass phenomenon in Europe at the beginning of the second millennium. Although this flow of people gradually decreased in volume, first with the split in Christianity with the Lutheran Reformation and then with modernity and the loss of the Church's earthly power, the fact is that pilgrims never disappeared, although they did become almost insignificant. However, the last decade of the 20th century witnessed the beginning of a truly golden age of pilgrimages to Santiago that has lasted until the present day, despite the limitations on mobility imposed by COVID-19. In 1980 only 209 pilgrims were registered in Santiago, in 1993 there were almost 100,000

*Corresponding author: xosemanuel.santos@usc.es

DOI: 10.1079/9781800621732.0009

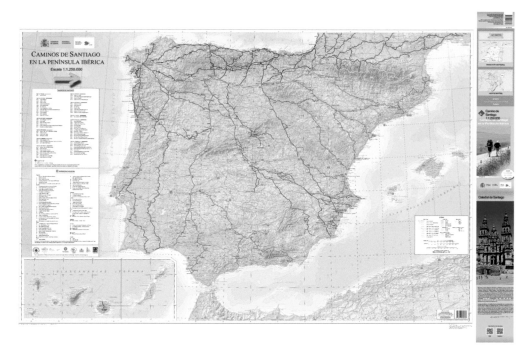

Fig. 9.1. Itineraries to Santiago.

and 347,000 in 2019; however the Covid pandemic meant that in 2020 only 54,000 pilgrims arrived in Compostela (see Fig. 9.2) (Pilgrim's Office, 2022). It is not easy to compare the pilgrimages to Compostela at the beginning of the second millennium with those taking place in this third millennium. The material conditions of life and the behaviour of human beings in their spiritual dimension have changed to a considerable extent. However, the parallels that can be found, despite the centuries of distance, between the two periods, are sometimes surprising.

One of the contemporary characteristics of the Camino de Santiago is its high degree of institutionalization. Beyond the regulations established by the Church to define what a pilgrim is, since the early 1990s the regional government of Galicia has created a tourist brand, Xacobeo, and has progressively developed a whole legislation that regulates the accommodation and the layout of the routes including the areas of protection. In fact, the Galician Cultural Heritage Act of 2016 devotes 10 articles to the Way of St James while revoking the 1996 Act on the protection of the

Pilgrims' Roads to Santiago de Compostela. This Act not only defines what the routes are, but also establishes protection mechanisms that affect, for example, urban planning policies, which depend on the municipalities. Therefore, the Pilgrims' Routes to Santiago are protected by a body of legislation, mainly in the case of Galicia, although it is not the only one.

The interest currently aroused by the phenomenon of pilgrimages and religious tourism in general focuses, in the case of academia, above all on understanding the motivations of those who make these journeys, as well as on the impact generated in the destinations. The large number of existing publications contain interesting research and reflections that help us to gain a more detailed understanding of this resurgence of pilgrimages (Durán-Sánchez et al., 2018). However, questions related to the governance of these routes and the power of the different groups and institutions involved are much less frequent.

Whatever the case, this historical link between pilgrimages to Compostela and power has scarcely been the subject of attention since

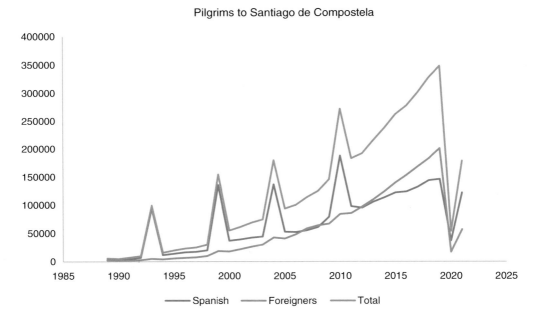

Fig. 9.2. Pilgrims to Santiago de Compostela.
Source: Pilgrim's Office, 2022, processing by the authors.

the 1993 revival. Only in the analyses of Franco's dictatorship (1939–1975) has the close relationship between power and the Church been emphasized, in this case focusing on Franco's use of the figure of the apostle to reinforce ideas about the unity of Spain and its unwaveringly Catholic character (Pack, 2008, 2010; Castro, 2015; Santos and Trillo-Santamaría, 2017). With these notable exceptions, periods such as the rediscovery of the apostle's remains in 1879 or the contemporary boom, which is usually dated to 1993, have not deserved prominent attention from the perspective of power relations.

Focusing on the current period, this lack of interest probably stems from several facts that have diverted attention elsewhere. Firstly, the need to understand how a pilgrimage route of medieval origin has managed to revitalize itself to become a very popular contemporary phenomenon. Second and connected to the above, there has been much insistence on linking the pilgrimage to Santiago with new forms of tourism, the latter being understood as a dynamic activity typical of the most advanced societies (Santos and Lois González, 2011; Nilsson and Tesfahuney, 2016; Lois González

and Lopez, 2020). In fact, if we focus exclusively on 1993, it is easy to see how the multiplication of pilgrims, almost 100,000 compared to very modest levels in previous years, is directly connected to the creation of a tourist offer with the characteristics of an event (Santos, 2016).

Some facts help us to understand this argument. The 1992 Olympic Games in Barcelona and the Universal Exhibition in Seville in the same year stimulated this concept of a great event which, like these two, led to the design of a mascot (pelegrín), a logo and a brand (Xacobeo). Large investments in infrastructures and equipment reinforced the discourse. In addition, a personal relationship was created between the relaunch of the pilgrimages and their political impetus, although the political intentionality was ignored. The leading figure who reflected this idea was Manuel Fraga, president of Galicia between 1990 and 2005. The dominant ideas about his role focus on three aspects: he was minister of tourism under Franco in the golden years of Spanish tourism in the 1960s and, therefore, a person with experience and interest in tourism; he was of Christian Democrat ideology and deep religious beliefs; and, finally, he was a man of very strong character who wished to leave his mark as a statesman.

The contemporary recovery of the Pilgrims' Roads to Santiago was not a spontaneous process. It is true that it was preceded by a historical interest in and curiosity for the phenomenon. However, we can affirm that there is a political intentionality, born of the Galician government and accompanied by legislation that regulates all aspects of the routes. In fact, the 1996 regional Act on the Protection of the Pilgrims' Routes to Santiago de Compostela states in Article 1 that its objective is the delimitation and regulation of the conservation, use and different levels of protection of the sections of the Pilgrims' Routes to Santiago de Compostela that run through Galicia. The regional government, in collaboration with the Church and the municipalities, will activate all the mechanisms for the creation and protection of a tourist cultural offer. Other autonomous communities, the Spanish government, other European governments and associations of Friends of the Way will gradually join this governance.

This personalization of the recovery of the pilgrimage, which also had Pope John Paul II as an *apolitical* figure, diverted the focus of attention towards other readings. In addition, the configuration of the route as an itinerary that crosses different countries and, in the case of Spain, autonomous communities with full jurisdiction in tourism, made it more difficult not only to manage but also to understand the Camino as a unit in which various public and private institutions are involved, sometimes with contradictory interests (Santos, 2017) and in which there are more or less overt power relations.

In this chapter we will focus mainly on the two institutions that are probably the weakest in the system that sustains the Way. On the one hand are the municipalities, which are political administrative units that are the closest to the population and often have to manage a large flow of visitors who quickly cross their territories, and over which they have very little decision making, management and organizational capacity. On the other hand, we will pay attention to the role of the associations of Friends of the Way, which are private and voluntary and often play an important role in the Jacobean culture with very limited means.

9.2 International Governance of the Camino

The different routes that lead to Santiago de Compostela cover thousands of kilometres throughout Europe. In the Iberian Peninsula there are 10 officially recognized routes. In many other countries of the continent we find a dense network of interconnected routes that were used by pilgrims to reach Compostela and that, in many cases, have been rediscovered for the transit of current pilgrims or as hiking routes. This is the case, for example, in France, Poland, Germany and the Czech Republic, to mention just a few cases where the shell marking is evidence of the extent of this continental network of paths. Shell markings are Jacobean symbols that mark the paths for pilgrims to take to complete their pilgrimage.

The international recognition of the Way of St James by institutions such as UNESCO or the Council of Europe means the implementation of actions aimed at encouraging the conservation and promotion of this itinerary. These two bodies do not have direct authority over the management of the route, but their vigilance over the conservation of the property, which is inscribed in the World Heritage List, entails the need to apply policies in this respect, both at national and regional level. Therefore, the role of these institutions is very important not only for the visibility they give to the route, but above all for understanding the governance of the route.

Regardless of the different definitions of the route, the Way of St James must be understood today as a cultural itinerary. This is what UNESCO or the Council of Europe does. This means that we should understand the Way as a unit in which the important thing is the route itself and not so much the final destination, which is simply the place where the itinerary (or itineraries) ends. This is a huge challenge in terms of management because there are many countries involved. In fact, when UNESCO itself recognized the French Way in 1993, it did so exclusively for its route in Spain. It was not until 1998 that it was incorporated as a new element in the so-called Routes of Santiago de Compostela in France, which initially included 64 monuments (cathedrals, abbeys, churches, etc.), seven urban areas and seven sections of routes of *grande randonnée*. Meanwhile, in Spain, four more routes corresponding to the north of the country were added to the World Heritage List in 2015 (UNESCO, 2022b).

In a different way to France, the Portuguese roads to Santiago are also trying to be recognized as World Heritage Sites by UNESCO. In this case, it is a joint action between the two countries, Spain and Portugal, whose initiative corresponds to the Eixo Atlántico do Noroeste Peninsular, a cross-border cooperation organization that develops different projects in the territory of Galicia and northern Portugal. The proposal has been taken up by the Portuguese government and, in the case of Spain, would only affect the Autonomous Community of Galicia. However, if this application is adopted, it remains to be seen whether the management of the routes will be coordinated (Ramos Loza, 2016).

At the international level, it is also worth highlighting the role of the Council of Europe, which in 1987 recognized the Way of St James as the first cultural itinerary, later incorporating other routes. Currently, the Council of Europe has recognized 48 cultural routes (CoE, 2023). The evaluations every three years serve to assess the state of the different routes. Unlike UNESCO, which considers cultural routes as a heritage category regardless of the number of countries participating, the Council of Europe is clearly directed towards collaboration and dialogue between several countries, hence the certification of the routes must include at least three states.

In the case of the Saint James Way, eight countries are involved (Spain, Belgium, France, Italy, Latvia, the Netherlands, Poland and Portugal). This network is articulated through the European Federation of Saint James Way (http://www.saintjamesway.eu/en/), which acts as the managing body. It is made up of representatives of European regions involved in this route. Among the actions it carries out are those of promotion and cooperation in the field of the Way of Saint James in areas such as tourism and culture. Another of these lines of collaboration is related to knowledge. Thus, we find agreements with organizations such as the Compostela Group of Universities, with the associations of Friends of the Way or with the International Committee of Experts of the Way of St James.

If UNESCO or the Council of Europe are relatively new players in their relationship with the Camino, without a doubt the institution that is most obviously connected to it and constantly claims its role is the Catholic Church. This universal institution is the owner of a very large part of the heritage found along the Camino. But it also administers and manages the cathedral of Santiago, which is the final point of the pilgrimage route and where the remains of the apostle rest. Even more importantly, as it is responsible for the delivery and verification of the pilgrim's credentials and the pilgrim's certificate, the Compostela, it sets its rules for those who request these documents.

This means that in order to achieve the *official* status of pilgrim it is necessary to satisfy certain standards not only in terms of physical distance travelled but also in terms of motivation. Hence the published statistics, which are those provided by the Church through a brief questionnaire when the Compostela is received, are so incomplete when it comes to reporting on motivation. It cannot be otherwise because, as specified on its website, to obtain the Compostela the first requirement is 'Make the pilgrimage for religious or spiritual reasons, or at least an attitude of search' (https://oficinadelperegrino.com/en/pilgrimage/the-compostela/).

The fundamental role of the Church can also be seen, for example, in the repetition of the 2021 Holy Year, which is the exclusive responsibility of the Vatican, following a request from the diocese of Santiago. It is true that there is, and seems to have always been, a very close connection between the ecclesiastical hierarchy and political power, and many decisions on both sides are conditioned by these relations. However, what is certain is that the role of the Church is fundamental to understanding not only the religious and spiritual but also the material dimension of the pilgrimage to Compostela.

Despite the international projection that UNESCO and the Council of Europe give to the Way of St James, at the level of the daily management of the route its impact is rather limited. It is true that UNESCO is always attentive to the proper conservation of the route and to ensuring that there are no actions that jeopardize the material and immaterial values that characterize it. Likewise, the Council of Europe, beyond promotion, is concerned with encouraging dialogue and initiatives that enhance the value of this route. However, we maintain, on a practical level, that the leading role in decision making falls to other institutions. The same can be said of the Church which, despite its great influence on all aspects of the pilgrimage, is in fact outside the management of the Way, although its rules, such as the need to walk at least 100 km to obtain a pilgrim's certificate, are decisive in understanding the functioning of the route.

9.3 National and Regional Governance of the Camino

Going from international to national and regional level organizations, we can observe different scenarios. Each country involved in the Way has the capacity to decide on specific policies for its territory, something that was lacking in the institutions mentioned in previous paragraphs. However, at least in the Spanish case, tourism and cultural policies are highly decentralized. This means that the attribution of competences corresponds to the autonomous communities (the political administrative regions). Specifically, the 15 peninsular autonomous communities are involved, as well as the two island communities (Balearic and Canary Islands), which have also been working on the enhancement of their itineraries.

In this complex panorama that includes the 17 autonomous communities, it has been those of the north that have played the most important role in the recovery of the Camino. These northern territories of Spain are crossed by the French, Primitive and Northern routes, i.e. those recognized by UNESCO. In 1991 they set up the Jacobean Council, on the basis of a 1987 Agreement for the recovery and revitalization of the Way, as a body for collaboration between the state administration and the autonomous communities involved. Subsequently, this first decree was modified until its current version, which dates from 2009. Its main objective, as stated in the official document, is to implement the provisions of the UNESCO guidelines on the need for mechanisms to ensure a coordinated management of the protected site, in this case the Pilgrims' Routes to Santiago de Compostela. This coordination has come about

through a Cooperation Committee, an Executive Commission, and a Plenary. In addition there are five working groups, in charge of different tasks in preparation for that specific Holy Year (Consejo Jacobeo, 2022).

In addition to the technical work and other coordination and cooperation tasks of the Jacobean Council, whose president is the head of the Ministry of Culture, at central government level there are also specific policies aimed at the promotion and support of the Pilgrims' Routes to Santiago, especially in relation to the Holy Years. For example, for the Holy Year 2021–22 the Sectoral Commission for Tourism, which brings together the Ministry with the 17 autonomous communities, decided in 2019 to create a specific Working Group for the year 2021. More recently, in 2021, the Spanish Ministry of Tourism passed the National Tourism Plan – Xacobeo 2021–2022, within the framework of the Spanish Government's Recovery, Transformation and Resilience Plan. The aforementioned National Tourism Plan is structured into four programmes with a budget of just over €121 million to be implemented over the next 3 years (Mincotur, 2021).

Although it is not exactly an institution linked to the Camino de Santiago, the Real Patronato de la Ciudad de Santiago, whose origin dates back to 1964 although it was reformulated in 1991, is a body that brings together the government of Spain, Galicia and the city of Santiago to coordinate and promote actions aimed at the revitalization and preservation of the city of Santiago and its cultural heritage. Its executing body is the Consortium of the city of Santiago, established in 1992. The work of this consortium is very important because it is responsible, for example, for a large part of the rehabilitation of the historic centre of Santiago de Compostela as well as the creation of cultural facilities that contribute to the dynamics of the final destination of the Way. At its meeting in July 2021, the Royal Board committed itself to an investment of €281.5 million until the Holy Year of 2032 in different urban, environmental and heritage projects, among others (Consorcio de Santiago, 2021).

As we have observed, despite the fact that responsibilities for tourism and culture belong to the autonomous communities, the Spanish government participates actively in initiatives related to the Camino de Santiago, especially in the holy years. However, it is the autonomous communities that are the most involved because they are responsible for the bulk of these policies. Obviously, the greater or lesser degree of interest is related to the importance they attach to the network of paths that cross their territory. In this sense, those regions crossed by the French Route are particularly involved. This is the case, for example, of Castilla y León with a specific plan for 2021 and an initial investment of €11.5 million for a total of 65 actions (Junta de Castilla y León, 2021). The same is true of Navarre and its more than 40 initiatives or La Rioja (Navarra, 2021).

However, it is the Autonomous Community of Galicia that is the most involved, since it is in this region that all the routes converge at the Compostela destination. It was also the Galician government who created the Xacobeo brand and promoted, in 1993, a whole series of actions and initiatives that had a direct impact on the growth of pilgrimages to the levels that exist today. It is true that the success of the Way as a cultural and religious itinerary has a whole series of antecedents that have little to do with the public policies developed by the Galician regional administration, but it cannot be denied that the influence of the latter has been critical to the consolidation of the route, at least as a tourist product.

There are several antecedents that can be cited to understand the contemporary success of the Camino. Very succinctly, it has been important, for example, in the ideological use of pilgrimages during the Franco dictatorship (1939–1975), which served to reaffirm the status of Spain as a Catholic and European country. During this period (Rodríguez, 2004), the holy years became major events that brought millions of people to Compostela, often channelled by parishes, schools or other types of associations of varying characteristics; in addition, Santiago became a place where the military, political and religious authorities converged. This convergence occurred regardless of the type of political regime Spain had. During both dictatorship and democracy, the figure of Santiago was used to reaffirm Europeanism and the Christian character that defines Europe.

In a different context, the role played by researchers from different countries was also relevant. The historical interest aroused by the Camino stimulated its academic study and even the recreation of traditional pilgrimages. From the beginning of the 20th century we find some interesting examples, such as that of the American Georgiana Goddard King, who published a three-volume work in 1917 on her pilgrimage to Compostela (King, 1920). But it was above all in the second half of the 20th century that works, initiatives and personalities appeared that began to make visible the importance of this pilgrimage route, thus helping to lay the foundations for its subsequent expansion (Santos, 2021). Many of these actions must be related to the appearance of the associations of Friends of the Camino, as we shall see below.

The political decentralization in Spain, with the creation of the autonomous regions, which assumed responsibility for tourism and culture, was a determining factor in understanding the role of Galicia in the revitalization of pilgrimages. We have already referred to the figures of Manuel Fraga and Pope John Paul II. The Way of St James proved to be the perfect excuse to unite tradition, religion, Europeanism, economy and uniqueness. This last concept refers to the need to establish differences with the rest of the autonomous communities but without questioning at any time that it belongs to Spain. The Way would serve to mark the role of Galicia in the history of Spain and Europe, to highlight Christianity as an element of identity, but also to contribute to the economic growth of Galicia.

It is important to consider that in the 1980s the world was already in the midst of a transition towards a service economy, with strong processes of industrial relocation and the disappearance of a large part of industry. In this context, tourism was increasingly becoming an alternative for the growth of cities, regions or countries. Spain's political decentralization was going to allow the autonomous communities to design strategies that were less dependent on the Mediterranean model of sun and sand. In the case of Galicia, rural tourism and, in particular, the Way of St James, constituted the most important offer at that time.

It is true that, at least initially, the Way of St James is not understood exclusively as a tourist product, or at least there are many nuances that give it a certain singularity. In 1991, a public company called Sociedad Anónima para la

Gestión del plan Jacobeo was created in Galicia with the mission of preparing the 1993 event, focusing on the French route. This celebration was understood as a great event, similar to a universal exhibition (Santos, 2016). The enormous success achieved prolonged and diversified its activities. From those initial moments to the present day, we have witnessed a progressive loss of management capacity of this public company. In fact, nowadays it is under the supervision of the Galician Tourism Agency and the objectives of the Sociedad Jacobea are mainly related to the public network of hostels – managed by a private company – to the associations of Friends of the Way and to the organization of events during the holy years.

The loss of relevance of the Jacobean Society is counterbalanced by the growing importance of the Way in the tourism policy of the Galician government, constituting one of its cornerstones, as it appears in the various strategic documents that have been passed in recent years. Even the public network of hostels, initially free or with a symbolic price to give meaning to the traditional concept of hospitality, is subject to pressures for privatization and, ultimately, for the conversion of the Camino into just another tourist offer.

9.4   Local Governance of the Camino

The municipalities and the associations of Friends of the Way are two institutions that participate very actively in the governance of the Jacobean routes but have very little visibility and, frequently, limited recognition of the work they carry out. Their role is often silenced by other institutions. In the first case, we are dealing with the public administration which is closest to the citizen and which has to manage basic services, normally with precarious means, ranging from cleaning to town planning. In the second case, we are dealing with private and voluntary organizations whose mission is to support pilgrims and disseminate the culture of St James.

In the case of Spain, municipalities constitute the basic scale of territorial division. In Spain there are 8131 municipalities of which 61.5% have less than 1000 inhabitants and

another 29.1% have between 1000 and 10,000 inhabitants (Ine, 2022). They are grouped into provinces whose representative bodies are the provincial councils which, among other functions, support small municipalities in the provision of services that they would not otherwise be able to provide, such as those related to water or waste, for example. In addition, the municipalities are grouped into a Spanish federation, and a federation of their own in the case of Galicia, which aims to defend and represent these entities before other public administrations.

As we have pointed out, the municipalities are in charge of the management of most of the basic services, as well as being responsible for the approval and implementation of urban planning, always in accordance with the regulations in force. Therefore, they play a fundamental role in the daily life of the resident population but also those in transit, as in the case of pilgrims. By way of example, we can point to the quality of municipal services or the programming of cultural activities as two aspects that can influence the satisfaction of pilgrims on their way to Compostela.

More specifically, the cleaning and maintenance of the route is also the responsibility of the municipalities which, in addition, have to adapt their urban planning to the protection required by higher regulations. In some cases, they have their own hostels or, when demand is very high, they have to offer alternative accommodation to pilgrims, such as sports pavilions. In short, they play a fundamental role in everything that has to do with the daily governance of the routes to Santiago.

However, the municipalities, as we have already pointed out, find themselves in a very precarious situation, especially those with a smaller population, which are the majority. Some of the most important complaints to other administrations have to do with the scarce funding they receive. At least, in the case of Galicia, one of the most recurrent concerns stems from the fact that the funds they receive often come from competitive calls for proposals. This means that, for many actions, they depend not on a fixed budget but on the municipality's ability to obtain grants or subsidies to hire staff for the tourist office or to maintain the paths, for example. They also emphasize that these subsidies are often used for investment purposes, but that it is then up to the municipality to maintain them, for which it does not always have the budget.

Another important element to bear in mind is that the provision of services does not always have a return in the form of benefits. In recent years there has been an increasing concentration of services to pilgrims at certain points along the Camino, mainly in small urban centres of a few thousand inhabitants. In these cases, the municipalities have to make a great effort that is rewarded with an improvement in the economic dynamics through the opening of businesses linked to the Camino. Meanwhile, the more rural municipalities or those without such a cluster of services see walkers pass through their territory without any kind of positive impact, which leads to a lack of interest on the part of the local population in the phenomenon of the pilgrimage. However, even in the latter cases, the municipalities have to exercise their obligations as public administration.

The municipalities along the Way have to face additional expenses derived from their status as Jacobean centres. We are referring to the maintenance of the Way, the municipal hostels, and cultural promotion, among many other things. The most effective way for municipalities to face the multiple challenges posed by the scarce funding they receive in relation to their needs is through collaboration with other institutions or municipalities. However, this strategy is almost always subject to obtaining subsidies and grants which, as we have seen, do not solve the structural problem of a lack of sufficient budgets to develop projects or provide services without depending on extra income. The specific problems faced by many of these municipalities led them to create the Association of Municipalities of the Camino de Santiago, officially constituted in 2015 and based in the city of Jaca. This association brings together just over 100 Spanish municipalities crossed by the French Way.

The aims of this association are focused on cooperation in the field of the protection and promotion of the Way, the development of projects on the Way and collaboration with other administrations. Its work in the few years that it has been active has been very intense. By way of example we can point to the publication of a protocol of actions of the hostels in relation to COVID-19 (Icte, 2020); the signing of an agreement with Spanish public television for the broadcasting of news; or the creation of a forum of companies that involves a continuous dialogue with the private sector aimed at improving services on the Camino, the promotion of economic activity, and increasing efficiency in the management of the cultural and environmental heritage of the Camino. Likewise, in 2017 a scientific committee was created in which people from different fields of knowledge were integrated with the aim of advising the association. Finally, it is important to point out the participation of the association in planning tasks, such as, for example, carrying out field work that allows progress to be made in the drafting of the Master Plan of the Property of Cultural Interest Camino de Santiago.

Along the same lines as the one mentioned above, there are other associations that work on other routes, although, due to their shorter length, the number of municipalities is smaller. We have the example of the Association of Municipalities of the Winter Way, which includes some 20 municipalities, mainly in Galicia; or the English Way. These types of initiatives, with greater or lesser success, seek collaborative work that gives a unitary meaning to the concept of itinerary while helping to overcome the great difficulties encountered by the municipalities when managing their territories. In fact, the role of these smaller associations of municipalities is often limited to providing general information on their websites, organizing seminars and little else.

The other institution to which we want to pay attention is that of the associations of Friends of the Camino de Santiago. They are of a private nature and are run by people who, on a voluntary basis, participate in activities organized for the promotion and dissemination of the Jacobean culture while giving support to the pilgrim. Although their contemporary origin is in the Société Française des Amis de Saint-Jacques de Compostelle, established in Paris in 1950, they are actually heirs to a medieval tradition of support for pilgrims. In any case, from that first French initiative, progress was made little by little, with a second association in Spain in 1962. It was mainly due to the success of the 1993 Holy Year that these associations multiplied. There are currently some 350 associations in some 40 countries, although almost half of them are in Spain, where they are grouped under a federation of associations (Santos, 2021).

Although they have very different characteristics in terms of their organization and functions, their role is vital to understand the Camino de Santiago today, having an undeniable role in the governance of it (Santos, 2021). Initially, in the first decades of the second half of the 20th century, when the Camino was still in an embryonic phase of development, these associations played an important role in the visibility of the Camino, not only with the organization of pilgrimages, but also with the carrying out and dissemination of studies and the recovery of the old routes, many of them lost in time or occupied by new infrastructures. In fact, one of the most important works carried out by these associations was to identify, recover, clean, signpost and maintain the paths, based on historical evidence and research.

These tasks, which in some cases continue to be carried out, are complemented by others no less important, such as the dissemination of Jacobean culture and support for pilgrims. In relation to the first, the dissemination of Jacobean culture, the organization of seminars and conferences is important, especially in those places where the Way is less well known. A very relevant aspect is that this dissemination work is based on the idea of the traditional pilgrimage. This latter concept is related, among other things, to the welcoming or non-commercial hospitality that would be framed in that sense of community and in the phase of liminality that Turner (1969) explained and that serves to create a special connection between pilgrims. Hence also, in this process of personal transformation, support for the other becomes fundamental. This support manifests itself in all its phases, before, during and after the transformative journey.

The significance of this traditional hospitality has led to the signing of a declaration on 25 July 2021 in the city of Astorga, with the participation of the Spanish Federation of Associations of Friends of the Camino de Santiago, to promote and support traditional hospitality as an Intangible Heritage of Humanity (Federación Española de Asociaciones de Amigos del Camino de Santiago, 2021). This can give us an idea of

the role played by the hostels along the route. Beyond their symbolism as accommodation, hostels are places of encounter and socialization where the experience of being a pilgrim, of forming a community and of being in a process of inner transformation is shared. This relevance is also manifested in the involvement of associations of Friends. The management of hostels or the training of hospitaleros are activities carried out by some associations. Through them, they help to transmit the value of this traditional welcome in order to understand the meaning of the Camino.

In short, the associations claim their role as heirs to a long historical tradition and help the Camino to be much more than just a tourist destination. The debate between false and authentic pilgrims or the one that criticizes the imposition of a minimum of 100 km to obtain the Compostela, receive many nuances by the associations. Although there are very different positions, there are associations that defend the idea that the transformative capacity of the Camino is so great that even in situations of overcrowding, strictly recreational motivations or short routes, walkers have the opportunity to absorb the spirit of the Camino and become pilgrims (Santos, 2021).

As is easy to deduce from what has been said so far, the associations are very diverse, although they share many common values about the Camino. Although there are exceptions, in general they do not have a religious connection, even though many of their members are often believers. In fact, one of their characteristics is their independence, both from public administration and from the Church. Their capacity for action lies, to a large extent, in their size, so that the smaller ones sometimes limit their activity to the distribution of credentials or the organization of pilgrimages. Meanwhile, the more powerful ones train hospitaleros, manage hostels, provide support before and after the pilgrimage, and even have financial assistance for pilgrims with fewer resources.

In summary, the associations of Friends of the Camino de Santiago are a fundamental institution in the governance of the Camino. Without them, the route would probably be a purely tourist itinerary without the uniqueness that gives it the conservation of certain traditional values. Moreover, on a practical level, they contribute to strengthening the international dimension of the Way and participate very actively in daily management tasks, from the maintenance and signposting of the routes to their work in the network of hostels and information points along the Way.

9.5   Conclusions

Throughout this text we have seen that the governance of the Camino de Santiago is organized on multiple levels, reflecting the complexity and the different interests that surround this route. From universal institutions, such as the Catholic Church, to small local associations, all of them make contributions that serve to configure a complex system of public and private actors that is not always easy to manage. In any case, it is important to understand that the current success of the Way of St James is by no means exclusively a consequence of a tourist campaign that designs, (re)creates and promotes a tourist product. Just as we must also assume that this success cannot be measured in number of walkers but must take into consideration other values that give the Camino its uniqueness.

UNESCO points out that governance is about the culture and institutional environment in which citizens and stakeholders interact among themselves and participate in public affairs (UNESCO, 2022a). The complexity of managing a route such as the Compostela route implies the need for coordinated governance at different scales. The involvement of multiple public and private actors and the hierarchy with which they act does not always facilitate this governance. The weak points are the municipalities that have responsibility for direct contact with pilgrims, and the associations of Friends of the Camino that represent the pilgrims themselves. In recent years progress has been made towards more coordinated governance through mutual recognition of the importance of each institution and we believe that this is the way forward for the future. The Way of St James is accompanied by all the difficulties of governance inherent to a cultural itinerary. UNESCO itself tries to point out the idea of unity in these routes, although it is aware of the problems in its management when it crosses different countries.

In our case, it is not only this circumstance but also those related to smaller territories within the same country. This is the case in Spain, where the autonomous communities, with competences in tourism and culture, do not always coordinate their actions or defend the same strategies, sometimes giving rise to discontinuities and fragmentation.

In this chapter we have focused primarily on two institutions that are often considered minor in relation to the Camino de Santiago but that are fundamental to understanding not only the governance of the Camino but also its uniqueness. First, we looked at the municipalities whose limited financial capacity, at least in Spain, does not prevent them from having to assume a large number of functions ranging from the provision of basic services, such as water or waste disposal, to those related to the care of pilgrims, for example in the form of accommodation in case of need. It is true that in recent years their work in relation to the Camino has been recognized, but this fact has not translated into a regular transfer of resources, which continue to arrive largely by way of exceptional contributions through, for example, competitive fundraising channels.

The second of the institutions to which we have paid most attention is the associations of Friends of the Way. It is a heterogeneous group of more than 300 associations distributed all over the world. Because of their private nature, they do not have the capacity to manage the Way themselves. However, their work is fundamental to understanding the uniqueness and even the success of this pilgrimage route. Initially, they were largely responsible for the recovery, signposting and maintenance of the routes. Nowadays, they also focus their efforts on disseminating the Jacobean culture, supporting pilgrims and, in particular, promoting traditional values, which are not necessarily religious. In this last respect, hospitality plays a very important role.

In short, municipalities and associations of friends are two institutions that participate very actively in the governance of the Camino, attending to those aspects closest to the pilgrim's experience. The weakening or failure of either of them would have a rapid and negative impact on the Camino. That is why not only their public recognition is necessary, but also, and above all, the implementation of instruments that allow them to develop their work efficiently without losing their independence as parts of a whole that is the Camino de Santiago.

References

Castro, B. (2015) The way of Saint James: memory, propaganda and power. In: Maddrel, A., Terry, A. and Gale, T. (eds) *Mobilities and Meaning in Sacred Journeys*. Ashgate Publishing, Farnham, UK, pp. 129–143. DOI: 10.4324/9781315607344.

CoE (2023) *Explore All Cultural Routes by Theme*. Available at: https://www.coe.int/en/web/cultural-routes/by-theme (accessed 18 January 2023).

Consejo Jacobeo (2022) Consejo Jacobeo. Available at: https://www.culturaydeporte.gob.es/consejo-jacobeo/en/presentacion.html (accessed 11 May 2022).

Consorcio de Santiago (2021) *Propuesta estratégica plurianual del Consorcio de Santiago para el periodo 2021-2027-2032*. Available at: http://www.consorciodesantiago.org/sites/default/files/documentos/2021/07/propuesta_estrategia_consorcio.pdf (accessed 11 May 2022).

Durán-Sánchez, A., Álvarez-García, J., del Río-Rama, M. and Oliveira, C. (2018) Religious tourism and pilgrimage: bibliometric overview. *Religions* 9(249), 2–15. DOI: 10.3390/rel9090249.

Federación Española de Asociaciones de Amigos del Camino de Santiago (2021) *La acogida tradicional jacobea, bien inmaterial de la Humanidad*. Available at: https://www.caminosantiago.org/cpperegrino/prensa/verprensa.asp?PrensaID=17152# (accessed 11 May 2022).

Icte (2020) *Medidas para la reducción del contagio por el coronavirus SARS CoV-2*. Available at: https://www.mincotur.gob.es/es-es/COVID-19/GuiasSectorTurismo/Restaurantes.pdf (accessed 11 May 2022).

Ine (2022) *Cifras oficiales de población*. Available at: https://www.ine.es/jaxiT3/Tabla.htm?t=2917&L=0 (accessed 11 May 2022).

Junta de Castilla y León (2021) *Plan Jacobeo 20–21*. Available at: https://patrimoniocultural.jcyl.es/web/es/patrimonio-bienes-culturales/plan-jacobeo-2021.html (accessed 11 May 2022).

King, G.G. (1920) *The Way of Saint James in Three Volumes*. J.P. Putnam's Sons, New York and London.

Lois González, R. and Lopez, L. (2020) The singularity of the Camino de Santiago as a contemporary tourism case. In: Pileri, P. and Moscarelli, R. (eds) *Cycling and Walking for Regional Development. Research for Development*. Springer, Cham, Switzerland, pp. 221–233.

Mincotur (2021) *Plan turístico nacional Xacobeo 2021–2022*. Available at: https://www.mincotur.gob.es/es-es/gabineteprensa/notasprensa/2021/documents/presentacion-plan-turistico-nacional-xacobeo-2021-%202022-%20vf%20(1).pdf (accessed 11 May 2022).

Navarra (2021) *Navarra pone en marcha un plan de trabajo para el año Xacobeo*. Available at: https://www.navarra.es/es/noticias/2021/01/12/navarra-pone-en-marcha-un-plan-de-trabajo-para-el-ano-xacobeo (accessed 11 May 2022).

Nilsson, M. and Tesfahuney, M. (2016) Performing the "post-secular" in Santiago de Compostela. *Annals of Tourism Research* 57, 18–30. DOI: 10.1016/j.annals.2015.11.001.

Pack, S. (2008) The Camino de Santiago and the paradox of national Catholicism in modern Spain. In: Bunk, B., Pack, S. and Scott, C.G. (eds) *Nation and Conflict in Modern Spain: Essays in Honor of Stanley G. Payne*. University of Madison Press, Madison, WI, pp. 65–80.

Pack, S. (2010) Revival of the pilgrimage to Santiago de Compostela: the politics of religious, national, and European patrimony, 1879–1988. *The Journal of Modern History* 82(2), 335–367. DOI: 10.1086/651613.

Pilgrim's Office (2022) *Statistics*. Available at: http://oficinadelperegrino.com/en/statistics/ (accessed 11 May 2022).

Ramos Loza, R. (2016) *Estudo de viabilidade da candidatura à UNESCO do Caminho Portugués a Santiago*. Eixo Atlântico-Interreg, Braga, Portugal.

Rodríguez, M.F. (2004) *Los Años Santos Compostelanos Del Siglo XX. Crónica de Un Renacimiento*. Xunta de Galicia, Santiago de Compostela, Spain.

Santos, X.M. (2016) The way of Saint James as an event: politics and nation. *Journal of Policy Research in Tourism, Leisure and Events* 8(3), 233–248. DOI: 10.1080/19407963.2016.1214960.

Santos, X. (2017) La construction touristique des Chemins de Saint-Jacques-de-Compostelle en Espagne: acteurs, regards et contradictions. *Sud-Ouest Européen* 43, 7–19. DOI: 10.4000/soe.2522.

Santos, X. (2021) Las asociaciones de amigos del Camino de Santiago. Altruismo y colaboración. *Cuadernos de Turismo* 48, 49–68. DOI: 10.6018/turismo.492661.

Santos, X. and Lois González, R. (2011) El Camino de Santiago en el contexto de los nuevos turismos. *Estudios Turísticos* 189, 87–110.

Santos, X.M. and Trillo-Santamaría, J.M. (2017) Tourism and nation in Galicia (Spain). *Tourism Management Perspectives* 22, 98–108. DOI: 10.1016/j.tmp.2017.03.006.

Stone, J. (1927) *The Cult of Santiago: Traditions, Myths, and Pilgrimages*. Longmans, Green and Co. Ltd, London.

Turner, V. (1969) *The Ritual Process: Structure and anti-structure*. Aldine Publishing Company, Chicago, IL.

UNESCO (2022a) *Concept of Governance*. Available at: http://www.ibe.unesco.org/en/geqaf/technical-notes/concept-governance (accessed 13 May 2022).

UNESCO (2022b) *Word Heritage Convention*. Available at: https://whc.unesco.org/en/list/868/ and https://whc.unesco.org/en/list/669/ (accessed 11 May 2022).

Vázquez de Parga, L., Lacarra, J.M. and Uría Riu, J. (1948) *Las Peregrinaciones a Santiago de Compostela*. CSIC, Madrid.

10 Religious Tourism in Malta Between Politics, Policies and Private Enterprise

Dane Munro*

Institute of Tourism, Travel and Culture (ITTC), University of Malta

Abstract

Malta has a cultural heritage of about 8,000 years, still possessing tangible, intangible and visible traces of that rich past, including religion, pilgrimage and at present, faith-based tourism. Although Malta has this massive cultural, tangible religious heritage, one may wonder why Malta has never become a pilgrimage destination or a magnet for faith-based tourism.

The theoretical framework of this chapter is based on evidence-based policy making (EBPM) and policy analytics. The chapter analyses and discusses the trajectory of the phenomenon of faith-based tourism and the various attempts to create a niche market by policy makers and stakeholders in Malta. There is an ongoing struggle whether to force faith-based tourism into the summer mass tourism segment or to decide on a quality-based shoulder and low season special interest market. The politics, policies and the private enterprise structure of the islands will be also discussed. This will lead to identifying several areas where improvements are probable, if not possible, depending on how far new insights are reaching, the severity of the resistance against change and the power of evidence.

10.1 Introduction

Globally, faith-based tourism has over the years become a mature niche in tourism and the forecasts are it will keep on growing, notwithstanding the volatile nature of tourism. After all, faith-based tourism, including pilgrimage and religious tourism, seems to be a 'thing' that humans are engaged with all over the world. According to Scott (2010), humans have engaged in pilgrimage since the Upper Palaeolithic times, some 70,000 years ago. At present, worldwide faith-based tourism destinations receive millions of visitors per year and global faith-based travel is one of the largest, fastest growing and crisis-resistant sectors. 'Nowadays, no one doubts about the importance of religious tourism, which allows us to safeguard our heritage and to contribute to the social and economic development of the area...' (M. Buch, as cited in Boz, 2018, p. 69). On a global scale, the faith-based tourism market is estimated to reach US$13.7 billion in 2022, while growth is foreseen to reach an estimated market valuation of US$37 billion by 2032 (Future Market Insight, 2022).

The theoretical framework of this chapter is written through the lens of evidence-based policy making (EBPM) and policy analytics (Head, 2008; De Marchi *et al.*, 2016; Richards, 2017) and explores the possibilities of informing faith-based tourism niche market policy makers and stakeholders in Malta. The imaginary and unofficial tourism niche in which religious tourism is now

*dane.munro@um.edu.mt

© CAB International 2023. *The Politics of Religious Tourism* (eds D. Bozonelos and P. Moira)
DOI: 10.1079/9781800621732.0010

currently placed was not the result of evidence-based decisions, as that was not practiced in the 1950s. It was more the result of opinion-based policy making, due to the dominant religious and societal ideas of the period. While it may have worked for a time, tourism demands have shifted such that it is time for structuring an independent faith-based tourism niche. Furthermore, the history of planned and unintentional niche development will be explored and its decision making basis will be discussed. Also, I have integrated my 25 years of experiences as a tourist guide in Malta into this chapter for a practitioner's perspective, to balance my theoretical views as a tourism academic.

10.2   Malta: Religio-Cultural Overview

Malta consists of a small archipelago, in the centre of the Mediterranean Sea, in total a little less than 316 km², with a total population of 519,562. Nearly 95% of the population lives in urban centres, with about 1649 people per km², making it the most densely populated country in the EU (NSO, 2022).

Malta became a crown colony of Great Britain in 1813. It gained its independence in 1964, becoming a parliamentary republic in 1974. Since 2004, Malta has been a member state of the EU and joined the Eurozone in 2008. Malta's economy, until the 1960s, relied mostly on British military spending at the Naval Dockyard and British military and civil services (Blake et al., 2003). Modern tourism in Malta started somewhere in the 1950s, with visitors from Great Britain taking up the lion's share of the arrival statistics, to compensate for the already decreasing British military spending and importance of Malta as a British military strongpoint.

The islands have been populated since the Neolithic era, some 7200 years (Malone et al., 2009), but recent discoveries made in the FRAGSUS (2015) archaeological project indicates that this might be pushed farther back in time by 700 years or so (Malta Independent, 2018). Since then, the Maltese islands have built up a very diverse tangible and intangible religio-cultural heritage. Pilgrimage has been around in Malta probably since the Neolithic

period (Zuntz, 1971) and from Bonanno (2005) we learn that Malta received visitors in the Classical period, leading to the idea of fusing pilgrimage and tourism. Sant Cassia (1993, pp. 358–359) claimed that Malta's national identity began in 60 CE when St Paul arrived on the island of $M\varepsilon\lambda\iota\tau\eta$, i.e. Malta, delivered by shipwreck. This event is narrated in the Acts of the Apostles 27 and 28 of the New Testament and is regarded as a winning narrative for faith-based tourism. During the era of the Order of St John (1530–1798), many chapels, churches and cathedrals were built, while an enormous amount of religious art was commissioned. These masterpieces can still be enjoyed in those places of worship and in other edifices built by the Order. The Order of St John, together with the Jesuits, also developed a serious pilgrimage industry centred around the cult of St Paul (Azzopardi and Blondy, 2012), targeting the Grand Tour of the privileged classes visiting Europe (Freller, 1995, 2006, 2009). At present, religious groups and individuals, such as Roman Catholics, Protestants and the followers of the New Religious Movements (NRMs), arrive at Malta to experience, among others, St Paul, St John, Our Lady, and the divinities from the Neolithic era. The islands of Malta are still considered to be Roman Catholic, although Sunday Mass attendance has dropped considerably. An increasing part of the population is either unchurched or secularized. Church research points out that 38% of all Maltese regularly attend Sunday Mass, while 74% claim to go once a month (Archdiocese of Malta, 2018).

At first glance, one may wonder why Malta, so rich in its authentic cultural and religious heritage, is not a main destination for faith-based tourism, notwithstanding its fully functional and continuously improving tourism infrastructure. Many people and organizations endeavoured, both in the past and in the present, to promote visits and pilgrimages to Malta, but it seems that the islands never managed to come out of the periphery of matters. Faith-based tourism in the Maltese context, is a very selective type, strongly linked to the islands' past. Unlike regular tourism, this type of tourism has a mediation function between the natural and the cultural world and between the natural and the supernatural world (Blackwell, 2007, pp. 38–39).

10.3 Malta: Politics, Policies and Tourism

Tourism policies have been in place in Malta since 1959 (Mangion, 2022). Subsequently, Malta has engaged in mass tourism, a blue economy destination of sea, sun, sand and fun (Ashworth and Tunbridge, 2017), relying mostly on high volume/modest quality. Subsequently, politics, policies and private enterprise have shaped Malta's tourism preferences and infrastructure accordingly, generally improving 'product Malta'. Concentrating on mass tourism also meant less attention for other travel motivations. Additionally, when among the decision making people there are those who have little or no affinity with religion, it is obvious that they do not pay attention to its value, although faith-based tourism is a travel segment like any other one. There is little political argument involved in creating an official experience-based niche for faith-based tourism. It is not controversial, while it connects deeply with the human condition and can bring healthy revenues (Head, 2008). 'Besides the economic benefits, religious tourism is also a powerful instrument... and a key agent of peace, fostering tolerance and understanding between visitors and host communities, in an amalgam of different faiths' (Secretary-General of the World Tourism Organization, Taleb Rifai, as cited in Boz, 2018, p. 69). As a policy research framework, EBPM is able to take an academic distance from political, religious or secular ideologies by looking at facts and evidence even if 'value, preferences and decisions should remain a political act' (De Marchi et al., 2016, p. 17).

In the late 1990s, when the realization had set in that Malta's religious and cultural heritage was an answer to the seasonality of its 'blue' economy, i.e. beach holidays, Malta changed over to a hybrid tourism destination, adding a 'grey' component, i.e. heritage based economy (Ashworth and Tunbridge, 2017), a sunny cultural heritage so to speak, which better brought out the unique selling points of Malta. It also became clear to the authorities that Malta's economy was suffering an overdependence on tourism and manufacturing, deciding that the islands needed a more diversified and higher value-added services-based economy. Currently, besides tourism, construction, retailing and banking, there are at present financial services, special interest tourism (SIT), professional services, shipping, transit container terminal, gaming, civil service, and IT hardware and software industries, all making Malta's economy less dependent on the tourism pillar (Grech, 2016). The Maltese Tourism Authority (MTA) also placed greater emphasis on a more diverse niche tourism market and a quality upgrading of the service provision. Nonetheless, Malta's economic dependence on tourism is still deemed very high, for instance, in 2017, it was 14.2% of the GDP, translating to about 31,000 jobs directly in Malta.

From 1950 to 2019, Malta saw an annual growth from a few thousand tourists to about 2.4 million in 2018. Tourism in 2019 hit an all-time high, with 2,771,888 arrivals and a total tourist expenditure of €2.2 billion (Attard, 2019), immediately followed by the Covid-19 slump. During the years up to 2019 there were a few crises which hit Malta rather hard, but thanks to its small size and economic diversity, they were handled well and the country recovered quickly. For instance, during the mid-1980s there was the second 'oil shock' and deep recession in the UK, and other sea-sun-fun destinations in the Mediterranean and the Adriatic became serious competitors. The years 2009/10 saw a sharp drop in arrivals due to the financial crises (Attard, 2019). Tourism in Malta is recovering from Covid-19 and the situation is once again being handled well despite inflation pressures and shortage of staff.

10.4 Faith-Based Tourism: Meaning, Value and Definitions

Notwithstanding the ongoing debate and discussions regarding definitions in this field, it is useful for policy makers and stakeholders to take notice of definitions in order to be able to identify the 'what' and the 'why' of the matter. There are many to choose from and Malta can develop its own understanding, which would help formulating faith-based tourism policies, informing questions for data gathering and statistical purposes and, on a practical level, exploring the boundaries of what is possible and suitable locally.

Faith-based tourism is an umbrella term which incorporates all kinds of religion-related and non-religion-related travel (Joo and Woosnam, 2022), including pilgrimage, secular pilgrimage, religious tourism, spiritual tourism, tourism for religious people, spiritual travel, retreats, seminars, festivals, holidays organized by the parish and some aspects of Dark Tourism. It may also include visits to both sacred and secular places imbued with meaning, for instance, related to World War II sites in Malta, where (re)visiting a site can provoke a highly emotional or spiritual reaction (Munro, 2017).

Faith-based tourism can be both of a transformational and of a transactional kind. Transformational is understood to allow the full-sensory, mystical, introspective and experiential mechanisms to work body, spirit and soul in a lived religious or spiritual experience. There are many faith-based tourists who are seeking new forms of spirituality or new ways to experience spirituality. This often means going beyond the social and religious constructs and transactional sides of the established and traditional religions. Transactional can relate to the formal nature of the traditional religions, where the experience comes from following a prescribed set of rituals, ceremonies, sacraments, etc., to fulfil certain obligations. Getting what you paid for is then also the transactional nature of the supplier side of tourism although the intangible rewards are of the highest value for the participants. Among many other things, faith-based tourism is also big business (Munro, 2017).

A common factor for all faith-based tourists is that they appreciate the destination, its religious and cultural heritage, its food, and its natural beauty. Besides, they are sensitive to how a destination handles its environment and are genuinely interested in the inhabitants of a destination (Sharma, 2013). Greenia's research finds that most importantly, pilgrimage or faith-based tourism is an undertaking available and accessible for every religion, gender and age. Even the depth of one's spirituality is immaterial and, as an activity, it leaves no shame, guilt, indebtedness or damaged reputation. Faith-based tourism is respectable and clean, since to reach fulfilment, one does not need drugs or alcohol. Experiences gained as faith-based

tourists and the achievement of fulfilment can be communicated and shared with others, while the experience is also repeatable (Greenia, 2014). There is also the issue of emotional solidarity, as faith-based tourists tend to look for communality and fairness (Joo and Woosnam, 2022).

Some pilgrimages require walking over long distances (route-based), as the walking is the transformational aspect and not a prolonged stay at the site (e.g. Santiago de Compostela). In view of Malta's size, this form of pilgrimage is perhaps less applicable. Nonetheless, efforts should be made to create longer walks in Malta. The benefits of walking are well researched, body, spirit and soul are rewarded when walking longer distances (Gros, 2015). When it comes to St Paul in Malta, such 'follow in the footsteps of' journeys may also be regarded as invented routes, because they quite often blend in with tourism interests (Greenia, 2014). For others, being at the shrine (site-based) holds the promise of a transformational effect (e.g. Medjugorje), and how one arrives there is irrelevant. Pilgrims usually do not undertake the journey primarily as a holiday for leisure, but rather for spiritual goals to a single route, shrine or other place of significance. Pilgrims yearn for fulfilment, healing, closure, acceptance, getting closer to one's divinity and possibly hope to receive a miracle.

One sample of an often-used formal definition of pilgrimage comes from Barber: 'A journey resulting from religious causes, externally to a sacred site and internally for spiritual purposes and internal understanding' (1991, p.1), which will certainly apply to Malta. A sample of an informal definition could be from Singh (2006, p. 220), defining Hindu pilgrimage as 'an inner journey manifest in an exterior space in which the immanent and the transcendent together form a complex spiritual and travel phenomenon,' although this could also be relevant for the adherents of the NRM who visit Malta for transcendental sessions in one of Malta's Neolithic temples. A very broad definition of faith-based tourism, adapted to modern times where one can experience a pilgrimage by means of virtual technology is given by Digance (2006, p. 36) as 'Undertaking a journey that is redolent with meaning.' This would also apply to people who cannot travel for various reasons, but still want to experience Malta in this manner.

Defining religious tourists becomes more problematic, as in Smith's continuum the religious tourist is placed between the pious pilgrim and the secular tourist (Smith, 1992) or between belief, culture and entertainment according to the continuum of Alecu (2010). Such tourists have the luxury to be a pilgrim in one moment and a shopper in the next. To take it a step further, combining traditional religious rituals with modern lifestyles is no longer frowned upon in a globalized world, as consumers, including faith-based tourists, are increasingly focused on buying experiences (Pine and Gilmore, 2020). The effect of an experience is immediate and permanent and there is a difference between an unforgettable experience and an experience which one cannot 'unforget'. A modern faith-based tourist is as much a product of a consumer-oriented society and faced with an abundance of choices, just like any other tourist (Collins-Kreiner, 2018).

10.5   Existing Faith-Based Tourism in Malta

Malta attracts foreign Roman Catholic parish priests who have taken the initiative to organize a trip with their parish. These foreign priests and their values are therefore key to the success of such trips. Parish groups, e.g. from Germany, France, Poland, Spain and Italy, are very much budget aware, as they often travel by coach in their own countries or when crossing Europe. Although individual families and youth groups are also present, many of these groups consist of travellers over 50 years of age. They share many characteristics with a comparable market, the 50+ Silver Economy (Zsarnoczky, 2017), which also prefers the low and shoulder seasons, as they are not burdened with school holidays and favour the least expensive airfares and accommodation rates. Youth groups tend to follow the school holidays, while individual travellers and family groups may arrive at any time of the year but would not easily be recognizable as faith-based tourists.

Malta is not only visited by Roman Catholic groups and individuals, but similarly also by Protestant ministers (male and female) and their congregations, who often regard themselves as 'faith travellers' rather than pilgrims (Munro, 2019b, Munro, 2020) and adherents of the NRM, arriving mostly from the English-speaking world. The latter may also be categorized as spiritual tourists (Munro, 2017, 2021). Of all religious visitors, the NRMs are the most eclectic, regularly using the Neolithic heritage and places of natural beauty of Malta as places of worship. They also represent a higher spending segment in faith-based tourism, as they prefer to stay in superior accommodations and demand high quality products and services. Faith-based tourists centring on St Paul may be called pilgrimage tourists, as there is a Biblical person and site involved.

Once in Malta, religious tourists would like to experience more of the islands, which of course must contain a certain amount of authenticity, leisure, history, originality, pageantry, entertainment, etc., to allow the holiday aspects to be enjoyed. Religious tourism in Malta has always been linked to traditional feasts of the patron saints celebrated in Malta during the summer, the so-called *festa* season, as this was regarded as a way of lifting religious tourism into an economy of scale. In order to deal with small island issues, the idea that religious tourism and 'normal' tourism were not so different probably originated from local Maltese stakeholders. Sea, sun and *festas* were available for free. In the past, and even at present, most churches do not demand an entrance fee, as they serve local communities. As a result, from the very start, churches appeared in every excursion programme. This led to the famous configuration of local tours, with at least two churches thrown in every day, earning them the title ABC tours (Another Blessed Church). This way of conducting tours was based on exploitation, as the churches hardly received any compensation, while the wear and tear increased disproportionally compared to that of the normal use by the parishioners. There is a certain ambiguity here. It can be regarded as a classic case of privatizing the profits (by the entrepreneurs) and socializing the costs (to the disadvantage of the parish). On the other hand, it has been noted that local parish priests would compete among themselves to bring in tour operators, because the offering box enjoyed the donations of the tourists.

For many years, this freebie aspect was tolerated by the churches, until St John's Co-Cathedral radically changed its policies. Church and state came together and on 31 July 2001 a notarial deed was signed, bringing into life St John's Co-Cathedral Foundation. It introduced an entrance fee outside church hours, turning the co-cathedral into a museum (Munro, 2019a). Within 15 years, most of the church, and its priceless collection of art, had been cleaned, preserved and restored. This political decision made some other churches, basilicas and cathedrals in Malta with a touristic value follow suit. Consequently, their financial situation is becoming healthier so that the buildings and collections are being prepared for a better future. These policy changes also upgraded these churches to a better-quality product and became part of every tour operator's excursion programme, with a structured income through entrance fees. Charging admission gives a message that the site is worth experiencing (Pine and Gilmore, 2020, p. 24).

10.6   Analysis and Discussion Regarding a Separate Niche Formation

Multiple forms of evidence, in favour of structuring an independent faith-based tourism niche, are presented here. Such evidence is essential for niche formation, linking the theoretical with practical and political knowledge, arguments and relevance (Head, 2008). Evidence in itself is irrelevant without acknowledging that other inputs and perspectives have validity too and that the policy-making process is not a pure and simple linear and rational process (Richards, 2017, p. 166). In analogy with the analysis of institutional and cultural seasonality of Rico *et al.* (2021) and the influence of agents of economy and stakeholders in tourism, one can understand why it had been decided over time in Malta, as an unwritten rule of opinion-based decision making, that religious tourism would be best placed in a segment which is all events based, carrying components of religion

tradition and 'Malteseness' such as the Maltese religious *festa* summer season, processions, fireworks, festivals, concerts, religious events, pageantry, etc. This inorganically grew into an unofficial but generally accepted concept of the *festa niche*. Later, historical re-enactments were added to this. It is suggested here, based on various strands of evidence, that *now* is the opportune moment to structure an official, independent niche for faith-based tourism.

The Tourism Policy for the Maltese Islands 2012–2016 (MTA, 2012) was a step closer to developing Malta as a destination for faith-based tourism and to create an independent niche. The document states that to 'attain our overarching goals we need...a mix of tourists that will make use of the spectrum of the niche offerings and products that our country offers...and...tourists that will respect Malta's uniquely constructed (from temples to hotels), natural (from marine to terrestrial) and intangible (from local customs to quality labels) heritage.' The policy further mentions (p. 30) that Malta will be promoted as a pilgrimage destination, presenting Malta as a Sacred Island (from prehistory to modern times), an emphasis on the Goddess of Fertility Cult in prehistoric Malta and Gozo, creating itineraries for the cult of St Paul and supporting traditional and village feasts. Also, certain sanctuaries, including those of the Virgin Mary, would be promoted as well as treasures of art at various sites. A following tourism policy 2015–2020 (MTA, 2015) emphasized low and shoulder seasons (p. 33) and brand identity for religious tourism (p. 44). These tourism policies (MTA, 2012; 2015) acknowledged that religious tourism would ideally not take place in summer. With ever-rising temperatures in summer, it is unlikely that those hot weather conditions would be helpful for people to engage in prayer, meditation or contemplative walks. Very recent tourism policies, both the 'Recover. Rethink. Revitalize' produced by the MTA (MTA, 2021) and the 'Rediscover', produced by the Tourism Operators Business Section at the Malta Chamber of Commerce, Enterprise and Industry (2021), come close to MacCannell, 1999, p. 181, who suggests that differentiation and independence of a niche provides more chances for growth.

Although the unofficial *festa niche* is still important to stakeholders in Malta, it not necessarily offering the right experiences for faith-based tourists since the essence of their experiences is found outside that niche. In this artificially constructed niche, faith-based tourism is the odd one out because most items found in the *festa niche* are events, while faith-based tourism consists of experiences. This is very much in line with the shift in trends in global tourism, away from goods and services, emphasizing high value experiences that engage tourists in personal and memorable ways. Moreover, the *festa niche* is a cultural expression and part of product Malta, with many commoditized and commercialized tangible products and intangible services. Although religious tourists have in general little issue with commoditized and commercialized tourism products and services (Scott, 2012), they would rather have their services commoditized into quality experience-time (Pine and Gilmore, 2020). When religious tourists visit churches, temples and other sites considered sacred, they not only seek the religious or spiritual matters these may have to offer (Pohner *et al.*, 2009), but also the exclusivity, innovation, novel context, storytelling or everything that providers can design or arrange to create memorable experiences and value for the participants (Jensen and Prebensen, 2015).

10.7 Policy Prescriptions: What Makes an Independent Faith-Based Tourism Niche?

Policy decisions are always about *what works* and *what are the consequences of applying changes*. Hence, policy decisions are influenced by politics, stakeholder interests, opinions and discussion, rather than coming from an empirical analysis. Evidence provided by a variety of stakeholders and communities will certainly differ from similar evidence produced by technocrats. This makes evidence simultaneously pliable and contestable. The results of a quantitative cost/benefit analysis maybe regarded and valued differently than a qualitative ethnography on

the same topic (Head, 2008). However, niche creation requires an interdisciplinary approach. As Cairney (2016, p. 2) puts it 'there can and should be a direct and unproblematic link between "the evidence" and the policy decisions and outcomes'.

For these reasons, evidence- based policy making can be relevant for religious tourism governance and policy formation. In paragrpah 10.2, the question was asked: 'At first glance, one may wonder why Malta, so rich in its authentic cultural and religious heritage, is not a main destination for faith-based tourism, notwithstanding its fully functional and continuously improving tourism infrastructure.' The contribution of this chapter is to inform the policy-making process, to identify aspects of faith-based tourism and suggest ways forward in structuring Malta's own independent faith-based tourism niche, to allow growth, diversity and to foster trust and cooperation (Fig. 10.1).

Part of what makes EBPM useful is that the framework focuses on the *effectiveness of the solution* (Cairney, 2016). In the past, some unstructured and uncoordinated initiatives were taken, remaining limited in scope. For example, when a problem was identified, such as the bulk of tourists entering for free at church sites, the goal was to address the *size of the problem*. The solution was to charge a justifiable entrance fee for tourists while accommodating those who come for prayer. Describing the potential issue only, rather than finding an effective answer, is part of the dissonance in modern policy making. This may be a consequence of the fact that evidence-based policy making does not exist independently from politics and private enterprise and that there are different interpretations of that evidence (Nutley *et al.*, 2013).

Using the EPBM's approach, the following suggested policy prescriptions are offered as effective solutions to initially populate Malta's independent faith-based tourism niche.

10.7.1 Policy prescription #1: definitions and statistics

It would be beneficial should localized definitions of pilgrimage, faith-based tourism and religious tourism be agreed upon. These can

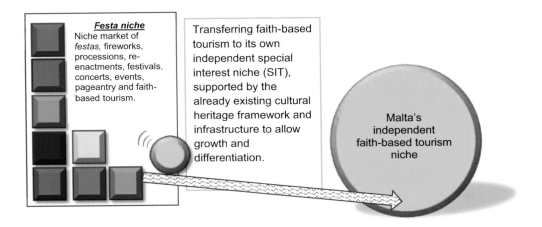

Fig. 10.1. Transferring faith-based tourism from the *festa niche,* a niche-within-a-niche, to its own independent faith-based tourism SIT niche.
Source: Author.

then inform policy makers and planners, as well as serve as a solid basis for quantitative and qualitative data gathering. It appears that neither the National Statistics Office (NSO) nor the MTA collect statistics related to incoming pilgrimage or faith-based tourism to Malta or Gozo. Therefore, the realistic number of visitors arriving at the islands for this purpose remains largely hidden. When one knows the definitions and the product, one can start formulating the right narratives to target audiences.

10.7.2 Policy prescription #2: IT, connectivity, pilot project, cooperation and trust

The usual question asked by local tourism entrepreneurs is whether going through all the trouble to create a faith-based tourism niche would pay off. Certainly, it will require initiative, cooperation and a modest initial investment to make it work. One regular occurring grave mistake is that when secular people, or people with a grudge against religion, obtain an influential position in tourism, their personal views may block their professional views. It might escape them that faith-based tourism and pilgrimage can be regarded as just any other

touristic product, and quite a profitable one at that.

One of the biggest uncertainties the formation of a faith-based tourism niche will face is the fragmented and decentralized character of the Church's management structure. Since faith-based tourism is also a tour operator driven phenomenon, the whole process of finding and booking a church for a group is very complicated. First, one needs to identify a fitting church for a particular itinerary, get in contact with the parish priest and hope he can make it on that day and time. Often, mishaps occur, and the priest has to cancel his appearance at the church and thus the advertised Holy Mass. Agencies, therefore, are facing difficulties because they cannot carry out the programme according to contract, leading to unsustainable situations. The Church in Malta does not have a central online booking and payment system or a central management team, making it a challenge to plan ahead. This fragmentation concerns also all monasteries, retreat houses and related products and activities.

The fragmented state relates also to all the different religious communities that have properties available for faith-based tourism, pilgrimages and retreats. In an ideal world, all these properties would have one central booking system for agencies and individuals, rather than a jumble of individual contacts. Without that, some will remain hidden and opportunities are missed. A demand for a technical solution is justified, i.e. a better website showing all that would be available, and more importantly, connectivity. This combined website would link then to the websites and connected booking engines of local tour operators, so that bookings can be made easily, and payments are made and automatically distributed. This would solve the usual bottlenecks of manual booking, payment by cheque and sending someone to collect the tickets. The introduction of e-tickets on mobile devices is also important for the sustainability reputation of the project. It also avoids inventing the wheel repeatedly, as there is already a centralized booking system with the required connectivity available at Heritage Malta, the national agency taking care of museums and cultural sites. As an affiliated authority, Heritage Malta could offer its assistance by allowing bookings through their website and booking engine. All tour operators have their systems connected to this site. Payment by card, issuing of e-tickets and redistribution of income will then facilitate the whole process.

It is further suggested that the Church, stakeholders and authorities set up a pilot project to identify two churches to be incorporated in a faith-based programme, both for groups and individuals. These churches, or chapels, should be part of a natural environment and part of an experience-oriented programme. An initial budget with the help of stakeholders and authorities would be welcomed. After agreeing on an opening-times schedule, a caretaker would be employed, who carries a master key to both churches. Tickets for groups and individuals (including booking a Holy Mass) for these two churches can then be done through the Heritage Malta booking engine. This step requires trust and cooperation but will work out for the benefit of all organizations involved. It is understood that giving up some of one's independence may cause an initial hesitance.

One of the aims and objectives of this faith-based tourism pilot project would be that the generated income is used to promote, maintain and restore those two churches and pay for the appointed staff, rather than engage volunteers. The choice of staff over volunteers is a professional preference, as there are contractual rights and duties involved, while standard operating procedures apply.

10.7.3 Policy prescription #3: marketing, branding and main marketing targets

In the most traditional form of religious tourism, it has been established that the parish priest or minister abroad is key to everything. These are the people who can make it happen. Precise targeting of such key people should be a priority in the marketing and branding strategy, as in every country there will be certain centralized communication platforms for Catholic priests and Protestant ministers. This micro-marketing approach is not much different to what the MTA does to reach their markets in EU countries and further afield.

10.7.4 Policy prescription #4: transformational and memorable experiences

Events require mostly passive audiences, while experiences mostly require active participation. All the items of the unofficial *festa niche* can of course be programmed in an itinerary as auxiliary items. Although in Christianity the Holy Mass must be respected for its passive character, a more active experience of faith can be achieved. In faith-based tourism we must honour both the faith and the tourism aspects. After all, there is the elements of competition among the stakeholders.

A few samples will suffice. A short walk through a landscape of choice before or after mass or celebrating mass in the open-air at sunset are just a few samples of what can make the difference. Rather than just watching a procession passing by, why not organize workshops to engage religious tourists in statue-carrying exercises, under the direction of an excellent storyteller who can share the meaning and value of the procession for the local community. Creating a bond between procession, bearers and religious tourists seems beneficial. St Paul's Island is another example. Although Malta is mentioned in the Scriptures, the exact location of St Paul's shipwreck remains unclear. However, in the meantime, in the absence of concluding archaeological evidence, the tradition of the shipwreck has been localized in St Paul's Bay for centuries. Nonetheless, experiences for the benefit of religious tourism have not been created there. How many countries have a biblical site? As a comparison, the Via Dolores in Jerusalem is no longer the same set of streets as in Christ's time, they have been commoditized and commercialized, but their inauthenticity does not make them less popular. Likewise, St Paul's Island is mostly about passion, devotion and the memorable experience, and not so much about scholarship and authenticity. Experiences must be designed and managed, hence there are numerous opportunities for creative minds. Experiences also do not happen on their own. Should they happen on their own, then policy prescription #5 applies.

10.7.5   Policy prescription #5: identify miracles, develop narratives and storytelling

One of the bigger issues that is seemingly holding back Malta is its own version of 'big' miracles and apparitions, which are push and pull factors in other pilgrimage sites such as Lourdes or Fatima. Malta does have its own apparitions and miracles, for instance at the shrine of Ta' Pinu in Gozo, but these are not readily available in widely published and distributed winning narratives for the visitors, as is the case with the big shrines (Haller and Munro, 2021). There is a need to identify all miracles, miraculous events and apparitions that have occurred in the Maltese archipelago and to publish winning narratives about them. Every successful pilgrimage and faith-based tourism site produces books, websites and apps.

Moreover, material is required to fill the gap in virtual pilgrimage. For instance, the St Olav Way in Norway and the Camino de Compostela can be followed virtually. Producing an app or a virtual 'in the footsteps of (St) Paul' may be a valid idea. This links to the consumer trend to first try out a destination's experience virtually before deciding to book their actual journey (Pine and Gilmore, 2020).

Tourist guides can engage different strategies, actions and role choices to create compelling themes, their content meaningfully

related to the participants' branch of religion or spiritual direction, which then can help in creating value and organizing transformational experiences (Jensen and Prebensen, 2015). All categories of faith-based visitors prefer tourist guides who understand their religious and spiritual needs, so that there can be a relationship of trust, support and safety. Such tourist guides must have a vision and a passion, able to engage in storytelling, linking to a higher purpose or something bigger than the participants themselves. When tourist guides are good storytellers, they can make things livelier and provide an unforgettable experience (Gallo, 2016).

10.7.6   Policy prescription #6: seasonality

Faith-based tourism will not eliminate seasonality, but it can be helpful in filling out the low and shoulder seasons. Creating a structured faith-based tourism demand outside the *festa* summer niche can be a good start, which eventually may see an overlap into the high season. Faith-based tourism can be navigated into the low and shoulder seasons by creating a proper independent niche, teaming up with knowledge banks and larger infrastructures, especially in IT and e-booking systems.

10.7.7   Policy prescription #7: training for tourist guides and tour operator staff

Being up to date with faith-based tourism will assist stakeholders in making informed decisions in view of the demand for faith-based tourism experiences. One other crucial group of service providers for experiences are tour operator staff and tourist guides. The tour operator will have to design the experiences found in the itinerary. For instance, the foreign priest will set out a few demands about what the tour should contain. Beyond that, he is depending on local knowledge and expertise. If the tour operator lacks insight or passion the programme will remain mediocre or artificial at best.

The Institute for Tourism, Travel and Culture at the University of Malta can mitigate a shortage of tourist guides specialized in faith-based tourism with short courses. The same can be organized for staff and representatives (reps) of tour operators so that they are well-informed about what there are advising and selling. Specialized industry reports can be produced and distributed.

10.7.8 Policy prescription #8: site-based destination and walking routes

As a destination for faith-based tourism, Malta seems to be more feasible as a site-based destination for religious tourism and pilgrimage, as it lacks most of the route-based characteristics. Nevertheless, around the Maltese archipelago there are many routes, shrines, sites and features of religio-cultural heritage and one can visit many of these in a week, e.g. 'follow in the footsteps of' Saint Paul (for Catholics) and Paul the exemplary man (for Protestants).

Regarding pilgrimage, efforts should be made to create longer walks in Malta. Many routes are already in place, but suffer from people illegally appropriating public land, a few self-entitled people blocking public entrance for their own private enjoyment (Ramblers Association Malta, 2022). It seems nothing more than logical to provide an interface whereby pilgrims and faith-based tourists can be connected to the routes and to the accumulated knowledge of the Ramblers' local experts to build up different narratives along the same routes.

10.8 Conclusion: Visualizing the Policy Prescriptions

In conclusion, the abovementioned policy prescriptions, based on evidence, suggests building blocks for structuring an independent faith-based tourism niche. According to expectation in a mature policy-making process, various consultation rounds will need to take place to discuss matters, to balance the interests of the public and the stakeholders, and come to a first workable model (Fig. 10.2).

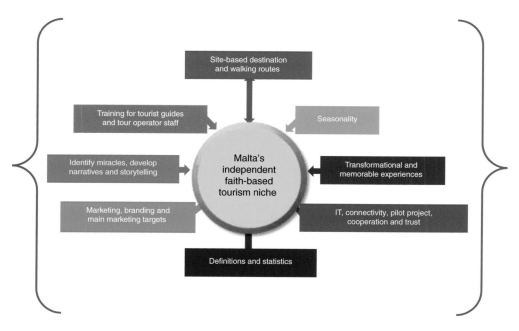

Fig. 10.2. Suggested structure elements for an independent faith-based tourism niche based on evidence and interpretation for Malta.
Source: Author.

No tourism policy is ever finished, as both tourism and policy making and planning are cyclical in nature. Over time, building blocks may be added or modified, due to the volatile nature of tourism, but they will always have to be interconnected, as in any practical formula.

References

Alecu, I.C. (2010) Epistemological aspects of religious tourism in rural areas. *Romania: International Journal of Business, Management and Social Sciences* 2(3), 59–65.

Archdiocese of Malta (2018) *Around 40% Attend Sunday Mass Regularly*. Available at: https://church.mt/around-40-attend-sunday-mass-regularly/ (accessed 17 August 2022).

Ashworth, G.J. and Tunbridge, J.E. (2017) From blue to grey? Malta's quest from mass beach to niche heritage tourism. In: Harrison, D. and Sharpley, R. (eds) *Mass Tourism in a Small World*. CAB International, Wallingford, UK, pp. 200–209.

Attard, S. (2019) The evolution of Malta's tourism sector. *Xjenza Online - Science Journal of the Malta Chamber of Scientists* 7, 37–48.

Azzopardi, J. and Blondy, A. (2012) *Marc'Antonio Haxac and Malta's Devotion to St Paul*. Fondation de Malte, Valletta.

Barber, R.W. (1991) *Pilgrimage*. The Boydell Press, Woodbridge, UK.

Blackwell, R. (2007) Motivations for religious tourism, pilgrimage, festivals, and events. In: Raj, R. and Morpeth, N.D. (eds) *Religious Tourism and Pilgrimage Management: An International Perspective*. CAB International, Wallingford, UK, pp. 35–47.

Blake, A., Sinclair, M.T., Sugiyarto, G. and DeHaan, C. (2003) The Economic Impact of Tourism in Malta. *Report for the Malta Tourism Authority*. The University of Nottingham. Available at: https://www.academia.edu/399013/The_Economic_Impact_of_Tourism_in_Malta (accessed January 2023).

Bonanno, A. (2005) *Malta: Phoenician, Punic, and Roman*. Midsea Books, Santa Venera, Malta.

Boz, M. (2018) Religious heritage tourism: the St. Paul trail project in Troas. *International Journal of Religious Tourism and Pilgrimage* 6(3), Article 9. Available at: https://arrow.dit.ie/ijrtp/vol6/iss3/9 (accessed 27 September 2022).

Cairney, P. (2016) *The Politics of Evidence-Based Policy Making*. Palgrave Macmillan, Stirling, UK.

Collins-Kreiner, N. (2018) Pilgrimage-tourism: common themes in different religions. *International Journal of Religious Tourism and Pilgrimage* 6(1), Article 3. Available at: https://arrow.tudublin.ie/ijrtp/vol6/iss1/3 (accessed 27 September 2022).

De Marchi, G., Lucertini, G. and Tsoukiàs, A. (2016) From evidence-based policy making to policy analytics. *Annals of Operations Research* 236(1), 15–38. DOI: 10.1007/s10479-014-1578-6.

Digance, J. (2006) Religious and secular pilgrimage: journeys redolent with meaning. In: Timothy, D.J. and Olsen, D.H. (eds) *Tourism, Religion and Spiritual Journey*. Routledge, Oxon, UK, pp. 36–48.

FRAGSUS (2015) *Fragility and Sustainability in Restricted Island Environments: Adaptation, Culture Change and Collapse in Prehistory*. Queen's University, Belfast. Available at: https://www.qub.ac.uk/sites/FRAGSUS/ (accessed 4 August 2022).

Freller, T. (1995) *St Pauls Grotto and Its Visitors: Pilgrims, Knights, Scholars and Sceptics*. Valletta Publishing Ltd, Santa Venera, Malta.

Freller, T. (2006) St Paul's Grotto, Malta and its antidotic earth in the awareness of early modern Europe. In: Azzopardi, J. (ed.) *The Cult of St Paul in the Christian Churches and in the Maltese Tradition*. PEG, San Gwann, Malta, pp. 191–218.

Freller, T. (2009) *Malta and The Grand Tour*. Midsea, Santa Venera, Malta.

Future Market Insight (2022) *Faith Based Tourism: Overview, Highlights, and Industry Outlook Overview, Faith Based Tourism Market*. Faith Based Tourism Market Size, Industry Share and Trends – 2032. Available at: https://www.futuremarketinsights.com/reports/faith-based-tourism-sector-overview (accessed 31 July 2022).

Gallo, C. (2016) *The Storyteller's Secret*. MacMillan, London.

Grech, A.G. (ed.) (2016) *Understanding the Maltese Economy*. Central Bank of Malta, Valletta. Available at: https://www.centralbankmalta.org/file.aspx?f=31385 (accessed 17 August 2022).

Greenia, G.D. (2014) What is pilgrimage? In: Harman, L.D. (ed.) *A Sociology of Pilgrimage: Embodiment, Identity, Transformation*. Ursus Press, London, ON, Canada, pp. 8–27. Available at: https://scholarworks.wm.edu/cgi/viewcontent.cgi?article=1666&context=aspubs (accessed 15 January 2023).

Gros, F. (2015) *A Philosophy of Walking*. Verso, London and New York.

Haller, S.F. and Munro, D. (2021) The winning narrative: the social genesis of pilgrimage sites. *International Journal of Religious Tourism and Pilgrimage* 9(3), Article 4. Available at: https://arrow.tudublin.ie/ijrtp/vol9/iss3/4 (accessed 28 September 2022).

Head, B.W. (2008) Research and evaluation: three lenses of evidence-based policy. *The Australian Journal of Public Administration* 67(1), 1–11. DOI: 10.1111/j.1467-8500.2007.00564.x.

Jensen, Ø. and Prebensen, N. (2015) Innovation and value creation in experience-based tourism. *Scandinavian Journal of Hospitality and Tourism* 15(1), 1–8. DOI: 10.1080/15022250.2015.1066093.

Joo, D. and Woosnam, K.M. (2022) Traveling to feel connected: origins and outcomes of potential faith-based tourists' emotional solidarity. *Journal of Travel & Tourism Marketing* 39(1), 42–57. DOI: 10.1080/10548408.2022.2045245.

MacCannell, D. (1999) *The Tourist*. University of California Press, Berkeley, CA.

Malone, C., Stoddart, S., Bonanno, A., Trump, D.H., and Gouder, T., et al (eds) (2009) *Mortuary Customs in Prehistoric Malta. Excavations at the Brochtorff Circle at Xaghra (1987–1994)*. McDonald Institute for Archaeological Research, Cambridge, UK.

Malta Chamber of Commerce, Enterprise and Industry (2021) *Rediscover: A Renewed Vision for Malta's Tourism Industry*. Available at: https://www.maltachamber.org.mt/en/the-malta-chamber-launches-rediscover-a-new-vision-for-the-tourism-industry-in-malta (accessed 9 August 2022).

Malta Independent (2018) *First Inhabitants Arrived 700 Years Earlier than Previously Thought—Research*, 3 March. Available at: https://www.independent.com.mt/articles/2018-03-03/local-news/First-inhabitants-arrived-700-years-earlier-than-previously-thought-research-6736185593 (accessed 4 August 2022).

Mangion, M.L. (2022) Malta's tourism development: themes, impacts, challenges, patterns and contrasts: pointers for a framework for short/long-term tourism development. In: Andriotis, K., Cardoso, C.P. and Stylidis, D. (eds) *Tourism Planning and Development in Western Europe*. CAB International, Wallingford, UK, pp. 32–50.

MTA (Malta Tourism Authority) (2012) *Tourism Policy 2012–2016*. Available at: https://tourism.gov.mt/en/Departments-Sections-Units/Pages/Departments-Sections-Units%20Sub%20Pages/EU%20Affairs%20and%20Policy%20Development/Grant%20Scheme%20for%20Tourism/Call4/Tourism_Policy_2012-2016.pdf (accessed 4 August 2022).

MTA (Malta Tourism Authority) (2015) *Tourism Policy 2015–2020*. Available at: https://tourism.gov.mt/en/Documents/FINALBOOKLETexport9.pdf (accessed 4 August 2022).

MTA (Malta Tourism Authority) (2021) *Tourism Policy 2021–2030: Recover, Rethink, Revitalize*. Available at: https://tourism.gov.mt/en/tourism/Pages/National-Tourism-Strategy-2021-2030.aspx (accessed 4 August 2022).

Munro, D. (2017) Historical perspectives of shifting motives for faith-based travel. *International Journal of Religious Tourism and Pilgrimage* 5(2), article 5. Available at: https://arrow.tudublin.ie/ijrtp/vol5/iss2/5 (accessed 27 September 2022).

Munro, D. (2019a) Managing St John's—Working for the greater good. In: Griffiths, M. and Wiltshier, P. (eds) *Managing Religious Tourism*. CAB International, Wallingford, UK, pp. 32–46.

Munro, D. (2019b) Managing Catholic Churches and sacred sites for protestant visitors to Malta. In: Dowson, R., Yaqub, J. and Raj, R. (eds) *Spiritual and Religious Tourism: Motivations and Management*. CAB International, Wallingford, UK and Boston, MA, pp. 144–152. DOI: 10.1079/9781786394163.0000.

Munro, D. (2020) A Pauline progress: Protestant post-pilgrimage reflections. In: McIntosh, I., Farra Haddad, N. and Munro, D. (eds) *Peace Journeys: A New Direction in Religious Tourism and Pilgrimage Research*. Cambridge Scholars Publishing, Newcastle upon Tyne, UK, pp. 243–256.

Munro, D. (2021) Modern full-sensory experiences and pilgrimage fulfilment in Malta's ancient temples. In: Liutikas, D. (ed.) *Pilgrims: Values and Identities*. CAB International, Wallingford, UK, pp. 150–163. DOI: 10.1079/9781789245653.0000.

NSO (National Statistics Office) (2022) *Census of Population and Housing 2021*. Census Office, National Statistics Office, Valletta. Available at: https://nso.gov.mt/en/nso/Media/Salient-Points-of-Publications/Documents/2022/Census%20of%20Population%20and%20Housing%20Preliminary%20Report/Census%20of%20population%202021.pdf (accessed 17 August 2022).

Nutley, S., Powell, A. and Davies, H. (2013) *What Counts As Good Evidence? A Provocation Paper for the Alliance for Useful Evidence*. Nesta, London.

Pine II, B.J. and Gilmore, J.H. (2020) *Welcome to the Experience Economy: Competing for Customer Time, Attention, and Money*. Harvard Business Review Press, Boston, MA.

Pohner, T., Berki, T. and Rátz, T. (2009) Religious and pilgrimage tourism as a special segment of mountain tourism. *Journal of Tourism Challenges and Trends* 2(1), 27–42.

Ramblers Association Malta (2022) Details of discussion to guarantee the accessibility of the foreshore at Fomm ir-Riħ, *Blog*, July, 24. Available at: https://www.ramblersmalta.org/blog/ (accessed 5 August 2022).

Richards, G.W. (2017) How research–policy partnerships can benefit government: a win–win for evidence-based policy-making. *Canadian Public Policy* 43(2), 165–170. DOI: 10.3138/cpp.2016-046.

Rico, P., Cabrer-Borrás, B. and Morillas-Jurado, F. (2021) Seasonality in tourism: do senior programs mitigate it? *Mathematics* 9(16), 2003. DOI: 10.3390/math9162003.

Sant Cassia, P. (1993) The discovery of Malta: nature, culture and ethnicity in 19th century painting. *Journal of Mediterranean Studies* 3(2), 354–377.

Scott, R.A. (2010) *Miracle Cures: Saints, Pilgrimages and the Healing Powers of Belief*. University of California Press, Berkeley, CA. DOI: 10.1525/9780520946200.

Scott, J.S. (2012) Representing sacred space: Pilgrimage and literature. In: Coomans, T., De Dijn, H., De Maeyer, J., Heynickx, R. and Verschaffel, B. (eds) *Loci Sacri: Understanding Sacred Places. KADOC Studies on Religion, Culture and Society (9)*. Leuven University Press, Leuven, Belgium, pp. 138–167.

Sharma, V. (2013) Faith tourism: for a healthy environment and a more sensitive world. *The International Journal of Religious Tourism and Pilgrimage* 1(1), 15–23.

Singh, R.P.B. (2006) Pilgrimage in Hinduism: historical context and modern perspectives. In: Timothy, D.J. and Olsen, D.H. (eds) *Tourism, Religion and Spiritual Journey*. Routledge, Oxon, UK, pp. 220–236.

Smith, V. (1992) The quest in guest. *Annals of Tourism Research* 19(1), 1–17.

Zsarnoczky, M. (2017) Developing senior tourism in Europe. *Pannon Management Review* 6(3–4), 201–213.

Zuntz, G. (1971) *Persephone, Three Essays on Religion and Thought in Magna Graecia*. Clarendon Press, Oxford, UK.

11 International Efforts to Secure Sacred Sites: Capacity and Autonomy Across Countries

Charlotte Lee[1]*, Masahiro Omae[2] and Dino Bozonelos[3]

[1]*Political Science & Global Studies, Berkeley City College, USA;* [2]*School of Behavioral and Social Sciences and Consumer and Family Studies, San Diego City College, USA;* [3]*Departments of Political Science and Global Studies, California State University, San Marcos, USA*

Abstract

There has been a growing call for the securitization of religious sites around the world, spurred by hundreds of high-profile terrorist acts committed at places of worship on an annual basis. In 2019, the United Nations published an ambitious Plan of Action to Safeguard Religious Sites. This chapter analyses the implementation of recommendations in the UN Plan. Comparative case studies of Sri Lanka, Germany and Iraq reveal how state capacity and autonomy determine the degree and type of protections implemented by various governments. The UN Plan of Action is a necessary, but insufficient, condition for the protection of religious sites from religious terrorism. If the goals of the UN Plan are to be achieved, states must increase their capacity and, in cases of weak states such as Iraq, also increase their autonomy.

11.1 Introduction

There has been a growing call for the securitization of religious sites around the world, spurred by hundreds of high-profile attacks committed at places of worship on an annual basis. Violence aimed at religious sites are inherently acts of political violence. In many countries, religious sites are especially 'soft' targets (UN Office of Counter-Terrorism, n.d.). Soft targets are defined as 'locations that are easily accessible to large numbers of people and that have limited security or protective measures in place making them vulnerable to attack' (US Department of Homeland Security, 2018). Religious sites are often minimally defended, unlike military installations, government buildings and even some private businesses such as professional sports venues. Howie (2014) writes that, 'sites of religion and pilgrimage, representing sites that attract mass gatherings of people, are often considered highly attractive for would-be terrorists' (p. 39).

Existing data on the connection between a particular form of political violence, terrorism and religious targets support this logic. Targets of contemporary terrorism are overwhelmingly religious institutions and figures. According to the University of Maryland's Global Terrorism Database, during the period from 1970 to 2019 over four in five (84%) reported terrorist incidents were intended to

*Corresponding author: clee@peralta.edu

© CAB International 2023. *The Politics of Religious Tourism* (eds D. Bozonelos and P. Moira)
DOI: 10.1079/9781800621732.0011

harm religious targets. Violent attacks rose precipitously in the 2010s, peaking at over 400 incidents on religious targets in 2014. This has fallen to over 200 incidents annually, which still implies, on average, at least one religiously motivated terrorist incident in the world every 2 days. In response to this targeted violence, strategies to secure religious sites have ranged considerably, from the hiring of private security firms, to heightened local policing, to coordination with international bodies (Sönmez *et al.*, 1999; Howie, 2014).

Violent actions at religious sites and places of pilgrimage have deleterious political, social and economic effects. Violence impacts the entire spectrum of those who visit these places, from those who are pious in their motivations, often referred to as pilgrims, to those who visit for other reasons, referred to as religious tourists. These visitors may be motivated by their individual faith and/or culture or for more profane reasons, such as the simple desire to visit a famous landmark (Smith, 1992; Stausberg, 2011; Raj and Griffin, 2015; Durán-Sánchez *et al.*, 2018). Regardless of motivation, violence at a sacred site both immediately and in the long-term reduces the number of pilgrims, religious tourists and profane tourists alike (Sönmez, 1998; Pizam and Smith, 2000). Chowdhury *et al.* (2017) demonstrate across diverse country cases the immense tourism losses incurred when religious sites are attacked. Baker (2014) adds that terrorist attacks can contribute to negative external images of the destination site, which directly shapes tourist motivation. This highlights the strong incentives for national governments protect religious sites.

While national-level governments are often the central institutions for governing religious sites, international intergovernmental organizations are important actors in their own right. There exist institutions at the international level that contribute to the management of religious sites. The United Nations is prominent among these. It comprises entities such as UNESCO (UN Educational, Scientific, and Cultural Organization) and UNAOC (UN Alliance of Civilizations), which support the preservation and safeguarding of humankind's cultural and natural heritage. Many religious sites fall within this remit.

International organizations fulfil several key functions that can complement the work of national governments. These include, at a material level, provision of resources such as monies and international advisors to ensure the protection of cultural heritage sites. One of the more widely known ways in which international organizations have shaped the management and governance of religious sites is through UNESCO's World Heritage List. In existence since 1972, this list includes sites 'of outstanding universal value'. In 2021 the World Heritage List included 1154 cultural and natural sites, of which nearly one in five were religious sites such as mosques, churches, temples, shrines and archaeological sites of religious significance (UNESCO, 2021a, b). Through its identification, support and promotion of sites, UNESCO's World Heritage List has shaped international tourism flows and local development patterns (Vrabel, 2014; Esposito, 2018). A UNESCO-led Initiative on Heritage of Religious Interest has outlined an international strategy regarding the specific histories, significance and needs for preserving religious sites.

The UNAOC has taken a different tack, focusing on dialogue and violence prevention. Since its creation, the UNAOC has sought to explore and defuse the sources of growing polarization in the world. The UNAOC coordinates member governments to engage in intercultural dialogue and preventive diplomacy, among other activities. Its Plan of Action for 2019–2023 focuses on three strategic priorities including 'prevention, mediation, [and] preventing and countering violent extremism conducive to terrorism' (UNAOC, 2019, p. 8). Nested within this latter priority is a call to safeguard religious sites worldwide. A 2019 plan of action issued by the UNAOC, entitled 'The United Nations Plan of Action to Safeguard Religious Sites: In Unity and Solidarity for Safe and Peaceful Worship,' offers a three-tiered process for national governments to respond systematically and deliberately to the growing security needs of religious sites. The drafting of this plan was spurred on by several high-profile attacks on religious sites, including 'horrific attacks on two mosques in Christchurch, New Zealand; the Tree of Life synagogue in Pittsburgh; three Catholic churches in Sri Lanka on Easter Sunday; and an increasing number of hate-based attacks targeting religious sites worldwide' (UN News, 2019). In crafting the plan, UN representatives consulted with religious leaders and faith-based organizations around the world, convening them at UN headquarters in New York and also conducting visits to member states. UNAOC coordinated with other UN bodies such as those focused on mapping religious sites (UN Operational Satellite Applications Programme, UNOSAT) and engaged in counterterrorism measures worldwide (UN Office of Counter-Terrorism, UNOCT). The plan is also meant to dovetail with the UN Strategy and Plan of Action on Hate Speech.

The UNAOC Plan of Action offers recommendations on prevention, preparedness and response. Prevention focuses on measures such as public education, anti-hate speech legislation, reduction in online hate speech and interfaith dialogue. Preparedness includes a call for robust national planning processes and establishing 'specialized units' for the safeguarding of religious sites. Specifically, the UN recommended member-states to 'consider establishing, where appropriate, in accordance with national legislation and procedures, specialized units in central and local administrations to safeguard religious sites' (UNAOC, 2019, p. 25). This recommendation is of importance as most tourism destinations, extending to sacred sites, are guarded by private security forces. Yet a paradox results, where societies have asked 'low-paid and undervalued workers to be on the frontline of some of our most important security operations' (Parfomak, 2004, p. 42). Security guards sometimes lack the proper training and equipment. They are asked to not only safeguard sites from potential terrorism, but also to crowd control, prevent petty theft and vandalism and in some cases provide emergency services. They 'fill the gap' (Parfomak, 2004, p. 5), especially in countries where state capacity is low. In the unfortunate case of a violent attack on a religious site, the Plan recommends strong national 'early-warning systems, emergency response, crisis management, security, and resilience' (UNAOC, 2019, p. 19). These three phases of activity, while logical as laid out in the Plan, demand a great deal of state capacity to implement on a short- and longer-term basis.

This chapter will examine the UN's recommendations, particularly regarding preparedness and response. A comparative case study approach illustrates how governments have responded and their proposed frameworks to secure sacred sites, which are often part of broader counterterrorism efforts. The goal of this chapter is to broaden and deepen the research on the nexus between international and national efforts to protect religious sites. Case studies of Sri Lanka, Germany and Iraq highlight the diverse approaches of national governments to this issue. In some instances, state-level actions are augmented by support from international organizations. Different state responses illuminate the ways in which security of religious sites intersects with varying levels of state capacity, state autonomy, state organization and counterterrorism efforts.

11.2 Understanding State Capacity and State Autonomy

State capacity and state autonomy are fundamental concepts in comparative politics. They serve to sharpen understanding of the quality of governance in a country as well as the power of the state. In a description given by the World Bank, state capacity refers to 'the capacity of the government to effectively formulate and implement sound policies,' (as quoted in Roller, 2020). State autonomy refers to a different aspect of state power, namely the ability of a state to function independently of domestic interest groups and external influences (Kersh, 2000). Many discussions of these concepts are grounded in the ideas of Max Weber, whose 1919 essay, *Politics as a Vocation*, helps provide basic definitions and understandings of politics, particularly the role of the state in society (Brett et al., 2017).

One starting point for applying these concepts is to sort states by whether they possess high vs low degrees of state capacity and state autonomy. A state with a high degree of capacity can devise and implement policies that enable a state to secure itself and protect its citizens. Conversely, a state with a low degree of capacity lacks the capability to protect itself and/or its citizens. A state with a high degree of autonomy will demonstrate the ability to enact policies despite pressure not to do so by domestic and international forces outside of that state.

These actions can occur at times without public consent, or with a disregard for public opinion. Conversely, a state with low autonomy is 'captured' by outside interests and lacks ability to act independently.

States with a high degree of capacity and autonomy can pursue any goals they want. In contrast, states with high capacity but lower autonomy have enough power to accomplish tasks but are more susceptible to public opinion. These states could accomplish more but are often stymied by internal opposition. Generally speaking, developed democracies, such as Australia, Germany or Japan, tend to fit into this category (Bäck and Hadenius, 2008). States with low capacity and high autonomy can make decisions independently, but they often lack the capability to adequately implement desired policies. A good example is Russia in the 1990s, when the Yeltsin government was unable to deliver basic services and most Russians saw their government as both unresponsive and inept. Finally, some states lack both capacity and autonomy. In political economy terms the state might be 'captured' whereby corporations, interest groups including ethnic or tribal groups, or other organized factions, shape state policies and regulations to selfishly fit their interests. This often leads to a high level of corruption and directly influences the capacity of a state (Hellman and Kaufmann, 2001). Table 11.1 offers examples of countries with varying levels of state capacity and autonomy.

11.3   Political Violence, State Capacity and Autonomy

The literature on political violence identifies the important role of state capacity and state autonomy in preventing violence against religious

Table 11.1. Comparing State Power: Examples of Capacity and Autonomy.

	High capacity	Low capacity
High autonomy	China Singapore	Russia Venezuela
Low autonomy	Australia Japan	Nigeria Libya

Source: The authors.

communities and religious sites. The importance of capacity is embedded in the definition of the state itself. Weber (1965) defined a state as a political entity that claims the monopoly on the legitimate use of violence in a given territory. This implies that a state's physical capacity to protect itself and its citizens is a measurement of how well the state functions. This framework suggests that when a state becomes unable to enforce this monopoly on violence, it may transition towards what has been referred to as a failed state (Rotberg, 2002). Oftentimes, the lack of governmental authority and capacity will lead to open warfare in society. Examples include the protracted civil wars in Somalia, Yemen and Syria. In failed states, religious sites are extremely vulnerable to attack.

However, political violence is not limited to low-capacity states. High-capacity states also experience political violence, particularly terrorism. Terrorist attacks on high-capacity states have often transpired on physical locations that represent the interests of high-capacity states outside their borders. These have included attacks on overseas missions and military installations. Ghatak (2016) observed that terrorism is a strategy of the weak and is most optimal when the group has little support for its actions in society.

Likewise, the way states respond to various types of political violence depends on the level of state capacity. High-capacity states, especially democracies, are more likely to only target the actual instigators of such politically violent acts (Kalyvas, 2006). High-capacity states can deploy selective violence, as opposed to indiscriminate violence, as the former requires a more complex administrative structure.

State capacity is not the only factor for understanding state responses to political violence. The level of state autonomy determines how states respond to various types of political violence. As discussed above, low levels of autonomy are common in democracies. Democratic state leaders are constrained in their responses to politically violent actions. These ruling groups answer to what are referred to as 'winning coalitions' (Bueno de Mesquita *et al.*, 2003). In democracies, winning coalitions consist of those who voted for state leadership. Thus, public opinion is both necessary and sufficient for state action. Otherwise, a state response could be seen as illegitimate and leaders could find themselves replaced in the next election. In contrast, states with high levels of autonomy are less constrained in their responses to political violence. Non-democratic leaders typically answer to a small winning coalition, which consists of a smaller subset of powerful individuals and groups within a society. Because of this, states with high autonomy may deploy unpopular measures to protect religious communities and sites and face few repercussions for doing so.

11.4 Capacity and Autonomy: A Framework for Understanding Efforts to Secure Sacred Sites

The literature on political violence suggests that governments that experience interfaith violence, particularly terrorist attacks by religious minorities against sacred sites of the majority faith, are most likely to invest in preventive measures to protect religious sites of the majority religion. This may be especially true of countries where governments invest in repression of minority religions; in these cases, minorities have stronger incentives to resort to violence. The UN Plan of Action, particularly its suggestion for national plans to protect religious sites, should be most applicable and its concomitant resources attractive to these countries. To better understand this, we ask the following research question:

> RQ: Under what conditions might a government invest resources in the protection of religious sites as expected in the UN Plan of Action?

To address this research question, we will engage in a diverse exploratory case study approach as outlined by Gerring (2017). Comparative case studies deepen understanding of context and invite possible future generalizations. According to Barlett and Vavrus (2016), 'no "place" is unaffected by history and politics; any specific location is influenced by economic, political, and social processes well beyond its physical and temporal boundaries' (p. 12). Thus, social practices and institutional developments in one country might vary from one context to the other, but comparative case studies can illuminate underlying patterns.

Our study will focus on two independent variables of interest: state capacity and autonomy. To test expectations derived from our state capacity

and state autonomy framework, and in combination with the coordinating role of international organizations, this section explores three cases of government protection of religious sites. These 'analytical vignettes' offer a starting point for probing the possibilities embedded in documents such as the UN Plan of Action.

The case studies focus on Sri Lanka, Germany and Iraq. All three are diverse and multi-confessional – if not deeply divided – societies, with major lines of conflict falling along ethnic and religious lines. Sri Lanka's decades of ethnic and sectarian violence, from the 1980s through 2000s, were followed by a period of national recovery and post-conflict rehabilitation. This country's past and present make it a strong candidate for the recommendations contained within the UN's Plan due to ongoing violence committed at religious sites. Germany's high state capacity, in combination with its dark history of genocide against religious minorities, offers a case study in robust state and international response to violence committed against religious sites. Our final country vignette, of post-conflict Iraq, highlights how weak state capacity creates an opening for non-state coercive units to engage in policing and protection of religious sites. A summary of these country cases and their levels of state capacity and autonomy is given in Table 11.2.

11.5 Country-Level Vignettes: National Action and Inaction

11.5.1 Sri Lanka: Post-conflict recovery and instability

Sri Lanka is a multi-confessional country that has been in the process of recovery and rehabilitation since the 2009 conclusion of

Table 11.2. Comparing capacity and autonomy in Germany, Sri Lanka and Iraq.

Country	Capacity	Autonomy
Germany	High	Low
Sri Lanka	Low	Medium/High
Iraq	Low	Low

Source: The authors.

a brutal multi-decade civil war. This conflict was driven by separatist territorial claims and ethnonationalist grievances. Major parties to the conflict were a separatist Tamil insurgency and the Sri Lankan government. The war, in which over 100,000 were killed, ended with the defeat of the Tigers of Tamil Eelam (LTTE). Nearly a decade of recovery, rehabilitation and relative calm followed, although it has been stained by ongoing evidence of major human rights violations (UN OHCHR, 2017).

Sri Lankan society is divided along ethnic, religious, linguistic and geographic lines. Nearly three-quarters of Sri Lankan society is Buddhist, and this overlaps with the majority-Sinhalese ethnic group that dominates Sri Lankan power structures. The Tamil ethnic minority, which comprises just over one-tenth of the population, is predominantly Hindu, with some Tamils subscribing to Roman Catholicism, Protestantism and Islam. Geographically, this minority is clustered in the northern and eastern parts of the country (Fig. 11.1). Major religions recognized by Sri Lankan law, and taught in the public school system, include Buddhism, Islam, Hinduism and Christianity.

Because of widespread terrorist tactics deployed by all parties during its recent civil war, government officials have issued public statements that express an awareness of the need to secure places of worship in Sri Lanka. These statements and government resources are skewed toward the protection of Buddhist sites. In 2018, Prime Minister Ranil Wickremesinghe stated, 'Temples in Sri Lanka with a majority of Sinhala Buddhists must be protected. ...It is the responsibility of the government to uplift religious sites.' Statements such as this pander to the Sinhalese Buddhist majority in the country, which due to prior decades of civil war is primed to believe that there exist grave internal threats to their national integrity (Herath, 2020). There has been no corresponding call to protect important sites of other religions, despite widespread reports of attacks on religious sites and figures. These have included Buddhist extremists carrying out anti-Muslim and anti-Christian violence and Muslim attacks on Catholic churches (Jenkins, 2019; Morrison, 2020; US Department of State, 2020b, 2021b).

Bias in favour of the Buddhist majority has perhaps led to willful ignorance of threats to sacred sites of religious minorities. The period of post-conflict stability in Sri Lanka was ruptured in April 2019 with a major terrorist attack carried out on Easter Sunday by Muslim suicide bombers. In a coordinated attack, three Christian churches and several tourist hotels were bombed, resulting in nearly 300 fatalities. Media coverage of the tragedy uncovered foreknowledge of the suicide attacks by the police, highlighting gaps in the prevention mechanisms across the country's intelligence, law enforcement and political leaders. In responding to the attacks, the government stationed army troops at sites of worship, the homes of religious leaders and government buildings.

Sri Lanka is thus a country primed to adopt the recommendations of the UN Plan of Action to Safeguard Religious Sites. There exists some expressed political will for such planning, though it is biased in favour of the religious majority. Yet to date there has been no significant evidence of planning to protect religious sites, and this may be due to at least two factors, one idiosyncratic and the other institutional. Most immediate was the onset of the Covid-19 global pandemic, which strained public resources and government attention worldwide.

A second factor is the lack of a national planning process that focuses on prevention, rather than response, in the protection of religious sites. This speaks to the political will of the country's majority-ethnic Sinhalese (mostly Buddhist) leaders, which is more narrowly focused on promoting and defending Buddhist-majority interests. There have been only ad hoc measures directed at the protection of vulnerable sites, such as the creation in 2020 of a Task Force for Archaeological Heritage Management in the Eastern Province (President of Sri Lanka, 2020). While this task force does have multi-confessional representation, it may be a pretext for pushing minority religions off sites deemed sacred for the Buddhist majority (US Department of State, 2021b). All of these factors speak to biases in state organizations and strained capacity in this post-conflict society.

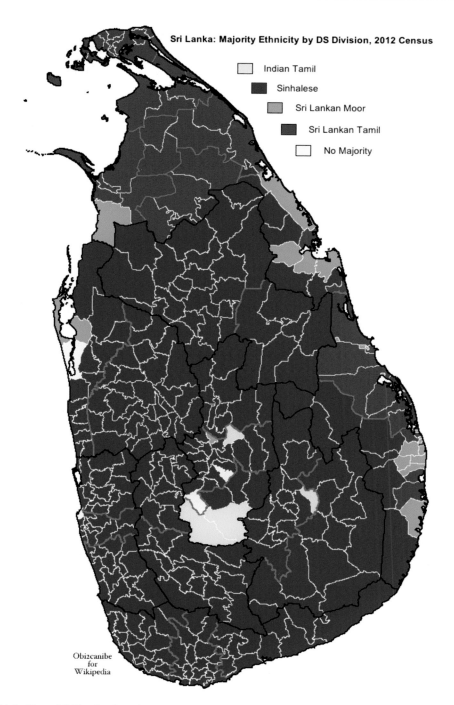

Fig. 11.1. Map of Sri Lanka denoting majority religions by region (2012 Census).
Source: Wikimedia Commons, Obi2canibe, from data provided by the Sri Lanka Department of Census and Statistics (Public Domain).

11.5.2 Germany: Managing tensions in an increasingly diverse society

Germany's history of state-sponsored genocidal acts against religious minorities continues to cast a shadow into the present. This history, particularly genocide of Jews and other minorities during the 20th century, along with subsequent state-building after the country's defeat during World War II, informs present policies regarding protection of religious sites. Germany today is a multi-confessional society where freedom of religion is constitutionally protected. Religious discrimination is also prohibited by the national constitution (US Department of State, 2020a, 2021a).

While approximately two-fifths of the German population is non-denominational (40.7%), an estimated one quarter of the population is Roman Catholic (26.7%) and one quarter is Protestant (24.3%). Estimates vary regarding the number of Muslims in Germany, which ranges from 3.5% to over 6% of the population when including non-citizens. The number of Muslims in the country has grown recently due to immigration spikes in the 2010s and is over 5 million (Pew Research Center, 2017). One final important ethno-religious group is the Jewish population. Despite the horrors of genocide committed against the German and, more broadly, European Jewish populations in the 20th century, there were an estimated 118,000 German-Jewish persons in 2019 (World Population Review, 2021).

There exist strong historical and political reasons for the German government to invest in the protection of religious sites. In contrast to Sri Lanka, Germany benefits from high state capacity and resources. There is also a deeper public willingness to grapple with the country's past genocide of religious minorities, specifically against Jews but also organized violence committed against ethnic groups such as Roma. Institutions have subsequently been put in place to protect religious minorities, with state resources devoted to education and allocation of public monies to preserve historical sites and support survivors. The German people and state have demonstrated a willingness to engage in a sustained way with the challenges inherent to building a dynamic, open and diverse society. Because of this alignment of interests, in the German case there is an expectation of a robust state response to politically motivated violence at religious sites.

This expectation is met to some degree. Antisemitism has been on the rise in recent years. An attempted mass shooting of worshippers at a synagogue in October 2019 spurred officials to issue a broad set of measures to combat religious extremists and far-right groups. In a show of state unity, these measures were issued jointly by all state-level interior ministers and the federal interior minister. They included calls for more information sharing on far-right and extremist groups and protection of places of worship by placing officers outside religious sites. In 2020, the federal government backed up this plan with an infusion of $26 million to a national Jewish organization to support the costs of securing synagogues and other Jewish community sites (Axelrod, 2020).

The efforts of German officials, local and national, are also buttressed by the resources of a powerful regional organization, the European Union. The union brings significant coordinating and organizational heft to state efforts to combat extremism and terrorist attacks on European targets. A 2020 technical paper released by the European Commission (EC) laid out a framework for assessing the likelihood of a terrorist attack (Table 11.3). Using a point system for risk assessment, where more points equate to more vulnerability, the paper considered six different categories of risk factors such as the symbolic importance of a site and how many people congregate at the site. The presence of security guards was identified as an important 'existing measure' to deter attacks.

Beyond problem analysis, the EU dedicated resources for action. In a 2020 statement following the release of this technical paper, the EC noted an allocation of €20 million toward enhancing the security of places of worship. The EC referenced the UNAOC Plan of Action in this statement on how EU member states might engage in threat identification, assessment of the likelihood of attack, assessment of target vulnerability and protection measures for places of worship.

Table 11.3. European Union point system to assess the likelihood of a terrorist attack.

	Allocated points	1	2	3	4
Indicators	Accessibility	– No public contact – No previous threats – Minor-crime area	– Little public contact – Some previous threats in the surrounding area – Low-crime area	– Normal public contact – Previous threats against the facility – Moderate-crime area	– High public contact – Usual presence of protests – Usual threats against the facility – High-crime area
	Importance	– Insignificant impact at national level in case of an incident – Activities only at local level	– Some impact at national level in case of an incident – Activities only at regional level	– Significant impact at national level in case of an incident – Activities at national level	– Very big impact at national level in case of an incident (e.g. critical infrastructure) – Activities at international level
	Facility size (A)	A<1000m²	1000 <A<10,000 m²	10000 <A<25,000 m²	A>25,000 m²
	People attendance (N)	N<100	101 <N<250	251 <N<750	N>751
	Site symbolism	– Not well-known facility	– Well-known at a local level – Symbolic only at a local level	– Well-known at a regional level – Symbolic only at a regional level	– Well-known at a national level – Symbolic at a national level (tourist attraction)
	Existing measures	– Elevated physical security measures – Presence of limited security guards	– Some physical security measures – Presence of limited security guards	– Basic physical security measures – Absence of security guards	– Absence of physical security measures – Absence of security guards

Source: Karlos and Larcher (2020) (CC BY 4.0).

11.5.3   Iraq's shrine militias

Sectarianism has become the most defining feature of Iraqi political society. The US invasion of Iraq unlocked long-simmering tensions between the three major groupings in Iraqi society: the Shi'a Arab majority, located mostly in the southern and eastern part of the country; the Sunni Arab minority, located mostly in the western al-Anbar province; and the mostly Sunni Kurdish minority, who form a majority in the autonomous region of Iraqi Kurdistan. These tensions are not just ethnic, but also ethno-confessional in nature. Ethno-confessionalism refers to when an ethnic identity develops out of a religious identity. One prominent example of this phenomenon is the ethno-confessional identities in Northern Ireland, between Catholics and Protestants. Both groups identify culturally as Irish, but due to their different confessions, see each other as competing ethnic groups.

In part because of the development of ethno-confessionism in the country, along with the US invasion and occupation of the country beginning in 2003, Iraq is today a consociational democracy. Consociationalism has been proposed as an effective solution in religiously fragmented countries. Hope existed that such a model would, if not entirely solve problems, at least it would reduce the potential for future violence. It is important to note that consociational systems violate the democratic principle of majority rule. Rights are provided to each community, rather than the individual, which allows each group enough power to negotiate on behalf of its members (Lijphart, 1969). Minority groups may then stall the political system, preventing a majority from making decisions, but also protect minority rights. Lijphart observed four pillars of consociationalism: grand governing coalitions, segmental autonomy, a semblance of proportionality in resource allocation and policy veto. Dodge (2020a) points out that the 2005 Iraqi Constitution provided for a 'light consociationalism'. This approach has not worked, however, as pervasive corruption and a hardening of identities through years of warfare have led Iraqis to have little faith in their government.

Consociationalism has left the Iraqi state with a low level of capacity where the government is unable to carry out basic tasks. But the government also has a low level of state autonomy as well. Temporary power-sharing measures, and a mix of federal and confederal practices between the central government and the regional governments, makes Baghdad dependent on intra-state squabbling. A good example is the attempt by the former Iraqi Prime Minister to curry favour with Iraqi military officers through promotions and acts of favouritism in the years leading up to the ISIS takeover (Dodge, 2020b). By politicizing the officer corps, he weakened the autonomy of the military to act in the best interests of the state.

These low levels of state capacity and state autonomy precipitated development of what are referred to as 'shrine militias' or *Saraya al-'Atabat* in the country. Shrine militias are non-state actors that were specifically organized to protect holy sites in Karbala, Najaf and other Iraqi cities. These forces are also referred to as *Hashd al-Marji'i*, or the 'holy' mobilization. Their official status is fluidly defined and they generally fall under what is referred to as the larger Hashd umbrella. Hashd is short for *al-Hashd al-Shaabi*. They are Shia-dominated Popular Mobilization Forces (PMF) that were called into action by Grand Ayatollah Ali al-Sistani in 2014 (Abbas, 2017). The Islamic State (IS) had quickly expanded geographically, having taken Mosul that same year. IS was threatening Shia holy sites in Iraq. Al-Sistani issued a fatwa, asking Iraqis 'to defend the country, its people, the honor of its citizens, and its sacred places' (Boduszynski, 2016).

The Hashd were formally integrated into Iraq's security forces in 2016, in what was referred to as the Hashd Law. However, that law also declared that the Hashd are 'independent'. This level of autonomy is quite visible with the shrine militias. The shrine militias manage their own finances, purchase military equipment and pay the salaries of their fighters. This makes them much less reliant on the Iraqi Ministry of Defence, which is not the case for other Hashd militias that have become more integrated. The shrine militias almost wholly answer to religious leaders, such as the Grand Ayatollah, reinforcing the low capacity of the state.

11.6 Conclusion

The COVID-19 pandemic derailed any potential responses to the 2019 UN Plan of Action. As international travel was suspended, and most domestic travel was limited, there was less immediate need to protect sacred sites. If anything, the pandemic highlighted the contingent nature of institutional action. On a practical level, it also highlighted the need to have robust planning mechanisms in place to minimize the disruption of such black swan events, or catastrophic events that by nature are difficult or perhaps even impossible to forecast (Taleb, 2007).

Comparative case studies of Sri Lanka, Germany and Iraq help illuminate why there may be only a limited response to the 2019 UN Plan of Action even after the pandemic subsides. Countries with low levels of capacity, such as Sri Lanka and Iraq, are less likely to invest resources in the protection of religious sites, such as the creation of government-managed special protection units. Likewise, countries with low levels of both state capacity and autonomy are also less likely to invest resources. In countries with religious strife, where sacred sites would need the most protection, state leaders might be unable to rise above the conflict. They might be 'captured' by the 'winning coalition' and prevented from addressing actualized or potential violence.

Conversely, a country with a high degree of capacity, such as Germany, has the capability to provide protection to religious sites. This is buttressed by the recommendations and resources of an international organization such as the European Union, which has aligned with the UN Plan. As a developed democracy, Germany has a lower degree of state autonomy, which can slow down decision making. Yet, this same low degree of autonomy can also be beneficial to smaller interest groups. In Germany, national Jewish organizations have consistently lobbied the government for protection of their synagogues (Sokol, 2021). They have been successful in garnering national attention and sympathy and the German government has responded positively.

In Sri Lanka, we see a country with low capacity and higher levels of state autonomy. The government feels obligated to protect Buddhist shrines, but less so when it comes to sacred sites of other religions. Higher levels of autonomy allow the government to be less responsive to the needs of the Hindu, Christian and Muslim minority populations. Sri Lankan president Gotabaya Rajapaksa, who served as Secretary of Defence during the last years of the civil war, made it clear that Buddhism is the country's primary identity. In a speech to Sri Lanka's parliament, he proclaimed,

> ...Defending the Buddhist order, protecting the Sinhalese, protecting the country's unity are all interlinked. ... Other religions can protect their religious freedom in this country only if the Sinhalese Buddhists are protected. (Lam, 2020).

In Iraq, a country with low capacity and low autonomy, non-state actors are emboldened. The development of independent shrine militias are a direct result of the Iraqi government's inability to act. It lacked both the institutional structures (capacity) and the political willpower (autonomy) to respond to religious terrorism propagated by IS militants. Iraq presents an example to other countries which have experienced or have the potential to experience terrorist actions linked to religious sites. The militarized non-state solution observed in Iraq could also happen where state capacity and state autonomy are low. One potential example is Nigeria, where tension between Christian and Muslim communities has led to attacks on holy sites and places of worship (Egwu, 2020).

If a low-capacity country does not follow the UN Plan of Action, this could lead to further fracturing and political violence within that country. Iraq's shrine militias illustrate this. While the Iraq case demonstrates protection of majority-religious sites as consistent with our theoretical expectations, it is also a cautionary case. Iraqi shrine militias are under the command of religious leaders, not the state. Furthermore, because Iraq's shrine militias predate the UN Plan of Action, it is unlikely that the Iraqi government will adopt any of the measures in the 2019 Plan.

On a deeper institutional level, should the protection of religious sites fall under existing coercive organizations such as police and military? This was the path taken by Germany and Sri Lanka. However, in religiously fractured countries this might not even be possible. The development of special protection units, designed to safeguard religious sites, may by their very definition have to exist outside of state structures, with implications for weakening state capacity.

We should also acknowledge the limits of protecting religious sites through policing or other such measures. As the UN Plan suggests, governments must create durable communication channels with different faith communities (Jasch, 2007). The German Islam Conference (Deutsche Islam Konferenz), begun in 2006, is an example of this institutionalized communication, where Muslim leaders can confer with state officials to promote the interests of their communities. With specialized protection units, religious groups might not feel the need to communicate with the state directly. These specialized units and their commanders may become interest groups themselves, by representing the interests of the local religious community to the state. This could further erode state capacity by siphoning away both coercive and coordination functions.

References

Abbas, H. (2017) *The Myth and Reality of Iraq's al-Hashd al-Shaabi (Popular Mobilization Forces): A Way Forward*. Friedrich-Ebert-Stiftung Jordan and Iraq, Amman, Jordan. Available at: https://library.fes.de/pdf-files/bueros/amman/13689.pdf (accessed 5 January 2022).

Axelrod, T. (2020) Germany pledges extra $26 million for Jewish security. *The Jerusalem Post*. Available at: https://www.jpost.com/diaspora/germany-pledges-extra-26-million-for-jewish-security-642842 (accessed 10 December 2021).

Bäck, H. and Hadenius, A. (2008) Democracy and state capacity: exploring a J-shaped relationship. *Governance* 21(1), 1–24. DOI: 10.1111/j.1468-0491.2007.00383.x.

Baker, D.M.A. (2014) The effects of terrorism on the travel and tourism industry. *International Journal of Religious Tourism and Pilgrimage* 2(1), 58–67.

Barlett, L. and Vavrus, F. (2016) *Rethinking Case Study Research: A Comparative Approach*. Routledge, New York.

Boduszynski, M. (2016) Fighting the Islamic state won't change the sectarian image of Iraq's militias. *The Washington Post*. Available at: https://www.washingtonpost.com/news/monkey-cage/wp/2016/12/28/fighting-the-islamic-state-wont-fix-the-sectarian-image-of-iraqs-militias/ (accessed 19 March 2022).

Brett, W., Xidias, J. and McClean, T. (2017) *An Analysis of Max Weber's Politics as a Vocation*. Macat Library, London.

Bueno de Mesquita, B., Smith, A., Siverson, R.M. and Morrow, J.D. (2003) *The Logic of Political Survival*. MIT Press, Cambridge, UK. DOI: 10.7551/mitpress/4292.001.0001.

Chowdhury, A., Razaq, R., Griffin, K.A. and Clarke, A. (2017) Terrorism, tourism and religious travellers. *International Journal of Religious Tourism and Pilgrimage* 5(1), 1–19.

Dodge, T. (2020a) Iraq's informal consociationalism and its problems. *Studies in Ethnicity and Nationalism* 20(2), 145–152. DOI: 10.1111/sena.12330.

Dodge, T. (2020b) Understanding the role of al-Hashd al-Shaabi in Iraq's national and transnational political field. In: *Project on Middle East Political Science*. Elliott School of International Affairs, George Washington University, Washington, DC.

Durán-Sánchez, A., Álvarez-García, J., del Río-Rama, M. and Oliveira, C. (2018) Religious tourism and pilgrimage: bibliometric overview. *Religions* 9(9), 249. DOI: 10.3390/rel9090249.

Egwu, P. (2020) Christian victims in Nigeria fear future attacks: religious violence is growing despite the pandemic. *Foreign Policy Online*. Available at: https://foreignpolicy.com/2020/10/09/christian-victims-in-nigeria-fear-future-attacks/ (accessed 9 June 2022).

Esposito, A. (2018) *Urban Development in the Margins of a World Heritage Site: In the Shadows of Angkor*. Amsterdam University Press, Amsterdam. DOI: 10.1515/9789048534050.

Gerring, J. (2017) *Case Study Research: Principles and Practices*. Cambridge University Press, New York.

Ghatak, S. (2016) The role of political exclusion and state capacity in civil conflict in South Asia. *Terrorism and Political Violence* 30(1), 74–96.

Hellman, J. and Kaufmann, D. (2001) Confronting the challenge of state capture in transition economies. *Finance and Development: A Quarterly Magazine of the IMF* 38(3). Available at: https://www.imf.org/external/pubs/ft/fandd/2001/09/hellman.htm (accessed 17 May 2022).

Herath, D. (2020) Constructing Buddhists in Sri Lanka and Myanmar: imaginary of a historically victimised community. *Asian Studies Review* 44(2), 315–334. DOI: 10.1080/10357823.2020.1717441.

Howie, L. (2014) Security guards and counter-terrorism: tourism and gaps in terrorism prevention. *International Journal of Religious Tourism and Pilgrimage* 2(1), 38–47.

Jasch, H. (2007) State-Dialogue with Muslim Communities in Italy and Germany - The Political Context and the Legal Frameworks for Dialogue with Islamic Faith Communities in Both Countries. *German Law Journal* 8(4), 341–380. DOI: 10.1017/S2071832200005642.

Jenkins, P. (2019) Microcosm of religious violence. *Christian Century* 136(22), 52–53.

Kalyvas, S.N. (2006) *The Logic of Violence in Civil War*. Cambridge University Press, Cambridge, UK. DOI: 10.1017/CBO9780511818462.

Karlos, V. and Larcher, M. (2020) *Guideline—Building Perimeter Protection*. European Commission JRC Technical Report. EUR 30346 EN. Publications Office of the European Union, Luxembourg.

Kersh, R. (2000) State autonomy & civil society: the lobbyist connection. *Critical Review* 14(2–3), 237–258. DOI: 10.1080/08913810008443559.

Lam, R. (2020) Sri Lankan government ties religious freedom to protection of Buddhism. *Buddhistdoor Global*. Available at: https://www.buddhistdoor.net/news/sri-lankan-government-ties-religious-freedom-to-protection-of-buddhism/ (accessed 17 May 2022).

Lijphart, A. (1969) Consociational democracy. *World Politics* 21(2), 207–225. DOI: 10.2307/2009820.

Morrison, C. (2020) Buddhist extremism, anti-Muslim violence and civil war legacies in Sri Lanka. *Asian Ethnicity* 21(1), 137–159. DOI: 10.1080/14631369.2019.1610937.

Parfomak, P. (2004) *Guarding America: Security Guards and U.S. Critical Infrastructure Protection*. Congressional Research Service Report for Congress. Available at: https://sgp.fas.org/crs/RL32670.pdf (accessed 17 May 2022).

Pew Research Center (2017) *The Growth of Germany's Muslim Population*. Report. Available at: https://www.pewforum.org/essay/the-growth-of-germanys-muslim-population/ (accessed 21 January 2022).

Pizam, A. and Smith, G. (2000) Tourism and terrorism: a quantitative analysis of major terrorist acts and their impact on tourism destinations. *Tourism Economics* 6(2), 123–138. DOI: 10.5367/000000000101297523.

President of Sri Lanka (2020) *Two Separate Presidential Task Forces to Ensure a Secure Country and for Archaeological Heritage Management*. Press Release. Available at: https://www.president.gov.lk/two-separate-presidential-task-forces-to-ensure-a-secure-country-and-for-archaeological-heritage-management/ (accessed 10 December 2021).

Raj, R. and Griffin, K.A. (2015) . : *Religious Tourism and Pilgrimage Management: An International Perspective*, 2nd edn. CAB International, UK. DOI: 10.1079/9781780645230.0000.

Roller, E. (2020) Political performance and state capacity. In: Berg-Schlosser, D., Badie, B. and Morlino, L. (eds) *The SAGE Handbook of Political Science*. Sage, Credo Reference, UK.

Rotberg, R. (2002) The new nature of nation-state failure. *The Washington Quarterly* 25(3), 3–96.

Smith, V.L. (1992) Introduction: the quest in guest. *Annals of Tourism Research* 19(1), 1–17.

Sokol, S. (2021) German Jews demand government protect synagogues after Israeli flag burnings. *Ha'aretz*. Available at: https://www.haaretz.com/world-news/europe/.premium-german-jews-demand-government-protect-synagogues-after-israeli-flag-burnings-1.9805455 (accessed 31 March 2021).

Sönmez, S. (1998) Tourism, terrorism, and political instability. *Annals of Tourism Research* 25(2), 416–456. DOI: 10.1016/S0160-7383(97)00093-5.

Sönmez, S., Apostolopoulos, Y. and Tarlow, P. (1999) Tourism in crisis: managing the effects of terrorism. *Journal of Travel Research* 38(1), 13–18. DOI: 10.1177/004728759903800104.

Stausberg, M. (2011) *Religion and Tourism: Crossroads, Destinations and Encounters*. Routledge, New York.

Taleb, N.N. (2007) *The Black Swan: The Impact of the Highly Improbable*. Random House, New York.

UN News (2019) *Reaffirm the 'sanctity' of Religious Sites, Says Guterres, Launching New Plan to 'counter hate and violence*. Available at: https://news.un.org/en/story/2019/09/1046182 (accessed 10 December 2021).

UN OHCHR (2017) *Preliminary Findings of the Visit to Sri Lanka*. UN Human Rights, Office of the High Commissioner. Available at: https://www.ohchr.org/en/NewsEvents/Pages/DisplayNews.aspx?NewsID=21883&LangID=E (accessed 10 December 2021).

UNAOC (2019) *The United Nations Plan of Action to Safeguard Religious Sites*. Available at: https://www.un.org/sg/sites/www.un.org.sg/files/atoms/files/12-09-2019-UNAOC-PoA-Religious-Sites.pdf (accessed 5 January 2022).

UNESCO (2021a) *World Heritage List Statistics*. Available at: https://whc.unesco.org/en/list/stat (accessed 8 December 2021).

UNESCO (2021b) *Heritage of Religious Interest*. Available at: https://whc.unesco.org/en/religious-sacred-heritage/ (accessed 8 December 2021).

US Department of Homeland Security (2018) *U.S. Department of Homeland Security Soft Targets and Crowded Places Security Plan Overview*. U.S. Department of Homeland Security. Available at: https://www.cisa.gov/sites/default/files/publications/DHS-Soft-Target-Crowded-Place-Security-Plan-Overview-052018-508_0.pdf (accessed 5 January 2022).

US Department of State (2020a) *2019 Report on International Religious Freedom: Germany*. Office of International Religious Freedom. Available at: https://www.state.gov/wp-content/uploads/2020/06/GERMANY-2019-INTERNATIONAL-RELIGIOUS-FREEDOM-REPORT.pdf (accessed 10 December 2021).

US Department of State (2020b) *2019 Report on International Religious Freedom: Sri Lanka*. Office of International Religious Freedom. Available at: https://www.state.gov/wp-content/uploads/2020/05/SRI-LANKA-2019-INTERNATIONAL-RELIGIOUS-FREEDOM-REPORT.pdf (accessed 10 December 2021).

US Department of State (2021a) *2020 Report on International Religious Freedom: Germany*. Office of International Religious Freedom. Available at: https://www.state.gov/wp-content/uploads/2021/05/240282-GERMANY-2020-INTERNATIONAL-RELIGIOUS-FREEDOM-REPORT.pdf (accessed 10 December 2021).

US Department of State (2021b) *2020 Report on International Religious Freedom: Sri Lanka*. Office of International Religious Freedom. Available at: https://www.state.gov/wp-content/uploads/2021/05/240282-SRI-LANKA-2020-INTERNATIONAL-RELIGIOUS-FREEDOM-REPORT.pdf (accessed 10 December 2021).

UN Office of Counter-Terrorism (n.d.) *Vulnerable Targets*. Available at: https://www.un.org/counterterrorism/vulnerable-targets (accessed 19 March 2022).

Vrabel, J. (2014) Tourism at UNESCO World Heritage Sites: protecting global treasures and the travelers who seek them. *Case Western Reserve Journal of International Law* 46(3), 675–710.

Weber, M. (1965) *Politics as a Vocation*. Fortress Press, Philadelphia, PA.

World Population Review (2021) *Jewish Population by Country 2021*. Available at: https://worldpopulationreview.com/country-rankings/jewish-population-by-country (accessed 21 January 2022).

12 Closure of Sacred Sites and Autonomous Organization of Religious Ritual: Re-Thinking the Geography of Sacred Space. Policies and Restrictions in Europe in the Age of COVID-19

Valentina Castronuovo*

National Research Council – Institute for Research on Innovation and Services for Development, Naples, Italy

Abstract

The policies and strategies adopted by governments to manage the COVID pandemic have caused changes in the management of public places, generating new user behaviour. Among the places affected by restrictions, sacred sites have been the object of closures and subsequently of restricted use, giving rise to tension between public health norms and the freedom to enjoy essential services. After an overview of the restrictive policies that have affected sacred sites, adopted by the European Union and local governments, this chapter reviews attempts to rethink the exercise of religious freedom in various countries. It also presents an initial characterization, from a geographical point of view, of the neo-spaces generated by alternative cult practices which, in the present as well as in the past, have reflected the resilience of the identity of religious communities.

12.1 Introduction

The global health emergency linked to the spread of the SARS-CoV-2 virus has led an increasing number of governments and international organizations to impose extraordinary regulatory measures to limit contagion. In this situation, to varying degrees, central and regional governments have, by these measures, brought about social and relational changes among populations and the emergence of new daily habits. The closure of businesses, schools and places where people gather for cultural and other purposes has resulted in various forms of substantial physical and social distancing. Among the activities considered to be at risk in terms of group gatherings, religious activities in general have been identified by many states as particularly prone to spread the viral infection. The imposition of preventive measures to contain COVID-19 has had a profound impact on the ability of individuals and communities to publicly manifest their beliefs, culture and identity, to observe religious festivities and rituals, and to participate in rituals associated with certain stages of life.

In terms of the restrictions introduced, in some cases, state authorities directly imposed

*valentina.castronuovo@gmail.com

© CAB International 2023. *The Politics of Religious Tourism* (eds D. Bozonelos and P. Moira)
DOI: 10.1079/9781800621732.0012

regulations for the management of sacred sites and the conduct of religious communities; in other cases, the authorities negotiated the forms and scope of restrictions with representatives of the main religious communities, directly granting religious leaders and communities autonomy and decision making responsibility (Leplongeon, 2020; Mazurkiewicz, 2021).

The disruption has thus interacted with the daily ritual and participatory dimension of religious communities. The experience of the various lockdowns has certainly highlighted the interruption of the social dimension of religious experience and the limitation of people's physical presence in the places where the relationship with the sacred traditionally unfolds (Carnevale and Girneata, 2021). Religious communities have thus had to reshape the aesthetics of ritual. In collective worship, the aesthetic relationship plays a predominant role in the circulation of meanings and the transmission of the symbolic system (Bartalesi, 2017). During the pandemic, we have seen rituality transformed in terms of its physical characteristics, namely the meeting of people in order to perform joint (and hence social) acts of worship in a dedicated place. Consequently, we have also seen a renegotiation of the ritual's own signifiers, based on a more intimate and subjective dimension of worship as well as on the metaphysical dimension of online 'social worship', which is the most innovative aspect of this historical moment.

This chapter first provides an overview of the measures enacted by states to regulate the opening and closing of sacred sites. It then presents some examples of the reorganization and self-organization of worship where restrictive measures have temporarily closed institutional places of worship. This reorganization has certainly affected the exercise of worship, giving rise to expressions of religious practice that have not yet been codified, centred on the operational dimension of religious activity. These are complex processes of adaptation – already recorded in other historical situations of deprivation of fundamental freedoms – with contextual and potentially long-lasting sociospatial effects.

12.2 Literature Review

This chapter is part of the growing literature on the topic of central and regional government restrictions on collective freedom of worship during the COVID-19 pandemic. Over the past 3 years, dozens of studies have analysed and discussed the fundamental individual rights and freedoms that were compromised following the enactment of laws to contain the coronavirus. Among these, religious freedom was among the most heavily affected, as the suspension of religious ceremonies, restrictions on mobility and, in some cases, the total closure of sacred sites, compromised the normal expression of religious freedom worldwide (Alves et al., 2020; Brzozowski, 2020; Lara, 2020; Martinez, 2020; Raimundo et al., 2020; Reyes, 2020; Bohler-Muller et al., 2021; Haynes, 2021; Kong, 2021; Madera, 2021; Martínez-Torrón, 2021; Milinković, 2021; Mosquera, 2021; Stanisz, 2021). Particular attention has also been paid to 'transitional law', i.e. regulations affecting religious freedom during the months of the state of emergency and then during the period of transition to the so-called new normality (Lara, 2020). From a comparative point of view, most courts around the world have approached the problem with insight and balance, reaching different conclusions however on the legitimacy of the restrictions (Movsesian, 2022).

In most cases, legal challenges to restrictive government measures have resulted in courts upholding their constitutionality and declaring religious freedom to be subordinate to the duty to protect life and health (Alves et al., 2020). However, many of the analyses of the constitutionality of the measures are ongoing. There is also the suggestion that some judicial bodies are changing the standards of states' powers under emergency conditions so as to permanently strengthen some rights and dilute others under normal circumstances (Mariner, 2021). The debate over the measures continues, with the possibility of a radical political experiment in which the very conception of religious freedom and its place in the hierarchy of human rights will change (Mazurkiewicz, 2021). The emergency measures taken in the context of the COVID-19 pandemic provided an opportunity, in the fields of law and religion, to examine the legality of restrictions on religious freedom, but also, more fundamentally, to observe, from the perspective of religious studies, the growing difficulties in understanding individual freedoms, in both their specificity and their diversity (Christians, 2020), and the modern components of religious institutions (Shah, 2021). The multidisciplinary nature of the issue has led to the exploration of the interrelationships between place, space and the spiritual (Bryson *et al.*, 2020), taking account of the 'do-it-yourself' mechanisms that have been developed by various religious institutions. Individual worship, online service provision and virtual inclusion have, to some extent, blurred the boundaries between sacred spaces and rituals.

12.3   Cross-National Research

In addition to a review of the literature, which revealed a fairly varied scientific landscape, the study is based on desk data regarding the type of measures introduced by central and regional governments concerning the use of sacred sites and the regulation of worship. The data were processed in accordance with the principle of the 'equivalent phenomenon' (Przeworski and Teune, 1966).

    This cross-national research (Kohn, 1987) aims to compare the 34 states participating in the European Union Civil Protection Mechanism (UCPM) in terms of the restrictive measures applied to religious worship. The study area was selected following verification of the availability, updatability and correctness of the data collected and processed by the Joint Research Centre (JRC), which supports the European Commission by providing independent scientific advice and monitoring with regard to the COVID-19 emergency. The JRC has published a timely overview of the containment measures adopted by the national authorities of the states participating in the European Union Civil Protection Mechanism (UCPM) (COVID, 2020). The relevant website (https://covid-statistics.jrc.ec.europa.eu/) contains information relating to the closure of public spaces and places of worship in particular (COVID, 2020), and offers a much more comprehensive transnational overview than other documentation portals. The data

collected by the platform was then compared and implemented with other secondary sources such as laws, directives and official documents available on central and regional government websites. This analysis revealed that the measures taken by the various states differed, in many cases reflecting the legislative conditions of the respective countries. The period examined was from March 2020 to June 2022.

12.4   Restrictions on the Use of Sacred Sites During the COVID-19 Pandemic: A European Overview

When it comes to restrictions on freedom of religion and the opening of sacred sites, the perception of the importance and urgency of the values to be protected and the concept of essential goods, which are understood differently in secular and religious perspectives, are both important. Another essential question is not only the scope but also the depth of state intervention in the life of religious communities. In Europe, there has been a wide variety of national approaches to the restriction of religious freedom to ensure public health. Some have pursued very restrictive policies, while others have been more moderate and still others have adopted a very light touch. In some cases, the regulatory measures involved the suspension of events of any kind, in places both closed and open to the public. Broadly, they banned, albeit temporarily, the celebration of religious rituals and faith-based events that could give rise to any concentrations of people. These measures, which were gradually extended, inflexibly included celebrations and funerals. To these was added a sort of civil self-regulation concerning how to attend places of worship in compliance with the rules on social distancing.

    After analysing the restrictive measures implemented by each state (at the time of JRC dashboards consultation, data were available for 24 out of 34 states in total), it was possible to identify six macro regulatory behaviours that were implemented in specific periods, sometimes simultaneously and cyclically (Table 12.1): full closure of sacred sites; opening for individual worship only; access subject to protective

Table 12.1. Types of restriction adopted by UPCM states during the first and second lockdowns.

Type of restriction	Country	
	First lockdown	Second lockdown
Full closure	Denmark, Latvia, Lithuania, Portugal, Romania	
Opening for individual worship only	Belgium, Czech Republic, France, Greece*, Ireland, Italy*, Netherlands*, Poland*, Slovenia	Austria*, Czech Republic, Germany, Slovakia*, Slovenia
Accessible with protective measures (masks, cleaning agents)	Austria*, Belgium, Czech Republic, Greece*, Germany, Italy*, Poland*	Austria*, Belgium, Czech Republic, Denmark, Estonia, France, Greece*, Ireland, Italy*, Latvia, Lithuania, Malta, Netherlands*, Poland*, Portugal, Romania, Slovakia*, Slovenia, Spain*
Accessible with restricted flow	Austria*, Czech Republic, Estonia, France, Germany, Iceland, Malta, Poland*, Slovakia*, Spain*	Austria*, Belgium, Cyprus, Czech Republic, Denmark, France, Germany, Greece*, Iceland, Ireland, Italy*, Lithuania, Netherlands*, Poland*, Portugal, Romania, Slovakia*, Slovenia, Spain*
Accessible with safety distance	Austria*, Germany, Malta, Poland*	Austria*, Belgium, Czech Republic, Denmark, Estonia, France, Germany, Greece*, Ireland, Italy*, Latvia, Lithuania, Malta, Netherlands*, Poland*, Portugal, Romania, Slovakia*, Slovenia, Spain*
Accessible with time and duration restrictions		Latvia

Source: Authors' presentation of Joint Research Centre (JRC) data (COVID, 2020).
*Hybrid rules. Within the country there are various arrangements arising from regional autonomy and 'zonal' distinctions decreed by the central government on the basis of regional trends.

measures; restricted flow; safety distancing; and restrictions on time and duration.

In many cases, the restrictions (COVID, 2020) confirm the experimental nature of the states' efforts as they sought to understand the extent of the pandemic and the effectiveness of the responses that were gradually adopted. It is also possible to observe differences in the decision making of most countries during the first and second waves of the pandemic.

As indicated in Table 12.1, there have been several countries, including Spain and Greece, in which the measures introduced by the central state have been accompanied, followed or even contradicted by laws enacted by regional and local government. In Spain, at the national level, from 14 March to 21 June 2020, the state of alert declared throughout the country included strict security measures governing attendance

at places of worship and religious ceremonies, including funerals. The central government and the autonomous communities agreed on coordinated public health measures in cities with more than 100,000 inhabitants with more than 500 cases. On 22 June 2020, the Autonomous Communities assumed exclusive competence for the adoption and execution of measures to contain the virus. This federal approach has resulted in a complex regulatory environment and a non-homogeneity of restrictions: the geographical level of application is regional or even local. The first communities in which the measures were lifted were Cataluña and Extremadura, which, as of 30 September 2021, had no restrictions on visiting sacred sites. Between October 2021 and February 2022, the Comunidad Foral de Navarra, Castilla y León, Galicia, País Vasco, Comunidad de Madrid, Ciudad Autónoma de

Melilla, Cantabria, Andalusia, Ciudad Autónoma de Ceuta, Aragón, Región de Murcia, Canarias and La Rioja all returned to normal (COVID, 2020).

As with Spain, Greece also saw regional and local directives. However, there was no shortage of measures enacted by the central authorities, which from 12 March to 10 May 2020 imposed a ban on religious services that lasted until 19 May 2020 (COVID, 2020). In general, in alternating periods, religious ceremonies were suspended or permitted for a limited number of participants in compliance with hygiene and safety regulations. In 2021, many regions renewed the cancellation of religious practices in 'high pandemic risk' areas such as Boeotia, where from 12 January to 5 February 2021 religious ceremonies were suspended, as well as Western Macedonia (Municipality of Eordaea, Municipal Unit of Siatista and City of Krokos), Attica (Municipalities of Aharnes and Aspropyrgos), the Peloponnese (Municipality of Sparta) and the North Aegean (Municipality of Lesvos). As of 4 March 2021, places of worship allowed the presence of one individual per $25\,m^2$ and no more than nine individuals in total for regions considered to be at high risk of SARS-CoV-2 transmission. As of 22 November 2021, entry into churches was only permitted with proof of vaccination, recovery or a negative test (COVID, 2020). The central state and regional governments have managed to deal with the pandemic without deviating from the constitutional order and the protection of fundamental rights, partly thanks to constant social pressure (Androutsopoulos, 2021).

In Spain and Greece, religious freedom on a personal level was certainly not affected, but the decision to temporarily suspend religious gatherings undermined religious coexistence. In France, these restrictions added to an already complicated historical moment for religious freedom within the country, considering the decision by the central government to dissolve by decree several Muslim organizations accused of 'inciting hatred, violence and discrimination', closing 672 Muslim institutions from February 2018 to October 2021, including 21 mosques from November 2020 (United States Department of State—Office of International Religious Freedom, 2022).

Although the overwhelming majority of religious institutions in France stopped collective services during the two lockdowns without raising any particular objections (Fornerod, 2021), after President Macron's announcement that starting in August, a 'health pass' would be required to enter public spaces – including sacred sites – some protesters wore the yellow Star of David or held signs comparing the treatment of unvaccinated people to that of Jews during the Holocaust; others protested with anti-Semitic signs. President Macron and other government officials continued to condemn anti-Semitic, anti-Muslim and anti-Christian acts, and the government continued to deploy security forces to protect religious sites and other sensitive locations (United States Department of State—Office of International Religious Freedom, 2022).

In the context of religious freedom during the COVID-19 pandemic, Romania was listed by the OSCE (OSCE Office for Democratic Institutions and Human Rights (ODIHR), 2020) as one of the countries that opted for the harshest measures. All indoor religious activities in the country were suspended from 18 March to 14 May 2020. From then on, all religious activities were permitted on condition of compliance with precautionary health regulations (disinfection of hands; use of masks; minimum distancing inside buildings). As of 9 March 2022, all restrictions were lifted (COVID, 2020). Some studies have noted how in Romania, during the pandemic, the restrictions imposed on religious life took little account of national law and international commitments to religious freedom, based on the rule of law (Raiu and Mina-Raiu, 2022).

States that are careful to balance individual freedoms with containment measures designed to safeguard public health include Germany, whose Federal Constitutional Court has emphasized the value of religious freedom (Muckl, 2020), and the Netherlands.

In the latter, from 16 March to 31 May 2020, religious communities reduced collective celebrations as much as possible. From 1 June 2020, the changed social context saw a cautious return to religious observance, with meetings of a religious or philosophical character possible in compliance with EU health and safety directives. With regard to the constitutionally guaranteed freedom to profess one's beliefs and practise them via religious meetings and other activities, religious organizations assume full responsibility for taking the necessary measures to prevent or limit new large-scale outbreaks. The Netherlands therefore started with containment and moved to mitigation within 3 weeks, implementing a 'mild' blockade, showing a way to effectively slow transmission through individual responsibility, while allowing more personal and economic freedom than most other countries (Hoekman *et al.*, 2020).

Countries such as Italy grasped the importance of negotiating intervention with representatives of religious communities from the very beginning. A Prime Ministerial Decree of 8 March 2020 stipulated that places of worship could open subject to the adoption of organizational measures to avoid crowds of people, considering the size and characteristics of the places and ensuring that attendees could maintain social distancing of at least one metre. Civil and religious ceremonies, including funeral ceremonies, were suspended. Decree-Law No. 19 of 25 March 2020, converted with amendments into Law No. 35 of 22 May 2020, confirmed these conditions, together with the adoption of health protocols, in agreement with the Catholic Church and other religious denominations regarding measures necessary for the performance of religious functions in conditions of safety. The Decree of the President of the Council of Ministers (Prime Minister) of 17 May 2020 made access to places of worship conditional on the adoption of organizational measures to avoid gatherings of people and ensure compliance with the protocols (Fig. 12.1.) signed by the government and the respective confessions in Annexes 1 to 7.

In this way, the Italian Government demonstrated that it interacted with the major religious communities present in the country including Catholics, Jews, Evangelical Christians, Anglicans, Orthodox Christians, Hindus, Buddhists, Muslims and Latter-day Saints (President of the Council of Ministers, 2020a, 2020b, 2020c, 2020d, 2020e, 2020f, 2020g, 2020h),establishing, by common agreement, shared guidelines to facilitate the exercise of religious worship.

This brief overview of the restrictive measures governing places of worship and religious buildings (COVID, 2020) adopted by the members of the UCPM shows that from March 2020 onwards, the opening of places of worship has almost always been conditional on the adoption of organizational measures to avoid crowds of people. Rarely have central or regional governments enacted total closures of places of worship, while they have frequently allowed their opening for individual use. More often than not therefore, access to sacred places has remained restricted, with a maximum number of people permitted. Moreover, most states have periodically reviewed the restrictions imposed, monitoring their impact and adjusting their level according to the evolving pandemic risk.

12.5   Self-Organization of Religious Freedom

In many cases, the limitations imposed by governments on the use of places of worship have been developed further by the leaders of religious communities who, in addition to confirming the directives, have provided a guide for the faithful regarding the self-organization of worship even in private spaces. To do this, permanent and non-permanent channels of communication have been created ad hoc, at national regional and local levels, in order to enable religious leaders to celebrate functions and rituals, and to maintain the relationship with their respective communities.

During the various lockdowns that have marked the daily lives of people all over the world, the world wide web and social media have made it possible to experiment online with certain types of services in ways that had hitherto been unexplored or, in any case, had always been subsidiary to 'de visu' practice. This has entailed 'proximity' solutions, where the areas adjoining places of worship have been fitted with loudspeakers, broadcasting the rite in stereo to the neighbourhood, and Pope Francis' decision to stream the Mass 'without the people' from Santa Marta (creating a historical precedent).

In addition, many religions in the world have used digital tools such as WhatsApp, Zoom, Google Meet, Facebook and Instagram live streams to maintain audio-visual contact with

Fig. 12.1. Way of the Cross procession in the old city of Taranto (Italy). Preparation for Holy Week after the 2 year suspension. April 2022.
Source: Antonello Cafagna.

the faithful, providing a further push towards digitalization. Individual dioceses, for example, have organized e-pilgrimages, online streaming of masses and online prayer aids for adults and children. Many apps are now being used, from Dindondan, which allows users to locate the nearest mass, to Follow JC Go, where players form an evangelization team made up of friends, biblical characters and saints. One of the most popular apps is Laudate, boasting more than one million downloads from the Google Play Store as of June 2022, which engages users in several ways. Besides providing – among other things – liturgies, prayers (in Latin if required), and readings of the day, the app allows the faithful to write prayers and save them as favourites. There

is also a 'confession' section with a check-list of sins to confess. The practice of video-preaching, which has been widespread in the United States for decades, has also taken hold.

A survey on the subject of 'Religious Freedom and Faith at the Time of Covid-19' (Palumbo *et al.*, 2020) was conducted by the 'Giustino Fortunato' University in collaboration with the Department of Law of the 'Luigi Vanvitelli' University of Campania and the Department of Canon Law of the Pontifical Theological Faculty of Southern Italy (St Thomas Aquinas Section). Its aim was to assess the degree of satisfaction derived from these alternative services among a sample of 4000 Italian Christian worshippers. Evident confusion was registered on the subject of access to places of worship for personal prayer during Phase 1 of Italy's lockdown. While 37.5% of the sample correctly perceived it to be permitted provided that a distance of no less than one metre between worshippers was maintained, 33.73% perceived it to be forbidden in all cases or permitted only in the context of essential travel. Indeed, during Phase 1, 65.20% of the sample never went to a church for personal prayer (Palumbo *et al.*, 2020). The greatest concern reported by the respondents was that of not being able to receive Holy Communion (32.38%), followed by the thought of not being able to receive a dignified funeral in the event of death (29.16%).

The temporary suspension of burial rituals was certainly one of the most discussed items among the religious communities, who adapted in the ways most congenial to their beliefs, in what was in any case an extraordinary situation. For instance, after the ban on communal Friday prayers and the call to all Muslims to pray in their homes (sallū fī buyūtikum), senior clerics in the European and international Islamic community agreed on special provisions concerning how to conduct Islamic funeral rites and burials in the face of the COVID-19 emergency. Pursuant to Article 10 of its Regulations, at its 24th regular session on 22 Rajab 1441/17 March 2020, in view of the situation caused by the coronavirus pandemic, the Mufti Council of the Islamic Community of Bosnia and Herzegovina issued a Fatwa on washing and dressing the deceased (Ghusl Mayyit) and the funeral prayer (Janazah) for those dying of infectious diseases. The Fatwa was taken up by the EuLeMa (European Muslim Leaders' Majlis), the Council of European Muslim Leaders, and proposed to the civil authorities in Germany, the United Kingdom, Ireland, Portugal, Slovenia, Denmark, Lithuania and Norway. The Council of Wise Men of the Al-Azhar University in Cairo and the Muslim Council of Britain (MCB) adopted broadly similar policies.

The introduction of virtual religious services has certainly altered the relationship between the individual and the broader co-creation of collective ritual. Indeed, there has been a shift in religious experience, including the temporary creation of worship spaces and rituals within the home, leading to the production of new and transitory geographies of worship (Bryson *et al.*, 2020). Adaptive worship practices have involved a new role, for instance, for domestic space. The home has become a part of the worship experience and has become intertwined with a more formal online worship space, although it is not clear how long this will last (Sharma, 2012).

12.6 Adaptation of the Geographical Space of Worship

In the history of humanity, the inherently relational nature of sacred sites has always been recognized. Indeed, in keeping with their spiritual character and use, they are goods that enable various types of relationship. The category of 'relational good' was only introduced into theoretical discussion in the second half of the 1980s (Donati, 1986; Gui, 1987; Uhlaner, 1989; Craven Nussbaum, 2004). Although there are varying definitions, what has distinguished and continues to distinguish the cultural approach to relational goods is precisely their 'relational' meaning: they are physical dimensions in which relations can neither be produced nor consumed by a single individual, as they depend on forms of interaction with others and can only be enjoyed if shared in reciprocity (Bruni, 2006). Reciprocity is therefore fundamental to this type of place: the relational good 'emerges' within a relationship (Bruni, 2006). It is defined as a good that does not come into being to satisfy an instrumental need, but rather emerges as a result of intrinsic needs linked to the cultural and social dimensions of human existence, in a given territorial context, with an important expressive value for all the subjects involved.

On this basis, in the context of the pandemic, we are faced with a transfer of the relational component from the good to the service it produces, giving rise to the extraordinary-in-the-ordinary, but also prompting the faithful to self-organize. While the pandemic has affected the ordinary interrelations between individuals and spaces, it has not affected the 'symbolic equipment' that enables communities to live not merely by virtue of their material, geographical and environmental characteristics, but by the normative codes and values that give rise to their members' sense of identity (Cohen, 1995).

The pandemic doesn't seem to have affected religious sentiment itself. Nor has it compromised the traditional intangible heritage linked to memory, history, festivals, rituals and shared symbols. In this sense, it may be said to have reinforced the existence of communities founded on scales of values that are independent of the physical availability of space. The new digital religious spaces that emerged during the pandemic, for instance, mediated between inter-action and 'web presence', offering religious communities the opportunity to invent new forms of participation in religious life (Mpofu, 2021).

Sharma (2012) had already shown how worship practices and family spaces can occupy the space of the sacred site and vice versa, becoming inter-penetrable (Della Dora, 2016). Overlapping practices and spaces have long characterized the religious and cultural identities of individuals. Like families, places of worship are not fixed. They are spaces in which a variety of rituals, routines and transitory phenomena are experienced. They are more or less fluid spaces in which people experience dynamic relationships, responding to social and cultural changes (Kong, 1990, 2002, 2010; Casanova, 1994). The movement of people brought about by macro-events (or conversely their near-total immobility, as in the case of the COVID-19 pandemic), results in the dispersal of individuals in space or their unprecedented relocation, causing an 'extension' of religious practices and, in general, of the bond with belief (Cloke, 2011; Sharpley and Jepson, 2011; Nilsson and Tesfahuney, 2016).

This extension tends to adapt to possible distances and/or impediments to collective religious exercise. Consider for example the experience of the Palestinian people, who for over 70 years under Israeli occupation have experienced varying restrictions on their right to worship, especially during the month of Ramadan: the intermittent closure by the Israeli authorities of the Haram al-Sharif, a place of collective worship par excellence, is associated with numerous clashes and injuries every year. For Palestinians physically dispersed and separated from their sacred places, ritual is nevertheless the mechanism through which inaccessible places are made central and kept alive in their consciousness during religious practice.

In reality, the religious rituals that permeate the daily life of Muslims have never depended on the accessibility or proximity of the place of worship. Whether in the mosque, one's residence or the workplace, in Saudi Arabia or China, Muslims symbolically turn to Mecca to pray (Mazumdar and Mazumdar, 2004). Thus, while sacred buildings can certainly inspire and nurture devotion and guide and regulate worship practices, we see how, within historical religious communities, spiritual practice may unfold irrespective of the physical availability of the sacred building (Mazumdar and Mazumdar, 2004).

Conditions that have long precluded many peoples from the normal use of physical places of faith need to be considered in this light, given that the extraordinariness of closure policies is in fact quite ordinary in many places and for many communities.

The 'remote' sacred space has thus materialized, worldwide, as part of a space that challenges existing routines and rules. A new temporary geography of home or 'other' place emerges through the creation of an 'intersacred' space (Bryson et al., 2020), a temporary extension of the sacred site (Hulme and Truch, 2006; Bittarello, 2009). New forms of worship space have been created, challenging existing theological conventions (Woods, 2013). 'In these new virtual churches, offices have become sanctuaries and kitchen tables altars, simultaneously transforming sacred sites and the homes of the faithful through webcams or other metaphysical extensions where all can gather and feel welcome' (Bryson et al., 2020, p. 370). During the pandemic, it was in this intersacred space that people acted and interacted with each other as they co-created shared online worship experiences. This new virtual normality helped reconnect people and places through shared beliefs and behaviours.

12.7 Conclusions

The health regulations introduced during the pandemic significantly affected the exercise of individual freedom. Their impact depended not only on the restrictions governing places of worship and sacred sites in general, but also on the willingness of individuals to respect the rules. In general, during the first wave of the pandemic, there were broadly four governmental approaches to religious freedom, characterized by a very high, high, moderate or low level of restrictiveness. In some countries, these approaches were adjusted during the second wave of the pandemic; in others, the original line was applied several times in alternating phases. The most complex situations, in terms of the asynchronicity of the restrictions imposed, seem to have occurred in Spain and Greece, where regional laws imposed different restrictions.

The measures taken to contain the COVID-19 pandemic in the sphere of collective practices and places of worship have had and continue to have varied and, in some cases, damaging results for collective needs. However, many groups have long had to live with restrictions on religious practice, deemed necessary as a result of geopolitical dynamics. In fact, the health emergency has brought the whole world face to face with an issue that has been affecting many people for decades.

Via virtual practices and the exercise of religion by the faithful even in private spaces, however, places of worship are seeing a regeneration. The online streaming of religious services from a sacred space *multiplies* the use of that space and *enhances* its accessibility, thereby confirming its nature as an available resource, despite its closure. Combining the features of traditional devotion with the experimentation of a new approach, the behaviour of the faithful all over the world has enabled the restoration of the function of otherwise inaccessible sacred buildings and revived the original meaning of religious life.

In this sense, we may conclude that places of worship temporarily rendered unavailable or partially inaccessible (and thus affected by a deprivation of identity) have nevertheless contributed to the regeneration of the socio-spatial dimensions of religious practice. The question remains as to whether this enrichment of the cognitive variety of religious space is restoring the original sense of a place of worship as a social, spiritual and cultural meeting point that is not purely physical. The situation is still very dynamic and requires continuous observation and analysis.

References

Alves, R.V.S., Guimaraes, A.L.C., Resende, J.R.F.V.P. and Do Carmo, G.D.X. (2020) Freedom of religion or belief and the Covid-19 pandemic: an analysis of the adoption of restrictive measures in Brazil. *Revista General De Derecho Canonico Y Derecho Eclesiastico Del Estado* 54, 24.

Androutsopoulos, G. (2021) The right of religious freedom in light of the coronavirus pandemic: the Greek case. *Laws* 10(1), 14. DOI: 10.3390/laws10010014.

Bartalesi, L. (2017) *Antropologia dell'estetico.* Mimesis Edizioni, Milan/Udine, Italy.

Bittarello, M.B. (2009) Spatial metaphors describing the internet and religious websites: sacred space and sacred place. Observatorio 3(4), 1–12.

Bohler-Muller, N., Roberts, B., Gordon, S.L. and Davids, Y.D. (2021) The 'sacrifice' of human rights during an unprecedented pandemic: reflections on survey-based evidence. *South African Journal on Human Rights* 37(2), 154–180. DOI: 10.1080/02587203.2021.2009740.

Bryson, J.R., Andres, L. and Davies, A. (2020) COVID-19, virtual church services and a new temporary geography of home. *Tijdschrift Voor Economische En Sociale Geografie* 111(3), 360–372. DOI: 10.1111/tesg.12436.

Bruni, L. (2006) *Reciprocità. Dinamiche di cooperazione, economia e società civile.* Mondadori, Milan, Italy.

Brzozowski, W. (2020) Poland: freedom of religion in times of Covid-19 pandemic. *Revista General De Derecho Canonico Y Derecho Eclesiastico Del Estado* 54, 29.

Carnevale, D.N. and Girneata, S.F. (2021) Comunità da remoto. Il laboratorio della diaspora cristiano-ortodossa davanti alla pandemia. *Comparative Cultural Studies - European and Latin American Perspectives* 6(13), 143–164. DOI: 10.36253/ccselap-12766.

Casanova, J. (1994) *Public Religions in the Modern World*. University of Chicago Press, Chicago, IL. DOI: 10.7208/chicago/9780226190204.001.0001.

Christians, L.L. (2020) Religion and the health crisis, the new certainties of law. *Revue Theologique De Louvain* 51(4), 566–595.

Cloke, P. (2011) Emerging postsecular rapprochement in the contemporary city. In: Beaumont, J. and Baker, C. (eds) *Postsecular Cities*. Continuum, London, pp. 237–253.

Cohen, A.P. (1995) *The Symbolic Construction of Community*. Routledge, London.

COVID (2020) *ECML Covid*. Available at: https://covid-statistics.jrc.ec.europa.eu/ (accessed 28 June 2022).

Craven Nussbaum, M. (2004) *La fragilità del bene. Fortuna ed etica nella tragedia e nella filosofia greca*. Il Mulino, Bologna, Italy.

Della Dora, V. (2016) Infrasecular geographies: making, unmaking and remaking sacred space. *Progress in Human Geography* 42(1), 44–71. DOI: 10.1177/0309132516666190.

Donati, P. (1986) *Introduzione alla sociologia relazionale*. Franco Angeli, Milan, Italy.

Fornerod, A. (2021) Freedom of worship during a public health state of emergency in France. *Laws* 10(15), 1–10. DOI: 10.3390/laws10010015.

Gui, B. (1987) Eléments pour une Définition d' «économie communautaire». *Notes et Documents* 19–20, 32–42.

Haynes, J. (2021) Donald Trump, the Christian right and COVID-19: the politics of religious freedom. *Laws* 10(1), 1–15. DOI: 10.3390/laws10010006.

Hoekman, L.M., Smits, M.M.V. and Koolman, X. (2020) The Dutch COVID-19 approach: regional differences in a small country. *Health Policy and Technology* 9(4), 613–622. DOI: 10.1016/j.hlpt.2020.08.008.

Hulme, M. and Truch, A. (2006) The role of interspace in sustaining identity. *Knowledge, Technology & Policy* 19(1), 45–53. DOI: 10.1007/s12130-006-1014-6.

Kohn, M.L. (1987) Cross-national research as an analytic strategy: American sociological association presidential address. *American Sociological Review* 52(6), 713–731. DOI: 10.2307/2095831.

Kong, J. (2021) Safeguarding the free exercise of religion during the Covid-19 pandemic. *Fordham Law Review* 89(4), 1589–1633.

Kong, L. (1990) Geography and religion: trends and prospects. *Progress in Human Geography* 14(3), 355–371. DOI: 10.1177/030913259001400302.

Kong, L. (2002) In search of permanent homes: Singapore's house churches and the politics of space. *Urban Studies* 39(9), 1573–1586. DOI: 10.1080/00420980220151664.

Kong, L. (2010) Global shifts, theoretical shifts: changing geographies of religion. *Progress in Human Geography* 34(6), 755–776. DOI: 10.1177/0309132510362602.

Lara, M.B.R. (2020) Religious freedom in Spain during the Covid-19 pandemic. *Revista General De Derecho Canonico Y Derecho Eclesiastico Del Estado* 54, 27.

Leplongeon, M. (2020) Pourquoi les catholiques n'ont plus le droit d'aller à la messe. *Le Point*. Available at: https://www.lepoint.fr/societe/pourquoi-les-catholiques-n-ont-plus-le-droit-d-aller-a-la-messe-17-11-2020-2401607_23.php (accessed 10 June 2022).

Madera, A. (2021) The implications of the COVID-19 pandemic on religious exercise: preliminary remarks. *Laws* 10(2), 44. DOI: 10.3390/laws10020044.

Mariner, W.K. (2021) Shifting standards of judicial review during the coronavirus pandemic in the United States. *German Law Journal* 22(6), 1039–1059. DOI: 10.1017/glj.2021.51.

Martinez, J.A.S. (2020) State of alarm and freedom of religion and worship. *Revista General De Derecho Canonico Y Derecho Eclesiastico Del Estado* 53, 40.

Martínez-Torrón, J. (2021) COVID-19 and religious freedom: some comparative perspectives. *Laws* 10(2), 39. DOI: 10.3390/laws10020039.

Mazumdar, S. and Mazumdar, S. (2004) Religion and place attachment: a study of sacred places. *Journal of Environmental Psychology* 24(3), 385–397. DOI: 10.1016/j.jenvp.2004.08.005.

Mazurkiewicz, P. (2021) Religious freedom in the time of the pandemic. *Religions* 12(2), 103. DOI: 10.3390/rel12020103.

Milinković, I. (2021) Extraordinary measures in extraordinary times: legal response to the COVID-19 crisis in Bosnia and Herzegovina. *Medicine, Law & Society* 14(2), 439–456. DOI: 10.18690/mls.14.2.443-460.2021.

Mosquera, S. (2021) The impact of the Church–State model for an effective guarantee of religious freedom: a study of the Peruvian experience during the COVID-19 pandemic. *Laws* 10(2), 40. DOI: 10.3390/laws10020040.

Movsesian, M.L. (2022) Law, religion, and the COVID-19 crisis. *Journal of Law and Religion* 37(1), 9–24. DOI: 10.1017/jlr.2021.82.

Mpofu, B. (2021) Transversal modes of being a missional church in the digital context of COVID-19. *HTS Teologiese Studies* 77(4), a6341. DOI: 10.4102/hts.v77i4.6341.

Muckl, S. (2020) Religious freedom and Covid-19: legal developments in Germany. *Revista General De Derecho Canonico Y Derecho Eclesiastico Del Estado* 54, 25.

Nilsson, M. and Tesfahuney, M. (2016) Performing the post-secular in Santiago de Compostela. *Annals of Tourism Research* 57(C), 18–30. DOI: 10.1016/j.annals.2015.11.001.

OSCE Office for Democratic Institutions and Human Rights, (ODIHR) (ed.) (2020) *Human Dimension Commitments and State Responses to the Covid-19 Pandemic*. Warsaw, Poland. Available at: https://www.osce.org/files/f/documents/e/c/457567_0.pdf (accessed 10 June 2022).

Palumbo, P., Santoro, R., Foderaro, A., Scognamiglio, E., Martini, E. *et al.* (2020) *Libertà religiosa e fede al tempo del Covid-19—Risultati dell'indagine-ricerca "Libertà religiosa e fede al tempo del Covid-19" Fase 1*. Available at: https://issuu.com/profpaolopalumbo/docs/indagine (accessed 10 June 2022).

President of the Council of Ministers (2020a) *Decreto del Presidente del Consiglio dei Ministri 17 maggio 2020—Disposizioni attuative del decreto-legge 25 marzo 2020, n. 19, recante misure urgenti per fronteggiare l'emergenza epidemiologica da Covid-19, e del decreto-legge 16 maggio 2020, n. 33, recante ulteriori misure urgenti per fronteggiare l'emergenza epidemiologica da Covid-19*. Available at: https://www.gazzettaufficiale.it/eli/id/2020/05/17/20A02717/sg (accessed 10 June 2022).

President of the Council of Ministers (2020b) Protocollo con la *Conferenza Episcopale Italiana circa la ripresa delle celebrazioni con il popolo*. (Annex 1—D.P.C.M. 17 may 2020). Available at: https://www.gazzettaufficiale.it/eli/id/2020/05/17/20A02717/sg (accessed 10 June 2022).

President of the Council of Ministers (2020c) *Protocollo con le Comunità ebraiche italiane*. (Annex 2—D.P.C.M. 17 maggio 2020). Available at: https://www.gazzettaufficiale.it/eli/id/2020/05/17/20A02717/sg (accessed 10 June 2022).

President of the Council of Ministers (2020d) *Protocollo con le Chiese Protestanti, Evangeliche, Anglicane*. (Annex 3—D.P.C.M. 17 may 2020). Available at: https://www.gazzettaufficiale.it/eli/id/2020/05/17/20A02717/sg (accessed 10 June 2022).

President of the Council of Ministers (2020e) *Protocollo con le Comunità ortodosse*. (Annex 4—D.P.C.M. 17 may 2020). Available at: https://www.gazzettaufficiale.it/eli/id/2020/05/17/20A02717/sg (accessed 10 June 2022).

President of the Council of Ministers (2020f) *Protocollo con le Comunità Induista, Buddista (Unione Buddista e Soka Gakkai)*. (Annex 5—D.P.C.M. 17 may 2020). Available at: https://www.gazzettaufficiale.it/eli/id/2020/05/17/20A02717/sg (accessed 10 June 2022).

President of the Council of Ministers (2020g) *Protocollo con le Comunità Islamiche*. (Annex 6—D.P.C.M. 17 may 2020). Available at: https://www.gazzettaufficiale.it/eli/id/2020/05/17/20A02717/sg (accessed 10 June 2022).

President of the Council of Ministers (2020h) *Protocollo con la Comunità della Chiesa di Gesù Cristo dei Santi degli ultimi giorni*. (Annex 7—D.P.C.M. 17 may 2020). Available at: https://www.gazzettaufficiale.it/eli/id/2020/05/17/20A02717/sg (accessed 10 June 2022).

Przeworski, A. and Teune, H. (1966) Equivalence in cross-national research. *Public Opinion Quarterly* 30(4), 551–568.

Raimundo, M.A., Adragao, P.P., Leao, A.C. and Ramalho, T. (2020) Covid-19 and religious freedom in Portugal. *Revista General De Derecho Canonico Y Derecho Eclesiastico Del Estado* 54, 30.

Raiu, C. and Mina-Raiu, L. (2022) How to cope with counter-performance in public administration. The case of freedom of religion or belief during the pandemic. *Transylvanian Review of Administrative Sciences* 66(E), 81–98.

Reyes, A.P. (2020) Religious freedom in the face of the COVID-19 pandemic in Mexico. *Revista General De Derecho Canonico Y Derecho Eclesiastico Del Estado* 54, 35.

Shah, T.S. (2021) Institutional religious freedom in full: what the liberty of religious organizations really is and why it is an essential service to the common good. *Religions* 12(6), 414. DOI: 10.3390/rel12060414.

Sharma, S. (2012) 'The church is … my family': exploring the interrelationship between familial and religious practices and spaces. *Environment and Planning A* 44(4), 816–831. DOI: 10.1068/a4447.

Sharpley, R. and Jepson, D. (2011) Rural tourism: a spiritual experience? *Annals of Tourism Research* 38(1), 52–71.

Stanisz, P. (2021) Restrictions on freedom of religious worship during the COVID-19 pandemic: between constitutionality and effectiveness. *Przeglad Sejmowy* 3, 143–165.

Uhlaner, C.J. (1989) Relational goods and participation: incorporating sociability into a theory of rational action. *Public Choice* 62(3), 253–285. DOI: 10.1007/BF02337745.

United States Department of State—Office of International Religious Freedom (2022) *2021 Report on International Religious Freedom: France*. Available at: https://www.state.gov/wp-content/uploads/2022/03/FRANCE-2021-INTERNATIONAL-RELIGIOUS-FREEDOM-REPORT.pdf (accessed 27 July 2022).

Woods, O. (2013) Converting houses into churches: the mobility, fission, and sacred networks of evangelical house churches in Sri Lanka. *Environment and Planning D: Society and Space* 31(6), 1062–1075.

13 Is Pilgrimage an Essential Service? The Conflict Over Congregational Worship and Health Governance

Maía Angélica Alvarez-Orozco* and Silvia Aulet Serrallonga
School of Tourism, University of Girona, Spain

Abstract

After COVID-19 many questions related to lifestyle and health have been raised. One of the meanings of pilgrimage can be associated with the search for balance and harmony between soul and body. The search for spirituality can also be described as the search for a harmonious or unity relationship with oneself, others (including other people, animals, earth, nature) and/or God or the transcendent. Today it is widely accepted that the quest for spirituality is closely related to the search for well-being, that also includes self-improvement and overcoming challenges, especially related to physical activities like walking. This chapter attempts to examine whether pilgrimage can be considered as an essential activity needed to reach a meaningful and healthy life. According to the WHO, the different dimensions of health are physical, mental, social well-being and spiritual. Apart from exploring the connections between pilgrimage, well-being and health, in-depth interviews with representatives of pilgrimage sites have been conducted to better understand the reality of pilgrimage and pilgrims after the pandemic.

13.1 Introduction

The emergence of the global pandemic caused by COVID-19 has led us to question many issues not only related to health but also our lifestyle. The World Health Organization (WHO) defines health as a complete state of physical, mental and social well-being, and not just the absence of diseases or illnesses. In 2013 spiritual health was recognized as a fourth dimension. According to some health academics, we are entering a new phase in health that requires a more holistic approach based on inclusive narratives, the promotion of social trust and the need of having meaningful lives.

In the presented research, the authors also apply this holistic approach regarding pilgrimage, health and governance. Pilgrimage has a strong healing power. Pilgrimages allow us to connect with ourselves, with others, and with nature and can help us to develop a sense of well-being that can be related to emotional and spiritual health. Therefore, in a context like the current one, the authors vindicate pilgrimage as an activity that is not only healthy but necessary and must be taken into consideration in governance policies and also included in the agenda of each representative site and country where you can find pilgrimage routes.

*Corresponding author: maalvarez889@gmail.com

© CAB International 2023. *The Politics of Religious Tourism* (eds D. Bozonelos and P. Moira)
DOI: 10.1079/9781800621732.0013

The way in which power and governance are exercised in each country, as well as the type of policies applicable in each area of action, is a clear representation of what the decision makers expect their country to be and what its citizens represent to them. Are they important to the construction of a new valuable society with strong values and sense of belonging and caring that could contribute to the development of better human beings committed to their personal growth and also to reach new and better goals as a society? Are governments committed to knowing the social problems that most afflict their citizens and looking for ways to improve their quality of life and well-being? Does it have any importance, politically speaking, to promote, preserve and encourage the community to learn about the different pilgrimage routes that exist in their destinations? Sometimes it tends to be difficult to think this through because an effective managed policy should be measured, controlled and give the right numbers to check its availability. In this scenario, how can you control a resource that until now has been seen just as a type of tourism that doesn't go beyond the economic income and statistics based on visitors to religious sites? The criteria needs to be understood, so that's why this chapter attempts to show why pilgrimage should be considered as an essential service focusing on the valuable and visible changes you perceive in those who participate in these retreats and pilgrimages. It is important to note the relevance of religious tourism worldwide and, in this sense, we can include pilgrimage as a type of activity within religious tourism.

Is it essential for individuals to go on pilgrimages? At this point, the immense importance of policies that revolve around the well-being of the community and its visitors, the effective dissemination and visibility of the natural environment and heritage, inside and outside the destination, and the conservation of these important resources is emphasized. This chapter helps to understand the relevance of pilgrimage as a lasting life changing event that should be taken into account when talking about these routes, their maintenance, their visibility, preservation (they're surrounded by nature and tangible and intangible heritage), their impact on people's lives, and how these should be properly managed.

One of the meanings of pilgrimage can be associated with the search for balance and harmony between soul and body. The quest for spirituality can also be described as the search for a harmonious or unity relationship with oneself, 'others' (including other people, animals, earth, nature), and/or God/higher power (Willson et al., 2013). Today it is widely accepted that the quest for spirituality is closely related to the research of well-being understood as a multidimensional concept (Bimonte and Faralla, 2012), that also includes self-improvement and overcoming challenges, especially related to physical activities like walking (Santos, 2002; Sachs, 2017; Eichberg et al., 2017).

This research aims to explore the connections between pilgrimage, health and governance, and to determine whether pilgrimage can be considered an essential service related to well-being and spirituality, and well proposed and managed policies by governments. For these purposes, the chapter is structured in four main sections after the introduction. First, a revision of the literature is presented connecting the main topics of the research, especially exploring the connections between pilgrimage and well-being, pilgrimage and health, and the connection with the concept of essential service in governance. This section is followed by the methodology, and then the main results and findings are presented. In the last section, the main conclusions the research are discussed.

13.2   Pilgrimage and Well-Being

Since the beginning of humanity, how people regained their sense of balance was through walking, creating a natural propensity for the path and what it represented to them (Esteve, 2009). Pilgrimage was the first method of mobility, born thousands of years ago, and indeed the development of tourism cannot be understood without understanding the practice of pilgrimage since ancient times (Collins-Kreiner, 2019). Even so, the connections between pilgrimage and tourism are sometimes contested. Most authors do not distinguish between pilgrims and tourists, and pilgrimage is accepted as a form of tourism because it shares the same characteristics in terms of the use of transport, services and infrastructure. According to Smith (1992), for example, contemporary pilgrimages and tourism have in common three operational elements that can vary according to intensity: adequate income and resources for travel, free time, and social appreciation (Jackowski, 1987; Rinschede, 1992; Jackson and Hudman, 1995; Vukonic, 1996). However, there is another approach that argues that pilgrimage and religious tourism are two differentiated realities, especially because of the final motivation and intensity of experiences. The idea that religious tourism is different from pilgrimages was born in Europe in the post-war period, as a result of the decline in religious practice, the increasing popularity of travel by car or coach, the secularization of society, and in some countries, the reduction of flows of traditional pilgrimages. This perspective places the pilgrim as a reality away from tourism (Ostrowski, 2002; Santos, 2002; Pardellas, 2005). Cohen (1992) argues that pilgrims move to a centre, which is the destination of pilgrimage, to obtain a transcendental experience; while tourists move to the periphery (routine escape) to obtain recreational experiences.

To this debate, it should be added that today tourism has become a form of approach to significant experiences, leading to the emergence of new trends like conscious tourism (Andriotis, 2002; Pollock, 2012), spiritual tourism (Cheer et al., 2017; Aulet, 2020), or regenerative tourism (Hussain, 2021), among others. The concept of meaningful experiences has transcended the realm of religion and spirituality and is used to refer to those tourist experiences where visitors are 'immersed by just being there or doing something actively' (Breiby et al., 2020, p. 337) or that promotes deeper understanding and transformation (Kottler, 1997). In the case of pilgrimage, it is a form of attraction to sacred places and their entire context, which provides, through its practice, a new meaning of life and offers the opportunity to live a period of transformation linked to an awakening of strong religious feelings that regenerates a secular vision to a more spiritual and transcendental vision. It is here that we find pilgrimage as an activity in search of meaning that contains deep transformational and lasting elements (Collins-Kreiner, 2019) based mainly on values.

Due to their nature, pilgrimages are massive social phenomena that move millions of people around the world. Although the experience is lived and perceived individually, pilgrimages are generally carried out in groups and at specific times of the year (Di Giovine and Choe, 2019). The apparent and latent absence of God is what has encouraged men to seek in the pilgrimage the recovery of divine closeness (Esteve, 2009). Pilgrimage is a spiritual retreat that brings with it entirely religious motivations that have nothing to do with a tourist excursion (Bauer, 1993) and that take place in unique and singular spaces that are completely outside daily life (Liutikas, 2017).

If pilgrimage seeks spiritual regeneration and the achievement of balance between body and spirit, the tourist trip seeks the recovery of the psychophysical balance and physical regeneration of human beings, which is commonly described as charging the batteries to be able to continue in the daily task of profane pursuits (Esteve, 2009).

According to Besecke (2001), two fundamental ideas must be exposed about the modernity that surrounds everyday life and is influenced by it. There is currently a crisis of sense; social differentiation and specialization that characterize modernity have deteriorated and pulled away from the sense of daily life. Second, modernity does not have to be this way, the agents in the hands of those who find the tools to provide meaningful experiences can turn preconceived discourses to support the construction of new narratives based on mutual understanding (Alvarez Orozco and Aulet Serrallonga, 2021). All this is based on the fact that through spiritual tourism and activities such as pilgrimage, new scenarios can be explored that develop spirituality and intentional desire for growth.

'Popular spirituality can seem shallow, indeed flaky; however, its currents creative, under the right conditions, can activate our deepest energies and commitments. Even in its most self-absorbed forms, today's spiritual ferment reflects a deep hunger for self-transformation that is genuinely and personally satisfying' (Roof, 1999, p. 9). It is a constant search for hopes and purposes that seem to have been lost amid consumerism and savage capitalism that governs socio-economic structures and policies of the new world tendencies.

Free time has become the ideal space in which individuals have developed their instinct to pursue spiritual goals, which generally include projects of personal meaning and life purpose, questions about identity, among others. That is, spiritual tourism is a subjective practice of well-being (Norman and Pokorny, 2017), which involves various elements that are found in the world and that can be related to religious symbols, as is the case of pilgrimages, rituals, new sources of wisdom, new images and stories, which in a particular way will help the construction of that path of spirituality and that will give meaning to new life purposes (Besecke, 2014).

Having meaning and a purpose in life is also close to the idea of well-being. Well-being is also a holistic concept that encompasses emotional, social, cultural, spiritual and economic needs, which allow individuals to realize their full potential and engage in society to their fullest capacity. The definitions of health and well-being are linked to each other and even when the concept of well-being is studied by a large number of areas of knowledge, it is scarcely used concerning tourism. Well-being has been a philosophical and sociological concern since the beginning of time, so it has been spreading to other areas to study its true relevance and impact, especially examined from the point of view of satisfaction and meaning of happiness (Hanlon *et al.*, 2013; Pyke *et al.*, 2016; Smith and Diekmann, 2017).

According to the above, Sheldon (2020) establishes that there are important factors that can dramatically affect an individual's life. Living from a state of consciousness or transformation has great significance for those who experience it, for society and tourism. The freedom, the feeling of connection with the world, the concern for higher issues and the detachment from egocentric thoughts are some of the results of the process of change to another state of mind, commonly associated with a permanent state of enlightenment. If pilgrimages can help us to reach this state, which is beneficial for human health, could they be considered as an essential service?

Normally essential services are considered the goods and supplies everyone should have access to, regardless of the ability to pay for them, and are related to different policy actions managed by governments in some specific aspects like health, education and culture, among others (Eddy, 1991). The Agenda for the Sustainable Development of the United Nations and the Sustainable Development Goals refer to some of the indicators, the need to guarantee essential services, for example, regarding health, education and others, mainly through the action of government investment. The European Pillar of Social Rights also states that everyone should have 'the right to access essential services of good quality, including water, sanitation, energy, transport, financial services and digital communications' (European Commission, 2017). But what is not clear at all is how to define what 'essential service' means in culture, health or education.

According to the World Health Organization (2022), there are 10 Essential Public Health Operations (EPHO) that should guide the action of states and governments when establishing essential services. These operations centre around three main areas of service delivery: health protection, disease prevention and health promotion. Even though the WHO defines health as a complete state of physical, mental and social well-being (including spiritual health) few policies have been developed to face the challenge of how to promote well-being among citizens. The policy framework for health stated by the European Commission (2017) calls for action to strengthen mental health promotion programmes and for further research to adapt to new challenges related to mental health.

EPHO's number 6: Assuring Governance for Health and Wellbeing, is helping us to get a closer look at pilgrimage as an essential service and to be understood as part of those actions to strengthen mental health promotion programmes not only because this itinerary is fully based on the search for spirituality, awareness, enlightenment, development of psychological strengths, new life resolutions and permanent changes of behaviour, but also because it has been proven that assuring governance and introducing policies that provide citizens with tools to have better lives can contribute to the development of a new healthier and strong society with a great sense of belonging and caring. This is challenging because the effects of the pandemic and the several lockdowns have not been researched enough (Boden *et al.*, 2021) and the connections between mental health, well-being and spirituality are not well established yet. What we can be sure of is that the pandemic has brought new questions on what mental health and well-being are and how they should be a relevant topic to talk about within policies and mostly related to the normative created by governments to rule the destination.

Authors like Berger (1969), Tolle (2004), and Nasr (2007), to mention a few, believe that the actual situation of pollution and climate change is the result of a deep spiritual crisis in human beings. Nature is no longer seen as a resource but as essential for human life. The rupture of ecological balances accelerated by current development models gives rise to activities whose sole purpose is to reconnect with nature and the search for an inner harmony of human beings with it (Bagri *et al.*, 2009). Nature and the environment offer the sense of inner peace and tranquillity that would explain, also, the increasing number of (young) people engaging in pilgrimage routes such as the Camino de Santiago (Collins-Kreiner and Kliot, 2017). Fedele (2013) states that new pilgrimage routes are emerging based on ecofeminism, Goddess or New Age movements that have in common a deep relation with nature.

Pilgrimage routes as cultural landscapes encompass different values like historical, symbolic, spiritual, aesthetic and social. These values are important in achieving a meaningful life that is key for well-being. According to Health Tourism Worldwide (2020), spirituality and nature represent the areas with a higher potential for growth. In the actual situation of restrictions and limitations, can we consider tourism connected to well-being practices as an essential activity?

13.3   Methodology and Presentation of a Case Study

This research is mainly based on qualitative methods such as semi-structured interviews with pilgrimage route representatives. To answer the research question 'can pilgrimage be considered as an essential service within health governance?' the first step is to connect pilgrimage with well-being and health. The elements identified in the literature review that conform to the pilgrimage experience are the shrines or places where pilgrimages take place and the pilgrims. The authors have focused on sanctuaries for this research.

Why sanctuaries? We could say that their nature is primarily defined by the meaning they hold for the faithful rather than for what they are. The reason that a place is a sanctuary lies in that it is somewhere that is frequently visited by tourists as well as by worshippers. The sanctuary aims to provide pilgrims and visitors with what they expect to find there Aulet, 2019, and these sites also have specific guidelines and policies that have been linked to the public administration as they can be also considered as cultural goods.

The authors have selected a sample of four pilgrimage routes in Europe located in Portugal, Spain, France and Italy. Semi-structured interviews were held with those responsible for each of the shrines. The shrines and routes analysed were the sanctuary of Our Lady of Fatima (Portugal), the Holy Cave in Manresa (Spain) linked with the Ignatian Way, the Via Francigena and the Assisi route (Italy), and the sanctuary of Our Lady of Lourdes (France).

The Shrine of Fatima is a place of pilgrimage located in central Portugal in La Cova da Iria, Fatima. It is one of the most important Marian Shrines in the world and also the world's fourth largest Catholic pilgrimage site, visited by over 5 million visitors every year. Among the various buildings associated with the sanctuary, the Basilica (Basílica de Nossa Senhora do Rosário) is a solid limestone church built between 1928 and 1953 in Neo-Baroque style. The story states that the Lady of Fatima appeared to three little shepherds and requested them to go to the Cova on the 13th day of each month, for 6 months. During their encounters, the Lady of Fatima foretold prophecies, miracles and revelations that became part of the basis of what is today the Basilica that moves millions of visitors, pilgrims and tourists from all over the world (Shrine of Fatima, 2022). The person interviewed was the one in charge of tourist promotion of Fatima, which is part of the government tourist commission.

The Ignatian Way, as its promoters indicate, is a pilgrimage for men and women of the 21st century. This path arises from the dynamics of

Ignatian spirituality recovering that 'spiritual' dimension previously referred to (Abad and Guereño, 2016, p. 12). El Camino was an initiative of a small group of laymen and Jesuits to recreate the pilgrimage made by Ignacio de Loyola in 1522 from Loyola to the city of Manresa. It has 27 different stages starting from the Basque lands, passing through La Rioja, Navarra, and Aragón, until reaching Catalan lands and ending in Manresa, Spain. The main idea of the pilgrimage is to offer pilgrims the opportunity to experience retreat, prayer, physical resistance and strength, travelling 540 km of the road (the totality of the way is 647 km), while soul, conscience, heart and spirit are exercised by spiritual exercises (Ignatian Way, 2019). Two representatives were interviewed who were the Jesuits in charge of promoting the Ignatian Way and the Cova de Manresa.

Via Francigena is an itinerary that connects some places that testify to the life and preaching of the Saint of Assisi (Francesco di Assisi); a pilgrimage that intends to re-propose the Franciscan experience in the lands that the Poverello walked: the landscapes on which the pilgrim's eye rests are the same ones that cheered the simple heart of Francis; the stopping places preserve the memory of his words and deeds; the people you meet along the way are mostly related to him. The Via di Francesco consists of two distinct paths that lead to Assisi. The Northern Route starts from La Verna and is 189 km long, the Southern Route starts from Rome and is 247 km long (Vie Francigene, 2022). The person interviewed was the one in charge of the tourist promotion of Via di Francesco and is also part of the government commission for tourism in Umbria.

The fourth shrine studied was the Sanctuary of Our Lady of Lourdes (France). When the Virgin Mary appeared to Bernadette Soubirous in 1858, Lourdes had little more than 4000 inhabitants. Between 11 February 1858 and 16 July of the same year, no less than 18 apparitions were recorded. Soon, pilgrims flocked to Lourdes to see the Grotto of the Apparitions. The Grotto of Massabielle is an obligatory passage for the pilgrimage to Lourdes. A statue of the Virgin is nestled in a cavity and marks the location of the apparition. Fountains make it possible to draw water from the miraculous source and a little further on, swimming pools welcome pilgrims who wish to bathe there. Nowadays, Lourdes is one of the main places of pilgrimage in the world. The Sanctuaries of Our Lady of Lourdes cover an area of 52 hectares and nearly 6 million visitors from all over the world gather in Lourdes each year (Lourdes Sanctuary, 2022). The person interviewed was a religious person in charge of diocesan pilgrimages at the Sanctuary of Our Lady of Lourdes.

From all the above shrines studied, two are strongly related to pilgrimage routes (Italy and Spain), while the other two are mostly known for being pilgrimage centres (France and Portugal) but there are different routes and ways to reach the site. Two of the shrines are devoted to Our Lady (France and Portugal) so they are attached to Marian pilgrimages while the other two are related to the figures of important saints for the Catholic faith (Saint Ignatius and Saint Francesco di Assisi). Two of the interviews were related to the religious administration of the shrine (France and Spain) while the other two were more focused on tourism management (Portugal and Italy). This sample, even small, provides examples of different cases and approaches to the sites and the pilgrims that allow authors to understand a bit more on the effects of the pandemic in pilgrimage and health. Interviews were done between June and September 2021.

The questions of the interview could be grouped into three topics or areas. Some of the questions were related to the impact and challenges that pilgrimage has on the sanctuary, the second group of questions were related to the pilgrims, their profile and what changes there have been during the pandemic, and the last group of questions was focused on the experience of pilgrimage, the connections with well-being and if pilgrimage could or should be considered as an essential service.

13.4 Results

To answer the question of whether pilgrimage can be considered as an essential service or not, and what the connections with health and policies are, the answers have been analysed considering three elements, as can be seen in Fig. 13.1.

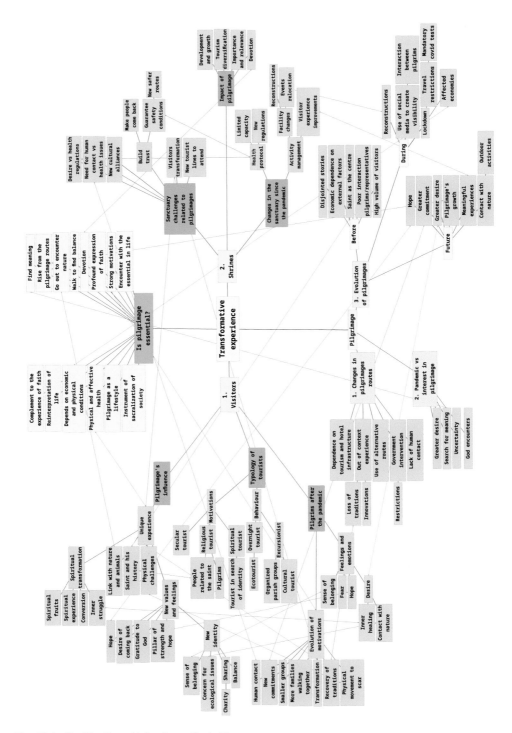

Fig. 13.1. Codification of interviews. Code Map.
Source: Authors (2022).

According to the answers obtained three main issues were addressed, the impact of pilgrimage on the site before and after the pandemic, the challenges the shrines are facing regarding pilgrimages, and the changes that they have implemented due to COVID-19.

As mentioned before, the identity of a sanctuary is not only defined by what it is but also strongly connected with the pilgrimage routes that lead to it and the experiences that pilgrims have. All the interviewees agreed that pilgrimages brought to the sanctuaries development and growth, and that public administration is now feeling more interested in ways to collaborate.

> The Sanctuary of Lourdes is one of the most important places in the world on any pilgrimage route
> **Lourdes Representative**

> The most visible impact of the pilgrimage routes in the Sanctuary are the manifestations of deep faith that pilgrims bring with them as they travel with great sacrifice, a path that can last days or weeks. The Sanctuary is clearly strengthened by the walks
> **Fatima Representative**

If in some cases it could be considered that a huge number of visitors could lead, also, to negative impacts, the perception of the interviewees was that pilgrimages were a positive element, and that they were very closely connected to the relevance and importance of the sanctuary. In some cases, for example, the Ignatian Way and the shrine of the Holy Cave, important modifications in the shrine have been done to adapt the infrastructure to the needs of visitors and the Municipality of Manresa has also made some changes in the city as they feel the Spirituality Centre is becoming a very important point of attraction for visitors and they needed to highlight the cultural importance of this place. Even though it was not mentioned in the interview, the same thing happened with the shrines of Lourdes and Fatima.

> All the impact that the Ignatian Way has had on the city of Manresa is immense, it has prompted an architectural renovation, a renovation at the level of structures, of infrastructures, a whole change that is being noticed in the city and that is going to live even longer
> **Ignatian Way Representatives**

Pilgrimages were cancelled because of COVID-19 and this is perceived as negative for the impossibility of moving to the sites. On the other hand, the sanctuaries had to come up with new fresh ideas to keep the visitors interested and linked to the sacred sites despite the physical impediment of travelling.

> I don't know if it is inventive or not, but it truly is an apostolic, missionary spirit of going out to meet people through social media, then we have been able to reach many people throughout the world, in English, in Spanish, in Italian, in French, praying the rosary online, through the site of the sanctuary. Many people have felt connected with us and have expressed how in this moment of uncertainty that we were experiencing worldwide, the prayers, the union and the virtual interaction with the sanctuary brought them closer to the hope of a better tomorrow
> **Lourdes representative**

> The pandemic has not only influenced pilgrimages but also the way of doing things in the sanctuary, they have developed new practices to bring people closer to the sanctuary, virtually, which has made people feel in communion with the place because they had already seen it
> **Ignatian Way Representatives**

Because of the pandemic, most of the changes done in the shrines studied were related to health protocols, where most of the efforts were put. Apart from the mobility restrictions that happened in different moments, the changes in regulations occurring in the different countries made the management of the sites difficult, and relate to the main challenges that shrines are facing. The main issues are related to changes in the visitors profile and how to deal with health issues. At the beginning:

> The desire to go on pilgrimage is postponed but not annulled the interest in pilgrimage has grown, although with scepticism for living the experience with restrictions that will not allow it to be lived well
> **Ignatian Way Representatives**

Before the pandemic, there were already different types of visitors attending the sites, but after the pandemic, this trend has been accentuated. Managers of the sites state that there are new visitors with new needs.

> People talk about the changes after walking 8, 11 or more days. They experience the essence of how life could be simpler, easier, thanking God for many things in their life
> **Assisi representative**

> Transition from organized religious groups to spiritual tourists, due to the appearance of new tourism trends and long paths to travel in nature
> **Assisi representative**

The other important issue is how to deal with the contradiction of people looking for human contact while caring for health issues. All the interviewees mentioned the fact that after the pandemic, people were struggling with this. Building trust was one of the main tasks of people in charge of shrines; they had to welcome visitors, make them feel at home, attend to their spiritual needs and, at the same time, be aware of not making people feel uncomfortable.

> People who walk need human contact along the way, so you can see it from different points of view. There's a security issue now because no one wants to wear the mask anymore, there's a security issue of course where they sleep, the usual tradition of eating together and things like that, but on the other hand, they want human contact, like hugs, for example. The experience has been transformed and the pilgrims do not want to live it that way
> **Assisi representative**

Visitors and their experiences were also considered by asking interviewees about the changes they noticed. While some changes in visitors' profiles were identified, few changes happened in pilgrims. Sanctuaries have seen a diversification of the typologies of tourists and visitors. In terms of behaviour, the main difference is between those that stay overnight at the site and those that are excursionists. This distinction existed already before the pandemic, the change is that before only the religious tourists and pilgrims spent the night in the place, while now we can find other types of visitors, especially those looking for contact with nature. In terms of motivations, we see also the differentiation between religious

motivations, spiritual motivations and secular motivations.

> Assisi is a religious place, but the pilgrims do not all identify themselves as such, they go in search of having contact with a transcendental identity in a spiritual way, interested in living the experience without ties or labels
> **Assisi representative**

The most interesting aspects were those related to the influence of pilgrimage in people's life. In general, pilgrimage was seen as a unique experience that provided meaningful insights. The main issues were that:

On one hand, pilgrimage fosters spiritual transformation, especially for those visiting the site for religious purposes. It was considered as part of life's essentials.

> Pilgrimage is for many pilgrims a pillar of strength and hope. Pilgrimages are remarkable experiences for pilgrims. They are such unique experiences that they provide many pilgrims with a new form of spiritual experience
> **Fatima representative**

On the other hand, the experience is linked with contact with nature, so it is not only about the shrine but the place where the shine is located. Nature is present on all pilgrimage routes and this is also where policies are needed as it is essential to preserve and apply the right regulations. This is a resource in which governments have noted some importance since the natural environment has become the best ally for spiritual retreats, use of natural resources as resources for energy and spiritual renewal, sports and nature tourism, which promote new forms of physical activity to improve physical and mental health.

> We receive people interested in nature, environmentalists, people who spiritually identify with the saint's sense of belonging to nature
> **Assisi representative**

Moreover, pilgrimage provides new values. It is not only about strengthening the faith but also feeling gratitude, hope and the desire to come back. It also helps to forge a new identity constructed on a sense of belonging, a concern for ecological issues and the concept of sharing.

Pilgrims have developed a great sense of belonging to the sanctuary, now it is not just any place, it is the place where they have believed, prayed. People arrive as having passed a tough test. They are seeking to be transformed and seek anchors where they can find this transformation, this new hope

Ignatian Way Representatives

The main changes in pilgrimage, as mentioned, were caused by the pandemic. The restrictions to movement affected pilgrimage in the same way as all the other tourist segments. Other changes were observed, for example, in summer 2021 the groups of pilgrims were smaller than normal and, because some remaining restrictions, there were some difficulties in finding accommodation in some places. Nevertheless, according to the interviewees, the most important changes were in the pilgrims. After the first lockdown, there was a greater desire for going on a pilgrimage. For example, in the case of the Way to Saint Francesco de Assisi, some people were doing the pilgrimage even during the lockdown and some international pilgrims were willing to self-quarantine for a week before starting the pilgrimage. Pilgrimage was part of the quest for meaning.

To answer the question of whether pilgrimage can be considered as an essential service, it is important to take into account the different perspectives that condition the term essential. In the interviews, it was observed that while the majority agreed that it was indeed an essential service, the pilgrimage could be conceived as an instrument of sacralization of society, as a way of rediscovering the meaning of what is essential in life, of undergoing a profound transformation of values and perspectives, which lasts over time and connects visitors with themselves, with others, with nature and with the environment itself. The link that is created between the pilgrim, the sanctuary and the path itself is a sign of deep devotion, strong enough to be considered an essential need. Others, on the other hand, affirmed that it was essential as long as it could be economically and physically assumed. This statement is an interesting point of discussion where future questions appear about the importance of activities in natural environments, with high heritage content, linked to spiritual issues that can contribute to the improvement of the physical and emotional

health of human beings. Likewise, it is important to consider what kind of efforts and initiatives are being carried out by governments to promote the improvement of habits and lifestyles by making use of the natural, cultural and heritage environments that surround the different destinations.

According to the World Economic Forum (2022) in countries like Canada, doctors prescribe trips to natural parks as a form of natural medicine. Patients annually receive a pass of approximately US\$57, which gives them free access to 80 natural parks and outdoor spaces. The outdoors are a part of the heritage environment of the country. According to scientific reports, people who spend at least 2 hours a week in contact with nature report high levels of health and well-being; reduced risk of heart attacks, heart disease, high blood pressure and even diabetes; decreased stress levels; and better spiritual and mental health, among many other benefits. This indicates that there are already governments promoting activities related to spirituality and physical and mental health. Not only activities are promoted, but within the government statutes there is already a clear policy designed for the well-being of society and the use of the natural resources available in the place, likewise, the population is being encouraged to learn more about their environment and to appropriate it culturally and socially.

In short, approaches have been made to what would be new health policies, from all areas, which could also approach the perfect trinomial between nature, heritage and spirituality; necessary factors when talking about pilgrimage. As time progresses and the narratives grow around spirituality and the need for humanity to rethink its values and ethical foundations, the urgency of a more conscious intervention by decision makers is evident. Society is undoubtably getting closer to this type of practice, pilgrimage, not necessarily seen from a religious point of view, but from the search for new experiences that bring greater and better benefits in terms of physical, mental and spiritual health. While this is happening, activities linked to spirituality, religiosity and well-being are imposed, from the autonomy of individuals, as a new way of finding a balance, of discovering new worlds, starting principally and prevailingly with one's spirituality and that it is only achieved in the deep inner search. In fact, according to the results, representatives are aware of the growing resurgence of pilgrimage routes around the world and the high increase in non-religious visitors interested in knowing the natural and heritage environment of the place, for them reaching the sanctuary is also the goal when taking the way.

> It is essential and society is looking for it, it is reflected in the resurgence of pilgrimage routes and the resurgence of Marian devotions
> **Ignatian Way Representatives**

> It is very important, essential? No, but it is very very important and it is essential as long as I am able to travel
> **Lourdes Representative**

> I consider the pilgrimage to be a profound expression of faith. As such, it is a complement to the experience of faith in the Shrine
> **Fathima Representative**

> Since Saint Francis left the song of the creature, there is a very strong bond between him and the animals and their care. We have a special certification in Assisi that we give if you walk with a dog. The testimony has an identity and a religious meaning. Of course, since you walk the dog all the way, it was right for the Franciscan priests to give the certificate for that
> **Assisi Representative**

13.5　Discussion/Conclusion

Destinations can help people to find themselves, and the opportunity to evolve into a better type of tourism that connects people to destinations in a much deeper and more sensitive way is in the hands of the ones creating experiences. If this connection is created, the bond established will be translated into loyalty, awareness, understanding and commitment within destinations and will also transform tourists with a new mindset, treasuring the new experiences that have led them to obtain a higher level of consciousness and an egocentric detachment that allows them to feel in constant connection with the world, develop concern for higher issues and seek well-being from that new and permanent state of enlightenment.

Spiritual values of religious sites and pilgrimage should be further researched, promoted and transmitted to visitors. If spirituality is the goal, travelling seems to be the ideal setting through which it can be sought and, in some cases, even found (Cheer *et al.*, 2017). Religious sites, as part of the cultural heritage of a destination, inherently include elements of spirituality and vibrant culture, and have long been a driving force for foreign travel (Diotallevi, 2015). Making visitors more aware of these values and involving them in specific practices can help to promote positive attitudes, including health but also respect, hope, justice or peace; helping to improve the spiritual, social and emotional dimensions of health (Alvarez Orozco and Aulet Serrallonga, 2021). Since some decades ago, we have been seeing an increasing interest in spirituality (many times under different names or labels). Several authors have already explored the connection between different forms of tourism (like religious tourism, pilgrimage or even rural tourism) and the quest for spirituality, and some authors point out that the current ecological crisis is a reflection of a deeper spiritual crisis affecting human beings.

Since the establishment of these pilgrimage routes, a great contribution is being made to the economic, socio-cultural, and tangible and intangible heritage of the communities directly impacted by the pilgrimage routes and sanctuaries. Likewise, tourism from its different branches, in this case through religious tourism, is contributing to the spiritual transformation of visitors, and is rescuing lives using one of the oldest tourism practices in the history of humanity, pilgrimage. In essence, the road is the vehicle that demonstrates the resurgence of a new spirituality (Abad and Guereño, 2016) based on the constant need of the human being to satisfy his shortcomings, to discover new forms of life, and to adopt new approaches to modern life.

Well-being and health are fundamental for the achievement of peace and social justice, which is one of the objectives of sustainable development. One of the elements that we often forget is the need to take a holistic view of reality. This holistic approach is not only considered in health; several philosophers have also reflected on this previously. The world cannot be understood without understanding the concept of interdependence. The world has become small but humankind has not grown big. The debate whether pilgrimages should be considered essential services or not could be extended to other forms of tourism that can provide meaningful experiences. The answer is not clear, but the reflection has to be done. As a society, we are facing important challenges, but they cannot be faced if we are not healthy and strong enough. As Gandhi said, there is no peace without inner peace.

In this scenario, can we consider tourism in religious heritage sites as an essential activity? Essential means that it refers to the essence, to the main characteristics of something or someone. We could mention Antonie de Saint Exupery's words, 'the essential is invisible to the eye', connecting the idea of essential to something precious and valuable. Could we consider visiting religious heritage sites and going on pilgrimages as an essential service for the improvement of health and well-being? After the study, even tourism itself could be considered as essential for mental and social health of people, so healthier ways of travelling like pilgrimages should be promoted and engaged with by governments.

The way in which governments are contributing to the improvement of mental health and well-being is of the utmost importance when it comes to establishing policies, included within government plans, that promote the development of these places, their preservation and the creation of incentives that allow citizens to visit and interact with destinations. It is also vital to point out not only how new policies are needed all over the world to create better environments for the next generations but to take actions in our actual situation to preserve, help and encourage our current generations to speak up and make their voice heard to be able to ask for a must-needed change of poor policies that are demanding more money and showing negative results for the communities impacted.

Policies that revolve around valuing what contributes to citizens improving their quality of life are the result of understanding the impact that governance has on achieving clear goals for citizens. The use of resources, the decentralization of tourism, the enhancement of rural areas with high cultural content and the economic, cultural and social spread that is generated, thus also bringing a new form of community-based tourism connected with pilgrimage, cultural tourism and spiritual and nature tourism are visible results that impact the development of a destination integrally.

Society must become aware that the first changes that must be done for social transformation are those that are made by the individual, the same individual concerned about their emotional, mental, spiritual and physical well-being, in order to later be able to contribute to the intervention of the community. Thus, according to the World Health Organization (2022), of the ten Essential Public Health Operations, number 6 (Assuring Governance for Health and Wellbeing) is a thoughtful tool that makes us reflect more deeply on how health services are governed and how institutions are committed to create quality and equity policies open to all, to facilitate actions to bring a healthier environment that recognizes the need of mental health, promotion of health care and the essentialness of well-being.

References

Abad, M. and Guereño, B. (2016) Needs of the Ignatian pilgrim: perceptions of an experience. *International Journal of Scientific Management Tourism* 2(3), 9–25.

Alvarez Orozco, M.A. and Aulet Serrallonga, S. (2021) Analysis of the spiritual impact of religious tourism on the tourist experience: the case of the Ignatian Way. *ROTUR, Leisure and Tourism Magazine* 15(2), 24–44.

Andriotis, K. (2002) Options in tourism development: conscious versus conventional tourism. *Anatolia* 13(1), 73–85. DOI: 10.1080/13032917.2002.9687016.

Aulet, S. (2020) Pilgrim's motivations: a theoretical approach to pilgrimage as a peacebuilding tool. *International Journal of Religious Tourism and Pilgrimage* 8(6), 59–74.

Aulet Serrallonga, S. (2019) L'acolliment turístic als santuaris: la importància de la custòdia. *Journal of Ethnology of Catalonia* 44, 135–147.

Bagri, S., Gupta, B. and George, B. (2009) Environmental orientation and ecotourism awareness among pilgrims, adventure tourists, and leisure tourists. *Tourism: An International Interdisciplinary Journal* 57(1), 55–68.

Bauer, M. (1993) Tourisme religieux ou touristes en milieu religieux. Esquisse d'une typologie. In: Cahiers Espaces 30: *Tourisme Religieux*. pp. 24–37.

Berger, P. (1969) *A Rumour of Angels: Modern Society and the Rediscovery of the Supernatural*. Doubleday and Co, New York.

Besecke, K. (2001) Speaking of meaning in modernity: reflexive spirituality as a cultural resource. *Sociology of Religion* 62(3), 365–381. DOI: 10.2307/3712355.

Besecke, K. (2014) *You Can't Put God in a Box: Thoughtful Spirituality in a Rational Age*. Oxford University Press, New York.

Bimonte, S. and Faralla, V. (2012) Tourist types and happiness a comparative study in Maremma, Italy. *Annals of Tourism Research* 39(4), 1929–1950. DOI: 10.1016/j.annals.2012.05.026.

Boden, M., Zimmerman, L., Azevedo, K.J., Ruzek, J.I., Gala, S., *et al.* (2021) Addressing the mental health impact of COVID-19 through population health. *Clinical Psychology Review* 85, 102006. DOI: 10.1016/j.cpr.2021.102006.

Breiby, M.A., Duedahl, E., Øian, H. and Ericsson, B. (2020) Exploring sustainable experiences in tourism. *Scandinavian Journal of Hospitality and Tourism* 20(4), 335–351. DOI: 10.1080/15022250.2020.1748706.

Cheer, J.M., Belhassen, Y. and Kujawa, J. (2017) The search for spirituality in tourism: toward a conceptual framework for spiritual tourism. *Tourism Management Perspectives* 24, 252–256. DOI: 10.1016/j.tmp.2017.07.018.

Cohen, E. (1992) Pilgrimage centres: concentric and eccentric. *Annals of Tourism Research* 19, 33–50.

Collins-Kreiner, N. (2019) Pilgrimage tourism-past, present and future rejuvenation: a perspective article. *Tourism Review* 75(1), 145–148. DOI: 10.1108/TR-04-2019-0130.

Collins-Kreiner, N. and Kliot, N. (2017) Why do people hike? Hiking the Israel national trail. *Tijdschrift Voor Economische En Sociale Geografie* 108(5), 69–68.

Di Giovine, M.A. and Choe, J. (2019) Geographies of religion and spirituality: pilgrimage beyond the 'officially' sacred. *Tourism Geographies* 21(3), 361–383.

Diotallevi, M. (2015) Intangible cultural heritage, spiritual tourism and sustainable development. In: *UNWTO First International Conference: Spiritual Tourism for Sustainable Development*, 21–22 November 2013, Ninh Binh City, Viet Nam. UNWTO, Madrid, pp. 69-74. https://doi.org/10.18111/9789284416738.

Eddy, D.M. (1991) What care is "essential"? What services are "basic"? *JAMA* 265(6), 782–788. DOI: 10.1001/jama.265.6.782.

Eichberg, H., Kosiewicz, J. and Contiero, D. (2017) Pilgrimage: intrinsic motivation and active behavior in the elderly. *Physical Culture and Sport. Studies and Research* 75(1), 35–42.

Esteve, R. (2009) Tourism and religion. Historical approach and evaluation of the economic impact of religious tourism. In: *Conference of Tourism Pastoral Delegates*. Spanish Episcopal Conference, Avila, Spain, pp. 1–10. Available at: https://xdoc.mx/preview/turismo-y-religion-aproximacion-historica-y-evaluacion-del-impacto-5e39d1588f311 (accessed 7 June 2022).

European Commission (2017) *The European Pillar of Social Rights in 20 Principles*. Available at: https://ec.europa.eu/info/strategy/priorities-2019-2024/economy-works-people/jobs-growth-and-investment/european-pillar-social-rights/european-pillar-social-rights-20-principles_en (accessed 7 June 2022).

Fedele, A. (2013) *Looking for Mary Magdalene: Alternative Pilgrimage and Ritual Creativity at Catholic Shrines in France*. Oxford University Press, Oxford, UK.

Hanlon, P., Carlisle, S. and Henderson, G. (2013) *Consumerism: Dissatisfaction Guaranteed Understanding Well-Being*. Glasgow University, Glasgow, UK.

Health Tourism Worldwide (2020) *Wellness and Travel 2030. A Pioneering Study*. Available at: https://www.life/references/studies-reports/ (accessed 7 June 2022).

Hussain, A. (2021) A future of tourism industry: conscious travel, destination recovery and regenerative tourism. *Journal of Sustainability and Resilience* 1(1), 1–10.

Ignatian Way (2019) *The Ignatian Way. Recreates the Route that Ignatius of Loyola, Being a Knight, Ran in 1522 from Loyola to Manresa*. Available at: https://caminoignaciano.org/en/the-ignatian-way/ (accessed 7 June 2022).

Jackowski, A. (1987) Les problèmes principales de la géographie des pèlerinages. *Geografia Roma* 10(2), 79–86.

Jackson, R.H. and Hudman L. (1995) Pilgrimage tourism and English cathedrals: the role of religion in travel. *The Tourist Review* 50(4), 40–48.

Kottler, J. (1997) *Travel That Can Change Your Life: How to Create a Transformative Experience*. Jossey-Bass, Hoboken, NJ.

Liutikas, D. (2017) The manifestation of values and identity in travelling: the social engagement of pilgrimage. *Tourism Management Perspectives* 24, 217–224. DOI: 10.1016/j.tmp.2017.07.014.

Lourdes Sanctuary (2022) *The Message of Lourdes*. Available at: https://www.lourdes-france.org/en/message-lourdes/ (accessed 7 June 2022).

Nasr, S.H. (2007) *The Essential*. World Wisdom, Bloomington, IN.

Norman, A. and Pokorny, J.J. (2017) Meditation retreats: spiritual tourism well-being interventions. *Tourism Management Perspectives* 24, 201–207. DOI: 10.1016/j.tmp.2017.07.012.

Ostrowski, M. (2002) Pilgrimage or religious tourism. III Congress of Sanctuaries and Pilgrimages. Sanctuary of Montserrat. Catalunya, Spain. Available at: http://www.mercaba.org/FICHAS/Evangelizacion/peregrinacion_o_turismo_religios (accessed 9 May 2023).

Pardellas, X. (2005) *Turismo Religioso: O Camiño de Santiago*. Universidade de Vigo, Vigo, Spain.

Pollock, A. (2012) Conscious travel: signposts towards a new model for tourism. In: *Contribution to the 2nd UNWTO Ethics and Tourism Congress Conscious Tourism for a New Era, September 12*. Quito. Available at: https://conscioustourism.files.wordpress.com/2011/02/conscious-travel-signposts-towards-a-new-model.pdf (accessed 7 June 2022).

Pyke, S., Hartwell, H., Blake, A. and Hemingway, A. (2016) Exploring well-being as a tourism product resource. *Tourism Management* 55, 94–105. DOI: 10.1016/j.tourman.2016.02.004.

Rinschede, G. (1992) Forms of religious tourism. *Annals of Tourism Research* 19(1), 51–67. DOI: 10.1016/0160-7383(92)90106-Y.

Roof, W.C. (1999) *Spiritual Marketplace: Baby Boomers and the Remaking of American Religion*. Princeton University Press, Princeton, NJ.

Sachs, W. (2017) The sustainable development goals and Laudato si. *Third World Quarterly* 38(12), 2573–2587.

Santos, X.M. (2002) Pilgrimage and tourism at Santiago de Compostela. *Tourism Recreation Research* 27(2), 41–50. DOI: 10.1080/02508281.2002.11081219.

Sheldon, P.J. (2020) Designing tourism experiences for inner transformation. *Annals of Tourism Research* 83(March), 102935. DOI: 10.1016/j.annals.2020.102935.

Shrine of Fatima (2022) *Shrine of Our Lady of the Rosary of Fatima*. Available at: https://www.fatima.pt/en/pages/narrative-of-the-apparitions (accessed 7 June 2022).

Smith, V.L. (1992) Introduction: the quest in guest. *Annals of Tourism Research* 19(1), 1–17.

Smith, M. and Diekmann, A. (2017) Tourism and wellbeing. *Annals of Tourism Research* 66, 1–13. DOI: 10.1016/j.annals.2017.05.006.

Tolle, E. (2004) *The Power of Now*. New World Library, New York.

Vie Francigene (2022) *Via Francigena Road to Rome: Cultural Route of the Council of Europe*. Available at: https://www.viefrancigene.org/it/ (accessed 7 June 2022).

Vukonic, B. (1996) *Tourism and Religion*. Elsevier, Oxford, UK.

Willson, G.B., McIntosh, A.J. and Zahra, A.L. (2013) Tourism and spirituality: a phenomenological analysis. *Annals of Tourism Research* 42, 150–168. DOI: 10.1016/j.annals.2013.01.016.

World Economic Forum (2022) *Why Doctors in Canada Now Offer Nature Prescriptions*. Available at: https://www.weforum.org/videos/why-doctors-in-canada-now-offer-nature-prescriptions (accessed 7 June 2022).

World Health Organization (2022) *The 10 Essential Public Health Operations*. Available at: https://www.euro.who.int/en/health-topics/Health-systems/public-health-services/policy/the-10-essential-public-health-operations (accessed 7 June 2022).

14 Religious Tourism as an Economic Development Policy: The Politics of Tourism Development

Anna Trono*

Department of Cultural Heritage, University of Salento, Italy

Abstract

Religious routes are a means of sharing ethical and religious values and feelings of peace and brotherhood. They can provide a response to the widespread need for spirituality and identity, and they can also be an essential means of socialization and generate quality sustainable tourism.

After an overview of the ancient and current meaning of religious tourism and faith itineraries, the chapter considers some tourism strategies designed to promote sustainable tourism and analyses a few case studies in an attempt to determine whether the blend of tourism, the desire for culture and religious sentiment can be reconciled not only with the search for spirituality, but also with a focus on sustainable tourism in the places visited. It will consider the need for tourism polices to create new market niches, new types of supply and demand, new tourist circuits and new entrepreneurial figures, acting as a dynamo of regional economic development.

14.1 Introduction

Travelling is not just about crossing geographical borders, it is also about experience, changing one's routine, dealing with the uncertainty of the new, talking to strangers, measuring oneself against others and, in some way, rewriting one's life story. The religious journey – unlike pilgrimage, which was driven above all by the need for expiation and penance in the early centuries of Christianity – is still today a journey of faith, but with its own characteristics and motives, topical and significant, linked to discovery, human sensitivity, authentic relationships and the value of hospitality, which make the experience richer and deeper. For those who undertake such a journey, it clearly represents a path of personal growth and cultural and environmental rediscovery; for those

who host such travellers, it is an opportunity to showcase the religious art and historical and artistic treasures present in places of worship as symbols of prayer that are often overlooked.

It is, however, also an excellent way to create the right synergy between those working in destinations that offer art, history and beautiful landscapes, and travellers who wish to focus on the contemplation and physical perception of the cultural and environmental context. Such travellers seek to establish an empathetic relationship with the inhabitants and fully enjoy humanity, because 'the other and the elsewhere always have something in store for us that we have not yet encountered' (Pace, 2017).

Recent events linked to the crisis affecting democratic institutions, widespread violence, environmental devastation caused by global

*anna.trono@unisalento.it

© CAB International 2023. *The Politics of Religious Tourism* (eds D. Bozonelos and P. Moira)
DOI: 10.1079/9781800621732.0014

changes in the ecosystem (particularly climate change) and last but not least, pandemics, have limited or prevented religious travel to certain destinations. In contrast, cultural and religious itineraries that follow ancient devotional routes and are the target of responsible, sustainable, eco-compatible and ethical tourism, as specified by the principles of the Word Tourism Organization, have benefited.

The COVID-19 pandemic has prevented visits to many places of worship, some of which were already denied to tourists due to the presence of armed conflict or poorly managed tourism and/or rampant urbanization (such as the Old City of Jerusalem and its Walls, which UNESCO has placed on its list of endangered World Heritage). It has posed complex challenges to the tourism sector but it has also highlighted new opportunities for reducing environmental impact and developing a new vision of resilience and safer, more sustainable forms of tourism.

The COVID-19 pandemic has disrupted all aspects of economic and social life, undermined established practices and accelerated the renewal, already under way, of the tourism sector, with a focus on new models of sustainable tourism (Angelini and Giurrandino, 2019). The result is an invitation to develop tourism strategies that defend and develop local environmental, social and cultural diversity and turn destinations into systems that are conscious, dynamic and open, but also resistant and resilient.

14.2 Research Aims

This chapter therefore proposes to analyse the value of religious and spiritual travel, which bears similarities to medieval pilgrimage and the Grand Tour and is increasingly recognized today as a remedy to health crises, social and environmental malaise and the uncertainty produced by the COVID-19 pandemic.

Religious routes, old and new, differ from conventional mass tourism, which is an expression of the artificial nature of modernity and a symbol of consumerism and alienation (Visentin, 2008). In contrast, they offer sustainable tourism in line with the principles indicated in Agenda 2030 for

Sustainable Development, which provide for job creation and the promotion of local culture and products, as well as the achievement of social equity and inclusiveness while respecting cultural values, diversity and accessibility (UNWTO, 2015; United Nations, 2019). Returning to the old normal after the health crisis, which continues to have a strong social and economic impact, is not considered a viable option. It will be necessary to modernize outdated policies and adopt new practices for planning and managing the tourism sector, in which cultural and religious routes and itineraries will increasingly play a leading role. In this new approach, aimed at improving the travel experiences of those who undertake such journeys, particular attention must be paid to the needs not only of walkers, without any discrimination between the able-bodied and the disabled, but also to the needs of host regions and operators in a sector that has been severely impacted by the COVID-19 pandemic.

14.3 Methodology

After a brief illustration of the ancient and current concepts of religious tourism and faith-based itineraries, the chapter considers how natural events, wars and pandemics have accelerated the regional reorganization of the tourist sector, prompting the development of new models of light and small-scale tourism, including religious itineraries and routes, which the crisis caused by the COVID-19 pandemic has made more urgent. Attention is therefore paid to the strategies adopted at various institutional levels, such as those of the Council of Europe and the Italian government, aimed at identifying new itineraries and tourist circuits, particularly in disadvantaged and peripheral regions, creating new market niches, new entrepreneurial figures and new wealth.

In order to better understand the implications of religious tourism as a development policy, a comparative approach, based on selected case studies of Italian itineraries, was adopted (Barlett and Vavrus, 2016; Bartlett and Vavrus, 2017).

Indeed, the present study examines the multilevel strategies adopted in Italy for the promotion and use of the Via Francigena, with particular reference to specific regional experiences in Puglia and Tuscany. Using desk analysis and the consultation of secondary sources – looking at the literature and ministerial and local government planning documents – the research compares two case studies, identifying their strong and weak points, as well as any reciprocal influence. The comparative method is designed to explore – in accordance with a 'horizontal' approach (Bartlett and Vavrus, 2017) – those processes that have more or less encouraged the creation of relationships and social networks in the regions in question and play a key role in regional economic development.

14.4 Literature Review

Cultural routes, which are a new category of heritage, a tool for protecting villages from depopulation and a specific product for promoting them for the purposes of tourism, are now the subject of great interest on the part of the scientific community, as evidenced by an extensive literature (see, for example, Briedenhann and Wickens, 2004; Majdoub, 2010; Berti, 2012, 2013; Zabbini, 2012; Beltramo, 2013; Trono, 2014; Bambi and Barbari, 2015; Graf and Popesku, 2016; Trono, 2017a), to which may be added a large body of studies of pilgrimage by both historians (on Christian pilgrimage, see, among others, Stopani, 1991; Lavarini, 1997; Caucci von , 1999; Sumption, 1999; Oldoni, 2005; Cardini, 2008; Arlotta, 2014) and scholars of social and economic disciplines.

Early theoretical works on the relationship between tourism and pilgrimage by Turner (1973), Cohen (1992) and Vukonic (1992) were followed by a substantial literature aimed at identifying the motives for pilgrimage and religious tourism, and the typology and dichotomous characteristics of the tourist-pilgrim (see, for example, Hitrec, 1990; Smith, 1992; Barber, 1993; Stoddard, 1997; Cohen, 1998; Santos, 2003; Blackwell, 2007; Griffin, 2007; Alecu, 2010).

Worthy of note are the studies aimed at determining the pilgrims' behaviour, partly with reference to their religious beliefs and degree of religiosity (see, for example, Collins-Kreiner and Kliot, 2000; Poria *et al.*, 2003). Of particular interest are works aimed at assessing their economic impact with reference to recreational activities, accommodation and services (see, for example Brayley, 2009; Gray and Winton, 2009; Cerutti and Piva, 2014). Research has also been produced on the capacity to manage the phenomenon (Shackley, 2001; Timothy and Olsen, 2006; Raj and Morpeth, 2007; Trono, 2017a).

A substantial literature is devoted to the consequences for religious tourism of the COVID-19 pandemic (Alaverdov and Bari, 2020; Ijaz, 2020; Raj and Bozonelos, 2020), and on public and private measures to enhance sustainable tourism in sacred sites during the pandemic and the accessibility of cultural and religious routes (see Mittal and Sinha, 2021; Trono and Castronuovo, 2021).

14.5 Strategies for Resilient and Conscious Tourism

Religious destinations geared towards pilgrimage (Fatima, Lourdes, etc.), supported mainly by the religious authorities and various local players interested in the high visibility of these sites, have generally developed good tourism promotion mechanisms managed mainly at local level. In contrast, itineraries and routes with a strong religious and cultural orientation, in order to compensate for their more limited popularity with respect to the holy sites, have preferred to take advantage of national support measures, regional tourism strategies and international development programmes.

The value of cultural heritage was first understood by UNESCO, and subsequently by the Council of Europe and the European Union. Attributing to cultural assets an 'exceptional universal value', as evidence of the values of civilization, UNESCO not only recognized the obvious tourist implications linked to the material nature of cultural assets, but also highlighted their ecumenical value. An excellent sign of this is the presence of numerous religious sites in UNESCO's list of World Heritage Sites (see Fig. 14.1).

As long ago as 1987, with the institution of the Cultural Itineraries, the Council of Europe

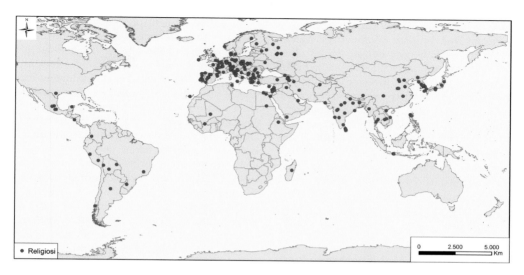

Fig. 14.1. UNESCO sites of religious interest in 2021.
Source: http://whc.unesco.org/en/syndication and authors' own work.

created a tool for the promotion of European values and the transnational dimension of European heritage and cultural diversity, by means of intercultural dialogue.

Religious itineraries not only promote the understanding of European identity but also consolidate the culture–tourism association, recognized, moreover, by the Holy See in its adhesion to the Agreement on European Cultural Itineraries in April 2018, the European Year of Cultural Heritage. Indeed, it is evident that religious experience, especially Christianity, is translated into culture, which is expressed in the combination of tangible and intangible heritage. This is clearly seen in the many religious itineraries established by the Council of Europe, including the Santiago de Compostela Pilgrim Route, the Via Francigena (an ancient route that joined Canterbury to Rome, forming a bridge between the cultures of Anglo-Saxon and Latin Europe), the Saint Olav Ways and many others. European cultural and religious itineraries create synergism between regional and local authorities, involving a broad range of socio-economic actors from both the public and private sectors. They provide an excellent opportunity for promoting local traditions, arts and crafts, and they are a source of income and development for the local population.

The focus on the role of citizens and the network of local authorities and stakeholders in the creation and management of cultural and religious routes has been emphasized by the European Commission which, in line with the principles of UNESCO and the Council of Europe, has noted their importance as a vector for cultural exchanges between peoples and as a strong factor in the performance of small and medium-sized enterprises and their capacity for innovation (European Commission, n.d.) .

Their economic impacts have recently been highlighted in the framework of the four macro-regional strategies implemented via the Routes4 project in connection with the 2017–2020 joint programme involving the Council of Europe (Directorate-General for Democracy) and the European Union (European Commission – DG REGIO). Routes4 promotes the regional development of the Adriatic–Ionian region, the Alps, the Baltic Sea and the Danube basin (Council of Europe, 2020).

Furthermore, the Cultural Routes network is expected to promote sustainable tourism in remote and lesser-known destinations via new management models for cultural routes and itineraries linked to themes of symbolic importance for European culture and identity.

The European Parliament's Committee on Transport and Tourism (Monteiro de Aguiar, 2021) has recently been moving in this direction, and its new strategy aimed at encouraging the recovery of the tourism sector after the pandemic seeks to steer consumer choices towards greener options that are more in touch with nature. The creation of itineraries accessible to all, on foot, by bicycle or on horseback and supported by European funding, should encourage the creation of specific networks linking up the less developed and peripheral regions of the various Member States.

14.6 The Slow Mobility Network of Cultural and Religious Paths in Italy

Cultural and religious routes and itineraries have become a central theme in Italian tourism. Referred to as 'Cammini' (in Mibact ministerial decree no. 567 of 16/12/2015), they enjoy widespread popularity, further fuelled since 2016 by the Jubilee year and the National Year of Paths. Considered to be instruments of knowledge of the history and heritage of Italy, but also an opportunity for slow and sustainable tourism, they have been the beneficiaries over the years of numerous measures implemented with both national and regional funding (Commissione Politiche del Turismo. Conferenza delle Regioni e Province Autonome, 2021). Subsidies amounting to tens of millions of euros have been granted to support initiatives, especially of an infrastructural nature, to create new 'soft mobility' networks and improve accessibility and intermodal transport. There have also been measures aimed at creating more widespread expertise in the area, in terms of both the public administration and associations and operators in the supply sector, and at supporting the promotion of thematic tourism products. For example, in 2016, by means of a resolution of the Interministerial Committee for Economic Planning, about 20 million euros were allocated to the religious paths of St Francis, St Benedict, and St Scholastica, and the same amount to both the Via Francigena and the Via Appia Regina Viarum (Comitato Interministeriale per la Programmazione Economica, 2016).

The development of routes and paths as instruments to promote widespread and ramified knowledge of the history and heritage of Italy was cited in the Strategic Plan for Tourism (STP) 2017–2022, aimed at strengthening the unified promotion of paths and slow tourism via a network of cultural routes crossing the country from north to south with a view to creating a real brand system. Particular attention is devoted to inland areas, minor destinations and southern Italy, involving local authorities through efficient and participatory governance (Nocifora et al., 2011). In line with the objectives of the Strategic Tourism Plan, in May 2021, local authorities in the Conference of Regions and Autonomous Provinces (Commission for Tourism Policies), decided to transform the paths into a product that can genuinely express the identity of the Italian tourism sector, in accordance with a model in which the regions can and must play a central role. To this end, adequate resources have been allocated to the creation of a fully-fledged network combining the main itineraries recognized today. Many regions have focused on religious tourism and on the development of artistic and religious itineraries within their territory, as shown by the Digital Atlas of Italian Paths (continuously updated), to which many inland areas in the centre-north have adhered (see Fig. 14.2). Created with the decisive encouragement of the Ministry of Cultural Heritage and Activities and Tourism in 2016 – proclaimed the Year of Paths – the Atlas presents maps with relevant information on distance, signposting and connections concerning 41 routes that showcase a country rich in natural, historical and cultural resources and promote an alternative and sustainable form of tourism. Containing itineraries that cross the country from north to south, the Atlas proposes a slow mobility network, helping travellers and tourists to get around on foot, by bicycle and with other forms of sustainable transport.

14.6.1 Italian religious routes and the Via Francigena

Religious (and cultural) ways and itineraries are the expression of new small-scale models of tourism, which were beginning to timidly

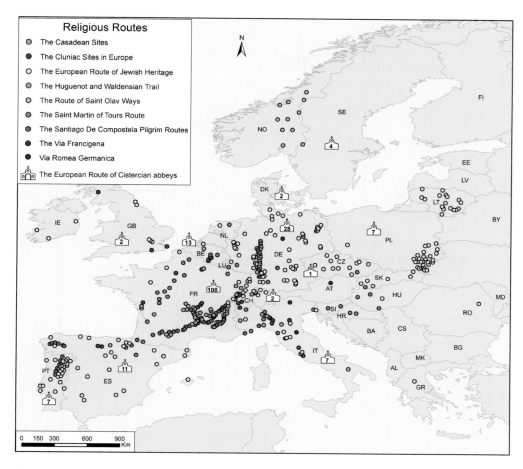

Fig. 14.2. Religious routes in the Atlante dei Cammini (Atlas of Paths).
Source: https://camminiditalia.cultura.gov.it/cammini/ and authors' own work.

emerge under the umbrella of 'light' tourism before the COVID-19 pandemic struck. Among them is the Via Francigena, one of the oldest and most popular pilgrimage routes in Europe, which has always attracted walkers and is growing in popularity. It has attracted walkers since time immemorial. Settlements, hostels and monasteries have sprung up along its route, but above all it has fostered the intermingling of people of different origins, languages and goals, giving rise to a civilization permeated and enriched by the most varied cultures. 'Testimony to man's desire to rediscover authenticity in relationships and actions through simplicity, slowness, solitude and poverty', the Via Francigena is also

a symbol of a great tourist 'product' that has yet to be fulfilled (Rizzi and Onorato, 2017, p. 11).

The Via Francigena in Italy has been and still is the recipient of million-euro funding targeted at impressive infrastructural improvement and the refurbishment of strategic points along the two thousand kilometres of the Italian section. This is a considerable opportunity for the Via Francigena, which is currently experiencing a moment of great dynamism and international recognition. The project aims to raise awareness among the institutions (at national, regional and local levels), improve the hospitality system and provide for the infrastructure and signposting of the route. In the regions crossed by the itinerary there is a growing awareness of the importance of investing energy and resources in a project that favours cultural, socio-economic and tourism development both along the route and in the surrounding areas. All the Italian regions included in the itinerary have committed to drawing up projects (with indications of technical feasibility) and to drafting an overall regional plan with the measures to be implemented in their areas and a proposed order of priorities.

14.6.2   The Southern Via Francigena

The southern regions benefiting from ministerial funding for the Via Francigena, officially recognized in October 2019 by the Vie Francigene European Association as regions crossed by the Southern Via Francigena (VFS) are Lazio, Campania and Puglia. The route, around 900 km long, winds through history, tradition and ancestral territory, following – with

consideration made for contemporary accessibility – the Itinerarium Burdigalese of 333, running from Rome to Santa Maria di Leuca at the tip of the Salento peninsula in Puglia (see Fig. 14.3).

The intervention of the national government will enable the southern regions to pursue the economic potential of the inland and peripheral areas crossed by the Via Francigena by offering services that facilitate its use and by raising awareness of this itinerary as an engine of local development. The Southern Via Francigena enables the community to develop social memory, consolidate local identity and prefigure the future development of small villages, inland areas and peripheral and marginal territories. This unfolds by means of a complex but increasingly important process that entails attracting experiential tourism and empowering local entrepreneurs and producers. Indeed, the route becomes an opportunity to promote local products, of both an agricultural/gastronomic and a craft nature, helping to build local and regional branding.

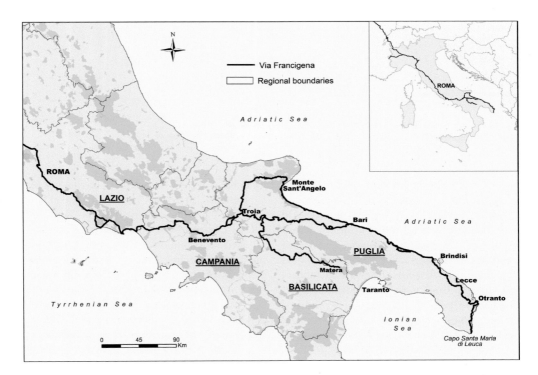

Fig. 14.3. The Southern Via Francigena.
Source: https://www.viefrancigene.org/it/ and authors' own work.

In line with the strategic objectives laid down in the agreement signed with the European Association of the Vie Francigene, the three southern regions are committed to carrying out a survey of its condition, continuity, conservation, suitability for use and accessibility in terms of infrastructure and services. The result is multilevel governance of the route involving participatory planning as a 'network within a network project', giving rise to 'participation heritage'. In this new model of cultural heritage, the itinerary is understood as a product (cultural and economic) and a tool for the co-creation of value, in accordance with guidelines that are drawn up by the authorities and adopted within the wider context of regional regeneration (Trono and Castronuovo, 2021, p. 5).

14.6.3 The Via Francigena in Puglia

The Southern Via Francigena is a route that is still in the process of being structured, with evident problems in terms of infrastructure, services and management. With the support of local stakeholders, regional authorities are seeking to overcome these issues by proposing projects and initiatives that can both meet the expectations of walkers and safeguard the interests of the local population. An example is Puglia, from whose ports the ancient pilgrims embarked for the Holy Land. With its undeniable landscape, and historical and cultural features, the region is active in proposing measures aimed at promoting the route. The Puglia stretch of the route ends at the Sanctuary of Santa Maria or de Finibus Terrae, which represents an important link with the East, but it is not the ultimate destination of the traveller on the Via Francigena who aspires to reach Jerusalem (Trono, 2017b).

The Puglia strategy for the promotion and management of the Via Francigena is expressed in the public–private partnership involving Puglia Regional Administration and a network of stakeholders (associations, companies, individual citizens) who aim to establish a system based on a unifying cultural theme that can generate cultural tourism and employment (see Fig. 14.4).

The strategy adopted by Puglia Regional Administration (partly via the LAGs benefiting

from European funding under the Leader programme) is aimed at stimulating slow tourism focused on rediscovering and learning about the areas through which the route passes: tourism suitable for visitors who like to immerse themselves in the ubiquitous heritage of art, good food, landscape and spirituality. In the process of structuring and promoting the route, stakeholders are the beneficiaries of various initiatives. They are involved in the management of the Southern Via Francigena by means of public tenders, which include the identification of the beneficiaries, knowledge of their interests and the use of influencing to achieve good results. Their active involvement is important to the infrastructure of the route (creation of signposting, installation of rest areas) and to the provision of information (creation of tourist information points, visitor centres, educational workshops), accommodation and catering (creation of hostels for walkers, pilgrim reception services) and transport services (workshops for cyclists and facilities for trekking, sailing, canoeing, diving, etc.). The planning of the Southern Via Francigena, as structured by Puglia Regional Administration and supported by local stakeholders, may constitute a good example of an innovative approach for other southern regions, indicating new opportunities for managing the tourism potential of the areas involved.

14.6.4 The Tuscan stretch of the Via Francigena

The Southern Via Francigena has great potential in terms of the success of tourism in the regions involved, but in some regions of central Italy such as Tuscany this promise has already been fulfilled. The Via Francigena crosses the whole region (see Fig. 14.5), boosting tourism but also and above all providing an opportunity for cultural development, justifying Fidei's remark that 'Tuscany cannot do without the Via Francigena' (Fidei, 2020).

With a wealth of landscapes and heritage reflecting relationships and influences unfolding over a long period among a variety of cultural groups, the Via Francigena runs safely for 380 km through 39 municipalities (20 of which

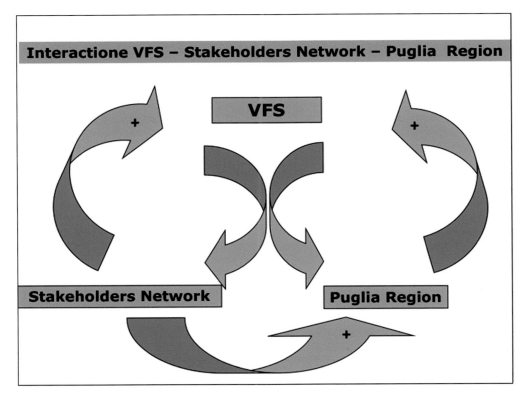

Fig. 14.4. Public–private interaction in the promotion of the Southern Via Francigena (VFS) in Puglia. Source: Authors' own work.

are of low tourist density) and offers over 1000 accommodation options (Regione Toscana, 2019b). From the point of view of tourism services, the areas concerned are heterogeneous. Unlike the internationally famous 'cities of art' with well-developed accommodation facilities, mainly hotels, such as Lucca, San Gimignano and Siena, and the coastal areas, which are characterized by extensive provision of accommodation and mainly mass tourism, the region crossed by the route is mainly rural and mountainous. Here there are minor towns, some very small, with low population density, affected by progressive depopulation and little tourist development. However, they have significant environmental resources, valuable landscape and widely distributed historical–artistic heritage that is often neglected, as shown by the low number of tourists (Conti *et al.*, 2014, p. 11).

For these towns, the Via Francigena offers excellent potential for development, as the regional administration has fully understood. As long ago as the Jubilee year of 2000, it launched an extensive regional programme of measures, including investment to improve the accommodation and hospitality system managed by the religious communities.

In 2006, Tuscany Regional Administration took the lead role in an interregional project based on the Via Francigena, working with Valle d'Aosta, Piedmont, Lombardy, Liguria, Emilia Romagna and Lazio. Starting in 2009, it planned and implemented a series of structural measures to ensure the recovery of the route, composed of 15 stages, creating a genuine tourist product (Bambi and Barbari, 2015). The Regional Administration's main objective was to ensure the safety of the route and make it immediately usable and accessible to all by means of a programme of investments already made, completed with improvements to the infrastructure.

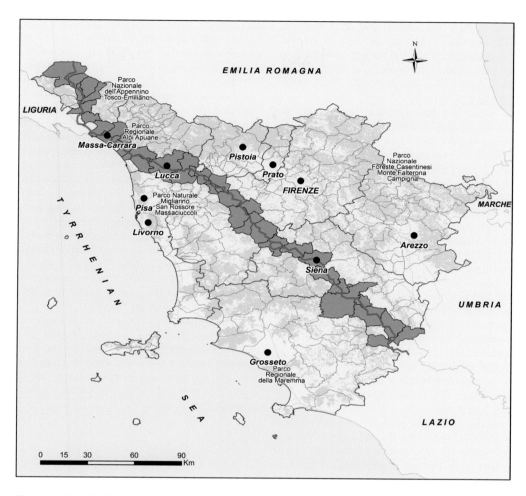

Fig. 14.5. The Via Francigena in Tuscany.
Source: Tuscany Regional Institute for Economic Planning (IRPET).

Of the extensive financial resources set aside for the management and fulfilment of the Via Francigena, mostly provided by the Regional Administration (17.4 million euros), with a congruous contribution by the local authorities, the lion's share (59%) was spent on infrastructure for the consolidation of the route. Significant amounts were also allocated however to the restoration of local architectural heritage (20%) and the provision of accommodation (17%) (Conti *et al.*, 2015, pp. 1–2).

The region has not only intervened with regard to the safety of the route, maintenance and support for hospitality, but has also sought to improve knowledge of the hospitality system along the route and aspects of identity values of a religious nature present in the communities crossed.

Important in this regard is the project entitled 'La Nostra Francigena', set up by the Regional Administration, which in 2015 grouped the 39 municipalities into four distinct areas with four lead municipalities: Pontremoli (north), Lucca (north-central), Fucecchio (south-central), and Siena (south), involving all the local stakeholders in the establishment of a 'homogeneous tourist product'. Their common goal is to enable, by minimizing management costs and planning activities, the functions of accommodation and tourist information to be handled on a supra-municipal level, together with periodic maintenance, the promotion and presentation of the tourist product and the monitoring and analysis of tourist flows (Associazione Europea delle Vie Francigene, 2019, p. 19).

Thus, the municipalities have begun to play a role in monitoring and reporting problems along the route and in the management of the Via Francigena itself. This has allowed some municipalities to obtain funding of about €4.3 million from the state, via the operational agreement stipulated between the region and the Ministry of Culture. The works, which will be completed by 2025, are designed to further improve the safety of the routes on foot, by bicycle and on horseback, especially in those areas which, partly for morphological reasons, have so far been affected by greater operational difficulties. The activities of the 'MontagnAppennino' Local Action Group, within the framework of the Leader programme, will also improve the capacity of the Via Francigena. The measures implemented on the historical–religious itineraries that are directly linked to the Via Francigena are aimed at developing among the operators and citizens the spirit of hospitality, enhancing and transmitting the cultural and historical traditions associated with the identity of their land. At the same time, they aim to improve and rationalize the governance of the local rural system, with particular emphasis on fulfilling the potential of its heritage (in terms of culture, nature and identity), improving the organization of the territory and local networks in order to promote and publicize the experiences, as well as refining the skills and the qualifications of its human capital (Regione Toscana, 2019a).

The joint efforts to make the most of the ancient route of the Via Francigena in recent years are now beginning to yield visible results, as shown by the study of the effects on tourism of the infrastructure and paths created along the route carried out by the Tuscany Regional Institute for Economic Planning (IRPET) (Conti, 2021a).

In the period 2000–2015, the Tuscan Via Francigena was one of the areas with the greatest expansion of tourism in terms of presences: about 15,000 walkers per year are estimated to travel part of the Via Francigena in that region. In fact, tourist flows are underestimated due to the statistical survey methods concerning data on overnight stays, which miss some forms of accommodation that are particularly common along the hiking routes (Regione Toscana, 2019b).

The recent update produced by IRPET regarding the assessment and estimation of tourist flows in 37 municipalities crossed by the Via Francigena, which the same body had conducted in 2014, confirms the positive effect of the infrastructural improvement carried out over the years, and estimates an increase in attributable tourist presences of about 614,000 in the 10 year period 2009–2019. The georeferencing of the accommodation structures by the Tuscan researchers and their descriptive analysis of the variation by distance from the route in the structures' arrivals and presences for the decade 2010–2019 confirm the hypothesis of a competitiveness differential attributable to the Via Francigena (Conti, 2021b, p. 3).

The minor towns along the Via Francigena are now seeing a completely new influx of 'pilgrims', mainly foreigners, attracted by the new possibility of an intense and direct relationship with the territory and its breath-taking landscapes (Ascheri and Turrini, 2017; Bambi and Iacobelli, 2019).

14.7 Conclusions

The COVID-19 pandemic has accelerated a process of renewal of both demand and supply in the tourism sector, generated by the rise of new experiential and educational motives among travellers, keen to satisfy a need for authenticity and escape from everyday life and isolation, as highlighted by the prevalence in the last 2 years of proximity tourism. The decline in the number of tourists visiting well-known cities such as Venice, Florence and Rome, and the cancellation of events such as festivals and fairs (e.g. the Oktoberfest in Munich), has been matched by greater interest in more remote and less crowded places, especially in inland and/or marginal areas with relatively low population density.

The comparative method enables a multisite analysis of the approaches adopted by central and regional governments to the creation of new sustainable tourism models on the regional scale. Our analysis favoured a simultaneous focus on both the methods used for the construction of resilient and 'slow' tourism areas and the replicability of the experiences. While the Via Francigena in Tuscany has proved to be a good model for tourism and economic development in inland areas throughout the region, the Southern Via Francigena is really still a work in progress, having been set up only in 2019.

Initiative and organizational efficiency have succeeded in bringing out the excellence of the regions involved in the Tuscan stretch of the Via Francigena by generating new forms of tourism and new trends that offer good prospects for local development. On the other hand, the promotion and management strategy of the Southern Via Francigena still requires considerable planning commitment on the part of institutions and local communities in order for it to become fully usable.

The southern Italian regions and, in general, all the areas hosting cultural routes and itineraries will need to overcome cultural and entrepreneurial barriers, assisted by regional management based on a systemic and synergistic approach, as demonstrated by other successful experiences. It will be necessary to develop networks and partnerships between operators to promote and integrate the area's resources (nature, culture, traditional products, etc.) by improving and rationalizing the governance of the local rural system. It will be necessary to devise policies and mechanisms to ensure solidarity and avoid giving in to oligopoly and control, while preserving all the diversity and creative capacity of local communities.

Acknowledgment

We would like to thank Mr Raffaele Mannelli, Project manager at Toscana Region, for the information provided on the activities and funding by the Toscana Region for the promotion of the Tuscan section of the Via Francigena.

References

Alaverdov, E. and Bari, M.W. (eds) (2020) *Global Development of Religious Tourism*. IGI Global, Hershey, PA.

Alecu, I.C. (2010) Epistemological aspects of religious tourism in rural areas. *International Journal of Business, Management and Social Sciences* 2(3), 59–65.

Angelini, A. and Giurrandino, A. (ed.) (2019) *Risorse culturali, ambientali e turismo sostenibile*. Franco Angeli, Milano, Italy.

Arlotta, G. (2014) La via francigena di mazara in Sicilia. prospettive di ricerca. *Dialoghi Mediterranei* 9, 6–16. Available at: https://www.istitutoeuroarabo.it/DM/la-via-francigena-di-mazara-in-sicilia-prospettive-di-ricerca/ (accessed 10 June 2022).

Ascheri, M. and Turrini, P. (2017) *Percorrendo La Francigena in Toscana*. Extempora edizioni, Siena, Italy.

Associazione Europea delle Vie Francigene (AEVF) (2019) *Vademecum Degli Standard Europei Del Percorso Della Via Francigena. Itinerario Culturale Del Consiglio d'Europa*. Comitato Europeo di coordinamento tecnico interregionale della Via Francigena. Available at: https://www.viefrancigene.org/wp-content/uploads/2021/04/vademecum__2019_it.pdf (accessed 9 June 2022).

Bambi, G. and Barbari, M. (eds) (2015) The European pilgrimage routes for promoting sustainable and quality tourism in rural areas. In: *Proceedings of the International Conference 4–6 December 2014*. Firenze University Press, Firenze, Italy. Available at: https://www.iris.unina.it/retrieve/handle/11588/755733/256479/2015_POLLONE%20S.%2C%20Between%20Permanence%20and%20Transformation.pdf (accessed 7 June 2022).

Bambi, G. and Iacobelli, S. (2019) Il sistema locale di cammini e itinerari culturali per la promozione del turismo sostenibile e di qualità nelle zone rurali: un esempio di metodologia di progettazione nella provincia di Arezzo-Toscana (Italia). In: Salvatori, F. (ed.) *L'apporto Della Geografia Tra Rivoluzioni e Riforme. Atti Del XXXII Congresso Geografico Italiano (Roma, 7–10 Giugno 2017)*. A.Ge.I, Roma, pp. 963–970.

Barber, R. (1993) *Pilgrimages*. The Boydell Press, London.

Barlett, L. and Vavrus, F. (2016) *Rethinking Case Study Research: A Comparative Approach*. Taylor and Francis Ltd., London.

Bartlett, L. and Vavrus, F. (2017) Comparative case studies. *Educação & Realidade* 42(3), 899–920. DOI: 10.1590/2175-623668636.

Beltramo, S. (2013) Itinerari Culturali e Reti di Conoscenza: Identità e Valorizzazione del Patrimonio Paesaggistico e Culturale Europeo. Il Caso Studio del Piemonte. *AlmaTourism. Journal of Tourism, Culture and Territorial Development* 4(7), 13–43.

Berti, E. (2012) *Itinerari Culturali Del Consiglio d'Europa: Tra Ricerca Di Identità e Progetto Di Paesaggio*. University Press Firenze, Italy. DOI: 10.36253/978-88-6655-142-3.

Berti, E. (2013) Itinerari Culturali del Consiglio d'Europa: Nuovi Paradigmi per il Progetto Territoriale e per il Paesaggio. *AlmaTourism. Journal of Tourism, Culture and Territorial Development* 4(7), 1–12.

Blackwell, R. (2007) Motivations for religious tourism, pilgrimage, festivals and events. In: Raj, R. and Morphe, N.D. (eds) *Religious Tourism and Pilgrimage Festivals Management. An International Perspective*. CAB International, Wallingford, UK, pp. 35–47.

Brayley, R.E. (2009) Managing markets, managing meaning: the contribution of tourist accommodations at sacred sites to the visitor experience and to the local tourism enterprise. In: Trono, A. (ed.) *Proceedings of the International Conference Tourism, Religion & Culture: Regional Development through Meaningful Tourism Experiences, Lecce, Poggiardo 27th–29th October 2009*. Congedo Ed., Galatina, Italy, pp. 169–178.

Briedenhann, J. and Wickens, E. (2004) Tourism routes as a tool for the economic development of rural areas—Vibrant hope or impossible dream? *Tourism Management* 25, 71–79.

Cardini, F. (2008) Il miraggio della Terrasanta tra pellegrinaggio e crociate. In: Civita, Banco di Napoli and Finmeccanica (ed.) *Roma Verso Gerusalemme Lungo Le Vie Francigene Del Sud*. Tipografia Ostiense, Roma, pp. 24–39.

Caucci von, P. (ed.) (1999) *Il Mondo Dei Pellegrinaggi—Roma, Santiago, Gerusalemme*. Jaca Book- F.lli Palombi, Milano-Roma.

Cerutti, S. and Piva, E. (2014) Gli eventi religiosi come leva di sviluppo turistico territoriale. *Ambiente Società Territorio—Geografia nelle Scuole* 6, 20–25.

Cohen, E. (1992) Pilgrimage and tourism: convergence and divergence. In: Morinis, A. (ed.) *Sacred Journeys*. Greenwood Press, Westport, CT, Ireland, pp. 47–61.

Cohen, E. (1998) Tourism and religion: a comparative perspective. *Pacific Tourism Review* 2, 1–10.

Collins-Kreiner, N. and Kliot, N. (2000) Pilgrimage tourism in the Holy Land: the behavioural characteristics of Christian pilgrims. *GeoJournal* 50(1), 55–67. DOI: 10.1023/A:1007154929681.

Comitato Interministeriale per la Programmazione Economica (2016) Delibera n. 3/2016schede 31 e 33 Gazzetta Ufficiale della Repubblica Italiana Serie generale—n.189, 13-8-2016. Available at: https://ricerca-delibere.programmazioneeconomica.gov.it/media/docs/2016/E160003.pdf (accessed 10 June 2022).

Commissione Politiche del Turismo. Conferenza delle Regioni e Province Autonome (2021) Documento presentatoin occasione dell'audizione alla 7° commissione del senato della repubblica. *Cammini E Turismo Lento*. Available at: https://www.senato.it/application/xmanager/projects/leg18/attachments/documento_evento_procedura_commissione/files/000/365/001/Conferenza_delle_Regioni_e_delle_Province_autonome.pdf (accessed 10 June 2022).

Conti, E. (2021a) L'impatto economico della Francigena. Un primo aggiornamento. *IRPET, Note Rapide* 5, 1–5. Available at: http://www.irpet.it/archives/60138 (accessed 7 June 2022).

Conti, E. (2021b) *Turismo & Toscana. L'impatto Della Via Francigena Sui Flussi Turistici in Toscana*. Available at: http://www.irpet.it/wp-content/uploads/2021/07/presentazione-via francigena_2021. pdf (accessed 7 June 2022).

Conti, E., Iommi, S., Piccini, L. and Rosignoli, S. (2014) The European pilgrimage routes as economic driver. The impact of the Francigena. In: *Tuscany International Conference-EPR*. International Conference Proceedings 4-6 December 2014. University Press, Firenze, Italy. Available at: http://www.irpet.it/storage/pubblicazioneallegato/581_paper%20IRPET.pdf (accessed 26 January 2023).

Conti, E., Iommi, S., Piccini, L. and Rosignoli, S. (2015) Itinerari culturali Europei e sviluppo sostenibile: il caso della Via Francigena. *EyesReg* 5(4), 1–6. Available at: http://www.eyesreg.it/2015/itinerari-culturali-europei-e-sviluppo-sostenibile-il-caso-della-via-francigena/ (accessed 7 June 2022).

Council of Europe (2020) *2017–20 / Joint Programme with the European Commission*—DGREGIO / Routes4U.

European Commission (n.d.) Cultural Tourism. Available at: https://ec.europa.eu/growth/sectors/tourism/offer/cultural_en (accessed 10 June 2022).

Fidei, F. (2020) *La Via Francigena in Toscana. Luoghi, Storie e Sapori*. Sarnus Editore, Firenze, Italy.

Graf, M. and Popesku, J. (2016) Cultural routes as innovative tourism products and possibilities of their development. *International Journal of Cultural and Digital Tourism* 3(1), 24–44.

Gray, M. and Winton, J. (2009) The effect of religious tourism on host communities. In: Trono, A. (ed.) *Proceedings of the International Conference Tourism, Religion & Culture: Regional Development through Meaningful Tourism Experiences, Lecce, Poggiardo 27–29 October 2009* Congedo Ed., Galatina, Italy, pp. 551–561.

Griffin, K.A. (2007) The globalization of pilgrimage tourism? Some thoughts from Ireland. In: Raj, R. and Morphet, N.D. (eds) *Religious Tourism and Pilgrimage Festivals Management. An International Perspective*. CAB International, Wallingford, UK, pp. 15–34.

Hitrec, T. (1990) Religious tourism: development—characteristics-perspectives. *Acta Turistica* 2(1), 9–49.

Ijaz, A. (2020) Types of religious tourism. In: Alaverdov, E. and Bari, M.W. (eds) *Global Development of Religious Tourism*. IGI Global, Hershey, PA, pp. 297–309.

Lavarini, R. (1997) *Il pellegrinaggio cristiano: dalle sue origini al turismo religioso del XX secolo*. Casa Editrice Marietti S.p.a., Genova, Italy.

Majdoub, W. (2010) Analyzing cultural routes from a multidimensional perspective. *AlmaTourism. Journal of Tourism, Culture and Territorial Development* 2, 29–37.

Mittal, R. and Sinha, P. (2021) Framework for a resilient religious tourism supply chain for mitigating post-pandemic risk. *International Hospitality Review* 36(2), 322–339.

Monteiro de Aguiar, C. (2021) *Relazione sulla definizione di una strategiadell'UE per il turismo sostenibile. Commissione per i trasporti e il turismo* (2020/2038(INI). Parlamento Europeo, 2019-2024.A9-0033/2021. Available at: https://www.europarl.europa.eu/doceo/document/A-9-2021-0033_IT.pdf (accessed 10 June 2022).

Nocifora, E., De Salvo, P. and Calzati, V. (eds) (2011) *Territori lenti e turismo di qualità. Prospettive innovative per lo sviluppo di un turismo sostenibile*. Franco Angeli, Milano, Italy.

Oldoni, M. (ed.) (2005) *Tra Roma e Gerusalemme nel Medioevo. Paesaggi umani e ambientali del pellegrinaggio meridionale. Proceedings Atti del Convegno Internazionale di Studi (26–29 ottobre 2000)*. Laveglia Ed, Salerno, Italy.

Pace, F. (2017) *Controvento. Storie e Viaggi Che Cambiano La Vita*. Einaudi, Torino.

Poria, Y., Butler, R. and Airey, D. (2003) The core of heritage tourism. *Annals of Tourism Research* 30(1), 238–254. DOI: 10.1016/S0160-7383(02)00064-6.

Raj, R. and Bozonelos, D. (2020) COVID-19 pandemic: risks facing Hajj and Umrah. *International Journal of Religious Tourism and Pilgrimage* 8(7), 93–103.

Raj, R. and Morpeth, N.D. (2007) *Religious Tourism and Pilgrimage Festivals Management: An International Perspective*. CAB International, Wallingford, UK. DOI: 10.1079/9781845932251.0000.

Regione Toscana (2019a) *Documento Strategico Operativo "I Cammini di Toscana*. Available at: https://www.montagnappennino.it/wp-content/uploads/2019/01/Delibera_n.663_del_18-06-2018-Allegato-A.pdf (accessed 10 June 2022).

Regione Toscana (2019b) *Via Francigena Toscana: Esperienza Unica*. Available at: https://www.regione.toscana.it/via-francigena (accessed 10 June 2022).

Rizzi, P. and Onorato, G. (2017) Introduzione. In: Rizzi, P. and Onorato, G. (eds) *Turismo, cultura e spiritualità. Riflessioni e progetti intorno alla Via Francigena*. Editore Educatt. Milano, Italy, pp. 11–15.

Santos, M.G.M.P. (2003) Religious tourism: contributions towards a clarification of concepts. In: Fernandes, C., McGettigan, F. and Edwards, J. (eds) *Religious Tourism and Pilgrimage*. Tourism Board of Leiria, Fatima, Portugal, pp. 27–42.

Shackley, M. (2001) *Managing Sacred Sites: Service Provision and Visitor Experience*. Continuum, London.

Smith, V.L. (1992) Introduction: the quest in guest. *Annals of Tourism Research* 19(1), 1–17.

Stoddard, R.H. (1997) Defining and classifying pilgrimages. In: Stoddard, R.H. and Morinis, A. (eds) *Sacred Places, Sacred Spaces, the Geography of Pilgrimages*. Geoscience Publications, Louisiana State University, Baton Rouge, LA, pp. 41–60.

Stopani, R. (1991) *Le Vie del Pellegrinaggio del Medioevo: Gli itinerari per Roma, Gerusalemme, Compostella*. Le Lettere, Firenze, Italy.

Sumption, J. (1999) *Monaci, Santuari, Pellegrini—La Religione Nel Medioevo*. Editori Riuniti, Roma.

Timothy, D.J. and Olsen, D. (eds) (2006) *Tourism, Religion and Spiritual Journeys*. Routledge, London and New York.

Trono, A. (2014) Cultural and religious routes: A new opportunity for regional development. In: Lois-González, R.C., Santos-Solla, X.M. and Taboada-de-Zúñiga, P. (eds) *New Tourism in the 21st Century: Culture, the City, Nature and Spirituality*. Cambridge Scholars Publishing, Cambridge, UK, pp. 5–25.

Trono, A. (2017a) Itinerari culturali e percorsi religiosi. Gestione e valorizzazione. In: Calò Mariani, M.S. and Trono, A. (eds) *The Ways of Mercy: Arts, Culture and Marian Routes between East and West*. Mario Congedo ed, Galatina, Italy, pp. 617–634.

Trono, A. (2017b) Itinerari culturali e turismo spirituale. Sfide ed opportunità della via Francigena Salentina. In: Rizzi, P. and Onorato, G. (eds) *Turismo, Cultura e Spiritualità—Riflessioni e Progetti Intorno Alla Via Francigena*. Editore Educatt. Milano, Italy, pp. 27–39.

Trono, A. and Castronuovo, V. (2021) The Via Francigena del Sud: the value of pilgrimage routes in the development of inland areas. The state of the art of two emblematic cases. *Revista Galega de Economía* 30(3), 1–18. DOI: 10.15304/rge.30.3.7701.

Turner, V. (1973) The center out there: pilgrim's goal. *History of Religions* 12(3), 191–230. DOI: 10.1086/462677.

United Nations (2019) *The Sustainable Development Goals Report*. New York. Available at: https://unstats.un.org/sdgs/report/2019/The-Sustainable-Development-Goals-Report-2019.pdf (accessed 10 June 2022).

UNWTO (2015) *Tourism in the 2030 Agenda*. Available at: https://www.unwto.org/tourism-in-2030-agenda (accessed 10 June 2022).

Visentin, C. (2008) Il viaggio perduto? Dal viaggio dei moderni alla fine dei viaggi. Viaggio e turismo, tra continuità e novità. In: Bonadei, R. and Volli, U. (eds) *Lo sguardo del turista e il racconto dei luoghi.*, Franco *Angeli*, Milano, Italy, pp. 217–226.

Vukonic, B. (1992) Medjugorje's religion and tourism connection. *Annals of Tourism Research* 19(1), 79–91.

Zabbini, E. (2012) Cultural routes and intangible heritage. *AlmaTourism. Journal of Tourism, Culture and Territorial Development* 3(5), 59–80.

15 Governing the Camino: Protecting Pilgrims During the COVID-19 Pandemic

Francisco Singul*

Xacobeo, Regional Government of Galicia, Spain

Abstract

The Camino de Santiago is one of the most relevant European historical phenomena, sustained for twelve hundred years, and through which the universal values of solidarity, hospitality, tolerance and mutual understanding can be gained. The success of this pilgrimage has been hobbled by the COVID-19 pandemic. As a communal event, in which people from more than 180 countries of the world participate, the health, safety and social distancing measures taken by public administrators work to safeguard this cultural and spiritual itinerary.

15.1 Introduction. Effects of the COVID-19 Pandemic and Governance Policies to Protect Pilgrims on the Camino

The surprise arrival of the COVID-19 pandemic in Spain in early 2020 led government authorities to take security measures to protect pilgrims on the Camino. On 14 March 2020, the Spanish Government declared a state of alarm to stop the pandemic (Government of Spain, 2020a). From 15 March to 2 May, the 47.4 million inhabitants of Spain were confined to their homes. Severe measures were taken regarding the movement of people and economic activities. On 2 May, the population was able to leave their homes wearing face masks and maintaining social distance. On 21 June, the borders with the European Schengen area were opened, with the exception of Portugal, whose borders remained closed until 1 July. On 22 June 2020,

Spain entered a 'new normal' phase, with the population out in the streets and resumption of economic activities.

This lack of mobility naturally affected the Camino de Santiago. During this period of confinement, it was not possible to cross borders between European countries or between regions of Spain. The pilgrims who were on the Camino on 15 March, like their non-pilgrim counterparts, had to suspend their activity. Those who could find a means of transport left, and those who lacked that opportunity were picked up by the Government of Galicia at the pilgrims' hostel in Monte do Gozo (Santiago). From there, the pilgrims looked for flights, trains and buses to return home. In the following months, concrete measures were taken to help the pilgrims, which proved to be effective, such as the layout of safe pedestrian corridors, the incorporation of a shock plan and the implementation of a coronavirus insurance.

---

*francisco.singul.lorenzo@xunta.gal

© CAB International 2023. *The Politics of Religious Tourism* (eds D. Bozonelos and P. Moira)
DOI: 10.1079/9781800621732.0015

15.2 A Brief History of the Pilgrimage to Santiago de Compostela

The Camino de Santiago, the First Cultural Route of Europe and a World Heritage Site, is a historical phenomenon full of vitality. It is a product of the history of Europe that achieved sharply renewed relevance during the final decades of the 20th century and into the opening decades of the 21st century. It is co-promoted by religious authorities and public entities, in particular in Spain and within Spain by the Autonomous Government of Galicia, and by multinational associations of Friends of the Way of Saint James which currently total more than 340 non-profit associations worldwide.

The discovery of the Tomb of St James the Elder in approximately 820–830 AD confirmed the influence of prior traditions and early medieval sources regarding the evangelization of the west of the Iberian Peninsula by St James (Van Herwaarden, 1980), and the translation of the remains of the apostle after his death at Jerusalem, according the *Acts of the Apostles*. During the early Middle Ages, Compostela (López Alsina, 1985a, b) as a settlement was a spontaneous by-product of the pilgrimage and the growing legacy of devotion and donations (Greenia, 2019) of the pilgrims (Greenia, 2011, 2018) who came from the most diverse corners of the kingdom and from other parts of Europe. The cult of St James and the success of the pilgrimage were consequences of the medieval Christian instrumental piety (Constable, 1996), the intensity of the religious experience and the other-worldly meaning the faithful found in sanctuaries where important relics were kept (Sumption, 2003; Singul, 2020). Other decisive factors for this development were the support from the ecclesiastical power and the contribution of the Benedictine order (Glass, 2008). The central period of the Middle Ages was the golden age of the pilgrimage to Compostela. Under the episcopate of Diego Gelmírez, in the first half of the 12th century (Fletcher, 1984), the city of Santiago was the centre of a world, at once devout and cosmopolitan, devoted to a collective experience, blending Christian piety, faith in the intervention of St James and the generous practice of hospitality (Gerson, 2006).

The several problems arising from the political situation of the late Middle Ages, specifically the war between France and England between 1337–1453 (Green, 2014), are the origin of maritime pilgrimages (Storrs, 1998): pilgrimages did not stop even in the most acute moments of crisis of the 14th century, despite the Black Death of 1348–1350 (Benedictow, 2004; Byrne, 2004).

15.3 The Recovery of the Common European Memory. Civilization Values

In general, along the history of this pilgrimage road, pilgrims' motivations were related to devotion to St James the Elder (Singul, 2019). In our times, people go to Compostela for religious tourism, cultural, sporting and natural tourism, as well as – according to the modern pilgrims – for making a personal, inimitable, intimate and, in short, very special human experience (Frey, 1998; Ozorak, 2006). The pilgrimage is indeed an important experience and is symbolically represented by the scallop shell, the emblem of Compostela and the Camino. The shell, natural or made from artificial materials symbolizes the good deeds made by the pilgrims, until the end of their lives (Caucci von Saucken, 2001); it is the symbol of the spiritual regeneration of the person.

In our times – at least up until the Covid-19 pandemic – pilgrims from all the countries of Europe and the world have travelled the Camino. Before the pandemic, more than 300,000 pilgrims walked at least the 100 km to the Cathedral of Santiago each year, coming from almost 160 countries, a factor which transcends races, beliefs, cultures (Badone and Roseman, 2004; Davidson, 2014) and sensitivities (Peelen and Jansen, 2007; Hesp, 2013; Hollander, 2014). It is the response of the rest of the world to a European framework of values which has become a universally known and admired reality in the last decades.

The current pilgrimage ways to Santiago, supported by approximately 340 associations of Friends of the Camino de Santiago extend throughout Europe and other countries of the five continents, with 85,000 km just in Europe. These ways are the result of a large European collective project involving the institutions and especially the civil society (Gitlitz and Davidson, 2000; Digance, 2006; Genoni, 2011; Harman, 2014), which study them, promote their signposting and conservation, encourage travelling them with a new sense of the spirit of coming together which fosters mutual European understanding.

15.4 Strategic Planning of the Camino and 'Xacobeo 2021–2022'

To manage this immense amount of material and intangible heritage (Pack, 2010), in 1992 the Galician Government created Xacobeo, a public limited company (Novello *et al.*, 2013), in charge of taking care of the Way of St James in Galicia and promoting the traditional pilgrimage to Santiago de Compostela. The company started its activity working for the Holy Year 1993, and since then it has continued its promotional programme, including the management of the roads of St James in Galicia, the building of public hostels for pilgrims, research on the Jacobean phenomenon, as well as publishing the research journal *Ad Limina*, which is one of the most important at the global level and is included in relevant international databases, and the publishing of books and brochures on the Camino. In addition, Xacobeo has also continued the international promotion of the pilgrimage in Europe, North and South America, Japan, and Australia, with exhibitions, international conferences, and participating in educational events and tourism trade fairs.

Xacobeo's permanent activities also include contacting and collaborating with all the associations of the Friends of the Way of St James around the world. The volunteer labour of these associations is key for promoting the Camino, and therefore Xacobeo keeps fluid relationships with the activities of these associations, especially by financing meetings, conferences and exhibitions.

In 2011 the European Saint James Ways Federation (European St. James Ways Federation, 2022) was established as an entity bringing together the regions and provinces situated along the Camino de Santiago in Europe; Galicia holds the vice-presidency of the Federation. In recent years, Xacobeo has taken part in meetings and international conferences organized by the Federation in Le Puy (France), Pavia (Italy), Paris, Lisbon (Portugal), Limbourg (the Netherlands) and others places in Europe.

The current vitality of the Camino (Collins-Kreiner, 2017) owes much to the enthusiasm of hundreds of thousands of pilgrims (or at least, so it was until the outbreak of the Covid-19 pandemic), as well as to the good practices implemented in the management of this cultural heritage. In the context of these good practices, a General and Strategic Plan of the Way of St James was designed in Galicia for the years 2015–2021 (Plan Directory Plan Estratégico del Camino de Santiago en Galicia, 2015–2021) as a Master Plan for the Camino that will now enter a new phase: 2022–2027 (work in progress). This Strategic Plan can be summarized in five general objectives. First, raising awareness and positioning of the essential values of the pilgrimage road to Santiago; second, enhancing this historical and cultural heritage; third, offering the pilgrims an excellent experience; fourth, strengthening the Camino as an axis of sustainable and responsible socio-economic development; and fifth, taking advantage of the prestige of the Way to reinforce the Galicia brand.

At the time of writing, in 2020, the Galician Government has issued some guidelines and different action programmes for the celebration of the Holy Year 2021–2022, as a part of the Strategic Plan Xacobeo 21–22. In addition to adapting the Covid-19 safety measures to the 'new normal', the Xacobeo 21–22 aims to facilitate reflection and multicultural dialogue in a privileged space such as the pilgrimage routes and the city of Santiago, based on the values of the Way of St James and of the Holy Year 2021. Another significant component is the active participation of both pilgrims and the local population in the celebration of the Holy Year 2021–2022. People will be the main subjects and the fundamental beneficiaries of the actions that will be implemented, during the Jubilee of Compostela. During the Jubilee, the various pilgrimage routes will be the physical space in which actions will take place that are essential to understand the importance of the Xacobeo 21–22, ensure its sustainability and the survival of the values inherent in the practice of the Camino and its history.

The Galician Government aims to celebrate the 2021–2022 Jubilee while ensuring the health and safety of both the pilgrims and the local population, so that the event may become a cultural benchmark in Europe for future years. The Holy Year of Compostela is therefore a project of enormous local impact for the territories through which the Camino passes, and in particular for Galicia, the region where the pilgrimage destination is situated.

We should therefore point out the importance of the Galician Government coordinating with the other public administration bodies, specially the Jacobean Council (Consejo Jacobeo, 2022), which is part of the Spanish Ministry of Culture, and the regions of the French Way and the North Way of Santiago, declared World Heritage by UNESCO. In spite of the difficulties, such as the Covid-19 pandemic, the attitude of the actors that will make Xacobeo 21–22 a success is positive and fosters optimism. There are seven major challenges to be faced in organizing this event, namely: preserving the sustainability of the Camino and preserving its values; generating pride and active participation in the local communities of the Jacobean world; turning pilgrims into ambassadors and promoters of the Way of St James; offering a pilgrimage experience based on the Jacobean culture; projecting the Way of St James and Galicia in general towards Europe and the world; promoting the local talent of the Jacobean communities and encouraging creative and cultural exchanges at the international level; and finally, creating new opportunities for sustainable development around the Camino, especially in rural areas.

At the opening ceremony of the Holy Door of the Cathedral of Santiago, on the afternoon of 31 December 2020, the Apostolic Nuncio to Spain announced that Pope Francis granted extension of the Compostela Jubilee to the year 2022. The goals of this extension is to ensure that pilgrims who cannot spiritually benefit from the Compostela Jubilee of 2021 due to the pandemic, can undertake the Way of St James or at least reach Santiago de Compostela in 2022 (Carballo, 2021; Religión Digital, 2021).

In general, the Camino experience should be multicultural, attractive, inclusive and respectful, and ensure the right of action and participation of everyone. Even in times of pandemic, people's motivations for travel are pluralistic, reflecting their different origins and values. That is why we should encourage participation in this event, an event that does not leave anyone out. Let it be the addition of personal and institutional efforts, betting on quality and innovation (Sánchez Bargiela, 2018). The Government of Galicia intends to use this event to organize an exceptional commemoration, a unique and different event – the Xacobeo 21–22 – with all possible health and safety measures in place, calling on people to participate with their own initiatives – music events, conferences, publications, meetings and exhibitions – which since 2018 have been financially supported by the O Teu Xacobeo programme (Xunta de Galicia, 2021).

15.5 Health Security Measures on the Camino de Santiago

The current Covid-19 pandemic has prompted public administrations to take health security measures on the Camino, both for pilgrims, shelter operators and the local population. This chapter was written in Spain, in 2020 and early 2021, which is the framework of the health security measures presented herein. On 14 March 2020, the Government of Spain declared a state of emergency throughout the national territory, to combat the Covid-19 pandemic, up until 21 June 2020. In the summer, mobility resumed and pilgrims were able to go to Santiago, but the situation worsened again in autumn. On 25 October 2020 the Spanish Government declared a state of emergency again, throughout the national territory, to contain the new spread of infections. The state of emergency was declared by Royal Decree 926/2020 and was to be lifted 9 November 2020 at midnight, but on 3 November, the Council of Ministers extended it for six months, from midnight of 9 November 2020 until midnight of 9 May 2021 (Government of Spain, 2020b).

15.5.1 The Camino in the summer of 2020

The inflow of pilgrims was relatively positive after the summer of 2020. According to statistical data from the Pilgrim's Office (Santiago Cathedral), the start was very timid, with 12 pilgrims arriving on foot in June. In July the figure increased to 9752 pilgrims, with a large majority of Spaniards (7859), accompanied by Europeans – especially Germans, Italians and Portuguese – and from the rest of the world (Pilgrim's Office, Santiago de Compostela, 2022b). Far from the figures of previous years, many pilgrims came in August, reaching the total number of 19,812, the majority of whom (10,446) arrived by the French Way, 3415 by the Portuguese Way, and the rest coming by the other routes. It should be noted that the majority of pilgrims in August were Spanish (15,168) and from other European countries, with only a few hundred from other continents. Mobility problems and poor air flow were very noticeable. The 10,428 pilgrims of September and the 6418 of October reflected the same composition by continents, as well as the downward trend which continued with 586 pilgrims reaching Santiago in November, 99 in December, and 60 in January 2021.

The statistical data from the Pilgrim's Office for the summer of 2020 reported this decline in the number of pilgrims, apparently less than expected. In the case of the Portuguese Way, at the end of August, with only a few days left to say goodbye to summer, the situation seemed positive, since the summer period is encouraging for them. In July, 2129 pilgrims travelled the Portuguese Way and the Portuguese Way of the Coast, while in 2019 there had been seven times more. In the summer of 2020, the profile of the pilgrims on the Portuguese Way changed, since in August there were few foreigners, while the Spanish pilgrims – the most numerous – were strongly interested in control and security measures. The pandemic had a decisive influence on this sector, which had been growing exponentially until then, and this year has left shelters on thin ice. A decade ago pilgrims who chose the Portuguese Way numbered 12,000, while before Covid-19 they were almost 100,000.

15.5.2 In search of higher quality for the way of St James. The Galicia safe destination programme: safe pedestrian corridors, best services on the Camino and a civil protection plan

The Galician Government designed a Plan to reactivate the culture and tourism sectors in the face of the effects of the Covid-19 pandemic. This Plan includes the main action measures for the Galician Tourism Agency in 2020, laid down in the Galicia, Safe Destination programme (Xunta de Galicia, 2022). This programme establishes the implementation of a series of measures that spread and disseminate the idea of Galicia as a safe territory and encourage safe visits to this Spanish autonomous community. Measure 15 should be noted in particular which lays out the 'design of actions for tourist municipalities, for the implementation of hygienic-sanitary measures', focusing on strengthening municipal coordination to promote the image of Galicia as a safe destination in terms of hygiene and sanitation.

The Camino is a paramount asset for the international dimension and promotion of Galicia. It covers a large part of the region and its values (improvement, contact with nature, open spaces, security, and solidarity) will have a great impact on the future tourism model. One of the actions that seeks to improve the pilgrimage to Compostela is the Collaboration Agreement between the Galician Tourism Agency and the ICTE, the Institute for Spanish Tourist Quality (Tudela Aranda, 2004), for the development of the project of safe pedestrian corridors on the Ways of St James and the implementation of prevention and hygienic-sanitary measures against Covid-19 as part of the value chain of the Camino in Galicia.

The scenario created by the epidemiological evolution of Covid-19 has motivated the adoption of hygienic-sanitary measures in the tourism sector, and the pilgrimage to Compostela is currently and officially associated with this activity. Protecting workers and consumers must be a priority in the post-health crisis context. One of the keys to the recovery phase and the establishment of a new normal is connecting the implementation of health security measures with the recovery of markets and consumer confidence. The Camino, due to its uniqueness, its level of territorial implementation and its international dimension, must be the object of special monitoring in the implementation of these measures, especially in fields such as accommodation, group management and mobility systems.

The general objective of this Agreement is the definition of safe corridors on the ways of St James in Galicia, as well as recommendations that help to improve the contagion risk containment processes and recommendations to achieve adequate security levels in these corridors. The specific objectives include guaranteeing security throughout the value chain of the pilgrims' journey on their way through Galicia, offering quality and safe tourist products and positioning Galicia and the Camino as safe destinations.

The aim of these measures is maintaining or improving the degree of satisfaction of pilgrims both with their experience in the natural and heritage environment as well as with the services offered. It is also important to improve communication and emotional closeness with the pilgrims, to increase their degree of trust. Regarding the specific aspect of safe corridors, the different elements or areas that make them up will be analysed for the greater sanitary security of the pilgrims, and an appropriate communication plan will be designed. It will also be relevant to offer recommendations and alternatives, especially based on risk diagnostics and analysis of the areas along the pedestrian corridors and their official layout; individual public spaces that may interfere with the corridor layout will also be identified; a risk analysis will be carried out of the public services provided to pilgrims (dedicated information offices, rest areas, public toilets); contingency plans will be created for pilgrim shelters and other public accommodation facilities along the route.

The Civil Protection volunteer services are essential for pilgrims' safety. With this conviction, an agreement was reached between the Autonomous Administration, the Provincial Council of A Coruña and the Santiago de Compostela City Council, for purchasing three off-road vehicles to be used for emergencies on the various pilgrimage routes to Compostela. The Galician Government will organize a Civil Protection plan for the Camino, to guarantee a safe pilgrimage with the support of volunteers

– some 90,000 operative – in the event of possible emergencies.

This project is carried out in collaboration with the municipalities and the Civil Protection Volunteer Groups (AVPC), in consideration of Covid-19-related risks, to promote a safe and sustainable path of pilgrimage. This plan has been renewed every year since 2017 in order to support the actions of the Civil Protection Volunteer Groups operating on the routes to Compostela. Despite the pandemic having reduced the number and influx of pilgrims on the Camino, the Galician AVPCs focus their work on the distribution of food and medicine, visiting people who live alone and the disinfection of public places.

15.5.3 Measures from the Cathedral of Santiago. The pilgrim's digital credential

The Pilgrim's Credential is one of the most recognized documents for those who undertake the Camino. Most pilgrims start the route with this personal and non-transferable credential, which accredits them as pilgrims to Santiago and with which they can obtain the Compostela, the certificate that the Pilgrim's Office of the Cathedral of Santiago issues to each pilgrim as irrefutable proof of their having made the pilgrimage to Compostela for religious and cultural reasons. The Pilgrim's Credential originated in the Middle Ages as a kind of safe-conduct that allowed pilgrims to travel freely and without risk along the Camino. This document has survived to this day and evolved into a booklet in which pilgrims register their trip with the stamps of the hostels and towns through which they pass. Future pilgrims will be able to get the credential from the different associations of Friends of the Camino in Spain, from some associations in other countries, as well as from shelters, parishes and brotherhoods of the Apostle St James and in the Pilgrim's Office of the Cathedral of Santiago (Camino Digital Pilgrim Passport, 2020). Pilgrims can also get this document from the first shelter where they spend the night, or from tourism offices in key points on the Jacobean route. The price of the Pilgrim's Credential ranges between 50 cents and €2, and is issued for free at hostels run by the associations of Friends of the Camino and at their headquarters, in exchange for a donation for the associations' activities to protect and improve the pilgrimage routes. To gain the Compostela on arrival at the Cathedral of Santiago, the Credential requires stamping at least twice a day in the last 100 km for pilgrims on foot or on horseback and in the last 200 km for those who travel the Camino by bicycle.

The Cathedral of Santiago and the Xunta de Galicia presented the new functionality of the Pilgrim's Digital Credential which will be managed through a mobile application and seeks to provide greater comfort to pilgrims, in addition to guaranteeing a safe Camino avoiding physical contact between hospitaleros and pilgrims. The Pilgrim's Digital Credential was implemented in 1 January 2021. It enables pilgrims to register their steps on any of the different Jacobean Routes, obtaining their stamps by capturing QR codes.

Pilgrims can download the mobile application, available for both iOS and Android platforms in eight languages. Through this app, pilgrims can get the two daily stamps necessary to prove their pilgrimage to Santiago. These stamps, also digital, can be obtained through the QR codes available at the different points of the Camino. The project will also have an official website where establishments with a seal can register and digitize their image to obtain the necessary QR code that pilgrims can scan with their mobile phones and incorporate it into their digital credentials. The mobile application managing the digital credential will display information on the different Jacobean Routes and, in addition to making it possible to capture the stamps through the QR code, and will allow the integration of the data into the Pilgrim Registry necessary to achieve the Compostela.

The incorporation of this digital certificate does not mean that the hardcopy Pilgrim's Credential will disappear. In fact, pilgrims who wish to do so can continue to use the traditional credential to collect the stamps that certify their passage through the different stages of the Camino. The virtual stamps will be as valid as the paper credential, with no difference between the two. However, the institutions that promote the Digital Credential – the Cathedral of Santiago and the Galician Government – believe that the digital version will offer greater comfort

to pilgrims, in addition to increasing health security, which is a priority in times of pandemic (Pilgrim's Office, Santiago de Compostela, 2022a).

The launch of the Pilgrim's Digital Credential is part of the growing implementation of new technologies on the Jacobean Routes. This process has been accelerated by the crisis caused by Covid-19 and aims to guarantee a safe path. Among the digital advances in recent months, it is worth highlighting the reservation platform for public pilgrim's hostels in Galicia, which will soon be joined by a new one for private accommodation. The Cathedral of Santiago has also made progress in the digitalization of the Camino with the incorporation of the Pilgrim Registry and the 'digital queue', two key steps to obtain the Compostela from the Pilgrim's Office. Since the summer of 2020, pilgrims are required to enter their data in the Registry so that their Compostela is ready upon their arrival in Santiago. A new system for obtaining accreditation of having completed the pilgrimage also includes an online appointment system. Thus, when arriving at the Pilgrim's Office, a QR code is obtained with the approximate time at which each pilgrim can pick up their Compostela. With this code it is also possible to see the progress of the queue in real time. With this measure, the Cathedral of Santiago aims to avoid the long queues that usually occur during some months of the year, especially in summer. To offer greater facility to pilgrims, the mobile app of the Pilgrim's Digital Credential will allow interaction with other web tools, such as the Pilgrim Registry. In addition, it will allow the Office to know the approximate volume of pilgrims that will arrive in Santiago in the near future in order to adapt the necessary resources to provide a better service.

15.6 Health, Safety and Cultural Activities. Shock Plan and Investments of the Autonomous Government of Galicia

Faced with an uncertain and atypical 2021 due to the Covid-19 pandemic, the Galician Government is experiencing a different Xacobeo which, however, is the best possible one. With this objective, the Autonomous Administration will focus its budget on five main areas. The first will be health security, to continue promoting Galicia as a safe destination, including road safety and security in general, with an emphasis on the Cathedral of Santiago and its surroundings. Secondly, the infrastructure and landscape will continue to be improved, with the completion of the Master Plan of the Way of St James 2015–2021, the latest works on the Camino de Invierno (the Winter Way), and continuing expansion of the public network of shelters on all Jacobean trails in Galicia, with the opening of six new shelters: Vilasantar and Sobrado (Northern Way), O Saviñao (the Winter Way), A Gudiña and Oseira (the Silver Way) and Vigo (the Portuguese Way of the Coast), and the start of work on the Piñor and Friol shelters, on the Silver Way and the Northern Way, respectively.

The third area on which the work will focus will be that of promotion, and the fourth that of programming, with more than 200 activities. Finally, the fifth area will focus on the participation of all Galician society, through participatory initiatives such as the O Teu Xacobeo programme (Your Xacobeo).

Likewise, the Galician Government emphasizes that the celebration of the Xacobeo will be an opportunity to promote the reactivation of the tourism sector which will also receive additional and specific support. Thus, in 2021, the Xunta de Galicia will allocate €35.7 million to implement a Shock Plan that will include the creation of important measures, such as 'Coronavirus insurance' to cover health, transport, and accommodation expenses to be borne due to a possible contagion situation, both for travellers who fall ill and their companions. It would also cover possible quarantine stays. The idea is to offer a specific Covid-19 insurance policy to all pilgrims and visitors who spend the night in hotels and tourist apartments, covering tests, possible hospital treatments and 10–12 days' quarantine stays at hotels.

This Shock Plan will act on more axes: direct aid to encourage consumption, with measures such as the Tourist Bonus or the 'Choose Galicia' programme; measures to promote the Galician Autonomous Community as a safe destination, such as the development of contingency plans, the promotion of tourist products that may have a better evolution in the current scenario,

natural spaces, hydrotherapy, and, in general, the promotion of training and offering quality tourism.

In January 2021, the pandemic worsened in Europe. Spain and Portugal experienced their worst days, and Galicia closed all its municipalities on the perimeter. The few pilgrims who were already travelling the Camino continued to Santiago de Compostela, but the difficult health situation and the consequent closure of the international borders with Portugal and France, in addition to the municipal perimeter closures in Galicia, made the arrival of new pilgrims impossible. In addition, all public and private shelters were ordered to close. However, the Pilgrim's Office remained open, although as a mere point of reference, and in the month of January 60 Compostelas were issued. On Sunday 31 January no pilgrims arrived. The pilgrims who received the Compostela in January came from every continent, although most of them were Spanish. The breakdown of certificates by nationality was: Spain, 27; Germany, 9; Portugal, 9; Argentina, 2; USA, 2, France, 2; the Netherlands, 2; Finland, Iceland, Lithuania, Brazil, Romania and Korea, one per country. Although the Galician Government ordered the closure of pilgrim shelters and imposed mobility restrictions, there were many people who called the shelters because they wanted to undertake the pilgrimage to Santiago in this Holy Year.

The above has confirmed the great attractiveness of the Camino de Santiago, with pilgrims unwilling to miss the special opportunity offered by the celebration of Compostela's Holy Year 2021, extended to 2022 thanks to the Pope's sensitivity.

15.7 Conclusion

For best safety practices along the Camino, for the future, in the Covid-19 pandemic context, it will be essential to cooperate with other public administrations; Galician, Spanish and international ones. It will therefore be necessary to involve the municipalities and provincial and regional governments located along the routes to Santiago, as well as the Government of Spain, the Catholic Church and the associations of Friends of the Camino de Santiago. The idea of cooperation is, therefore, one of the main axes of management, and another fundamental goal is preserving the health of both pilgrims and the local people. In order to develop these guidelines, health security measures have been applied to recover markets and the confidence of the pilgrims, defining safe corridors on the Camino to guarantee health security throughout the journey, boosting consumption with a Shock Plan promoting natural spaces and spas – the Way is, to a large extent, a natural space in itself – and the taking out (before possible contagion) of the 'Coronavirus insurance policy' to cover all hospital, pharmacy, accommodation, and transportation expenses.

To summarize, Galicia will continue to promote the universal values that are implicit in the western pilgrimage since the Middle Ages, dealing with physical infrastructure, the natural environment, pilgrims' health and safety, the route's historical heritage, and the traditional hospitality for pilgrims, and will continue to promote the Camino at the international level, as well as historical research on it and collaboration with other historical routes and the associations of Friends of the Way of St James from all over the world.

The efforts put in place by the Government to protect pilgrims during the harsh months of the pandemic are bearing fruit. In 2022 the Camino is recovering, reaching figures that are close to pre-pandemic ones; in May this year, more than 1500 pilgrims reached Compostela every day. This shows that the recovery is real. However, in the immediate future it will be essential to continue with prevention plans, which have proven effective, to ensure that the health of pilgrims is protected, and Galicia continues to be perceived as a reliable and safe destination.

References

Badone, E. and Roseman, R. (eds) (2004) *Intersecting Journeys: The Anthropology of Pilgrimage and Tourism*. University of Illinois Press, Urbana, IL.

Benedictow, O.J. (2004) *The Black Death, 1346–1353. The Complete History*. Boydell Press, Woodbridge, Suffolk, UK.

Byrne, J.P. (2004) *The Black Death*. Greenwood Press, Westport, CT and London.

Caucci von Saucken, J. (2001) *Il Veneranda Dies Del Liber Sancti Jacobi. Senso e Valore Del Compostellano*. Xunta de Galicia, Santiago, Spain.

Collins-Kreiner, N. (2017) Epilogue: pilgrimage tourism in the twenty-first century. In: Pazos, A.M. (ed.) *Translating the Relics of St James. From Jerusalem to Compostela*. Routledge, London and New York, pp. 222–233.

Constable, G. (1996) *The Reformation of the Twelfth Century*. Cambridge University Press, Cambridge, UK.

Davidson, L.K. (2014) Reformulation of the pilgrimages to Santiago de Compostela. In: Pazos, A.M. (ed.) *Redefining Pilgrimage. New Perspectives on Historical and Contemporary Pilgrimages*. Routledge, Farnham, UK and Burlington, VT, pp. 159–181.

Digance, J. (2006) Religious and secular pilgrimage. Journeys redolent with meaning. In: Timothy, D.J. and Olsen, D.H. (eds) *Tourism, Religion and Spiritual Journeys*. Routledge, London and New York, pp. 36–48.

Fletcher, R.A. (1984) *Saint James's Catapult: The Life and Times of Diego Gelmírez of Santiago de Compostela*. Clarendon Press, Oxford, UK.

Frey, N.L. (1998) *Pilgrim Stories: On and Off the Road to Santiago*. University of California Press, Berkeley, CA. DOI: 10.1525/9780520922464.

Genoni, P. (2011) The pilgrim's progress across time: medievalism and modernity on the road to Santiago. *Studies in Travel Writing* 15(2), 157–175. DOI: 10.1080/13645145.2011.565580.

Gerson, P. (2006) Art and pilgrimage. Mapping the way. In: Rudolph, C. (ed.) *A Companion to Medieval Art: Romanesque and Gothic in Northern Europe*. Blackwell Publishing, Oxford, UK, pp. 599–617.

Gitlitz, D.M. and Davidson, L.K. (2000) *The Pilgrimage Road to Santiago: The Complete Cultural Handbook*. St. Martin's Griffin, New York.

Glass, D. (2008) Revisiting the Gregorian reform. In: Hourihane, C. (ed.) *Romanesque Art and Thought in the Twelfth Century*. Penn State University Press-Index of Christian Art, Princeton, NJ, pp. 200–218.

Green, D. (2014) *The Hundred Years War. A People's History*. Yale University Press, New Haven, CT and London.

Greenia, G.D. (2011) Being a pilgrim: art and ritual on the medieval routes to Santiago. *La Corónica: A Journal of Medieval Hispanic Languages, Literatures and Cultures* 39(2), 250–253.

Greenia, G.D. (2018) What is pilgrimage? *International Journal of Religious Tourism and Pilgrimage* 6(2), 7–15.

Greenia, G.D. (2019) Bartered bodies: medieval pilgrims and the tissue of faith. *International Journal of Religious Tourism and Pilgrimage* 7(1), 38–51.

Harman, L.D. (ed.) (2014) *A Sociology of Pilgrimage. Embodiment, Identity, Transformation*. Ursus Press, London and Ontario, Canada.

Hesp, A. (2013) Creating community: diary writing in first-person narratives from the Camino de Santiago. *Studies in Travel Writing* 17(1), 78–94. DOI: 10.1080/13645145.2012.747243.

Hollander, P. (2014) Heaven on earth: political pilgrimages and the pursuit of meaning and self-trancendence. In: Pazos, A.M. (ed.) *Redefining Pilgrimage. New Perspectives on Historical and Contemporary Pilgrimages*. Routledge, Farnham, UK and Burlington, VT, pp. 71–86.

López Alsina, F. (1985a) Compostelle, Ville de Saint-Jacques. In: *Santiago de Compostela, 1000 Ans de Pèlerinage Européen*. Crédit Communal, Bruxelles, pp. 53–60.

López Alsina, F. (1985b) Evolution urbaine de la Compostelle mediévale (IX au XII siècle). In: *Santiago de Compostela, 1000 Ans de Pèlerinage Européen*. Crédit Communal, Bruxelles, pp. 230–232.

Novello, S., Roget, F.M., Murias Fernández, M.P. and de Miguel Dominguez, J.C. (eds) (2013) *Xacobeo. De Un Recurso a Un Evento Turístico Global*. Andavira, Santiago de Compostela.

Ozorak, E.W. (2006) The view from the edge: pilgrimage and transformation. In: Swatos, W.H. (ed.) *On the Road to Being There: Studies in Pilgrimage and Tourism in Late Modernity*. Brill, Leiden, The Netherlands, pp. 61–81.

Pack, S.D. (2010) Revival of the pilgrimage to Santiago de Compostela: the politics of religious, national and European patrimony, 1879–1988. *The Journal of Modern History* 82(2), 349–354.

Peelen, J. and Jansen, W. (2007) Emotive movement on the road to Santiago de Compostela. *Etnofoor* 20(1), 75–96.

Sánchez Bargiela, R. (2018) La gestión del Camino de Santiago: la experiencia del Xacobeo. In: Alonso Ibáñez, M.R. (ed.) *Los Caminos de Santiago En Asturias. Miradas Cruzadas Sobre Su Tratamiento Jurídico y Gestión Patrimonial*. Universidad de Oviedo, Oviedo, Spain, pp. 145–161.

Singul, F. (2019) Compostela and the way of St. James: a view of the world, 1300–1600. In: Fiorani, D., Franco, G., Kealy, L., Musso, S.F. and Calvo-Salve, M.A. (eds) *Conservation-Consumption. Preserving the Tangible and Intangible Values*. European Association for Architectural Education, Hassel, Belgium, pp. 9–28.

Singul, F. (2020) *Camino que vence al tiempo. La peregrinación a Compostela*. Europa Ediciones, Madrid.

Storrs, C.M. (1998) *Jacobean Pilgrims from England to St. James of Compostella from the Early Twelfth to the Late Fiteenth Century*. Confraternity of St. James, London.

Sumption, J. (2003) *The Age of Pilgrimage. The Medieval Journey to God*. Hidden Spring, Skillman, NJ.

Tudela Aranda, J. (2004) La problemática jurídica de la calidad turística. In: Melgosa, F.J. (ed.) *Derecho y Turismo*. Universidad de Salamanca, Salamanca, Spain, pp. 85–91.

Van Herwaarden, J. (1980) The origins of the cult of St. James of Compostela. *Journal of Medieval History* 6(1), 1–35.

Websites

Camino Digital Pilgrim Passport (2020). Available at: https://caminoways.com/camino-digital-pilgrim-passport-credential (accessed 16 May 2022).

Carballo, I. (2021) El nuncio apostólico leyó el decreto al término de los actos religiosos de apertura de la Puerta Santa. *La Voz de Galicia*, 2 January. Available at: https://www.lavozdegalicia.es/noticia/galicia/2020/12/31/santa-sede-decreta-prolongacion-ano-santo-durante-2022-efectos-pandemia-coronavirus/0003160943676271317 9523.htm (accessed 18 May 2022).

Consejo Jacobeo (2022). Available at: https://www.culturaydeporte.gob.es/consejo-jacobeo/presentacion.html (accessed 18 May 2022).

European St. James Ways Federation (2022). Available at: https://saintjamesway-lociiacobi.eu/the-european-saint-james-ways-federation/ (accessed 31 May 2022).

Government of Spain (2020a) *Crisis sanitaria COVID-19: Normativa e información útil*. Available at: https://administracion.gob.es/pag_Home/atencionCiudadana/Crisis-sanitaria-COVID-19.html (accessed 16 May 2022).

Government of Spain (2020b) *Gobierno de España. Presidencia del Gobierno*. Available at: https://www.google.es/url?esrc=s&q=&rct=j&sa=U&url=https://www.lamoncloa.gob.es/covid-19/Paginas/estado-de-alarma.aspx&ved=2ahUKEwjDj8awotz3AhUCIc0KHVX_B18QFnoECAIQAg&usg=AOvVaw0hr-L0wB0OqdyVTguPXQHK (accessed 16 May 2022).

Pilgrim's Office, Santiago de Compostela (2022a) *The Credential*. Available at: https://oficinadelperegrino.com/en/pilgrimage/the-credencial/ (accessed 16 May 2022).

Pilgrim's Office, Santiago de Compostela (2022b) *Statistics*. Available at: http://oficinadelperegrino.com/en/statistics/ (accessed 16 May 2022).

Plan Directory Plan Estratégico del Camino de Santiago en Galicia (2015–2021). Available at: https://www.turismo.gal/canle-profesional/plans-e-proxectos/plan-director-camino-de-santiago?langId=es_ES (accessed 16 May 2022).

Religión Digital (2021) *El Papa prorroga el Año Santo jacobeo recién iniciado hasta A 2022,* 1 January 2021. Available at: https://www.religiondigital.org/diocesis/Papa-prorroga-Ano-Santo-iniciado-compostela-santiago-xacobeo_0_2301069871.html#:~:text=El%20Nuncio%20de%20Su%20Santidad%2C%20Bernardito%20Auza%2C%20anunci%C3%B3,Santo%20Jacobeo%20reci%C3%A9n%20inaugurado%20durante%20el%20a%C3%B1o%202022 (accessed 16 May 2022).

Xunta de Galicia (2021) *Xacobeo 21–22, O Teu Xacobeo*. Available at: https://xacobeo2021.caminodesantiago.gal/es/programacion/o-teu-xacobeo (accessed 16 May 2022).

Xunta de Galicia (2022) *Galicia safe destination*. Available at: https://www.turismo.gal/covid19 (accessed 18 May 2022).

16 What's Next? Politics of Religious Tourism: Emerging and Future Directions

Dino Bozonelos[1]* and Polyxeni Moira[2]

¹Departments of Political Science and Global Studies, California State University, San Marcos, USA; ²Department of Tourism Management, University of West Attica, Greece

Abstract

This concluding chapter reviews three potential growth areas. The first growth area is peripheral political science which includes contentious politics, conflict resolution, and extending the literature on political economy. The second growth area is the incorporation of core political science concepts, theories, and frameworks through the various subfields of political science. These include international relations, comparative politics, and political methodology. Finally, there is public policy discourse, which has been studied at length regarding tourism policy, but less so with religious tourism policy.

16.1 What's Next?

This edited volume has provided a discussion of religious tourism, pilgrimage, and politics at length. However, we see this book more as a beginning, rather than the culmination of research. The field of religious tourism and pilgrimage represents a unique intersection of several disciplines: political science, public policy, religious studies, sociology, psychology, anthropology, environmental studies and economics. It also involves three disciplines that have been researched at length in religious tourism: geography, political economy and development, and management. Few areas of academia provide such richness from which to pursue consistent study, from a strict disciplinary perspective to a multidisciplinary and interdisciplinary one. This book has attempted to provide insight from a particular discipline – political science, but also from many areas of research that relate to politics, such as human rights, governance, and crisis management.

Given this, there are three potential growth areas. The first growth area is the continued research into areas that involve politics and political actors but are at times peripheral to the discipline of political science. This could be referred to as 'peripheral' political science. The second growth area is the application of core concepts and theories developed in political science to religious tourism. This can be subdivided through the subfields found within the discipline itself. The third and most potential growth area, involves the implementation of concepts and theories within the public policy discourse. This area has tremendous potential given the impact of religious tourism development and

*Corresponding author: dbozonelos@csusm.edu

© CAB International 2023. *The Politics of Religious Tourism* (eds D. Bozonelos and P. Moira)
DOI: 10.1079/9781800621732.0016

the growing infrastructure that comes with it (Kim *et al.*, 2020).

16.2 Peripheral Political Science

Peripheral political science research in religious tourism and pilgrimage tends to focus on sacred sites, particularly their role in contentious politics. Contentious politics is defined by Tilly and Tarrow (2015) as 'interactions in which actors make claims bearing on other actors' interests, leading to coordinated efforts on behalf of shared interests or programs, in which governments are involved as targets, initiators of claims, or third parties' (p. 7). Olsen, in Chapter 2 in this edited volume, states that sacred spaces and places, are 'often sites of contestation within or between social, political, and religious groups in terms of ownership and narrative control or are utilized to promote and protest – or counter-protest – political or religious ideologies – often in violent terms'. Given this, Tilly and Tarrow's outline of existing political opportunity structures can help reveal the major constraints and incentives that surround contentious events and episodes. These same mechanisms within these structures can be used then to help understand the contentions within sacred sites, as well as how to solve them.

Peripheral political science research can also involve the use of conflict resolution techniques regarding contested religious destination sites. Conflict resolution goes hand-in-hand with peace studies research (Wallensteen, 2019). Quite a few contested sites have also been the subject of intense rivalries that sometimes spills over into violence (Barkan and Barkey, 2015). Given this, techniques used to end conflict can be used to address religious places that are targets of political violence, such as terrorism. In addition, spaces that have been negatively impacted by wartime conditions, such as churches and monasteries in Ukraine, could benefit from these inquiries.

It also involves to some extent extending the political economy discourse to religious tourism development, including infrastructure and issues of sustainability. Political economy approaches, such as regulation theory, can help with better understanding how future regulation might work in religious tourism.

Other peripheral approaches include world systems theory, where the concept of the semi-periphery may help explain some features of religious tourism (see Wallerstein, 2004). Semi-peripheral regions have a significant role when it comes to mediating the social, political, and economic activities linking the periphery with the core places. Regions and certain locales that are semi-peripheral to sacred places often act as staging areas for religious travel and can be vital to the success of a religious destination site.

16.3 Application of Core Political Science

Within the discipline of political science, there are plenty of core concepts and frameworks that can be adapted to better explain religious tourist and pilgrim phenomena. The discipline is often subdivided into several subfields, including, but not limited to: international relations, comparative politics and political methodology. Within international relations, theories such as realism or liberalism, and frameworks such as constructivism or rational-choice explanations can be incorporated to explain state, organizational, and/or individual behaviour. As religious travel tends to be international, foreign policy decision making, inter-state relations, and international regime making regarding religious relations, all directly impact how this travel will look. Border control and entry visas are a salient part of travelling to a religious destination site and contemporary international politics is a key variable.

Still, researchers should not overly focus on the state, as the individual behaviour and motives of religious tourists and pilgrims matter in international relations. Gillen and Mostafanezhad (2019) note that a tourism encounter is 'an everyday, fleeting, and interactive experience with political undercurrents that reinforces as well as challenges ideologies of people and places' (p. 71). Thus, constructivist approaches where individuals can forge, shape, and change culture through ideas and practices are relevant for religious travel. How pilgrims choose to talk about themselves, and others influences interpretations of state identities, as well as others' interpretations of those state identities. These state identities in turn then affect government policy, particularly in countries with democratic regimes where public opinion carries more weight in policy formation.

Comparative politics is a potentially rich field from which to study religious tourism. Whereas international relations is about the relationships between countries, comparative politics looks within countries, and compares across them. Comparativists will often look at the governing institutions and structures of a country and try to understand why similarities and differences may exist. Areas within comparative politics that are of interest are: identity politics, theories about nationalism, democratization and democratic backsliding, and psephology or the study of elections. Recent developments in political ideologies, such as the rise of national populism, are going to become quite salient for explaining state policy in religious travel. Neoliberal assumptions about religious tourism will undoubtedly regress under the leadership of national populists.

Another major area of application is methodology. While quantitative tools, such as statistical analyses of survey datasets and mathematical models have been utilized, qualitative methodology, such as case study selection techniques and process tracing, are largely absent. As a high number of religious tourism journal articles and chapters consist of individualized case studies, there is surprisingly little justification explaining why certain cases are selected for the analysis. Many cases appear to be chosen based on their ease of access, or due to researcher interest. While this approach can add a richness and provide much needed context, it is difficult to draw any meaningful inferences about sacred sites in general. Using well-articulated qualitative methodology, such as qualitative comparative analysis (QCA), can potentially help in this effort. For example, Gerring (2017), categorized case studies into two broad types: descriptive and causal. His typologizing of case study selection methods is quite relevant for religious tourism field researchers.

Geopolitics is a growing area of research that invites analysis. Geopolitics, which is also the study of power, but through the lens of geography (Dodds, 2019) revolves around 'the struggle for political dominance of space' (Hall, 2017, p. 15), where the struggle often includes both international and global dimensions. As Flint (2017) notes, geopolitics is the 'use of such geographical entities for political advantage' (p. 16). Understanding the geopolitical power that is inherent in these religious destinations, and how this power is utilized by various domestic and international actors, can help inform a range of stakeholders, including tourism ministry officials, planners, policy makers, and vested private industry and religious organizations. Additionally, all of this complexity often occurs within a defined geographical space, usually in quite small physical locations.

16.4 Public Policy Discourse

The final area of growth is that of public policy. Public policy can be thought of as applied political science, where the concepts, theories, and frameworks are put into practice. Hall and Jenkins (1995) note that public policy is 'first and foremost a political activity' and is a 'consequence of the political environment, values and ideologies, the distribution of power, institutional frameworks, and of decision making process' (p. 5). Tourism public policy has been studied at length (see Hall, 1994; Hall and Jenkins, 1995; Elliott, 1997; Edgell and Swanson, 2019), yet this literature has yet to be fully extended to religious tourism and pilgrimage. Given the inherent unique qualities that exist within religious travel, religious tourism public policy needs further examination. This includes how the state regulation of religion itself affects religious tourism. Some of this was briefly explored in Chapter 8 in this volume by Bozonelos, Cerutti and Piva. However, there are quite a few more aspects to research, including the effect of religious liberty, existing and changing church–state relationships, and the treatment of minority and deviant faiths within sacred spaces.

Finally, there is the implementation of religious tourism policy, which stresses the importance of public sector management (PSM) in the tourism industry. Elliott (1997) defines the public sector as the 'whole range of public organizations from national government ministries and departments to government business enterprises and local government tourism departments (p. 37). PSM is different from bureaucratic studies as it can take on the more traditional administrative approach and can involve a managerial approach more commonly studied in the private sector. It allows for the public–private dynamic that characterizes tourism. PSM formulation, implementation, and control understandings are easily applicable, and could allow for better conceptualizations in religious tourism, particularly when both state and private actors are involved.

16.5 Conclusion

There is quite a bit of potential for continued research in the politics of religious tourism. From peripheral political science areas to core discipline specific concepts, theories and frameworks, to public policy discourse, there is enough relevant material to keep scholars engaged for years to come. More importantly, unlike other disciplines, where research is quite esoteric and often limited to just a small audience of academics, political science is rather accessible. If politics is the study of power and how that power is distributed, then that analysis is not limited to just political scientists. Scholars in sociology, business management, ecology and other fields all incorporate understandings of political arrangements in their work. Indeed, it can feel like reaching into political science writings is somewhat unavoidable. If they study power, they will find themselves reading something written by a political scientist. Yet, in political science, one often hears how the discipline borrows heavily from other disciplines as well. From methodologies in sociology to conceptualizations in psychology to econometric models, the joke is that political scientists will beg, borrow or steal any tool they can get their hands on to solve their particular puzzle. Given this tendency, it is only fair that others take freely from political science as well.

References

Barkan, E. and Barkey, K. (2015) *Choreographies of Shared Sacred Sites: Religion, Politics, and Conflict Resolution*, Series Religion, Culture, and Public Life. Columbia University Press, New York, pp. 1–32. DOI: 10.7312/bark16994.

Dodds, K. (2019) *Geopolitics: A Very Short Introduction*. Oxford University Press, Oxford, UK. DOI: 10.1093/actrade/9780198830764.001.0001.

Edgell, D.L. and Swanson, J.R. (2019) *Tourism Policy and Planning: Yesterday, Today, and Tomorrow*, 3rd edn. Routledge, New York.

Elliott, J. (1997) *Tourism: Politics and Public Sector Management*. Routledge, New York.

Flint, C. (2017) *Introduction to Geopolitics*, 3rd edn. Routledge, New York.

Gerring, J. (2017) *Case Study Research: Principles and Practices*, 2nd edn. Cambridge University Press, Cambridge, UK.

Gillen, J. and Mostafanezhad, M. (2019) Geopolitical encounters of tourism: a conceptual approach. *Annals of Tourism Research* 75, 70–78. DOI: 10.1016/j.annals.2018.12.015.

Hall, C.M. (1994) *Tourism and Politics: Policy, Place and Power*. Wiley, New York.

Hall, C.M. (2017) Tourism and geopolitics: the political imaginary of territory, tourism, and space. In: Hall, D. (ed.) *Tourism and Geopolitics: Issues and Concepts from Central and Eastern Europe*. CAB International, Wallingford, UK.

Hall, C.M. and Jenkins, J.M. (1995*) Tourism and Public Policy*. Routledge, New York.

Kim, B., Kim, S. (Sam) and King, B. (2020) Religious tourism studies: evolution, progress, and future prospects. *Tourism Recreation Research* 45(2), 185–203. DOI: 10.1080/02508281.2019.1664084.

Tilly, C. and Tarrow, S.G. (2015) *Contentious Politics*, 2nd revised edn. Oxford University Press, Oxford, UK.

Wallensteen, P. (2019) *Understanding Conflict Resolution*, 5th edn. Sage Publications, Newbury Park, CA.

Wallerstein, I. (2004) *World-Systems Analysis: An Introduction*. Duke University Press, Durham, NC. DOI: 10.2307/j.ctv11smzx1.

Index

CABI – who we are and what we do

This book is published by **CABI**, an international not-for-profit organisation that improves people's lives worldwide by providing information and applying scientific expertise to solve problems in agriculture and the environment.

CABI is also a global publisher producing key scientific publications, including world renowned databases, as well as compendia, books, ebooks and full text electronic resources. We publish content in a wide range of subject areas including: agriculture and crop science / animal and veterinary sciences / ecology and conservation / environmental science / horticulture and plant sciences / human health, food science and nutrition / international development / leisure and tourism.

The profits from CABI's publishing activities enable us to work with farming communities around the world, supporting them as they battle with poor soil, invasive species and pests and diseases, to improve their livelihoods and help provide food for an ever growing population.

CABI is an international intergovernmental organisation, and we gratefully acknowledge the core financial support from our member countries (and lead agencies) including:

Ministry of Agriculture
People's Republic of China

Australian Government
Australian Centre for
International Agricultural Research

Agriculture and
Agri-Food Canada

Ministry of Foreign Affairs of the
Netherlands

Schweizerische Eidgenossenschaft
Confédération suisse
Confederazione Svizzera
Confederaziun svizra

Swiss Agency for Development
and Cooperation SDC

Discover more

To read more about CABI's work, please visit: **www.cabi.org**

Browse our books at: **www.cabi.org/bookshop**,
or explore our online products at: **www.cabi.org/publishing-products**

Interested in writing for CABI? Find our author guidelines here:
www.cabi.org/publishing-products/information-for-authors/